Contrastive Discourse Analysis

Functional Linguistics

Series Editor: Robin Fawcett, Cardiff University

This series publishes monographs that seek to understand the nature of language by exploring one or other of various cognitive models or in terms of the communicative use of language. It concentrates on studies that are in, or on the borders of, various functional theories of language.

Published
Functional Dimensions of Ape-Human Discourse
Edited by James D. Benson and William S. Greaves

System and Corpus: Exploring Connections
Edited by Geoff Thompson and Susan Hunston

Meaningful Arrangement: Exploring the Syntactic Description of Texts
Edward McDonald

Explorations in Stylistics
Andrew Goatly

From Language to Multimodality:
New Developments in the Study of Ideational Meaning
Edited by Carys Jones and Eija Ventola

Text Type and Texture
Edited by Gail Forey and Geoff Thompson

An Introduction to the Grammar of Old English: A Systemic Functional Approach
Michael Cummings

Morphosyntactic Alternations in English: Functional and Cognitive Perspectives
Edited by Pilar Guerrero Medina

Reading Visual Narratives: Image Analysis of Children's Picture Books
Clare Painter, JR Martin and Len Unsworth

Systemic Functional Perspectives of Japanese: Descriptions and Applications
Edited by Elizabeth A. Thomson and William S. Armour

Choice In Language: Applications in Text Analysis
Edited by Gerard O'Grady, Tom Bartlett and Lise Fontaine

Systemic Phonology
Recent Studies in English
Edited by Wendy L. Bowcher and Bradley A. Smith

Contrastive Discourse Analysis

Functional and Corpus Perspectives

Edited by
Maite Taboada, Susana Doval Suárez
and Elsa González Álvarez

SHEFFIELD UK   BRISTOL CT

Published by Equinox Publishing Ltd.

UK: Unit S3, Kelham House, 3 Lancaster Street, Sheffield, S3 8AF
USA: ISD, 70 Enterprise Drive, Bristol, CT 06010

www.equinoxpub.com

The Introduction and Chapters first published in Volume 6, Numbers 1-3 of the journal *Linguistics and the Human Sciences*.

First published in book form 2013.

ISBN 978-1-908049-75-9 (hardback)

British Library Cataloguing-in-Publication Data

A catalogue record for this book is available from the British Library.

Library of Congress Cataloging-in-Publication Data

Contrastive discourse analysis : functional and corpus perspectives / Edited by Maite Taboada, Susana Doval Suarez, and Elsa Gonzalez Alvarez.
     pages cm. -- (Functional Linguistics)
 Includes bibliographical references and index.
 ISBN 978-1-908049-75-9 (hb)
 1. Contrastive linguistics. 2. Functionalism (Linguistics) 3. Discourse analysis. I. Taboada, María Teresa, editor of compilation.
 P147.C665 2013
 401'.41--dc23
                              2013006743

Printed and bound in Great Britain by Lightning Source UK Ltd., Milton Keynes and Lightning Source Inc., La Vergne, TN

Contents

List of contributors

Séverine Adam teaches German and comparative linguistics at the University of Paris-Sorbonne since 2008. From 1999 to 2008 she worked at the department of French language and literature of the University of Freiburg im Breisgau (Germany). She received her Ph.D from the Universities of Paris-Sorbonne and Freiburg. She is a member of the research team CoVariUs/'Contextes, variations, usages'. Her work currently focuses on comparing information structure devices in German and French.

Elsa González Álvarez is a tenured Lecturer in the Department of English Philology at the University of Santiago de Compostela (Spain). She holds a BA and a PhD in English Philology from the University of Santiago de Compostela. Elsa teaches courses in morphology and syntax, in addition to postgraduate courses in second language acquisition and methodology in linguistic research. Elsa's PhD thesis was on lexical innovation in the interlanguage of second language learners, an area in which she has also published a book and several articles.

Marta Carretero is Associate Professor in English Language and Linguistics at the Universidad Complutense, Madrid, where she currently lectures on the areas of pragmatics and functional linguistics. She has done extensive research on modality, including English-Spanish contrastive analysis, the influence of genre on modality and the relationship between modality and evidentiality, among other issues. Within this area she authors articles and reviews in international and Spanish periodical journals. She also has contributions in collective works, such as *English Modality in Perspective: Genre Analysis and Contrastive Studies* (2004), *Perspectives on Evidentiality and Modality* (2004) and *Studies on English Modality: In Honour of Frank Palmer* (2009). She has directed two research projects on modality in English and Spanish. She is co-editor of the collective work *A Pleasure of Life in Words: A Festschrift for Angela Downing* (2006), and was managing editor of the academic journal *Atlantis* (2006–2008).

Martine Dalmas studied German language and literature in France (Aix-Marseille) and Germany (Heidelberg). After her Ph.D in linguistics at the University of Lyon 2, she received her Habilitation degree in German linguistics from the university of Paris-Sorbonne, where she now teaches German and comparative linguistics as full professor and leads a research team that focuses the syntax-semantic interface (CoVariUs/'Contextes, variation, usages'). She has collaborated for many years with the German Institut für deutsche Sprache

(Mannheim). Specialization: Discourse markers, information structure, synonymy, formulaic language.

Angela Downing holds BA Honours and MA degrees in French and Spanish from the University of Oxford. She is also a graduate of the Universidad Complutense de Madrid, where she obtained her PhD. She held the Chair in English Language and Linguistics at the Universidad Complutense from 1986 until 2003, when she became Professor Emerita. Her research interests and numerous publications centre on functional grammar, discourse and pragmatics. With Philip Locke she co-authored *A University Course in English Grammar* (Prentice-Hall 1992), which in 1993 won First Prize in the Grammar and Dictionaries category of the Duke of Edinburgh's Award and also the Premio de Investigación Enrique García Díez granted by AEDEAN. A new edition was published by Routledge in 2002, followed by a second revised edition in 2006 under the title *English Grammar. A University Course*. She was Editor-in-Chief of the journal *Estudios Ingleses de la Universidad Complutense* from its foundation in 1992 through 2006, and was General Editor of *Atlantis* from 2006 through 2012.

María de los Ángeles Gómez González is Full Professor of English Language and Linguistics at the University of Santiago de Compostela. She is also the principal investigator of the research group SCIMITAR and has published articles in numerous scholarly journals as well as the following books: *The Theme-Topic Interface: Evidence from English* (John Benjamins, 2001), *A New Architecture for Functional Grammar* (Mouton de Gruyter, 2004), *Studies in Functional Discourse Grammar* (Peter de Lang, 2005), *The Dynamics of Language Use: Functional and Contrastive Perspectives* (Benjamins, 2005), *Languages and Cultures in Contrast and Comparison* (Benjamins, 2008a), and *Current Trends in Contrastive Linguistics: Functional and Cognitive Perspectives* (Benjamins, 2008b).

Mike Hannay is professor of English language at the Vrije Universiteit in Amsterdam. His research interests lie in the relation between grammar and discourse, particularly with regard to the organization of information at the level of the complex written sentence, and he seeks to incorporate insights from relevant research into training programmes for writers, editors and translators.

Jennifer Herriman is professor of English at Gothenburg University, Sweden. Her research is within the theory of Systemic Functional Linguistics. Her main areas of investigation are Swedish advanced learners' writing in English and contrastive studies of English and Swedish texts and their translations.

Raquel Hidalgo is Associate Professor in Linguistics at the Universidad Complutense de Madrid. Her research has centred in functional theories applied to the study of grammar, in particular to the grammar of spoken Spanish; some of her works in this line are 'The pragmatics of transitive voice in Spanish:

from passive to inverse' (T. Givón (ed.), *Voice and Inversión*. Amsterdam, John Benjamins, 1994) and the book *La tematización en el español hablado* (Madrid, Gredos, 2003). She has also carried out research in discourse analysis, with special attention to rhetoric and political discourse, and applied linguistics.

Jorge Arús Hita teaches English language and linguistics at the Facultad de Filología Inglesa, Universidad Complutense de Madrid. His publications include articles on contrastive linguistics and second-language teaching, within the systemic functional framework, in various national and international journals and edited volumes. He has been copy-editor of *Atlantis* and is currently b-learning coordinator at the School of Language of Linguistics, UCM.

Kerstin Kunz holds a diploma in translating and finished her PhD studies on English and German Nominal Coreference in October 2009. Currently, she is a researcher and lecturer at the Dept. of Applied Linguistics, Translation and Interpreting at Saarland University. She has been teaching various seminars in contrastive text linguistics and translations studies and courses in translation and has been working in projects concerned with eLearning, properties of translation and register variation. At present, she is involved in the project GECCo (German English Contrasts in Cohesion).

Julia Lavid is Full Professor in English Linguistics and Head of the Department of English Philology I, Universidad Complutense of Madrid (Spain), where she teaches several courses on English Linguistics, Computational and Corpus Linguistics, and the contrastive analysis and translation of English and Spanish. She has been team leader of several international projects financed by the European Commission and is now the team leader of a research group on Functional Linguistics and its Applications at UCM with the participation of both national and international researchers. Her research expertise focuses on functional and corpus-based approaches to the study of English in contrast with other languages, as well as their application to educational and computational contexts. Her most recent research focuses on the creation and validation of English-Spanish contrastive descriptions through corpus analysis and annotation, financed by the Spanish Ministry of Science Innovation within the CONTRANOT project. She has an extensive record of publications in international volumes and is the author of the book *Lenguaje y Nuevas tecnologías: Nuevas Perspectivas, Métodos y Herramientas para el lingüista del siglo XXI* (Madrid, Cátedra, 2005), and coauthor of the research monograph *Systemic-Functional Grammar of Spanish: a Contrastive Account with English* (London: Continuum, 2010).

Ana Mansilla is Professor of German in the Department of Translation and Interpretation at the University of Murcia (Spain). She has been a member of the research project FRASESPAL, directed by Dr Carmen Mellado Blanco of the University of Santiago de Compostela and is currently director of the research group FRASEMIA (Phraseology, Paremiology and Translation) at the University of Murcia. Her research focuses on contrastive phraseology (German-Spanish), cognitive linguistics applied to phraseology, teaching German as a second language, and German literature and music.

Lara Moratón is affiliated to Universidad Complutense de Madrid.

Gabrina Pounds (PhD in Linguistics, 2003) is lecturer in linguistics at the University of East Anglia Norwich, UK. Her research focuses on (comparative) discourse analysis, particularly the expression of attitude and subjectivity. She has published articles on the expression of opinion in Letters to the Editor (*Pragmatics*, 2005 and *Discourse and Society*, 2006), attitude and subjectivity in hard-news reporting (*Discourse Studies*, 2010), evaluation in advertising (*Text and Talk*, 2011) and expression of empathy in physician-patient interactions (*International Journal of Applied Linguistics and Professional Practice*, 2011).

Dr **Juan Pedro Rica** is an English teacher in the English Studies department and the Translation and Interpreting department at the Complutense University. His main research areas are corpus linguistics, phraseology and audiovisual translation English-Spanish. He holds a degree in English Studies by the UCM and a PhD in English Linguistics. He also holds a Master's degree on Teaching English as a Foreign Language by the University of Illinois at Urbana-Champaign (USA) and a Master's degree on Audiovisual Translation by the Autonoma University (UAB) in Barcelona (Spain). He is currently teaching in the English and Translation and Interpreting departments at the UCM and in the Master's degree on English Linguistics (UCM) and Audiovisual Translation (UAB).

Jesús Romero-Trillo is an Associate Professor at the English Philology Department (Universidad Autónoma de Madrid). He obtained an MSc in Applied Linguistics at the University of Edinburgh (1990) and a PhD at the Universidad Complutense de Madrid (1994). He specializes in the pragmatics-intonation interface in English and Spanish. In 2008 he edited Pragmatics and Corpus Linguistics (Mouton de Gruyter) and has also edited the volume Pragmatics and Prosody in English Language Teaching (Springer, 2012). At present he leads the interdisciplinary CLAN Project (Corpus of Language & Nature) and is the Editor-in-Chief of the *Yearbook of Corpus Linguistics and Pragmatics* (Springer)

Erich Steiner, born 1954 in Heidelberg (Germany), studied English and German Philology in Freiburg and Saarbrücken, with extended periods in Cardiff, Reading and London while doing research for his PhD in English Linguistics. He has held posts in Saarbrücken, Luxembourg and Darmstadt. Since 1990, he has been Chair of English Linguistics and Translation Studies, Department of Applied Linguistics, Translating and Interpreting, University of Saarland, Saarbrücken. His major research interests include Functional Linguistics, Translation Theory and Comparative Linguistics, as well as Computational

Linguistics. He has attracted major research projects from the European Union (ESPRIT/FRAMEWORK, LEONARDO, MINERVA) and from the Deutsche Forschungsgemeinschaft (DFG/German Research Council). He has been Visiting Professor at Rice University in Houston, Texas (1986), Visiting Professor at the University of Southern California in Los Angeles (1988), Socrates Lecturer at Dublin City University (1998) and Visiting Professor several times at the University of Sydney, Macquarie University Sydney and the University of Technology, Sydney, as well as the Universities Oslo, Hong Kong City University and Hong Kong Polytechnic University over the past 15 years.

Anna-Brita Stenström is Professor Emerita of English Linguistics at the University of Bergen, Norway. Her research interests include corpus linguistics, sociolinguistics, pragmatics and discourse analysis. She has initiated and (co)directed three online corpora of adolescent language The Bergen Corpus of London Teenage Language (COLT), Ungdomsspråk och språkkontakt i Norden (UNO) and Corpus Oral de Lenguaje Adolescente (COLA). Her current research focuses on adolescent language in a contrastive perspective.

Susana Doval Suárez is a tenured Lecturer in the Department of English Philology at the University of Santiago de Compostela (Spain). She holds a BA and a PhD in English Philology from the University of Santiago de Compostela. Susana teaches courses in phonetics, phonology, morphology and syntax. Her area of interest is second language learning, in particular acquisition of orthography and discourse competence.

Maite Taboada is Associate Professor of Linguistics at Simon Fraser University (Canada). She holds MA and PhD degrees from the Universidad Complutense de Madrid (Spain), and an MSc in Computational Linguistics from Carnegie Mellon University. Maite works in the areas of discourse analysis, systemic functional linguistics and computational linguistics.

Juan Rafael Zamorano-Mansilla is lecturer in English Studies (Language and Linguistics) at the Universidad Complutense de Madrid. He received his PhD in English Linguistic Studies from this university in 2006. He has co-authored *A Systemic-functional Grammar of Spanish: A Contrastive Study with English* (Continuum 2010) with Julia Lavid and Jorge Arús. His interests include functional and cognitive grammar and the expression of tense, aspect and modality.

Introduction
Functional and corpus perspectives
in contrastive discourse analysis

Maite Taboada, Susana Doval Suárez and Elsa González Álvarez

This book offers a collection of original contributions to the study of languages in contrast from discourse, corpus, and functional perspectives. The original papers were presented at the Sixth International Conference on Contrastive Linguistics, held in Berlin 29 September–3 October 2010, in the context of two panels: 'Discourse analysis and contrastive linguistics' (organized by Maite Taboada, Simon Fraser University and María de los Angeles Gómez-González, Universidade de Santiago de Compostela), and 'Contrastive linguistics, corpus analysis and annotation' (organized by Julia Lavid, Universidad Complutense de Madrid, and Erich Steiner, Universität des Saarlandes).

Much of the 'new wave' of contrastive linguistics has focused on aspects of the grammatical system, examining phonological, morphological, lexical and syntactic similarities and differences across two or more languages. As with many other areas of linguistics, there exists a renewed interest in discourse perspectives in the study of languages in contrast, and much of that work uses corpora and corpus linguistics techniques to study language.

By 'new wave' of contrastive linguistics, we mean a renewed interest in the contrast and comparison of languages. The framework of the International Conferences in Contrastive Linguistics, initiated at the Universidade de Santiago de Compostela in the late 1990s, has provided a venue for the dissemination of such work. A number of volumes out of those conferences (Butler *et al.*, 2005; Gómez-González *et al.*, 2008b, 2008c; González Álvarez and Rollings, 2004; Iglesias Rábade and Doval-Suárez, 2002) have summarized the innovative research being carried out in contrastive linguistics. As Gómez-González and Doval Suárez (2005) point out, contrastive linguistics is taking shape as its own discipline, distinct from the 'old style' of contrastive analysis, which focused on contrastive comparisons for the purpose of teaching languages, or took a diachronic view (see Gómez-González and Doval-Suárez, 2005 for an overview of the old style and the 'revival' of contrastive linguistics). It is also different from typological studies, which tend to involve more than two languages, and centre on language structures at levels below the sentence.

We see the interaction of discourse analysis and contrastive linguistics as a two-way channel. On the one hand, the contrastive linguistics methodology can serve as a helpful method in the analysis of discourse, highlighting the ways in which discourse organization, as a functional constraint, may be similar across languages, and pinpointing what linguistic constraints lead to different discourse structures. On the other hand, discourse analysis has long studied the way in which language in general is organized, and contrastive analyses can bring more richness to that kind of analysis.

In the rest of this introductory article, we outline how contrastive linguistics has grown out of earlier approaches that had a focus on second language teaching, and describe how discourse and corpus perspectives have contributed to the contrastive study of languages. Much of the ground covered here has already been explored in introductions to other compilations, and in the volumes themselves (Iglesias Rábade *et al.*, 1999; Iglesias Rábade and Doval Suárez, 2002; Butler *et al.*, 2005; Gómez-González and Doval-Suárez, 2005; Gómez-González *et al.*, 2008a, 2008c). Johansson (2007) also offers a good summary of the history of contrastive analysis.

1. The new wave of contrastive linguistics

Broadly defined, contrastive linguistics is the study of one or more languages, for applied or theoretical purposes (Johansson, 2000). We mentioned above that we see a new wave of contrastive linguistics, distinct from earlier approaches known under the umbrella terms 'contrastive linguistics' or 'contrastive analysis', where the focus was the teaching of languages. The discipline was probably started by Lado (1957), and a number of studies tried to predict difficulties that native speakers of language X would have in learning language Y by examining the differences between the two languages (Wardaugh, 1970; di Pietro, 1971; Eckman, 1977). The concepts of *interference* (or negative transfer), where structures from one language have a negative impact on the learning of a second language, and (positive) *transfer,* where the structures of the two languages match and can therefore be transferred from the native into the target language (Ellis, 1994), were central to this view of contrastive and applied linguistics, and related work on error analysis (Corder, 1981).

These fundamental concepts were what eventually led to the partial rejection of contrastive analysis, because they were found to be too strong and narrow. Ultimately, the behavioural roots of the approach were rejected in favour of theories of second language acquisition that took into account pragmatic and contextual phenomena, such as the learner's motivation or the context in which the learning takes place (Long and Sato, 1984; Sajavaara, 1996). More recently the concept of interlanguage has been modified to include some of those aspects (Selinker, 1992), and more higher-level discourse aspects have been addressed by contrastive rhetoric (Connor, 2002).

Another area where contrastive linguistics had an influence was in translation (Beekman and Callow, 1974; Enkvist, 1978). The goal was to help translators identify the differences between languages, with the goal of achieving better translations.

The new wave that we refer to constitutes a broadening and reinterpretation of the term *contrastive linguistics* to refer to any study, from different theoretical perspectives, that takes as point of departure the comparison of two (typically, although more are possible) languages. Pioneers in this area are the studies of Hawkins on English and German (Hawkins, 1986), or the cross-cultural pragmatics of Blum-Kulka *et al.* (1989). These new studies often make use of corpora in their comparisons, and, although they tend to be applied to second language teaching and learning, they do attempt to draw more general conclusions (König and Gast, 2009).

2. Contrastive discourse studies

Gast (forthcoming) points out that the fact that most recent papers (e.g., those published in the journal *Languages in Contrast*) have a discourse orientation may be related to the fact that they use corpora, so we will see many connections between the work mentioned in this section, which is mostly in the area of discourse analysis, and the work in the next section, devoted to corpus-based work.

It would be impossible to survey all the existing work on discourse with a contrastive focus. We will simply mention that many of the functional approaches to discourse take a contrastive perspective, from studies on Theme and information structure across languages (Hatcher, 1956; Steiner and Ramm, 1995; McCabe-Hidalgo, 1999; Caffarel, 2000; Lavid, 2000) and rhetorical structure (Rösner, 1993; Delin *et al.*, 1994; Grote *et al.*, 1997; Salkie and Oates, 1999; Ramsay, 2001) to characterizations of different aspects of genres across languages and cultures (Mitchell, 1957; Koike and Biron, 1996; Luzón Marco, 2002; Taboada, 2004).

Within the studies on contrastive discourse it is worth mentioning the work of the Multilingualism group based at the University of Hamburg, some of which has an emphasis on translation. Many of their publications deal with contrastive issues in discourse, in particular two of the volumes in the Hamburg Studies in Multilingualism published by John Benjamins[1] one on connectivity (Rehbein *et al.*, 2007) and one on multilingual discourse production (Kranich *et al.*, 2011).

3. Corpus-based contrastive studies

Johansson (2007) makes a compelling case for the use of corpora in contrastive studies, attributing, in part, the resurgence of contrastive work to the availability of corpora. It is certainly the case that corpora, whether small-, medium- or large-scale, have given us new insights into the comparison of languages. Multilingual corpora are useful because they provide information about all aspects of the language, from morphological to discourse-level comparisons. The composition of the corpora may also shed light on differences across genres and cultures, translated versus original texts, and those written by native and non-native speakers.

In terms of the origin of the corpus texts, there is a clear two way distinction between translation and comparable corpora (Johansson, 2007), also referred to as parallel and comparable. The former are translated versions of the same texts, sometimes aligned (parallel) at the sentence level, whereas the latter are original texts in each language, collected to be comparable in terms of genre and register (in the sense of Halliday, 1989), that is, in terms of type of text, subject matter, formality and mode of delivery.

Modern corpus-based approaches have proven most fruitful in the original pursuit of contrastive analysis, that of second language learning. In particular the work of Granger and colleagues has resulted in a number of corpora, and studies on contrastive corpora with the goal of helping the second language learner and teacher (Granger, 1998a; Granger *et al.*, 2002, 2003, 2009). Most Computer Learner Corpora (CLC) research adopts the methodology of *Contrastive Interlanguage Analysis*, which may involve two types of comparison: a comparison of native language and learner language (L1 vs. L2) and a comparison of different varieties of interlanguage (L2 vs. L2). The result is a view of learner language in terms of the words, phrases, grammatical items or syntactic structures that are either over- or underused by learners and therefore contribute to the foreign-sounding characteristics of advanced interlanguage even in the absence of errors. The topics dealt with range from modals (Aijmer, 2002; McEnery and Kifle, 2002), high frequency vocabulary (Ringbom, 1998, 1999; Altenberg, 2002), connectors (Milton and Tsang, 1993; Granger and Petch-Tyson, 1996; Altenberg and Tapper, 1998) collocations and prefabs (Howarth, 1996; Granger, 1998b; De Cock, 2000; Nesselhauf, 2003) to information structure (Boström Aronsson, 2001; Callies, 2009). This approach has been criticized for presenting interlanguage as an incomplete version of the target language. Granger (2004: 133) justifies the approach arguing that 'most CLC research so far has involved advanced EFL learners (…). For this category of learners more than any other, it makes sense to try and identify the areas in which learners still differ from native speakers and which therefore necessitate further teaching.'

4. The chapters in this book

The chapters included here have been organized around four themes: studies of discourse markers; information structure; registers and genres; and phraseology.

The first theme, discourse markers, includes four chapters that examine the differences in the use of discourse markers across languages. Recent research has shown the fruitful perspective that contrastive studies can bring to the study of discourse markers and their use in signalling coherence relations (Knott and Sanders, 1998; Altenberg, 2002; Degand and Pander Maat, 2003; Taboada, 2004; Fabricius-Hansen, 2005; Degand, 2009, among others). These contrastive studies add to a large existing body of research that has focused primarily on English, some of it with a historical perspective (Brinton, 1996). Much territory remains to be covered in contrastive studies of discourse markers, from a discourse point of view, or from the point of view of translation studies, into how discourse markers are translated, added or omitted across languages, and what their role is in the interpretation of coherence relations.

The first chapter in this group, by Taboada and Gómez-González, takes as a starting point the study of one particular coherence relation, Concession, and examines how it is signalled through discourse markers. The chapter compares English and Spanish, across two different genres, one written and one spoken. The authors conclude that the genre (written or spoken) seems to be more important in the selection of functions for the concessive relation than the languages themselves. That is, the use of concessive relations is very similar across languages, but varies more across genres.

The chapter by Stenström makes use of two rich corpora: the Corpus Oral del Lenguaje Adolescente de Madrid (COLAm), and the Bergen Corpus of London Teenage Language (COLT). Stenström compares the use of the discourse marker *venga*, a very frequent item in informal and teenage talk, with functions both at the discourse and interactional level of conversation. She shows that, given its multifunctionality in Spanish, it has more than one equivalent in the English corpus.

The third chapter, by Adam and Dalmas, compares discourse markers in French and German, first from a general point of view, thus abstracting from existing studies in either language, and then in the two languages in contrast, with focus on three particular markers. Adam and Dalmas propose that the differences in the use of discourse markers rest with two characteristics of French that make it different from German. First, in French, the signs of discourse organization on the part of the speaker tend to be more explicit. Second, the verbal element in French has a more central global role than it does in German.

The final chapter in this section, by Romero-Trillo, examines the use of Pragmatic Markers as a tool to support interpretation and verify the current interpretation of the communicative act, in a process labelled 'communicative triangulation'. Romero-Trillo studies the English of native and non-native speakers, showing that there are subtle intonation differences in the production of Pragmatic Markers across those groups. His analyses can contribute to pedagogical aims and help improve intercultural communication.

The volume continues with a section on information structure. Previous research shows that there is a great deal of variation in the morpho-syntactic realization of information structure categories (theme, topic, focus, etc.) across speech and writing (e.g., Hannay, 1994; Gómez-González, 2001, 2004). Contrastive investigations (e.g., Gómez-González and Gonzálvez García, 2005; Hannay and Martínez Caro, 2008a, 2008b) can bring to light systematic differences between languages in the encoding of such categories, in their frequency of usage, and with regard to the 'competing motivations' (Du Bois, 1985) that prioritize one choice over another. Examples of competing motivations may be the expression of 'alternative linguistic construals' (Goldberg and Del Giudice, 2005), the manifestation of different degrees of (inter)subjectivity (Stein and Wright, 1995; Scheibman, 2002; Verhagen, 2005), or the implementation of different perspectivizing strategies (Langacker, 1985, 1989, 1990).

The first chapter in this section, by Hannay and Gómez-González, examines an understudied aspect of language, the use and function of parentheticals. In particular, the authors study thematic parentheticals, those occurring between elements of the Theme, or immediately following the Theme (as defined by Halliday and Matthiessen, 2004). Their analysis of an English-Dutch corpus shows that thematic parentheticals have similar functions in the two languages, but that both genre-specific and language-specific differences also exist. The authors suggest that there is an interesting interplay between the syntactic features that a language allows and the stylistic differences that arise as a result.

Herriman's chapter has as a starting point the similarities in presentation order in English and Swedish. Both languages make use of the principle of end-weight, and both languages rearrange elements following that principle, with rearrangements resulting in fronting, extraposition, existential constructions and cleft sentences. However, upon close inspection, she discovers that Swedish makes much more frequent use of fronting and it-clefts, which she attributes to language-specific constraints (V2 in Swedish, and SV in English). As with many of the other chapters, her careful study of fine-grained aspects of discourse has applications for second language teaching.

Doval Suárez and González Álvarez also concern themselves with structure of information, in their case the use of it-clefts in learner corpora. They contrast use, frequency and structural complexity of it-clefts in the Spanish portion of the International Corpus of Learner English with the native equivalent in the Louvain Corpus of Native English Essays. They conclude that, contrary to the findings of previous studies carried out with learners with different L1s, Spanish learners underuse it-clefts. It is suggested that this underuse may point to the fact that the learners are overusing other focus constructions such as pseudoclefts. The chapter is an excellent example of a type of contrastive analysis that examines learner's language, or interlanguage, but unlike older approaches to interlanguage, does so from a quantitative point of view.

The structure of Theme and Rheme, both in English and Spanish, has been well researched (Gómez-González, 2001; Lavid *et al.*, 2010; Taboada, 2004). The differences across the two languages are well known, as are the challenges that more flexible word order and subject ellipsis bring to the application of an English-based notion (Theme as the first ideational element, Halliday and Matthiessen, 2004) to the study of Spanish. In the chapter by Arús, Lavid and Moratón, however, new insights are brought to bear, stemming from the annotation of thematic structure in a contrastive corpus of English and Spanish. Arús and colleagues propose the notion of Pre-Head and Head to account for the split nature of the verbal element in Spanish (containing both the Participant and the Process). The chapter describes the process of rigorous annotation of the thematic structure of the clause in a corpus of newspaper discourse, and puts forward proposals for the large-scale annotation of such a complex phenomenon.

The chapter by Hidalgo and Downing is also part of the same project, an annotation effort at the Universidad Complutense de Madrid. Hidalgo and Downing examine the pragmatic notion of topic, and annotate it in a contrastive corpus of assorted genres in English and Spanish. They also annotate the information status of discourse referents (Gundel *et al.*, 1993), with the two-fold goal of creating an annotated corpus and obtaining insights about topic organization in the two languages.

The third set of chapters deal with discourse and contrastive issues from the point of view of genre or register. Although most of the other chapters also consider genre as an important variable in contrastive analyses, the chapters in this section take the notion of genre as the point of departure for the analysis. The uncovering of recurrent lexico-grammatical patterns in different text types and genres, and across different languages and socio-cultural settings, raises speakers' awareness of how different discourse roles, discourse strategies and power statuses are enacted in their linguistic choices. This has been a continuous preoccupation among discourse analysts and grammarians (e.g., Swales, 1990; Biber *et al.*, 1999; Bhatia, 2002), but it clearly is still a hot issue that deserves further investigation. The chapters in this section make an important contribution to the study of genres from a contrastive point of view.

Kunz and Steiner open the section with a study of cohesion in English and German. They consider cohesion from the point of view of language contact, and study texts in either language and their translations in the other, analysing the influence that translation has on language change. Cohesion analyses have a long tradition in English, starting with the seminal work of Halliday and Hasan (1976), but there exists little work comparing studies of cohesion in English based in that framework to analyses in other languages. Kunz and Steiner propose a framework, methodology and corpus annotation process that will facilitate the systematic comparison of cohesive resources across languages and genres.

In Pounds' chapter we find a contrastive analysis of an everyday genre, real estate advertisements, in English and Italian. Given the culture-specific context of the genre, Pounds uncovers interesting differences in the way the persuasive nature of the texts is conveyed in the two languages. She uses the Appraisal framework (Martin and White, 2005) to study how evaluative language is expressed in the two sets of corpora. Appraisal and evaluative language are particularly interesting cross-linguistically because, as pointed out by Hunston and Sinclair (2000: 74), 'evaluation appears parasitic on other resources and to be somewhat randomly dispersed across a range of structural options shared with non-evaluative functions'. Evaluation tends to be highly implicit and discourse-dependent (Hunston, 2000: 199–201), which makes a contrastive analysis particularly well-suited to uncovering general properties of evaluation across languages. Pounds finds interesting differences between English and Italian, in particular in the degree of explicitness of the evaluation.

Taboada and Carretero also study evaluative language from the perspective of Appraisal. In their work, a corpus of informally-written reviews of books and movies is analysed, contrasting English and Spanish texts. The genre is particularly interesting because it is also persuasive and argumentative, but informal in this case (the reviews were posted online, on consumer-oriented sites). Theirs is part of a large-scale annotation effort, and their chapter discusses, in particular, how the categories of Appraisal need to be very well defined, so that the corpus can be reliably annotated by different coders.

Zamorano-Mansilla and Carretero close this section with a chapter within the same research project, aimed at creating a large annotated corpus of English and Spanish. Their chapter focuses on the annotation of modality in the two languages, and in particular the issues of annotator reliability when specifying types of modality conveyed by modal verbs and particles. This chapter focuses on dynamic modality, showing that, although it is comparable in English and Spanish from a definition point of view, in practice its annotation leads to the most disagreements.

The final section of the book contains two chapters that focus on phraseology, as a bridge between lexico-grammar and discourse. Rica Peromingo analyses lexical bundles in two corpora, one of non-native writers of English, and another one of professional native writers (containing English and Spanish subcorpora). The study uncovers interesting results, showing that non-native writers resort to multi-word units more frequently than native speakers of English, but that they show both over- and under-use of certain multi-word units, in particular those present in the native language. Rica Peromingo emphasizes the importance of multi-word units as topics in the teaching of English as a second language.

Mansilla also studies phraseology, but this time with a Spanish-German contrast, and focusing on an interesting semantic field, that of lying, falsehood and deceit. She approaches the concept of falsehood as a metaphor (Lakoff and Johnson, 1980), and explores the different expressions of falsehood in the two languages, and the different cognitive models that they reveal.

5. Conclusion

The chapters in this book, in summary, provide examples of cutting-edge research in contrastive analyses of different languages, all of them with a discourse and functional perspective. The languages included (Dutch, English, French, German, Italian, Spanish and Swedish) cover a range of European languages, showing not only diversity in their grammatical structures, but also subtle differences that are the focus of many of the chapters. The techniques used, from concordancing and careful annotation to painstaking qualitative analysis, showcase the variety of approaches to the study of languages in contrast.

Note

1.   http://www.benjamins.com/cgi-bin/t_seriesview.cgi?series=HSM

Acknowledgements

We would like to acknowledge support from a number of research agencies who helped fund the participation of different researchers in two panels at the International Contrastive Linguistics Conference (Berlin, 29 September–3 October 2010). One panel, organized by M. Taboada and M. Gómez-González, was supported with funds from the Natural Sciences and Engineering Research Council of Canada (Discovery Grant 261104-2008; PI: Maite Taboada), and from several projects with M. Gómez-González as PI: HUM2007-62220 (Spanish Ministry of Education and Science); FFI2010-19380 (Spanish Ministry of Education and Science); and INCITE09 204 155PR (Xunta de Galicia). The other panel, organized by Julia Lavid and Erich Steiner, was supported with funds from the German Research Foundation (GECCO project, PI: Erich Steiner), the Spanish Ministry of Science and Innovation (CONTRANOT project FFI2008-03384; PI: Julia Lavid), and the BSCH-UCM Consortium (Research Grant 2010-2011; PI: Julia Lavid). Thanks also to Jennifer Hinnell for careful copyediting.

References

Aijmer, K. (2002) Modality in advanced Swedish learners' written interlanguage. In S. Granger, J. Hung and S. Petch-Tyson (eds), *Computer Learner Corpora, Second Language Acquisition and Foreign Language Teaching*, 55–76. Amsterdam: John Benjamins.

Altenberg, B. (2002) Concessive connectors in English and Swedish. In H. Hasselgård, S. Johansson, B. Behrens and C. Fabricius-Hansen (eds), *Information Structure in a Cross-Linguistic Perspective*, 21–43. Amsterdam: Rodopi.

Altenberg, B. and Tapper, M. (1998) The use of adverbial connectors in advanced Swedish learners' written English. In S. Granger (ed.) *Learner English on Computer*, 80–93. London: Longman.

Beekman, J. and Callow, J. (1974) *Translating the Word of God.* Grand Rapids, MI: Zondervan Publishing House.

Bhatia, V. K. (2002) Professional discourse: Towards a multi-dimensional approach and shared practices. In C. N. Candlin (ed.) *Research and Practice in Professional Discourse*, 39–59. Hong Kong: Hong Kong University Press.

Biber, D., Johansson, S., Leech, G., Conrad, S. and Finegan, E. (1999) *Longman Grammar of Spoken and Written English.* Harlow, Essex: Pearson Education.

Blum-Kulka, S., House, J. and Kasper, G. (eds) (1989) *Cross-Cultural Pragmatics: Requests and Apologies.* Norwood, NJ: Ablex.

Boström Aronsson, M. (2001) *It*-clefts and pseudo-clefts in Swedish advanced learner English. *Moderna Språk* 95 (1): 16–23.

Brinton, L. J. (1996) *Pragmatic Markers in English: Grammaticalization and Discourse Functions*. Berlin: Mouton de Gruyter.

Butler, C., Gómez-González, M. de los Ángeles and Doval-Suárez, S. (eds) (2005) *The Dynamics of Language Use: Functional and Contrastive Perspectives*. Amsterdam: John Benjamins.

Caffarel, A. (2000) Interpreting French Theme as a bi-layered structure: Discourse implications. In E. Ventola (ed.) *Discourse and Community*, 247–272. Tübingen: Gunter Narr.

Callies, M. (2009) *Information Highlighting in Advanced Learner English*. Amsterdam: John Benjamins.

Connor, U. (2002) New directions in contrastive rhetoric. *Tesol Quarterly* 36 (4): 493–510. http://dx.doi.org/10.2307/3588238

Corder, S. P. (1981) *Error Analysis and Interlanguage*. Oxford: Oxford University Press.

De Cock, S. (2000) Repetitive phrasal chunkiness and advanced EFL speech and writing. In C. Mair and M. Hundt (eds) *Corpus Linguistics and Linguistic Theory. Papers from the Twentieth International Conference on English Language Research on Computerized Corpora (ICAME 20)*, 51–68. Amsterdam: Rodopi.

Degand, L. (2009) Describing polysemous discourse markers: What does translation add to the picture? In S. Slembrouch, M. Taverniers and M. Van Herreweghe (eds) *From Will to Well. Studies in Linguistics Offered to Anne-Marie Simon-Vandenbergen*, 173–184. Ghent: Academia Press.

Degand, L. and Maat, H. P. (2003) A contrastive study of Dutch and French causal connectives on the Speaker Involvement Scale. In A. Verhagen and J. van de Weijer (eds) *Usage Based Approaches to Dutch*, 175–199. Utretcht: LOT.

Delin, J, Hartley, A., Paris, C., Scott, D. and Vander Linden, K. (1994) Expressing procedural relationships in multilingual instructions. *Proceedings of 7th International Workshop on Natural Language Generation (IWNLG 7)*, 61–70. Kennebunkport, Maine.

di Pietro, R.J. (1971) *Language Structures in Contrast*. Rowley, MA: Newbury House.

Du Bois, J. W. (1985) Competing motivations. In J. Haiman (ed.) *Iconicity in Syntax*, 343–365. Amsterdam: John Benjamins.

Eckman, F. R. (1977) Markedness and the contrastive analysis hypothesis. *Language Learning* 27 (2): 315–330. http://dx.doi.org/10.1111/j.1467-1770.1977.tb00124.x

Ellis, R. (1994) *The Study of Second Language Acquisition*. Oxford: Oxford University Press.

Enkvist, N. E. (1978) Contrastive text linguistics and translation. In L. Grähs, G. Korlén and B. Malmberg (eds) *Theory and Practice of Translation*, 169–188. Berne: Peter Lang.

Fabricius-Hansen, C. (2005) Elusive connectives: A case study on the explicitness dimension of discourse coherence. *Linguistics* 43 (1): 17–48. http://dx.doi.org/10.1515/ling.2005.43.1.17

Gast, V. (forthcoming) Contrastive analysis: Theories and methods. In B. Kortmann and J. Kabatek (eds) *Dictionaries of Linguistics and Communication Science: Linguistic Theory and Methodology*. Berlin: Mouton de Gruyter. Available from http://www.personal.uni-jena.de/~mu65qev

Goldberg, A. E. and Del Giudice, A. (2005) Subject auxiliary inversion: A natural category. *Linguistics Review* 22 (2–4): 411–428. http://dx.doi.org/10.1515/tlir.2005.22.2-4.411

Gómez-González, M. d. l. Á. (2001) *The Theme-Topic Interface: Evidence from English.* Amsterdam and Philadelphia: John Benjamins.

Gómez-González, M. d. l. Á. (2004) A three-dimensional account of it-clefts in discourse: A corpus-based study. *Southwest Journal of Linguistics* 23 (2): 1–40.

Gómez-González, M. d. l. Á. and Doval-Suárez, S. (2005) On contrastive linguistics: Trends, challenges and problems. In C. Butler, M. d. l. Á. Gómez-González and S. Doval-Suárez (eds) *The Dynamics of Language Use*, 19–45. Amsterdam: John Benjamins.

Gómez-González, M. d. l. Á. and Gonzálvez García, F. (2005) On clefting in English and Spanish. In C. S. Butler, M. d. l. Á. Gómez-González and S. Doval-Suárez (eds) *The Dynamics of Language Use: Functional and Contrastive Perspectives*, 155–196. Amsterdam: John Benjamins.

Gómez-González, M. d. l. Á., Mackenzie, J. L. and González Álvarez, E. (2008a) Introduction. In M. d. l. Á. Gómez-González, J. L. Mackenzie and E. González Álvarez (eds) *Current Trends in Contrastive Linguistics: Functional and Cognitive Perspectives*, xv–xxi. Amsterdam: John Benjamins.

Gómez-González, M. d. l. Á., Mackenzie, J. L. and González Álvarez, E. (eds) (2008b) *Current Trends in Contrastive Linguistics: Functional and Cognitive Perspectives*. Amsterdam: John Benjamins.

Gómez-González, M. d. l. Á., Mackenzie, J. L. and González Álvarez, E. (eds) (2008c) *Languages and Cultures in Contrast and Comparison*. Amsterdam: John Benjamins.

González Álvarez, E. and Rollings, A. (eds) (2004) *Studies in Contrastive Linguistics*. Santiago de Compostela: Universidade de Santiago, Servicio de Publicacións.

Granger, S. (1998a) *Learner English on Computer*. London: Longman.

Granger, S. (1998b) Prefabricated patterns in advanced EFL writing: Collocations and formulae. In A. P. Cowie (ed.) *Phraseology: Theory, Analysis and Applications*, 145–160. Oxford: Oxford University Press.

Granger, S. (2004) Computer learner corpus research: Current status and future prospects. In U. Connor and T. A. Upton (eds) *Applied Corpus Linguistics: A Multidimensional Perspective*, 123–145. Amsterdam: Rodopi.

Granger, S., Dagneaux, E., Meunier, F. and Paquot, M. (2009) *The International Corpus of Learner English. Version 2.* [Corpus]. Louvain-la-Neuve: Presses universitaires de Louvain.

Granger, S., Hung, J. and Petch-Tyson, S. (eds) (2002) *Computer Learner Corpora, Second Language Acquisition and Foreign Language Teaching*. Amsterdam: John Benjamins.

Granger, S., Lerot, J. and Petch-Tyson, S. (eds) (2003) *Corpus-based Approaches to Contrastive Linguistics and Translation Studies*. Amsterdam: Rodopi.

Granger, S. and Petch-Tyson, S. (1996) *Extending the Scope of Corpus Based Research: New Applications, New Challenges.* Amsterdam: Rodopi.

Grote, B., Lenke, N. and Stede, M. (1997) Ma(r)king concessions in English and German. *Discourse Processes* 24: 87–117. http://dx.doi.org/10.1080/01638539709545008

Gundel, J. K., Hedberg, N. and Zacharski, R. (1993) Cognitive status and the form of referring expressions in discourse. *Language* 69: 274–307. http://dx.doi.org/10.2307/416535

Halliday, M. A. K. (1989) Context of situation. In M. A. K. Halliday and R. Hasan (eds) *Language, Context and Text,* 3–14. Oxford: Oxford University Press.

Halliday, M. A. K. and Hasan, R. (1976) *Cohesion in English.* London: Longman.

Halliday, M. A. K. and Matthiessen, C. M. I. M. (2004) *An Introduction to Functional Grammar* 3rd edn. London: Arnold.

Hannay, M. (1994) The theme zone. In R. Boogaart and J. Noordegraaf (eds) *Nauwe betrekkingen. Voor Theo Janssen bij zijn vijftigste verjaardag,* 107–117. Amsterdam: Stichting Neerlandistiek VU.

Hannay, M. and Martínez Caro, E. (2008a) Last things first: A FDG approach to clause-final focus constituents in Spanish and English. In M. d. l. Á. Gómez-González, J. L. Mackenzie and E. González Álvarez (eds) *Languages and Cultures in Contrast and Comparison,* 33–68. Amsterdam: John Benjamins.

Hannay, M. and Martínez Caro, E. (2008b) Thematic choice in the written English of advanced Spanish and Dutch learners. In G. Gilquin, S. Papp and M. B. Díez-Bedmar (eds) *Linking up Contrastive and Learner Corpus Research,* 227–253. Amsterdam: Rodopi.

Hatcher, A. G. (1956) Syntax and the sentence. *Word* 12: 234–250.

Hawkins, J. A. (1986) *A Comparative Typology of English and German: Unifying the Contrasts.* Austin, TX: University of Texas Press.

Howarth, P. (1996) *Phraseology in English Academic Writing: Some Implications for Language Learning and Dictionary Making.* Tübingen: Max Niemeyer.

Hunston, S. (2000) Evaluation and the planes of discourse: status and value in persuasive texts. In S. Hunston and G. Thompson (eds) *Evaluation in Text: Authorial Distance and the Construction of Discourse,* 176–206. Oxford: Oxford University Press.

Hunston, S. and Sinclair, J. (2000) A local grammar of evaluation. In S. Hunston and G. Thompson (eds) *Evaluation in Text: Authorial Distance and the Construction of Discourse,* 74–100. Oxford: Oxford University Press.

Iglesias Rábade, L. and Doval Suárez, S. (2002) *Studies in Contrastive Linguistics.* Santiago de Compostela: Universidade de Santiago de Compostela: Servicio de Publicacións.

Iglesias Rábade, L. and Doval-Suárez, S. (eds) (2002) *Studies in Contrastive Linguistics.* Santiago de Compostela: Universidade de Santiago, Servicio de Publicacións.

Iglesias Rábade, L., Núñez Pertejo, P., Díaz Pérez, J., Doval Suárez, S., Gómez Penas, D., González Álvarez, E., Mourón Figueroa, C., M. Oro Cabanas, J. and Palacios Martínez,

I. (1999) *Estudios de Lingüística Contrastiva*. Santiago de Compostela: Universidade de Santiago de Compostela: Servicio de Publicacións.

Johansson, S. (2000) *Contrastive Linguistics and Corpora* (Report from the project Languages in Contrast No. 3). Oslo: University of Oslo.

Johansson, S. (2007) *Seeing Through Multilingual Corpora: On the Use of Corpora in Contrastive Studies*. Amsterdam and Philadelphia: John Benjamins.

Knott, A. and Sanders, T. (1998) The classification of coherence relations and their linguistic markers: An exploration of two languages. *Journal of Pragmatics* 30 (2): 135–75. http://dx.doi.org/10.1016/S0378-2166(98)00023-X

Koike, D. A. and Biron, C. M. (1996) Genre as a basis for the avanced Spanish conversation class. *Hispania* 79 (2): 290–296. http://dx.doi.org/10.2307/344921

König, E. and Gast, V. (2009) *Understanding English-German Contrast*. Berlin: Erich Schmidt.

Kranich, S., Becher, V., Höder, S. and House, J. (eds) (2011) *Multilingual Discourse Production*. Amsterdam: John Benjamins.

Lado, R. (1957) *Linguistics Across Cultures: Applied Linguistics for Language Teachers*. Ann Arbor, MI: University of Michigan Press.

Lakoff, G. and Johnson, M. (1980) *Metaphors We Live By*. Chicago, IL: University of Chicago Press.

Langacker, R. W. (1985) Observations and speculations on subjectivity. In J. Haiman (ed.) *Iconicity in Syntax,* 109–150. Amsterdam and Philadelphia, PA: John Benjamins.

Langacker, R. W. (1989) *Subjectification* (No. A 262). Duisburg: Linguistic Agency University of Duisburg.

Langacker, R. W. (1990) Subjectification. *Cognitive Linguistics* 1 (1): 5–38. http://dx.doi.org/10.1515/cogl.1990.1.1.5

Lavid, J. (2000) Text types, chaining strategies and Theme in a multilingual corpus: A cross-linguistic comparison for text generation. In J. Bregazzi, A. Downing, D. López and J. Neff (eds) *Homenaje a Jack C. White: Estudios de filología inglesa,* 107–122. Madrid: Universidad Complutense.

Lavid, J., Arús, J. and Zamorano, J. R. (2010) *Systemic Functional Grammar of Spanish: A Contrastive Study with English*. London: Continuum.

Long, M. H. and Sato, C. J. (1984) Methodological issues in interlanguage studies: An interactionist perspective. In A. Davies, C. Criper and A. P. R. Howatt (eds) *Interlanguage,* 253–280. Edinburgh: Edinburgh University Press.

Luzón Marco, M. J. (2002) A genre analysis of corporate home pages. *LSP and Professional Communication* 2 (1): 41–56.

Martin, J. R. and White, P. R. R. (2005) *The Language of Evaluation*. New York: Palgrave.

McCabe-Hidalgo, A. (1999) *Theme and Thematic Patterns in Spanish and English History Texts*. Ph.D. dissertation, Aston University.

McEnery, A. M. and Kifle, N. A. (2002) Epistemic modality in argumentative essays of second-language writers. In J. Flowerdew (ed.) *Academic Discourse*, 182–215. London: Longman.

Milton, J. and Tsang, E. S. (1993) A corpus-based study of logical connectors in EFL students' writing. In R. Pemberton and E. S. Tsang (eds) *Studies in Lexis*, 215–246. Hong Kong: Hong Kong University of Science and Technology.

Mitchell, T. F. (1957) The language of buying and selling in Cyrenaica: A situational statement. *Hesperis* 26: 31–71.

Nesselhauf, N. (2003) The use of collocations by advanced learners of English and some implications for teaching. *Applied Linguistics* 24 (2): 223–242. http://dx.doi.org/10.1093/applin/24.2.223

Ramsay, G. (2001) What are they getting at? Placement of important ideas in Chinese newstext: A contrastive analysis with Australian newstext. *Australian Review of Applied Linguistics* 24 (2): 17–34.

Rehbein, J., Hohenstein, C. and Pietsch, L. (eds) (2007) *Connectivity in Grammar and Discourse*. Amsterdam: John Benjamins.

Ringbom, H. (1998) Vocabulary frequencies in advanced learner English: A cross-linguistic approach. In S. Granger (ed.), *Learner English on Computer*, 41–52. London: Longman.

Ringbom, H. (1999) High frequency verbs in the ICLE corpus. In A. Renouf (ed.), *Explorations in Corpus Linguistics*, 191–200. Amsterdam: Rodopi.

Rösner, D. (1993) Intentions, rhetoric, or discourse relations? A case from multilingual document generation. In O. Rambow (ed.) *Proceedings of Workshop on Intentionality and Structure in Discourse Relations, ACL,* 106–109. Ohio State University: ACL.

Sajavaara, K. (1996) New challenges for contrastive linguistics. In K. Aijmer, B. Altenberg and M. Johansson (eds) *Languages in Contrast. Papers from a Symposium on Text-based Cross-linguistic Studies,* 17–36. Lund: Lund University Press.

Salkie, R. and Oates, S. L. (1999) Contrast and concession in French and English. *Languages in Contrast* 2 (1): 27–56. http://dx.doi.org/10.1075/lic.2.1.04sal

Scheibman, J. (2002) *Point of View and Grammar: Structural Patterns of Subjectivity in American English*. Amsterdam and Philadelphia, PA: John Benjamins.

Selinker, L. (1992) *Rediscovering Interlanguage*. London: Longman.

Stein, D. and Wright, S. (eds) (1995) *Subjectivity and Subjectivisation: Linguistic Perspectives*. Cambridge: Cambridge University Press.

Steiner, E. H. and Ramm, W. (1995) On Theme as a grammatical notion for German. *Functions of Language* 2 (1): 57–93.

Swales, J. M. (1990) *Genre Analysis: English in Academic and Research Settings*. Cambridge: Cambridge University Press.

Taboada, M. (2004) *Building Coherence and Cohesion: Task-Oriented Dialogue in English and Spanish*. Amsterdam and Philadelphia, PA: John Benjamins.

Verhagen, A. (2005) *Constructions of Intersubjectivity: Discourse, Syntax, and Cognition.* Oxford: Oxford University Press.

Wardaugh, R. (1970) The contrastive analysis hypothesis. *TESOL Quarterly* 4 (2): 123–130. http://dx.doi.org/10.2307/3586182

1 Discourse markers and coherence relations: Comparison across markers, languages and modalities

Maite Taboada and María de los Ángeles Gómez-González

We examine how one particular coherence relation, Concession, is marked across languages and modalities, through an extensive analysis of the Concession relation, examining the types of discourse markers used to signal it. The analysis is contrastive from three different angles: markers, languages and modalities. We compare different markers within the same language (but, although, however, etc.), and two languages (English and Spanish). We aim to provide a contrastive methodology that can be applied to any language, given that it has as a starting point the abstract notion of coherence relations, which we believe are similar across languages. Finally, we compare two modalities: spoken and written language. In the analysis, we find that the contexts in which concessive relations are used are similar across languages, but that there are clear differences in the two modalities or genres. In the spoken genre, the most common function of concession is to correct misunderstandings and contrast situations. In the written genre, on the other hand, concession is most often used to qualify opinions.

1. Introduction

A great deal of the study of discourse markers has been linked to their role as markers of coherence relations. By coherence relations we mean relations in discourse that join clauses or sentences with rhetorical purposes (cause, condition, elaboration, justification or evidence), as defined in Rhetorical Structure

Theory (Mann and Thompson, 1988), and in similar or related theories (e.g., Sperber and Wilson, 1995; Asher and Lascarides, 2003).

At the same time, recent research has shown the fruitful perspective that contrastive studies can bring to the study of discourse markers and their use in signaling coherence relations (Knott and Sanders, 1998; Altenberg, 2002; Degand and Pander Maat, 2003; Taboada, 2004a; Fabricius-Hansen, 2005; Degand, 2009, among others). These contrastive studies add to a large existing body of research that has focused primarily on English, some of it with a historical perspective (Brinton, 1996). Much ground remains to be covered in contrastive studies of discourse markers, from both a discourse point of view and from the point of view of translation studies, into how discourse markers are translated, added or omitted across languages, and what their role is in the interpretation of coherence relations.

In this study we focus on the Concession relation, and examine the types of discourse markers used to signal it. The analysis is contrastive from three different angles: markers, languages, and modalities. The analysis involves different markers, within the same language and across languages (English and Spanish), and across two modalities: spoken and written language. We aim at providing a contrastive methodology that can be applied to any language, given that it has as a starting point the abstract notion of coherence relations, which we believe are similar across languages.

We analyze two contrastive corpora, one written and one spoken. The written corpus is a collection of 200 texts (100 per language) that evaluate movies and books, taken from web portals that collect and distribute different types of products: Ciao.es for Spanish, and Epinions.com for English, part of the SFU Review Corpus (Taboada, 2008). The spoken corpus, also contrastive, contains 10 telephone conversations (five in each language), from each one of which five minutes have been transcribed (Wheatley, 1996; Kingsbury *et al.*, 1997).

The methodology we follow consists of identifying all the markers that indicate a Concession relation, extracting them from the corpora, and calculating frequencies and other characteristics, such as placement of the marker (e.g., at the beginning or end of the clause). We define Concession as a relation that joins two clauses or units in a potential or apparent contradiction (see Section 3). Finally, we compare the usage of each marker in the two languages and modalities.

2. Coherence relations

One of the fundamental issues in the study of discourse is the phenomenon of coherence. In discourse studies, coherence is described as the way in which a discourse 'hangs together', with pieces relating to other pieces. Mann and

Thompson (1988) defined it as the absence of non-sequiturs, i.e., a coherent text is one where all the parts form a whole: 'for every part of a coherent text, there is some function, some plausible reason for its presence, evident to readers, and furthermore, there is no sense that some parts are somehow missing' (Mann and Taboada, 2010). Renkema (2004: 103) indicates that coherence refers to 'the connections which can be made by the reader or listener based on knowledge outside the discourse.' Those connections are often captured in the form of coherence relations.

The relations that we are concerned with here are referred to as coherence relations, discourse relations, or rhetorical relations. They are paratactic (coordinate) or hypotactic (subordinate) relations that hold across two or more text spans. When building a text or any instance of discourse, just as when building a sentence, speakers choose among a set of alternatives that relate two portions of the text. The two parts of the text that have been thus linked can then enter, as a unit, into another relation, making the process recursive throughout the text. Coherence relations have been proposed as an explanation for the construction of coherence in discourse. It is not clear how much speakers and hearers are aware of their presence, but it is uncontroversial that hearers and readers process text incrementally, adding new information to a representation of the ongoing discourse (e.g., van Dijk and Kintsch, 1983).

There are many classifications and a variety of labels for coherence relations. To better define these relation, we will be making use of Rhetorical Structure Theory, a theory of text organization (Mann and Thompson, 1988). In Rhetorical Structure Theory (RST), texts are understood as coherent wholes, made up of parts that stand in rhetorical relations to each other. The parts are typically clauses or sentences, and the relations are those that capture the perceived coherence of most texts. Examples of relations are: Concession, Condition, Cause, Result, Elaboration, Antithesis, Summary and Background. Units are called spans, and they may be atomic (one clause or one sentence), or composed of other spans.

Another fundamental aspect of RST is the relative status of spans. In most relations, one part of the relation, that is, one span, is considered to be the main part, and the other one is secondary. These are called nucleus and satellite, respectively, and are analogous to main and subordinate clauses in a hypotactic syntactic relation. Some relations are paratactic, consisting of two or more nuclei, just like coordinated clauses. Example (1) shows a typical Concessive relation from our corpus, with the nucleus and satellite marked in square brackets.

(1)   [S] Kiss the Girls was OK, [N] but there were too many unbelievable points about it that made it a bad story all together. [W, Books, no24]

Relations hold at all levels in a text from the clause up.[1] Typically, the clause is considered the minimal unit of analysis.

Space precludes a more extensive discussion of the theory itself. More detail can be found in the original paper on RST (Mann and Thompson, 1988), a recent overview (Taboada and Mann, 2006a, 2006b), or the RST web site (Mann and Taboada, 2010).

The main focus of this paper is the Concession relation, a relation that we have observed is very frequent in the review genre, one of the genres in this study (Trnavac and Taboada, 2010). We also include related relations, such as adversative and contrast relations. The next section outlines the family of concessive relations in Spanish and English.

3. Concessive, adversative and contrast relations

The term 'concession' generally refers to a special kind of adverbial subordinate clause, illustrated in (2), which: (a) is introduced by conjunctions somewhat aprioristically considered as concessive; (b) can be pre- or post-posed to the main clause or verb; and (c) cannot be replaced by a semantically equivalent adverb.

(2)   a.   Although the ending was a happy one, it was also a little sad. [M, no3]

        b.   La banda sonora es excelente, aunque se repite. [P, no_2_20]
            The soundtrack is excellent, although repetitive.

These characteristics have been identified in numerous studies of concessives in English (Quirk *et al.*, 1985; Rudolph, 1996: 4–6; Biber *et al.*, 1999; Couper-Kuhlen and Thompson, 2000; Crevels, 2000b; Huddleston and Pullum, 2002) and Spanish (Gili Gaya, 1955, § 239, § 249; Gutiérrez Ordóñez, 1977–1978; Álvarez Martínez, 1987; Narbona Jiménez, 1990; Kovacci, 1992: 29; Alarcos Llorach, 1994: 441–442; Hernández Alonso, 1995; Di Tullio, 1997: 337; López García, 1999; Carbonell Olivares, 2005; Real Academia Española, 2009, ch. 54). However, on closer inspection, the picture becomes rather more complex, as there still has not been a general consensus on the exact number, nature and realization of these relations.

In what follows it will be shown that concessive relations show a wide variety of realizations in English and Spanish ranging from subordinating ((*al*)*though*, *aunque*) and coordinating (*but*, *pero*) conjunctions to adverbial items (*nevertheless*, *nonetheless*, *all the same*, *sin embargo*, *después de todo*, *pese a todo*), phrasal (prepositional) expressions (*in spite of*, *a pesar de*), parenthetical elements, mainly impersonal clauses or adverbial items ((*it's*) *true*, *true enough*, *si bien es cierto*, *ciertamente*), or even combinations with the previous and/or other markers (*even though it is true that …*, *si bien es cierto que*).

We shall also see that, although it is common for concessives to be adverbial adjuncts at the matrix clause level of syntactic analysis, it is also quite common for both concessives and their conjoined segments to be expressed in two juxtaposed matrix clauses. In addition, concession can be expressed by certain lexico-syntactic realizations other than discourse markers such as special uses of tenses or impersonal constructions. It can also be left implicit in the discourse with no overt marking, a possibility that transcends the scope of this chapter.

From a semantic point of view, confusion emerges because such terms as 'contrastive', 'adversative', 'concessive' and 'corrective' have been used interchangeably in the Spanish and English literature when, in our view, these labels represent distinct notions (Rivarola, 1976; Abraham, 1979; Traugott, 1986, 1995; Spooren, 1989; Lavacchi and Nicolás, 1994; Moya Corral, 1996; Fuentes Rodríguez, 1998; Flamenco García, 1999; Crevels, 2000a, 2000b). In this study *concessive relations* fall within the triadic category of *relations of opposition* together with *contrast relations* ('adversative') and *corrective relations* (Lakoff, 1971; Foolen, 1991; Izutsu, 2008), as opposed to *alternative* or *otherwise* relations, the meaning of which emphasize a sense of alternativeness rather than opposition (Mann and Thompson, 1988). Both opposition and alternative relations belong to the ideational structure of the discourse (together with those expressing time, space, condition, etc.), and in the Spanish tradition they are mostly regarded as *causativity relations* (cause-effect or condition-consequence), within which concessives would express inefficient cause, conditionals hypothetical cause, final clauses intentional cause and reason clauses efficient cause (Gutiérrez Ordóñez, 1997: 76 and ff.). Therefore, excluded from this study are those discourse markers that belong to the interpersonal and/or textual dimension of discourse (e.g. *well, so, then, I mean, you know* and their Spanish equivalents (*bueno, entonces, quiero decir, ya sabes*). This distinction concerns the 'source of coherence' and has received different labels in the literature such as *ideational* vs. *pragmatic* discourse markers (Redeker, 1990), *subject-matter* vs. *presentational relations* (Mann and Thompson, 1988), *external* vs. *internal* uses of conjunctions and relations (Halliday and Hasan, 1976; Martin, 1992), or *semantic* vs. *pragmatic* connectives (van Dijk, 1977; Briz, 1994).

Focusing on ideational or subject-matter relations of opposition, the contrastive-concessive dichotomy endorsed here derives from Lakoff's (1971) study of *but*, distinguishing between 'the semantic opposition *but*' and 'the denial of expectation or concessive *but*' (for an application of this dichotomy to Spanish, see Rivarola (1976)). In the former, two clauses are directly opposed to each other (*Mary is tall, but Peter is short*), whereas the latter denies a presupposed expectation (or assumption) evoked from the semantic content of one clause. In *John is Socialist, but you can trust him* the *but*-concessive clause denies the implicit assumption that 'if John is Socialist, then he is not trustworthy' evoked in the first clause.[2] The third type, corrective, is obtained from the lexical distinction between such connectors as *pero* and *sino* in Spanish or *but* and *instead* or *rather* in English, of which only the latter (*sino, instead* and *rather*) are exclusively used for corrective purposes (Anscombre and Ducrot, 1977, 1983).

Besides lexical differences, these three types of relations of opposition also show syntactic differences that support their consideration as distinct semantic categories. As pointed out by Lakoff (1971), contrast differs from concessive and corrective under three syntactic operations: reversing two connected segments, paraphrasing with *and*, and omitting a connective.

Salkie and Oates (1999), in their study of *but* and *although*, distinguish between two meanings for *but*: contrast and denial of expectation. Contrast and concession are also distinguished by Quirk *et al.* in their classification of adverbial subordinate clauses (Quirk *et al.*, 1985).

In summary, and following Izutsu (2008), we propose that the family of opposition relations that includes concessive, contrast and corrective indicate a conflict or clash between the two (or more) parts of the relation. In particular, what is mutually exclusive in concessives is found between the propositional content of one clause and an assumption evoked in the other segment ('If John is a socialist, (then normally) he cannot be trusted.')

Our work is grounded in Rhetorical Structure Theory, where the Concession relation is defined as follows, with the fields (constraints and effect) suggested for an RST definition (Mann and Taboada, 2010):

> (3)   Concession
> **Constraints on the nucleus:** The writer[3] has positive regard for the nucleus.
> **Constraints on the satellite:** The writer is not claiming that S does not hold; the writer acknowledges a potential or apparent incompatibility between nucleus and satellite; recognizing the compatibility between nucleus and satellite increases the reader's positive regard for the nucleus.
> **Effect:** The reader's positive regard for the nucleus is increased.

Note that, in this case, 'positive regard' does not mean that the writer agrees with a potential (positive) evaluation expressed in the nucleus; it implies that the writer believes that the nucleus is more likely or more the case than the potentially conflicting situation presented in the satellite.

4. Markers of concession in English and Spanish

In this chapter, we deal mostly with discourse markers as signals of concessive relations. We use the term 'discourse marker' in a loose sense, to refer to any conjunction, adverb, adverbial phrase or other type of phrase that frequently links two or more units of discourse.

We extracted relations automatically, using discourse markers that indicate concessivity in each language. This has the advantage that the extraction can be done automatically. The disadvantage is that some relations that are 'implicit', or signaled by means other than a discourse marker (Taboada, 2009), will be missed. Markers were drawn from a number of sources, and from our own corpus analysis (Rivarola, 1976; Quirk *et al.*, 1985; Narbona Jiménez, 1990; Moya Corral, 1996; Knott, 1996; Rudolph, 1996; Marcu, 1997; Fuentes Rodríguez, 1998; Flamenco García, 1999; Crevels, 2000a; Montolío Durán, 2001; Carbonell Olivares, 2005; Taboada, 2006). In some cases, the automatic extraction returned cases of these markers that indicated something other than a concessive. Those cases were excluded from the study.

4.1. English markers

The following are general categories of English markers that indicate a concessive relation, classified according to part of speech.

(4) **Conjunctions and conjuncts:** albeit, although, but, but even so, come what may, despite (everything), despite the fact that, even if, even though, even when, even while, howbeit, much as, though, when, whereas, whether, while
a. It's the same message as 'It's a Wonderful Life', **albeit** delivered with a lot more f-words and flying liquor bottles. [W, M, yes23][4]
b. … felt a little funny he felt a little funny in the chest **but** that could be a reaction because of the heat [S, en_4315]

(5) **Sentence adverbials:** above all, after all, and even then, anyway, at any cost, even, even yet, for all that, for one thing, however, in any case, in spite of all things, in spite of everything, nevertheless, no matter what, nonetheless, of course, only, over all, rather, regardless, still, too, withal, yet
a. Kelly Preston has little to do and not much time to do it in. Baldwin, **however**, is a convincing bad guy. [W, M, yes15]

(6) **Gerunds introducing subordinate clauses or noun phrases:** admitting, allowing that, even supposing, gra`nting (all this), supposing, without considering
a. Miranda the patient was a more plausible impression, **considering** Halle Berry has a natural confused look on her face which enhances this role. [W, M, no23]

(7) **Prepositional phrases with certain prepositions:** against, aside from, distinct from, even after, even before, even as, even with, in contempt of, in defiance of, in spite of, in the face of, notwithstanding, regardless of, without regard to
a. **Regardless** of whether they like him or not, Luke is forced to keep many secrets the workers have told him or made evident to him. [W, B, no6]

4.2. Spanish markers

Below are summarized the Spanish markers of concession that are analyzed in this study. This list is not exhaustive but it does contain the most common markers.

(8)   **Concessive conjunctions/conjuncts**: a pesar de (que), a pesar de todo, a pesar de + Inf., así, aunque, cuando, no obstante, (Conditional / Future +) pero, pese a (que), si bien, sin embargo, (tan) siquiera.

    a.   **A pesar de que** para mi Almudena Grandes es una escritora genial (yo me he leído toodos sus libros aunque este no lo he podido terminar) este libro me ha parecido un coñazo, el argumento no me iba para nada y me parecía lento y monótono. [W, L, no_1_16]
    Although to me Almudena Grandes is a great author (I've read aaall of her books although I couldn't finish this one) this book was a pain, I didn't like the plot at all and I found it slow and monotonous.

    b.   Algo que me ha gustado de la película es que aparecen todos los personajes, o casi todos, **aunque** sólo sea en una imagen global de todos los habitantes del pueblo. [W, P, yes_4_2]
    One thing that I liked in the movie is that all the characters are there, or almost all, **although** it's only in a global image of all the town's inhabitants.

    c.   algunas escenas de la película son sencillamente magistrales, como la transformación del Hombre de Arena. **No obstante,** lo espectacular de algunas escenas (especialmente las de acción) en ocasiones resulta excesivo. [W, P, no_1_9]
    some scenes from the movie are simply masterful, like the transformation of the Sandman. **However,** what is spectacular in some scenes (especially action ones) in some others becomes excessive.

    d.   Realmente Prometía con Amor, curiosidad, prozac y dudas **pero** luego intentó vivir de rentas y en este mundillo: renovarse o morir. [W, B, no_1_11]
    [She] really showed promise with Amor, curiosidad, prozac y dudas [Love, curiosity, Prozac and doubts] **but** then [she] tried to live off of her success and in this world: either do something new or die.

    e.   En un principio, tengo que reconocer que tenía mis reservas, pues **si bien** es cierto que últimamente el cine español está abordando el género de terror con bastantes buenos resultados, esa no es siempre, ni de lejos, una característica aplicable a todas las películas del género que se ruedan en nuestro país. [W, P, yes_4_6]
    First of all, I have to acknowledge that I had my reservations, since **although** it's true that as of late Spanish cinema is venturing into horror with pretty good results, that is not at all a characteristic that can be applied to all the movies in that genre that are shot in our country.

(9)   *por + AdjP / AdvP + que-*relative clause: e.g., *por más que, por mucho que*
    a.   Otra razón radica en que intenta explicar al lector todo lo que ocurre **por más que** diré que esto no hacía falta alguna. [W, L, no_2_17]
    Another reason is that [the author] tries to explain everything to the reader **although** I'd say that this was not necessary at all.

b. Tampoco se debería manejar de forma absurda: sólo encaja perfectamente en el relato cuando se sabe utilizar. Si no, un 'intento de' contamina el resto de las páginas, **por muy bien escritas que** estén. [W, L, no_2_17]
It shouldn't be treated in an absurd way either: it only fits perfectly in the narration when one knows how to use it. Otherwise, an 'attempt to' corrupts the rest of the pages, **no matter how well written they are**.

(10) *para* + NP / InfP / *que*-relative clause
a. Es una niña muy inteligente **para la edad que tiene**, responsable y concienciada con el medio ambiente. [W, P, yes_4_2]
She's a very intelligent girl for her age, responsible and engaged with the environment.

(11) *con* + NP / InfP / *que*-relative clause or *con lo* + AdjP / AdvP + *que*-relative clause
a. Por otro lado, tb destaco como positivo, la interpretación del actor que dá vida al joven Lecter, lo cierto es que, no era nada fácil, y menos **con el antecedente de lo bien que bordó Hopkins al personaje**. [W, L, no_2_25]
On the other hand, I also point out as positive, the performance by the actor who plays the young Lecter, the truth is that, it wasn't easy at all, and least of all **with how well Hopkins played the character**.

(12) **Gerund**
a. **Siendo** tan fácil de recolectar en el campo o de cultivar en nuestro huerto, es una lástima que no se incluya como una verdura más de una manera habitual en la dieta diaria saludable.
Being so easy to pick in the countryside or to grow in a garden, it is a shame that it isn't included as a vegetable on a regular basis in a daily healthy diet.

(13) **Gerund / Participle / AdjP +** *y todo*
a. Guille como excelente padre que es, el viernes, **enfermo y todo**, se arrastró hasta el colegio para ir a buscarlo.
Guille, being the excellent father that he is, on Friday, **sick and all**, dragged himself to the school to pick him up.

(14) **Repetition** of two (identical or different) verbal expressions, in the same or different tenses, in which the second verb may be: *sea cual sea, (lo) quieras o no,*
a. Hecho que, la verdad, no da muy buena espina porque suena un poco a desesperación y a colarte el libro lo **quieras o no** para luego poder ir diciendo que si es un best seller que si tal y cual [W, L no_1_8]
A fact that, truth be told, doesn't bode well because it sounds of desperation and of trying to sell the book **whether you want it or not** so that then [they] can say that it's a best seller and such.

(15) **Impersonal clausal**: (si) bien es cierto, lo cierto es que, la verdad es que, está claro que
a. **Bien es cierto que** es cortito, pero tambien es cortito todo lo demas: los personajes, la trama, el desenlace, etc. … [W, L, no_2_21]

> **It is true that** it is short, but everything else is short too: the characters, the plot, the ending, etc.…

(16)   **Adverbs and adverbial expressions**: *ciertamente, efectivamente*
a.   Hace un tiempo, me llamaron la atención unos libros, que, **ciertamente**, no es que tengan una presentación que entre por los ojos, pero fué precisamente eso lo que me hizo fijarme en ellos.
Some time ago, I was struck by some books, which, **certainly**, do not have the most attractive presentation, but it was precisely that which led me to pay attention to them.

(17)   **Combination of markers** (cf. Luscher's (1994) distinction between compositional and additional sequences): *aún así, aún con eso/esto, aún cuando, aún +* Gerund, *así y todo, pero no obstante, y sin embargo.*
a.   **Aún con** esto no voy a dudar de la capacidad de la Iglesia seguire confiando en el, y espero que la proxima vez que lo veamos en pantalla me sorprenda como otras muchas veces. [W, P, no_2_12]
Even despite that, I don't doubt the capacity of de la Iglesia I will continue to trust him, and I hope that the next time we see him on the screen I will be surprised, like I have been in the past.

5. Corpus study: Corpus and methodology

In this section, we discuss the configuration of our corpus and the parameters studied. In our corpus study we are concerned with connections between clauses rather than smaller constituents, and contrast the behavior of concessives in English and Spanish along the following parameters:

  i.   **Distribution of concessives across written and spoken texts.** Our assumption is that differences in mode result in differences in the frequency and type of concessive markers. Writing requires a careful evaluation and an effective marking of the intended connections among segments in order to preserve the right logico-pragmatic interpretation of the text, which will be reflected in the choice of concessive connectors (Montolío Durán, 2001). In oral texts, on the other hand, the interactive nature of concession becomes more evident.

  ii.   **Realization of the concessive relation** in terms of (a) **concessive marker** and (b) position of concessives with regard to the conjoined element: **post-posed** or **pre-posed concessives**. We will argue that these realizational differences also encode semantico-pragmatic differences. In English some scholars claim that pre-posed and post-posed (*al*)*though*-clauses are variants of the same underlying structure, analyzing the former construction as being derived from the latter by the so-called 'adverb-preposing' (Ross, 1986; König, 1988; Winter and Rimon, 1994; Lagerwerf, 1998). We believe, however, that different placements in initial or thematic and final or rhematic position may involve different sources for the assumptions evoked, from the propositional content of the main clause (in post-posed *although* clauses) or from the concessive clause (in pre-posed *although* clauses). In addition, these positional tendencies can also be explained in relation to other factors such as the encoding of information as Given or New, or the implementation of different strategies of perspectivization in the discourse.

The written corpus is part of the Simon Fraser University Corpus,[5] which, in its latest version, consists of 1,600 reviews of movies, books, music, hotels and consumer products (cars, telephones, cookware, computers), 800 reviews for each language. For this study, we selected a portion of the movie and book review sections, because they tend to be the longest texts, and contain the most elaborate arguments. There are 50 reviews in each of the movie and book parts of the corpus for each language, with 25 having been labeled by the author as positive, and 25 as negative towards the movie or book being reviewed (a label of 'recommended' or 'not recommended').

The spoken corpus is part of the large CallHome set of corpora in different languages distributed by the Linguistic Data Consortium.[6] The Call-Home corpus was an effort by the Linguistic Data Consortium to collect spontaneous telephone conversations. Participants were given 30 minutes of long-distance calling time, to call relatives or friends, provided they agreed to being recorded. There are CallHome-style recordings for a variety of languages. Each of the Spanish and English versions of the corpus contain 120 conversations, about 30 minutes long, but with only five minutes of transcription (Wheatley, 1996; Kingsbury *et al.*, 1997). For this particular study, we chose the transcripts of five conversations in (American) English and five in Spanish. There is no detailed information on place of origin for the Spanish speakers, but we were able to identify a variety of dialects. In this sense, the English corpus is more homogeneous, since most callers were speakers of American English. Table 1 shows the number of texts or conversations per language, and the total number of words and sentences. Sentence count is approximate. For the written texts, we counted end-of-sentence punctuation. For the spoken conversations, the count corresponds to the number of turns in the transcripts. Most turns contain only one sentence, although often complex or compound.

Table 1: Corpus statistics

	Written		Spoken	
	English	**Spanish**	**English**	**Spanish**
Texts/conversations	100	100	5	5
Sentences	3,869	5,768	1,708	1,322
Words	62,090	90,338	11,457	8,694

Using the discourse markers presented in Section 4, we extracted sentences and their context from the corpus. We examined the sentences extracted, and discarded those where the presumed marker was not, in fact, a connective indicating concession. That left us with the following number of examples for English: 326 relations in the written part of the corpus, and 101 in the spoken part. For Spanish, the counts are 628 for the written, and 24 for the spoken parts, respectively.

For each marker, we then examined its frequency of realization and context of usage. We outline the main results of this study in the next section.

6. Results

We will first discuss some basic statistics about the number of relations and the presence of markers. Then we compare the spoken and written parts of the corpus, and the two languages.

Table 2: Markers in the English corpus

Marker	**Written**	**Spoken**
but	216	96
although	27	0
while	20	0
however	17	0
yet	10	0
even though	8	1
despite (the fact that)	6	0
though	6	4
even if	5	0
regardless	4	0
still	3	0
when	3	0
no matter	1	0
Total	326	101

Table 3: Markers in the Spanish corpus

Marker	Written	Spoken
pero	348	22
aunque	137	0
(y) sin embargo	45	1
aun así/ aún con/ aún + Ger	15	0
a pesar de (que) / a pesar de + Inf	17	0
Impersonal clausal	12	1
a pesar + Inf	9	0
Gerund	6	0
por mucho/más/muy x que	8	0
(pero) no obstante	7	0
si bien	7	0
cuando	5	0
para/con NP + que /Inf	4	0
a pesar de todo	3	0
pese a (que)	2	0
tan siquiera	1	0
Repetition	1	0
ciertamente, efectivamente	1	0
Total	628	24

The first observation from the tables is the lack of diversity in the spoken versions of the corpora, with *but* and its equivalent *pero* accounting for the majority of the types of concessive markers. Although the spoken corpus is much smaller in size, it is clear that the markers used are more restricted in type. To better compare written and spoken frequencies, we normalized the frequency of markers to presence per thousand words (Table 4). We can see then that spoken English has a slightly higher frequency of markers, but that, overall, written English and Spanish, and spoken English are comparable. The outlier is spoken Spanish, with a very low frequency of markers. We cannot draw good conclusions about this, since the spoken Spanish part of the corpus is the smallest, but it does seem to indicate that the type of interaction in the casual Spanish conversations does not require extensive use of concessive relations.

Table 4: Frequency of markers per thousand words

Written		Spoken	
English	Spanish	English	Spanish
5.25	6.95	8.82	2.76

6.1. Comparison between genres

The relations are used differently in the two different genres. In the written genre, they most often serve to qualify an opinion or dismiss potential objections to the author's opinion. In (18), the author expresses an opinion (a children's movie can appeal to adults), but acknowledges that there may be different viewpoints, in a sort of claim-response pattern (Hoey, 2001). The concession serves as a dismissal of those viewpoints, by including them in the author's statement. A different example is presented in (19), where the negative opinion (that some passages are tedious and long) is qualified by the acknowledgment that some passages are good. In this case, the result of the concession seems to be a balanced opinion, and one that is much more credible, because it is not polarized.

(18)   Despite what some people think, a kids movie can be good and appeal to adults, such as Toy Story or Space Jam. [W, M. no20]

(19)   Reconozco que tiene 'pasajes' muy guapos, pero también hay otros (la mayoría) muy pesados y otros que ni siquiera resultan creíbles. [W, P no1_15]

I acknowledge that it has very good 'passages', but also that there are others (most) [that are] very tedious and others that are not even credible.

In the spoken corpus, on the other hand, concessive relations are most often used to indicate a contrast between two situations, such as (20) and (21).[7]

(20)   B: it's hot I mean Tiberius is very hot too but it's dry
and this is humid
I don't know what's worse [S, en_4315]

(21)   A: Estamos gordos, no más, pero aparte de eso, estamos bien. [S, sp_0082]
We are fat, that's all, but apart from that, we are well.

Another function of concessives in speech is the correction of potential misinterpretations, such as in (22). This example is interesting because the concessive relation is built collaboratively across speakers' turns. Speaker A starts the main clause (*oh she's away now*), and speaker B adds the satellite or subordinate clause, which helps to clarify a potential misunderstanding. In (23) and (24), there seems to be an anticipation that the hearer will be worried upon hearing news of somebody 'feeling a little funny' in (23), or having spots all over in (24). This possible misunderstanding is then corrected with a concessive clause.

(22)   B: Susan's away this week so I might I'm going to my sister's tomorrow she needs a babysitter on Thursday
A: yeah
B: so I'm going tomorrow but I I feel like I'm (( ))

    A: I thought she was going away for vacation this week
    B: she's away now
    A: oh she's away now
    B: but she's coming back tonight [S, en_4315]

(23) B: felt a little funny
         he felt a little funny in the chest
         but that could be a reaction because of the heat [S, en_4315]

(24) B: Estoy lleno de granos por todos lados, pero ahí ya, ya me siento bien, como
         puedes oír, más o menos. [S, sp_0291]

         I'm covered in spots all over, but it's okay, I already feel better, as you can hear,
         more or less.

Concessives fulfill topic-management strategies in the spoken data, as in (25), where the clause that contains *sin embargo* changes topics from one child that has been discussed to another child, Mónica.

(25) B: y sigue igual, así bien despierta, igual a como era mamá
      A: ahá
      B: sólo que más despierta
         y Mónica sin embargo ha crecido un montón. [S, sp_0753]

         And she's the same, like really lively, just like Mom was (A: uh-huh) only more
         lively, and Monica, on the other hand, has grown a lot.

Finally, concessives in the spoken data may also have similar functions to those in the review texts, such as acknowledgment of a different viewpoint. In (26), the speaker discusses her husband's job opportunities as a teacher, and states that one of them would be good because the job is full-time. She acknowledges, however, that there may be a perception that the job is not desirable because the school is not the best.

(26) B: because it is a regular fulltime job
         even though it might not be the great the great school [S, en_4808]

6.2. Order of spans

Certain coherence or rhetorical relations are argued to have a canonical order, in terms of the position of the main and subordinate units. In RST, the canonical order does not tie to the syntactic status of the spans (whether they are independent main clauses or not), but to the tactic relations, that is, to the order of nucleus and satellite in a hypotactic relation. Nucleus and satellites tend to correspond to main and subordinate units respectively, at the lower level of analysis (within the clause). The distinction, however, applies to relations across clauses. In a concessive relation, the nucleus is the unit for which the reader has positive regard, and the satellite is the unit that presents a potentially conflicting situation (cf. definition in Section 3).

In some concessive relations, then, the nucleus-satellite distinction coincides with main-subordinate clause. This is the case in most *although* relations, as in Example (27).

(27)   [N] At the end of the film, kids were calling the Cat 'cool', [S] although Thing One and Thing Two seemed to get more praise than the Cat himself did. [W, M, yes15]

In other cases, and with other markers, the nucleus-satellite distinction from RST still applies, although the relation does not hold across clauses, but across sentences, as in (28), where the satellite is made up of two sentences ('although the idea is not new, because it is a different version of another film').

(28)   [S] The idea of the film is not new either. It was like a different version of the Sixth Sense, but in a more perverse way. [N] However, I forgive that because it seemed to work out at the end. [W, M, yes17]

With such distinction in mind, we annotated each example from our corpus to determine whether the nucleus-first or satellite-first order was the most frequent. According to Mann and Thompson (1988: 256), in Concessive relations, the most frequent order is satellite first.

Before we discuss the results of the annotation, we would like to point out that the annotation was not as straightforward as could be assumed. In the informal writing style of the reviews in particular, sentence boundaries are not always easy to determine. Punctuation is used irregularly, and run-on sentences are frequent, many of them involving concessive relations. A particularly difficult example is presented in (29), where arguments are strung together, with frequent use of suspension points and brackets as linking devices. The most interesting cases in this example are the two uses of the conjunction *pero* ('but'). In both cases, it is unclear whether a real concessive or adversative relation is intended, and what the satellite of that relation would be.

(29)   Un 7… porque aunque me fue algo más indiferente que las otras, me mantuvo entretenida y a pesar de ser YA la tercera parte… ¡En tensión! [Como nos gusta pasarlo mal, ¿verdad?… Ainss…] Pero sinceramente, tampoco encuentro demasiadas diferencias de las otras… solamente una [-en su final-] que lógicamente no puedo contaros porque si no os destriparía esta a veces desagradable película [y nunca mejor dicho]… Pero quiero decir que a mi parecer es tal vez el final más bestia de las tres partes…

A 7… because although it left me more indifferent than the other ones, it kept me entertained and despite the fact that it was ALREADY the third part…

In suspense! [How we enjoy suffering, right? Ouch…] But honestly, I didn't find many differences with the other ones… only one [-in the ending-] that of course I cannot tell you about because otherwise I would spoil this sometimes unpleasant movie [literally]… But I want to say that in my opinion is perhaps the most horrendous ending of the three parts…

We now turn to a discussion of the general results of presentation order (Table 5). For both languages, and across both genres, the table shows clearly that the canonical order proposed by Mann and Thompson (1988) holds: The majority of relations have satellite first. In some cases, we see a relation inserted in the middle. That happens when the satellite interrupts the clause that forms the nucleus. This seems to be more frequent in Spanish, of which we present an example in (30). Neither language shows any middle relations in the spoken genre, presumably because of the higher processing load that they involve.

(30)   Flaubert escribe con un estilo exquisito que, a pesar de que no lo hace inmune a las traducciones, sí facilita su excelente consideración fuera del original francés.

Flaubert writes in an exquisite style that, despite the fact that it does not make him immune to translation, does enable its excellent reputation outside of the original French.

Table 5: Order of presentation

	Written		Spoken	
	English	**Spanish**	**English**	**Spanish**
Nucleus first	31 (9.51%)	108 (17.20%)	1 (0.99%)	1 (4.17%)
Satellite first	294 (90.18%)	504 (80.25%)	100 (99.01%)	23 (95.83%)
Satellite middle	1 (0.31%)	16 (2.55%)	–	–

With respect to markers, most markers seem to have a preferred canonical order, with a typical satellite-first or nucleus-first order. Some markers are more evenly distributed across both (or all three) positions. For instance, in English *although* and *even if* occur in similar proportions in nucleus-first or satellite-first position. The markers *even though* and *when* appear most frequently in examples with the nucleus first. Markers with satellite-first ordering are: *but, despite, however* and *while*. The only example of a marker positioned in the middle in English is *although*.

In Spanish, *a pesar de (que)* seems to occur in all three positions, and *por mucho/muy/más (que)* both with nucleus-first and satellite-first. Other markers are more frequent with the nucleus-first ordering, *aunque* being the most salient. Most other markers tend to have a satellite-first distribution (*a pesar de (todo), aún (así), cuando, pero, sin embargo*).

An interesting follow-up to this work would be to examine the thematic development of the texts, and determine whether the order satellite-nucleus obeys contextual constraints, relating to how the information progresses (see also Spooren, 1989 on thematic continuation after *but* clauses), or to cognitive constraints. Noordman (2001) observed that in *although* clauses the preferred order is subordinate clause first, and proposed this was because of a correlation between cognitive and linguistic structures. He interpreted concessive relations as a type of causal relations, and as such, the most congruent order, from a cognitive point of view, is cause first, and then consequence.

6.3. Multiple markers

In some cases, more than one marker is present for the same relation. In our quantitative study, we have counted them as two markers. The most frequent instance of such cases is in Spanish, where a combination of *pero* and *es cierto/ lo cierto es que/ciertamente* is present, as in (31). In other cases, it is *a pesar (de) (que)* plus *pero*, as in Example (32).

(31)   Es cierto que en los capítulos de la serie de vez en cuando también aparecen personajes famosos y cosas así, pero en el filme se juntan muchos detalles de este tipo que hacen que sea una película muy ingeniosa. [W, M, yes_4_2]

It is true that in the chapters of the series there are every now and then famous characters and such, but in the movie many details of that type are put together, which makes it a very ingenious movie.

(32)   A pesar estar destinada a un público claramente infantil, lo cierto es que con Ratatouille pasa lo que pasa con muchas otras películas de animación… [W, P, yes_5_7]

Despite (the fact that) it is clearly geared towards a children's audience, the truth is that with Ratatouille you get what you get with many animation movies…

The combination of *pero* and *aunque* to signal the same relation is common in some languages, such as Farsi (Wilson and Wilson, 2001), but ungrammatical in Spanish, as in Example (33)

(33)   Aunque todas sus amigas y familia la dijeran que era lo mejor que la había podido pasar, pero ella seguía dando vueltas a la cabeza si Iain aun amaba a su ex. [W, B, yes_5_15]

Although all her friends and family told her that it was the best thing that could have ever happened to her, but she was still considering whether Iain still loved his ex.

7. Discussion and conclusions

We have presented a study of concessive relations in two languages (English and Spanish) and two modalities (spoken and written). First of all, we present a methodology for studying coherence relations starting with the abstract notion of coherence relations, which makes the methodology applicable to any language. We extracted relations based on markers used to signal them, which likely underestimates the number of relations, but which makes the automatic process much easier. An extension of this work would involve analyzing each text carefully, looking for other instances of relations that are not explicitly signaled, or that are signaled by means other than discourse markers.

We focused on the concessive relation, because we believe that it plays an important role in what we could call vernacular argumentation, especially in the case of informal online reviews. Concession fulfills the role of the classical thesis-antithesis structure, and helps writers and speakers express opinions, while mitigating their strength, or acknowledging potential alternative viewpoints.

We found that differences in usage are more pronounced across genres than across languages. In the spoken genre, the most common function of concession is to correct misunderstandings and contrast situations. In the written genre, on the other hand, concession is used to qualify opinions. This type of distribution is very similar across languages, showing that genre guides and constrains the types of coherence relations used, and that those constraints are constant across similar genres in different languages.

With regard to the variety of markers, it is striking that speech used only a handful of markers, most notably *but* and *pero,* whereas the written version of the corpus showed more type diversity.

We also quantified the ordering of spans, and confirmed the claim in Rhetorical Structure Theory that the most frequent order in concessive relations is satellite-nucleus.

Future work will involve a larger corpus, in particular for speech. We would also like to explore the relationship of coherence relations in general, and concession in particular, to the staging structure of the genre. Our intuition is that, at least in the review genre, concessions tend to occur towards the middle and end stages of the genre, that is, the most heavily argumentative stages. Finally, we will explore the semantic and pragmatic implications of a non-canonical order, that is, when the nucleus precedes the satellite.

Notes

1.   In RST, and in our work, minimal units (spans) are simple sentences or clauses, main and subordinate. Typically, though, complement clauses do not constitute a segment on their own. Thus, we do not segment subject and object clauses, reported speech and the like, but do consider adverbial clauses as minimal units of discourse.

2.   This distinction between simple contrast and concession involving an assumption has been variously termed in the literature, such as 'contrast' and 'violated expectation' (Kehler, 2002), 'contrast' and 'denial' (Blakemore, 1987, 1989), and in Spanish 'contraste' vs. 'objeción inoperante', 'obstáculo ineficaz', 'condición insuficiente' or 'relación de preferencia' (Kovacci, 1992; Moya Corral, 1996; Flamenco García, 1999; López García, 1999).

3.   RST was mainly developed with written texts in mind. We have shown that it can be extended to spoken language (Taboada, 2004b). When we use the terms 'writer' and 'reader', 'speaker' and 'hearer' are also possible.

4.   All the examples from our corpus are reproduced verbatim, including typos and grammatical errors for the written corpus and hesitations or repetitions in the spoken. The examples are marked with their source: W (written), S (spoken); M (movies), B (books), P (películas), L (libros); and with file identifying information. In addition, the review corpus examples contain information about whether the review was overall positive ('yes') or negative ('no'). When the example has no source specified, then it is invented.

5.   Available from http://www.sfu.ca/~mtaboada/research/SFU_Review_Corpus.html

6.   http://www.ldc.upenn.edu

7.   The spoken data is broken down by intonation units. Each line represents an independent intonation unit (Wheatley, 1996; Kingsbury *et al.*, 1997).

References

Abraham, W. (1979). But. *Studia Linguistica* 33 (2): 89–119. http://dx.doi.org/10.1111/j.1467-9582.1979.tb00678.x

Alarcos Llorach, E. (1994) *Gramática de la lengua española*. Madrid: Espasa–Calpe.

Altenberg, B. (2002) Concessive connectors in English and Swedish. In H. Hasselgård, S. Johansson, B. Behrens and C. Fabricius-Hansen (eds) *Information Structure in a Cross-Linguistic Perspective*, 21–43. Amsterdam: Rodopi.

Álvarez Martínez, M. Á. (1987) Las oraciones subordinadas: Esbozo de clasificación. *Verba* 14: 117–148.

Anscombre, J-C. and Ducrot, O. (1977). Deux 'mais' en français? *Lingua 43*: 23–40. http://dx.doi.org/10.1016/0024-3841(77)90046-8

Anscombre, J-C. and Ducrot, O. (1983) *L'argumentation dans la langue*. Brussels: Pierre Mardaga.

Asher, N. and Lascarides, A. (2003) *Logics of Conversation*. Cambridge: Cambridge University Press.

Biber, D., Johansson, S., Leech, G., Conrad, S. and Finegan, E. (1999). *Longman Grammar of Spoken and Written English*. Harlow: Pearson Education.

Blakemore, D. (1987) *Semantic Constraints on Relevance*. Oxford: Blackwell.

Blakemore, D. (1989) Denial and contrast: A relevance theoretic analysis of BUT. *Linguistics and Philosophy*, 12 (1): 15–37. http://dx.doi.org/10.1007/BF00627397

Brinton, L. J. (1996) *Pragmatic Markers in English: Grammaticalization and Discourse Functions*. Berlin: Mouton de Gruyter.

Briz, A. (1994) Hacia un análisis argumentativo de un texto coloquial: La incidencia de los conectores pragmáticos. *Verba* 21: 369–388.

Carbonell Olivares, M. S. (2005) *Estudio semántico-pragmático de las relaciones de contraste y sus marcas en lengua inglesa*. Unpublished Ph.D. dissertation, Universidad de Valencia, Valencia.

Couper-Kuhlen, E. and Thompson, S. A. (2000) Concessive patterns in conversation. In E. Couper-Kuhlen and B. Kortmann (eds), *Cause, Condition, Concession, Contrast: Cognitive and Discourse Perspectives*, 381–410. Berlin: Mouton de Gruyter.

Crevels, M. (2000a) *Concession: A Typological Study*. Unpublished Ph.D. dissertation, University of Amsterdam, Amsterdam.

Crevels, M. (2000b) Concessives on different semantic levels: A typological perspective. In B. Kortmann (ed.) *Cause, Condition, Concession, Contrast: Cognitive and Discourse Perspectives*, 313–339. Berlin: Mouton de Gruyter.

Degand, L. (2009) Describing polysemous discourse markers: What does translation add to the picture? In S. Slembrouch, M. Taverniers and M. Van Herreweghe (eds), *From Will to Well. Studies in Linguistics offered to Anne-Marie Simon-Vandenbergen*. Ghent: Academia Press.

Degand, L. and Pander Maat, H. (2003) A contrastive study of Dutch and French causal connectives on the Speaker Involvement Scale. In A. Verhagen and J. van de Weijer (eds), *Usage Based Approaches to Dutch*, 175–199. Utretcht: LOT.

Di Tullio, Á. (1997) *Manual de gramática del español*. Buenos Aires: Edicial.

van Dijk, T. A. (1977) *Text and Context: Explorations in the Semantics and Pragmatics of Discourse*. London: Longman.

van Dijk, T. A. and Kintsch, W. (1983). *Strategies of Discourse Comprehension*. New York: Academic Press.

Fabricius-Hansen, C. (2005). Elusive connectives: A case study on the explicitness dimension of discourse coherence. *Linguistics*, 43 (1): 17–48. http://dx.doi.org/10.1515/ling.2005.43.1.17

Flamenco García, L. (1999) Las construcciones concesivas y adversativas. In V. Demonte (ed.), *Gramática descriptiva de la lengua española* (Vol. 3: Entre la oración y el discurso. Morfología), 3805–3877. Madrid: Espasa.

Foolen, A. (1991) Polyfunctionality and the semantics of adversative conjunctions. *Multilingua* 10 (1–2): 79–92.

Fuentes Rodríguez, C. (1998) *Las construcciones adversativas*. Madrid: Arco.

Gili Gaya, S. (1955) *Curso Superior de Sintaxis Española*. Barcelona: Spes.

Gutiérrez Ordóñez, S. (1977–1978) A propósito de 'Cláusulas y oraciones'. *Archivum* XXVII–XXVIII: 529–547.

Gutiérrez Ordóñez, S. (1997) *Temas, remas, focos, tópicos y comentarios*. Madrid: Arco.

Halliday, M. A. K. and Hasan, R. (1976) *Cohesion in English*. London: Longman.

Hernández Alonso, C. (1995) *Nueva sintaxis de la lengua española*. Salamanca: Ediciones Colegio de España.

Hoey, M. (2001) *Textual Interaction: An Introduction to Written Discourse Analysis*. London: Routledge.

Huddleston, R. and Pullum G. K. (2002) *The Cambridge Grammar of the English Language*. Cambridge: Cambridge University Press.

Izutsu, M. N. (2008) Contrast, concessive, and corrective: Toward a comprehensive study of opposition relations. *Journal of Pragmatics* 40 (4): 646–675. http://dx.doi.org/10.1016/j.pragma.2007.07.001

Kehler, A. (2002) *Coherence, Reference, and the Theory of Grammar*. Stanford, CA: CSLI.

Kingsbury, P., Strassel, S., McLemore, C. and McIntyre, R. (1997) CallHome American English Transcripts, LDC97T14 [Corpus]. Philadelphia, PA: Linguistic Data Consortium.

Knott, A. (1996) *A Data-Driven Methodology for Motivating a Set of Coherence Relations*. Unpublished Ph.D. dissertation, University of Edinburgh, Edinburgh, UK.

Knott, A. and Sanders, T. (1998) The classification of coherence relations and their linguistic markers: An exploration of two languages. *Journal of Pragmatics* 30 (2): 135–175.

König, E. (1988) Concessive connectives and concessive sentences: Cross-linguistic regularities and pragmatic principles. In J. A. Hawkins (ed.) *Explaining Language Universals*, 145–166. London: Blackwell.

Kovacci, O. (1992) *El comentario gramatical II*. Madrid: Arco.

Lagerwerf, L. (1998) *Causal Connectives Have Presuppositions: Effects on Coherence and Discourse Structure*. The Hague: Holland Academic Graphics.

Lakoff, R. (1971) If's And's and But's about conjunctions. In C. J. Fillmore and D. T. Langendoen (eds), *Studies in Linguistic Semantics,* 114–149. New York: Holt, Rinehart and Winston.

Lavacchi, L. and Nicolás, C. (1994) Oraciones de 'aunque' y 'pero'. *Verba* 21: 257–278.

López García, Á. (1999) Relaciones paratácticas e hipotácticas. In V. Demonte (ed.) *Gramática descriptiva de la lengua española* (Vol. 3: Entre la oración y el discurso. Morfología), 3507–3547. Madrid: Espasa.

Luscher, J-M. (1994) Les Marques de connexion: Des guides pour l'interprétation. In J. Moeschler (ed.) *Langage et Pertinence*. Nancy: Presses Universitaires de Nancy.

Mann, W. C. and Taboada, M. (2010). *RST Web Site*, from http://www.sfu.ca/rst

Mann, W. C. and Thompson, S. A. (1988) Rhetorical Structure Theory: Toward a functional theory of text organization. *Text,* 8 (3): 243–281.

Marcu, D. (1997) *The Rhetorical Parsing, Summarization, and Generation of Natural Language Texts.* Unpublished Ph.D. dissertation, University of Toronto, Toronto, Canada.

Martin, J. R. (1992) *English Text: System and Structure.* Amsterdam and Philadelphia, PA: John Benjamins.

Montolío Durán, E. (2001) *Conectores de la lengua escrita.* Barcelona: Ariel.

Moya Corral, J. A. (1996) *Los mecanismos de la interordinación: a propósito de 'pero' y 'aunque'.* Granada: Universidad de Granada.

Narbona Jiménez, A. (1990). *Las subordinadas adverbiales impropias en español.* Málaga: Agora.

Noordman, L. (2001). On the production of causal-contrastive *although* sentences in context. In T. Sanders, J. Schilperoord and W. Spooren (eds), *Text Representation: Linguistic and Psycholinguistic Aspects,* 153–180. Amsterdam and Philadelphia, PA: John Benjamins.

Quirk, R., Greenbaum, S., Leech, G. and Svartvik, J. (1985) *A Comprehensive Grammar of the English Language.* London: Longman.

Real Academia Española. (2009) *Nueva Gramática de la Lengua Española.* Madrid: Espasa.

Redeker, G. (1990) Ideational and pragmatic markers of discourse structure. *Journal of Pragmatics,* 14 (3): 367–381. http://dx.doi.org/10.1016/0378-2166(90)90095-U

Renkema, J. (2004) *Introduction to Discourse Studies.* Amsterdam and Philadelphia, PA: John Benjamins.

Rivarola, J. L. (1976) *Las conjunciones concesivas en español medieval y clásico.* Tübingen: Max Niemeyer.

Ross, J. R. (1986) *Infinite Syntax.* Norwood, NJ: Ablex.

Rudolph, E. (1996) *Contrast: Adversative and Concessive Relations and their Expressions in English, German, Spanish, Portuguese on Sentence and Text Level.* Berlin: Mouton de Gruyter.

Salkie, R. and Oates, S. L. (1999) Contrast and concession in French and English. *Languages in Contrast* 2 (1): 27–56. http://dx.doi.org/10.1075/lic.2.1.04sal

Sperber, D. and Wilson, D. (1995) *Relevance: Communication and Cognition* (2nd edn). Oxford: Blackwell.

Spooren, W. (1989) *Some Aspects of the Form and Interpretation of Global Contrastive Coherence Relations.* Unpublished Ph.D. dissertation, Nijmegen University, Nijmegen.

Taboada, M. (2004a) Rhetorical relations in dialogue: A contrastive study. In C. L. Moder and A. Martinovic-Zic (eds), *Discourse across Languages and Cultures,* 75–97. Amsterdam and Philadelphia, PA: John Benjamins.

Taboada, M. (2004b) *Building Coherence and Cohesion: Task-Oriented Dialogue in English and Spanish*. Amsterdam and Philadelphia, PA: John Benjamins.

Taboada, M. (2006) Discourse markers as signals (or not) of rhetorical relations. *Journal of Pragmatics* 38 (4): 567–592. http://dx.doi.org/10.1016/j.pragma.2005.09.010

Taboada, M. (2008) SFU Review Corpus [Corpus]. Vancouver: Simon Fraser University, http://www.sfu.ca/~mtaboada/research/SFU_Review_Corpus.html.

Taboada, M. (2009) Implicit and explicit coherence relations. In J. Renkema (ed.), *Discourse, of Course*, 127–140. Amsterdam and Philadelphia, PA: John Benjamins.

Taboada, M. and Mann, W. C. (2006a) Rhetorical Structure Theory: Looking back and moving ahead. *Discourse Studies* 8 (3): 423–459. http://dx.doi.org/10.1177/1461445606061881

Taboada, M. and Mann, W. C. (2006b). Applications of Rhetorical Structure Theory. *Discourse Studies*, 8 (4), 567–588. http://dx.doi.org/10.1177/1461445606064836

Traugott, E. C. (1986) On the origins of 'and' and 'but' connectives in English. *Studies in Language,* 10 (1): 137–150. http://dx.doi.org/10.1075/sl.10.1.08clo

Traugott, E. C. (1995) Subjectification in grammaticalisation. In S. Wright (ed.), *Subjectivity and Subjectivisation: Linguistic Perspectives,* 31–54. Cambridge: Cambridge University Press.

Trnavac, R. and Taboada, M. (2010) *The Contribution of Nonveridical Rhetorical Relations to Evaluation in Discourse.* Paper presented at the 37th International Systemic Functional Congress, Vancouver, Canada.

Wheatley, B. (1996). CallHome Spanish Transcripts, LDC96T17 [Corpus]. Philadelphia, PA: Linguistic Data Consortium.

Wilson, L. and Wilson, M. (2001) Farsi speakers. In M. Swan and B. Smith (eds), *Learner English: A Teacher's Guide* (2nd edn), 179–194. Cambridge: Cambridge University Press.

Winter, Y. and Rimon, M. (1994) Contrast and implication in natural language. *Journal of Semantics,* 11 (4): 365–406. http://dx.doi.org/10.1093/jos/11.4.365

2 Pragmatic triangulation and misunderstanding: A prosodic perspective

Jesús Romero-Trillo

This chapter presents 'pragmatic triangulation' as the main tool used by speakers to avoid misunderstanding and reformulate ideas in speech. The study will delve into the prosodic features used by native and non-native speakers of English in the prevention of misunderstanding and describes their functional differences in both groups of speakers. The article will first make a theoretical account of the notion of understanding and misunderstanding and will discuss the characterization of pragmatic markers in the communication process. Second, the study will select the most frequent pragmatic markers used by speakers for this purpose, and will describe their frequency and relevance in the corpus. And third, the paper will look into the prosody and pragmatic asymmetry of the use of these elements by native and non-native speakers on the basis of statistical data. The final section will discuss the results of the analysis and will highlight the importance of invigorating this type of research for the benefit of contrastive and pedagogic studies.

1. Introduction

Misunderstanding in communication is a pervasive phenomenon that can find its roots in the cognitive or linguistic discrepancy of the expectations between addressers and addressees in conversation. Very often, speakers are not aware of these misunderstandings until communication reaches an incomprehensible peak that shows the incompatibility of their positions. At this point, interactants must engage in a clarification process to untangle confusion which can be costly in terms of social rapport and cognitive effort. To avoid such risks, speakers make use of 'pragmatic triangulation' to help verify and rearrange the communicative load of a message. The present study will describe the realization of pragmatic triangulation through pragmatic markers, and their prosodic contours, in a corpus of native and non-native speakers of English.

2. Understanding in conversation

Understanding is, from a cognitive perspective, a slippery conceptualization because we, as speakers, can attest to our understanding of an idea, but can only rely on the other's certification of (not) having understood a certain concept or proposition. This communication quandary implies that speakers are fragile in their discourse construction and are always exposed to face-loss, as they must interpret the listeners' behaviour and (non)linguistic signals, and can only assume that correct communication is taking place.

The conceptualization of understanding in conversation has traditionally been approached from two main perspectives: the cognitive approach and the conversation analysis (CA) approach. The former has studied the relationship between cognitive processes and meaning, as for example in the works by Panther and Thornburg (1998), Ponterotto (2000), etc., while the latter has delved into the systematics of conversation and the identification of conversation rules (Sacks *et al.*, 1974). In its analysis, CA has paid special attention not to the use of conversational rules, but mainly to their violation as the key to the lack of correct understanding. From a propositional perspective, understanding has been related to the semantic adequacy in the emission or reception of a message. This phenomenon has also been the subject of study by conversation analysts who have studied this phenomenon from the perspective of repair strategies (Schegloff *et al.*, 1977).

The presence of repair strategies in turn-taking is basic for conversation analysts as it is the only method to test understanding (Sacks *et al.*, 1974). For these authors, repair is always locally-based because speakers produce their 'next' turn on the basis of the prior turn, as also described by Hutchby and Wooffitt (2008: 13) with the expression 'next turn proof procedure'. As opposed to the cognitive approach, for CA practitioners the verification of correct understanding is not a major concern, as they believe that the system self-regulates and eventually leads to the correct interpretation. For these authors, conversation should be dissected turn by turn and contemplated unit by unit, because each new step is a notional challenge that needs testing against the prior context.

The fragility of what I shall term 'unilateral discourse building' increases when the contextual parameters that are usually shared by speakers of a language are hindered by cross-cultural differences and, therefore, by pragmatic distance. In other words, when the native languages of the speakers are different, and one of the interactants is communicating in a second or foreign language, the linguistic output can be disrupted by pragmatic deficiencies due to lack of fluency in the transmission of ideas. The problem at stake at this point is to decide the degree of 'nativeness' of the linguistic behaviour of the second/ foreign language speaker, and the extent to which extra-linguistic factors dealing with contextual features play a decisive role in the full understanding of a message. For example, Moeschler (2004) uses a cognitive approach to study non-standard cases of misunderstanding, specifically intercultural misunderstanding, and states that within intercultural communication the greatest risk of misunderstanding comes when the non-native speaker has a strong mastery of the primary language in the interaction, as the native speaker will assume that the non-native speaker also has the cultural grounding of the language.

From a more philosophical perspective, some philosophers of language consider that understanding is inextricably linked to believing in a tradition derived from Spinoza, for whom comprehension includes acceptance of content. In other words, explicit communication would be categorized as content preserving and would not challenge the ideas contained in the message by means of any inferential process. This approach would marginalize context – as understood for example in the Dynamic Model of Meaning (Kecskes, 2008) – as this is created by the speaker and the listener simply assumes (believes to be true) what is understood, and vice-versa. Against this traditional view of the philosophy of language, Sperber *et al.* (2010) propose the notion of 'epistemic vigilance' in which speakers start by understanding and then check the trustworthiness of a message, i.e., understanding and believing are separated cognitive processes in which listeners first decode the linguistic information and do not believe it by default. Moreover, only through 'epistemic vigilance' can speakers guarantee truthful communication.

Romero-Trillo and Maguire (2011: 234) propose a socio-cognitive description of context and communication and aver that 'it is very important to underline the fact that lexical information can run parallel or even collide with context, and that to avoid misunderstanding, the understanding of lexical and pragmatic units must then be revised dynamically in the interaction'. In other words, for these authors pragmatic processing runs parallel to lexical processing. The cognitive mechanism that speakers use to systematize the concomitant pragmatic and lexical information is called 'Adaptive Management' (Romero-Trillo, 2007). Adaptive Management shows that context is the only objective element in communication, because it is external, objectifiable and negotiable; in this model, context is so autonomous that it can collide with the lexical information or with the pragmatic information put forward by speakers. In other words, Adaptive Management is a process in which speakers participate to mould the context cooperatively, as they cannot exert any control over this process individually.

In fact, I contend that the question of understanding might be more influenced by the contextual history and inferences of the speaker than by linguistic parameters that can be remedied through direct linguistic strategies.

From this perspective, the existing cognitive abyss between a speaker and a hearer, no matter whether with the same or different mother tongues, can be filled through the exercise of pragmatic triangulation. Pragmatic triangulation can be defined as the mechanism that the participants in a conversation implement for the verification of the correct transmission of a message. In other words, triangulation is the linguistic tool that specifically helps a participant in a conversation agree or disagree with the new context promoted by the message and, thus, add or modify the pragmatic or lexical information presented by the other speaker. This confirmation is mandatory as it is the only means available to the speaker to know if he/she can proceed with a message. It can be realized vocally and kinetically (in conjunction or isolation) according to the model shown in Figure 1

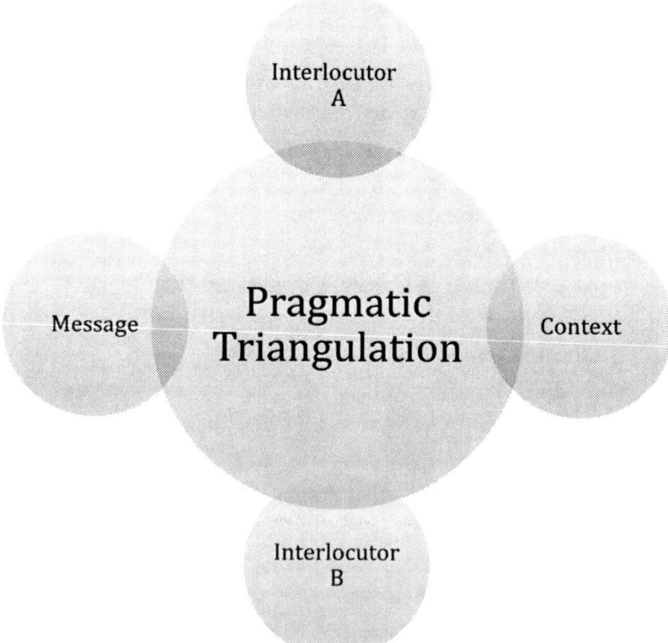

Figure 1: Pragmatic triangulation

The model works bi-directionally, in the sense that when the message is uttered by interlocutor A, the triangulation process works in one direction: Context-Message-Interlocutor B. Conversely, when interlocutor B intervenes, the process works in the other Context, Message and Interlocutor A. However, the schema links the four elements, including interlocutors A and B, because communication is a continuum between the participants in a conversation.

In this approach, pragmatics can be described as the mechanism that helps bridge the gap between what is literally said in an utterance and the meanings that can be implied, when speakers share a certain type of information and function in a shared context. Therefore, triangulation belongs to the domain of pragmatics, since the confirmation of understanding is not usually verbalized through the complete repetition of what is being said, as in the following example:

(1)   A: … I believe that the new degree in linguistics offered by our department will be very popular

          B: I understand that what you say is that the new degree in linguistics will be very popular, and that you are contrasting your ideas with your opinion about the present or previous degrees, or other departments' degrees. This, in your opinion, might imply more students and more funding for our department to have, etc. …

To avoid this linguistic meandering, speakers use triangulation as an effective pragmatic tool to alleviate communication verbosity and enhance smooth cognitive processing. Through pragmatic triangulation obscure language and semantic density can be simplified with gestural mechanisms, like nodding, or with pragmatic markers that help continue communication without excessive disruption.

Therefore, pragmatic triangulation merges the cognitive and conversation analysis traditions and focuses on the role of the cognitive component in conversation insofar as it justifies the verifiable correct transmission of knowledge through interactional linguistic data. This approach tries to describe the psychological status of interaction behind the speakers' turns through the study of the elements that guarantee understanding and cognitive adjustment.

The basis of triangulation is that understanding does not only have to be enacted in our minds, but that it has to become public and overt to be effective. In other words, there must be an overt link between cognition and interaction, and this has to be reflected in the analysis of conversation, otherwise cognition will play an inert role in the weight of interaction. In this model, the performance of understanding through triangulation is always localized and context-bound in a conversation, otherwise its acknowledgement is not always guaranteed, as certain ideas can be understood at a certain moment and misunderstood later (or vice-versa).

3. Triangulation and pragmatic markers

According to Romero-Trillo (in press):

> Pragmatics markers can be described as those constructions, such as *you know, I mean, you see, well, yeah*, etc., that are present in speech to support interaction, [...] have modified their original propositional meaning and have adopted a communicative status that weaves the net of discourse between the addressor, the addressee, and the context of a given message.

The fact that these elements are independent from any propositional relationship and are equidistant from the other three elements of communication (the addresser, the addressee and the context) is because they constitute, in my opinion, the prototypical tools for pragmatic triangulation. In other words, they contribute to scaffold the pragmatic coherence of discourse via feedback, i.e. the use of 'linguistic elements to show that [the listener] is following the ideas expressed in the message' (Romero-Trillo, 2001: 536).

The use of pragmatic markers for triangulation is crucial for the cognitive and interactional processing of the conversation, as they indicate that the message is being processed and accepted by the recipient. Also the type of feedback, which is realized primarily by prosodic features and not so much by the choice of the marker, indicates the extent to which the information is perceived as something predictable in the flow of the conversation (neutral feedback), or as something completely new or subject to surprise or emotion (emphatic feedback). In fact, triangulation shows that taking a turn in a conversation is an achievement of understanding, so the speakers can evaluate what an on-going turn is doing, and if it has any prospects of becoming an 'apt, relevant, cogent and sensible next turn' (Macbeth, 2011: 440). In this sense, authors differ in the way understanding is performed in conversation. For example, Fele (1992), Heritage (2007) and Mondada (2011) claim that overt recognition is not the most usual case in an interaction and that understanding is generally tacit and subsumed in the next turn construction. Other authors suggest that participants in a conversation need an ostensive proof of understanding that is sufficient to create new contexts (Hindmarsh *et al.*, 2011).

From a conversational perspective, the explicit formulation of understanding through pragmatic markers like 'yeah, ok, mhm', etc., needs a profound analysis of the different functions that these elements can realize in interaction, as the same element can realize more functions than showing understanding (Romero-Trillo, 2001), depending on the register where the markers appear (Lindwall and Lymer, 2011). In this sense, conversation analysts have explained how the completion of a Turn Constructional Unit can be in itself the realization of understanding in what is called the 'understanding position'

(Sacks, 1992: 426), as a preface to the possibility to initiate a turn or to initiate repair. In interaction, these pragmatic markers are accompanied by a whole array of prosodic contours that are essential for the analysis of the relationship between prosody and pragmatics.

For the present analysis I will adopt the description of English intonation developed by Halliday (1967, 1970) and Cruttenden (1997) *inter alios*. Their approach, the Nuclear Tone Theory, is based on the study of the tone as a perceptible element for all speakers, as opposed to the Autosegmental Theory (Gussenhoven, 1984; Ladd, 1996), which analyses the relative comparison of high or low pitch accents in an utterance. The Nuclear Tone Theory considers that there is a hierarchical semantic order in the way meaning is assigned to the tonic element, i.e., the most prominent accented syllable in a tone unit (Halliday, 1967). This element realizes this prosodic function intertwined with a semantic value, as it carries the most significant meaning in a specific speech segment. From a prosodic perspective, pragmatic markers have a distinct prosodic entity when they appear in first position and can be realized with multiple prosodic patterns. In propositional terms, they are not pronounced inside the same tone unit as the message they accompany, although they usually appear embedded in the same tone unit if they are at the end (Romero-Trillo, 2001). These prosodic features, with their variation in pragmatic meaning, are the reasons why they are difficult to process for non-native speakers of a language. To illustrate this point, the analysis in the London-Lund corpus of the 54 most frequent pragmatic markers presented in Romero-Trillo (2001) showed, for instance, that the element 'well' can appear with the five primary tones described by Halliday (1967). This multiple prosodic value certainly opens a new window for the pragmatic interpretation of language in use.

4. Analysis of the data

The data for the analysis comes from the Spanish section of the Louvain International Database of Spoken English Interlanguage (LINDSEI) compiled by Romero-Trillo and Fernández-Agüero. The LINDSEI corpus (Guilquin *et al.*, 2010) is a collection of spoken language data from interviews with intermediate to advanced speakers of English of 11 mother tongues. The interviewers are always native speakers of English. In order to make conversations comparable topic-wise, all interviews follow the same recording procedure according to the following outline: warming-up activity, informal discussion on a personal experience and a picture description. The Spanish section has a total number of 50 interviews (84,749 words), and for the present study we have selected five of these conversations with the following details: all the participants (interviewers and interviewees) in this study are female speakers, of a similar age, and of similar educational background (university students).

Table 1. Description of the data : duration of the file and number of pragmatic markers

File	Duration (min)	No. Feedback PM's
SP-001	15:11	75
SP-002	15:32	89
SP-003	16:18	81
SP-006	15:08	85
SP-014	14:47	85

For the acoustic analysis, we have used the acoustic analysis software Praat (Boersma and Weenink, 2010) and, as mentioned above, the intonation contours (primary tones) used to identify the different pitch movements are based on Halliday's model:

Tone 1:	falling
Tone 2:	rising
Tone 3:	level-rise
Tone 4:	rise-fall-rise
Tone 5:	fall-rise-fall
Tones 13 and 53:	compound tones (1+3 and 5+3)

The pragmatic markers that function as feedback under analysis are: 'mhm', 'ok', 'yeah' and 'yes'. An initial auditory perception of the markers in the corpus indicated that there was a difference in the pitch used by the native female speakers (Group A) compared to the non-native female speakers (Group B). In fact, the impression was that the non-native speakers were more assertive in their use of feedback than the native speakers, i.e., they used a lower pitch level. To test this impression, I computed the mean initial and mean final pitch of native and non-native speakers.

The comparison of the initial pitch between both groups was the following: the mean of the native speakers was 277.88 Hz, and of non-natives 262.80 Hz. The t-test had an almost significant result – although not in statistical terms – between both groups ($t = 1.73$; $p = 0.060$), as can be seen in Figure 2.

The mean result for the final pitch of pragmatic markers was 277.98 Hz for the native speakers, and 249.44 Hz for the non-natives. The results of the t-test showed a high significant difference ($t = 3.19$; $p = 0.001$) between both groups, which did confirm the initial auditory impression that non-native speakers had a lower tone in their use of the pragmatic markers. Here follows the figure with the visual differences of the final pitch level between both groups.

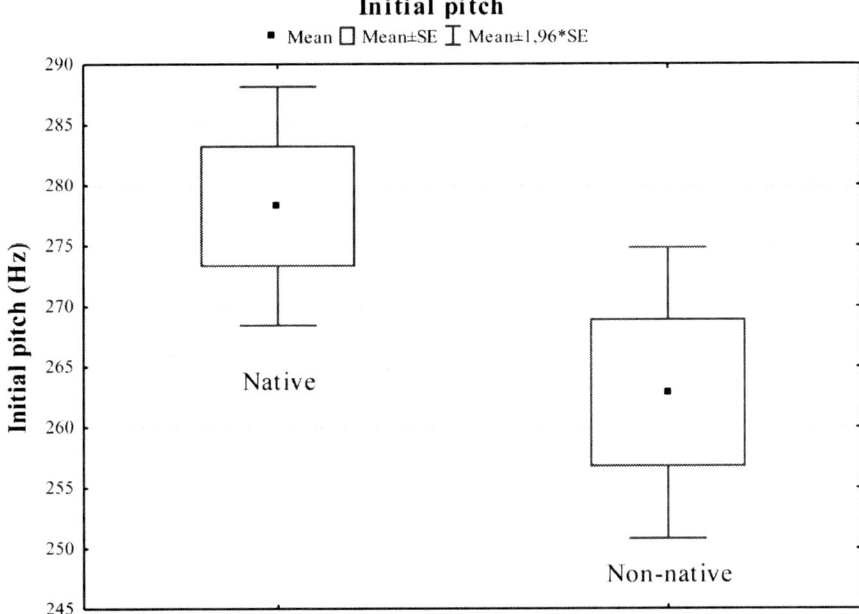

Figure 2: Initial pitch of Pragmatic Markers in native and non-native female speakers.

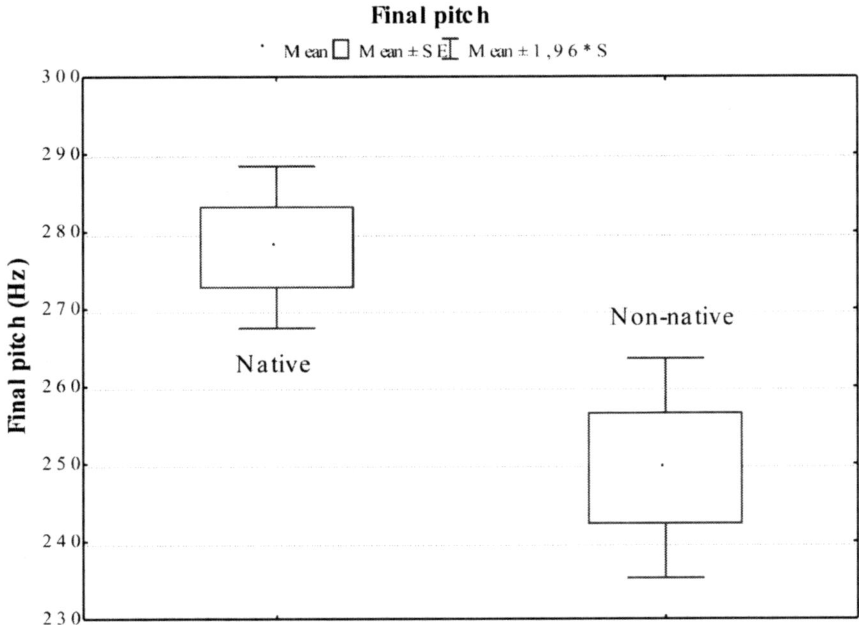

Figure 3: Final pitch of Pragmatic Markers in native and non-native female speakers.

After this initial analysis, I compared the different uses of the pragmatic markers in relation to the tones used to test the preferences of the native speakers and the assimilated use of non-native speakers.

1. The pragmatic marker 'mhm' appears as feedback in the speech of the native and non-native speakers with the tones 1, 2, 3, 4, 5 and 13. It is interesting that both groups of speakers use this marker with tone 1, 3, 5 and 13 with a similar frequency, and that the differences between native and non-native speakers appear with the tones that imply a final rising contour, 2 and 4. In fact, the t-test shows the high significance for tone 2 ($t = 2.659$; $p = 0.03$), which increases dramatically for tone 4 ($t = 4.008$; $p = 0.005$).

2. As regards the pragmatic marker 'ok', it has a common appearance in both groups with the tones 1, 3, 4 and 5. It is important to mention that the non-native speakers do not use it with the rising tone 2. The pattern of use for the rest of the tones shows non-significant results, which means that non-native speakers use this element in a similar way.

3. The element 'yeah' is used with the same contours by native and non-native speakers, namely with tones 1, 2, 3, 4 and 5. Again, the analyses showed interesting differences in the use of this marker with rising tones. In the case of tone 2 we find a statistical significance ($t = -2.392$; $p = 0.04$), which – as in the case of 'mhm'– increases with tone 4 ($t = 3.118$; $p = 0.01$).

4. To finish the analysis of the markers, the element 'yes' appears with tones 1, 2, 3, 4 and 5 in the native speakers, while only with tones 1 and 2 in the non-native group. We did not find significant differences in the cases of the shared contours, but it is important to highlight the absence of the three tones (3, 4 and 5) in the non-native speakers, two of which (tones 3 and 4) have a rising final pitch.

The results show that native speakers use more rising tones in the markers 'mhm' and 'yeah' because, in my opinion, they have a less transparent lexical link, i.e., they are more 'discourse-grammaticalized' (Romero-Trillo, 2001), while the other markers, 'yes' and 'ok' have a similar use of the tones. This result also correlates with the analysis of the mean initial final pitch of all the markers in which non-native speakers have a tendency for lower pitch levels. This indicates that these markers are pragmatically equivocal when used by non-natives, because they equate understanding with showing belief or agreement, i.e., they are not used as elements that contribute to enact fluency in communication through triangulation.

5. Conclusion

In the present article, I have presented the use of pragmatic markers as crucial elements in triangulation strategies for adaptive management in conversation. I have differentiated between (mis)understanding and believing – or agreeing – as triangulation helps interlocutors make overt signals to escape from interactional solipsism and engage in the process of contextual dynamism. The results show that there exists a difference in pitch level in the pronunciation of pragmatic markers between native and non-native speakers. The difference is slightly audible at the beginning of the marker, but it becomes clear at the end of the markers. The reason is the less frequent use of tones with a rising contour (2 and 4) by non-native speakers, which native speakers use more frequently for feedback as they are less pragmatically commissive with the content of the message than the elements with a falling tone. In this sense, non-native speakers sometimes conflate the agreement and feedback function and sound too assertive in contexts in which the mere confirmation of understanding would be enough to signal correct triangulation. In sum, the study shows that the use of correct intonation of pragmatic markers for feedback is an essential element to consider in the speech of non-native speakers of English, as their lower pitch level in comparison with the native speakers might indicate agreement or believing more than feedback, and therefore, their feedback cues might sound too rotund to be interpreted as such.

References

Boersma, P. and Weenink, D. (2010) Praat: Doing phonetics by computer [Computer program]. Version 5.1.07, from http://www.praat.org/

Cruttenden, A. (1997) *Intonation* (2nd edn). Cambridge: Cambridge University Press.

Fele, G. (1992) La comprensione nell'interazione. *Rassegna Italiana di Sociologia* 33 (3): 425–438.

Guilquin G. (ed.) *LINDSEI Corpus*. Louvain: Louvain la Neuve Press.

Gussenhoven, C. (1984) *On the Grammar and Semantics of Sentence Accents*. Dordrecht: Foris Publications.

Halliday, M. A. K. (1967) *Intonation and Grammar in British English*. The Hague: Mouton.

Halliday, M. A. K. (1970) *A Course in Spoken English*. Oxford: Oxford University Press.

Heritage, J. (2007) Intersubjectivity and progressivity in person (and place) reference. In N. J. Enfield and S. Levinson (eds) *Person Reference in Interaction: Linguistic, Cultural, and Social Perspectives*, 255–280. Cambridge University Press, Cambridge.

Hindmarsh, J., Reynolds, P., Dunne, S. (2011) Exhibiting understanding: The body in apprentices. *Pragmatics* 43 (2): 489–503. http://dx.doi.org/10.1016/j.pragma.2009.09.008

Hutchby, I. and Wooffitt, R. (2008) *Conversation Analysis.* Polity Press, Cambridge.

Kecskes, I. (2008) Dueling contexts: A dynamic model of meaning. *Journal of Pragmatics* 40 (3): 385–406. http://dx.doi.org/10.1016/j.pragma.2007.12.004

Ladd, D. R. (1996) *Intonational Phonology.* Cambridge: Cambridge University Press.

Lindwall, O. and Lymer, G. (2011) Uses of 'understand' in science education. *Pragmatics* 43: 452–474. http://dx.doi.org/10.1016/j.pragma.2010.08.021

Macbeth, D. (2011) Understanding understanding as an instructional matter. *Journal of Pragmatics* 43: 438–451. http://dx.doi.org/10.1016/j.pragma.2008.12.006

Moeschler, J. (2004) Intercultural pragmatics: A cognitive approach. *Intercultural Pragmatics* 1 (1): 49–70.

Mondada, L. (2011) Understanding as an embodied, situated and sequential achievement in interaction. *Journal of Pragmatics* 43 (2): 542–552. http://dx.doi.org/10.1016/j.pragma.2010.08.019

Panther, K. U. and Thornburg, L. (1998) A cognitive approach to inferencing in conversation. *Journal of Pragmatics* 30 (6): 755–769. http://dx.doi.org/10.1016/S0378-2166(98)00028-9

Ponterotto, D. (2000) The cohesive role of cognitive metaphor in discourse and conversation. In A. Barcelona (ed.) *Metaphor and Metonymy at the Crossroads, a Cognitive Approach.* Berlin: Mouton de Gruyter.

Romero-Trillo, J. (2001) A mathematical model for the analysis of variation in discourse. *Journal of Linguistics* 37 (3): 527–550. http://dx.doi.org/10.1017/S0022226701001050

Romero-Trillo, J. (2007) Adaptive Management in discourse: The case of involvement discourse markers in English and Spanish conversations. *Catalan Journal of Linguistics* 6: 81–94.

Romero-Trillo, J. (in press) Pragmatic markers. *Encyclopedia of Applied Linguistics.* Oxford: Blackwell.

Romero-Trillo, J. and Agüero, M. F. (2010) Spanish subcorpus. In Gäetanelle Guilquin (ed.) *LINDSEI Corpus.* Louvain: Louvain la Neuve Press.

Romero-Trillo, J. and Maguire, L. (2011) Adaptive context, the fourth element of meaning. *International Review of Pragmatics* 3 (2): 228–241. http://dx.doi.org/10.1163/187731011 X597523

Sacks, H. (1992) *Lectures on Conversation [1964–72],* 2 Vols. Oxford: Basil Blackwell.

Sacks, H., Schegloff, E. A. and Jefferson, G. (1974) A simplest systematics for the organization of turn-taking in conversation. *Language* 50 (4): 696–735. http://dx.doi.org/10.2307/412243

Schegloff, E. A., Jefferson, G. and Sacks, H. (1977) The preference for self-correction in the organization of repair in conversation. *Language* 53 (2): 361–382. http://dx.doi.org/10.2307/413107

Sperber, D, Clément, F., Heintz, C., Mascaro, O., Mercier, H., Origgi, G. and Wilson, D. (2010) Epistemic vigilance. *Mind and Language* 25 (4): 359–393. http://dx.doi.org/10.1111/j.1468-0017.2010.01394.x

3   Spanish *Venga* and its English equivalents: A contrastive study of teenage talk

Anna-Brita Stenström

The Spanish marker *venga* is frequently used in casual conversation in general and in teenage conversation in particular. Like other pragmatic markers, it is a multifunctional item. It is also an extremely versatile marker, which functions on the discourse level as well as on the interactional and interpersonal levels of conversation. Consequently, it can be expected to have more than one corresponding marker in English, depending on the speaking situation, the context and position in the discourse. This chapter focuses on the various uses of *venga* in Madrid teenagers' conversations and the way these uses are realized in London teenage conversations. As the paper will show, the closest English equivalent of the pragmatic marker *venga* in most of its uses is come on.

1. Introduction

Pragmatic markers are indispensible in oral communication. They help us to start a conversation, to keep it going and to arrive at a smooth ending. But although we master the use of pragmatic markers in our own language, how to use them in a foreign language may cause problems. Consequently, if we want to achieve communicative competence in other languages, contrastive analyses of pragmatic markers are absolutely necessary.

Since pragmatic markers are expected to be more frequent in young speech than in adult speech, I have concentrated on teenage conversation. The online accessibility of the two corpora representing Spanish and

English teenage conversation, respectively, which are described in Section 1.4, has been a great advantage for the study. Moreover, the main division of the various functions of *venga* suggested by Blas Arroyo (1998), and the detailed classification proposed by Santos Río (2003), referred to by Cestero Mancera and Moreno Fernández (2008) and their own adoption of this classification, have been of invaluable influence for my own classification (see Section 2).

Before entering on the study proper, let me give some crucial background information.

1.1. *Venga*

Originally, *venga* is the grammaticalized version of the third person subjunctive of the verb *venir* ('come') used as an imperative. An overview of the way it is dealt with in the literature shows that its present status in conversation is slightly controversial, however. Going by chronology, Blas Arroyo (1998) discusses the various uses of *venga* in terms of a discourse marker with various pragmatic functions, stressing its recent use as a closing marker, while Herrero (2002: 73–74) regards it as an interjection marking agreement (*Me ayudas a fregar? – Vale. Venga.* 'Will you help me mop? – OK. Fine') and, as a deictic marker, signalling that which provokes a particular emotional reaction (*Venga con esos bultos!* 'Come on with those bumps').

Cortés and Camacho (2005) agree with Blas Arroyo (1998) that *venga* is intended to generate a reaction from the addressee, which points to its function as an interactional marker. They view *venga* as a purely interactive marker, with a comforting and bonding effect on the addressee by showing straightforward support, which leads to confidence and mutual understanding. But they emphasize that, like other pragmatic markers, *venga* can acquire very different functional nuances, including contradictory, depending on how it is uttered, for instance with humour or irony or in an aggressive tone. As a result of the actual context, it can serve as an emphatic marker intended to change the addressee's attitude and can even reveal hostility (e.g., *venga idiota*). In other words, the effect is sometimes the opposite of comforting and bonding, resulting in reproaches, objections, and even anger.

Cestero Mancera and Moreno Fernández (2008: 7), with reference to Vigara Tauste (1992), Alonso-Cortés (1999) and Casamiglia and Tusón (1999), describe ¡*venga*! as 'una interjección impropia de tipo instativo' ('an improper interjection signalling urgency'), which performs such pragmatic functions as acceptance, rejection, instruction, entreaty, appeal, and encouragement (cf. Martín Zorraquino and Portolés Lázaro, 1999; Herrero, 2002; Santos Río, 2003). With reference to Casamiglia and Tusón (1999), Santos Río (2003) and Cestero (2005), they state that *venga* often serves as a turn-transitional and conversation-closing device. The main purpose, however, is to serve as a discursive attenuator and a cooperative index in the interaction.

All in all, despite the different labels used, from discourse marker to interactional marker and improper interjection, there seems to be general agreement that *venga* is used for pragmatic purposes.

1.2. Come on

Come on has aroused very little attention and is nowhere referred to as a 'pragmatic marker', as far as I am aware. In *Longman Dictionary of Contemporary English* (1987: 197), it is unlabelled and said to mean 'Try harder!', 'Make an effort!', 'Hurry up!' and 'Cheer up!'. *Collins Cobuild English Language Dictionary* (1987: 273) refers to *come on* as a 'phrase' that is used 'when you want to encourage someone to do or say something they are reluctant to do or say'. In the *New Oxford Dictionary of English* (1998: 365) it is referred to as an imperative used to encourage someone to do something or to hurry up, or when we think that what somebody has done is wrong. Green (2000: 261), in his dictionary of slang, describes *come on* as an exclamation of disbelief, disapproval or irritation, while the internet-based *Wiktionary* treats it as an interjection expressing encouragement (*Come on George! You can't win!*), or disbelief (*Come on! You can't possibly expect me to believe that.*), and as an expression meaning 'hurry up'. In other words, the way *come on* is looked upon varies from an unlabelled expression via a phrase, an imperative and an exclamation to an interjection – with no explicit reference to it as a pragmatic marker.

1.3. Definition of pragmatic markers

In this chapter both *venga* and *come on* are regarded as pragmatic markers in line with, for instance, Spanish *vale* ('okay') and *sabes* ('you know') and the well-established English pragmatic markers *right* and *well*. I have adopted the all-inclusive definition suggested by Carter and McCarthy (2006: 208), where 'pragmatic marker' is regarded as a cover term including 'discourse markers', for items that 'operate outside the structural limits of the clause' and that 'indicate the speaker's intentions with regard to organizing, structuring and monitoring the discourse', in addition to reflecting the speaker's attitude to the message.

1.4. The data

The various uses of the pragmatic marker *venga* in the Madrid teenagers' conversations in *Corpus Oral de Lenguaje Adolescente de Madrid* (COLAm; www.COLAm.org) will be compared with the way the same uses are realized in the London teenagers' conversations in *The Bergen Corpus of London Teenage Language* (COLT; www.hit.uib.no/colt). These two corpora are highly comparable due to the fact that COLAm[1] was collected with COLT as a model. They both contain roughly half a million words of spontaneous conversation recorded by student 'recruits' in various environments, for instance at home, in the street, in the school yard or at a café. The speakers are 13 to 19 year-old boys and girls, friends of the recruit, with a high, mid- or low sociolinguistic background. What distinguishes the corpora is time of collection: COLT was collected in 1993, while COLAm started being collected ten years later, a circumstance that ought not to have an effect on the outcome of the present study.

2. A model of analysis

The classification suggested by Blas Arroyo (1998) and Santos Río (2003), which is further elaborated by Cestero Mancera and Moreno Fernández (2008) will serve as a model for my analysis. According to Blas Arroyo, *venga* occurs with various pragmatic values in three main types of sequences: *directive, reactive* and *evaluative,* as illustrated in Examples (1) to (3):

Directive

(1)   A: venga date prisa que llegamos tarde
            come on hurry up we'll be late

       B: voy voy
            I'm coming I'm coming (Blas Arroyo, 1998: 7)

Reactive

(2)   A: Juani nos podrías cantar esa canción de+?
            Juani could you sing this song of+? for us

       B: no sé si voy a acordarme
            I don't know if I'll remember

       A: venga mujer
            come on woman (Blas Arroyo, 1998: 8)

Evaluative

(3)   A: el niño se viene con nosotros que su madre ya sabe lo que tiene que hacer con él
            como siempre ha hecho
            the child comes with us since his mother already knows what has to be done to
            him as usual

       B: pero yo no quiero (llorando)
            but I don't want to (crying)

       A: tú calla niño! que no sabes nada de esto
            you be quiet child! you don't know what it's all about

C: bue: no venga que le vamos a hacer una prueba muy sencilla que además no duele
      nada, no se preocupe
      good come on we're going to take a very simple specimen which doesn't hurt
      at all don't worry
      (Blas Arroyo, 1998: 9–10)

In addition, a recent use of *venga* observed by Blas Arroyo (1998) is as a conversational routine in *closing* sequences, which lead to the end of the interaction, as illustrated in (4). By using *venga* in this position, the speaker not only shows that s/he wants to end the conversation but also that s/he wants to do this as smoothly as possible (1998: 14).

(4) A: *venga*
           okay then
     B: *venga* un abrazo (Blas Arroyo, 1998: 17)
           right a hug

Serrano (2002: 160), too, sees *venga* as a form of leave-taking, though she describes the main function of *venga* as indicating assertion (A: *Te mando por correo el original* – B: **Venga** *y yo te acuso recibo*. A: 'I'll send you the original in the mail' – B. 'Okay and I'll send you a receipt'), a view that is also reflected in Herrero (2002: 73–74),

In what follows, I will adopt the three uses of *venga* discussed by Blas Arroyo (1998) in terms of 'directive', 'reactive' and 'evaluative' moves as a main division, supplemented with the more specific categorization of functions suggested by Santos Río (2003). Figure 1 presents an overview of the main division and the sub-functions.

DIRECTIVE	REACTIVE	EVALUATIVE
Instruct	object	reorient
Insist	reject	follow-up
encourage	accept	
Appeal	agree	
pre-close	close	

Figure 1: Classification of functions.

The directive-reactive-evaluative 'chain' has a parallel in the IRF-sequence (Introduction-Response-Follow-up) introduced by Sinclair and Coulthard (1975) for the description of classroom interaction and adopted by Stenström (1984) for describing questioning exchanges in natural conversation (cf. also Stenström, 1999).

3. Spanish venga and its English equivalents in teenage talk

Each of the functions of *venga* listed in Figure 1 will be illustrated by an example from COLAm and accompanied by what I regard as an equivalent example from COLT. The two corpora are comparable in that they both consist of spontaneous conversations produced by teenagers and recorded by the students themselves in similar surroundings, and that the topics of conversation are very similar. With the pragmatic functions of *venga* in various situations as a starting-point, I have looked for similar situations in COLT, realizing that *come on* would be the closest equivalent in most cases.

3.1. Directives

As a directive, the marker occurs in the initiating move of a conversational exchange (cf. Stenström, 1999: 31), where it typically occupies the first slot. This is illustrated in Examples (5) to (8), where *venga* serves to instruct, insist, encourage and appeal:

Instruct

COLAm. Situation: At home where Ana tells Juan to take a shower so that they can go down for supper, but Juan refuses.

> (5a)   Ana: *venga* dúchate y bajamos a cenar
>   come on take a shower and let's go down to supper
>   Juan: no (MALCC2[2])

COLT. Situation: Tom asks Chris to listen to a tape, but Chris is not interested.

> (5b)   Tom: come on Chris listen. It's funny [man I te=]
>   Chris: can't be bothered (35602[3])

In both examples above the speaker tells the addressee in a straightforward way what to do, but without the desired effect, as reflected in the responses. In the next two examples, the speakers' eagerness to get the addressees to do what they want them to do is reflected in the repeated requests.

Insist

COLAm. Situation: Isabel and Marta are trying in vain to persuade Miguel to sing on the tape.

> (6a)   Marta: hace eh ah eh ah
>   sing eh ah eh ah
>   Isabel: *venga* canta
>   come on sing
>   Migual: no
>   no
>   Marta: canta
>   sing

   Isabel: sí *venga* (MABPE2)
       yes come on

COLT. Situation: Ben wants Jock to reveal a secret.

 (6b) Ben: come on Jock tell me I wanna know.
    Jock: I don't know
    Tom: come on you tell you're probably just trying to put it in a different way
       now (42002)

The next brief dialogues, (7a) and (7b), are from the beginning of a recording session. It is obvious that the recruits have some difficulty getting their friends to collaborate by saying something. But unlike a similar situation illustrated in (6a), the added expressions *no desesperes* ('don't give up') and *Don't be shy* have an encouraging effect.

Encourage
COLAm. Situation: José (the recruit), Diego and Judy start joking about Norwegians for lack of topic of conversation.

 (7a) José: venga cuenta algo
       come on tell me something
    Diego: *venga* aun no desesperes
       come on don't give up
    Judy: venga noruegos a ver si estáis buenos y venís a visitarme (MALCC2)
       come on Norwegians let's see if you are nice and come and visit me

COLT. Situation: Sylvia (the recruit) has difficulties getting her friends to talk.

 (7b) Sylvia: So come on, talk to me. Tell me your dreams. You are! Come on! …
       Don't be shy, it's just a microphone (32909)

The speakers in (8a) and (8b) are obviously very eager to persuade the addressees to do what they want them to do, as is reflected in the use of the combinations *venga anda* in (8a) and *come on please* in (8b), with an appealing effect:

Appeal
COLAm. Situation: Jorge has got hold of a list of taboo expressions from which he is reading aloud.

 (8a) Jorge: … coños lavados coños con costra coños viscosos como una ostra …
       … cunts washed, cunts with scab, cunts viscous like an oyster …
    Pablo: *venga* Jorge pásame la hoja anda (MALCB2)
       come on Jorge let me have the page please

COLT. Situation: Betty has some sweets that she first refuses to share with Sue.

(8b)   Betty: no you can't I've only got two left.
      Sue: Oh come on
      Betty: Oh shall I open it right
      Sue: Equal share
      Betty: Look, no it's for you, [it might look, cos that's the thing for {unclear}]
      Sue: [Come on, please please please] come on
      Betty: No, no, no, screw you (32503)

As these examples show, *come on* seems to be the closest and perhaps only English marker that corresponds to *venga* in its various directive functions. Like *venga, come on* is the grammaticalized version of the imperative use of a verb, which has developed into a pragmatic marker. In addition to encouraging someone to do something, it is used, for instance, when we want somebody to hurry up, to change his/her mind, to make an effort or to cheer up (cf. *Longman Dictionary of Contemporary English* (1987: 197)). But as will be seen in Section 3.2, *come on* is also used as a reactive device, when we think that somebody is doing or saying something silly (cf. *Collins Cobuild Dictionary* 1987: 273), or as expressed by Green (2000: 261), as 'a general excl. of disbelief, disapproval, or irritation'.

3.2. Reactive

A reactive utterance is realized by the responding move in a conversational exchange, elicited by another speaker's immediately preceding directive utterance (cf. Stenström, 1999), but as Example (9a) shows, a reactive utterance can also be triggered by a nonverbal action. *Venga* in reactive utterances realized by an 'object' or a 'reject', reflecting a negative reaction, is best translated by *come on* in English. By contrast, *come on* is not a suitable candidate when *venga* is used to express acceptance or agreement, as in (10a) and (11a).

Object

In (9a), Antonio is apparently objecting to what is actually happening in an awkward situation, and not merely to what is being said, while Anne (9b) objects to what Lucy said about Neil.

COLAm. Situation: Antonio and Salvador have got hold of a 'forbidden' drink that they want to taste in secret and realize that they need a straw.

(9a)   Antonio: es frío
                is it cold
    Salvador: como de calambre
                ice cold

Antonio: la pajita has echado en casa
did you leave the straw at home

Salvador: <risa>

Antonio: [laughter] venga esto es infantil … (MASHE3)
come on this is childish

COLT. Situation: Lucy and Anne are talking about a boy at school who had overheard their conversation.

(9b)   Lucy: Wish you hadn't said that I felt really embarrassed.

         Anne: Oh only Neil heard it and he really didn't mind.

         Lucy: {laughing} Oh he didn't mind what, how could he show if he did mind though.

         Anne: Oh come on it's not like he's mind you, he's, he's like one of these natural {unclear}: need women. Oh come on, you know he is! You know it! (42603)

In (10a) and (10b) *venga* and *come on* object more strongly to what was said, very much like expressions such as *stop it!* or *lay off!*.

Reject

COLAm. Situation: Four 15 year-old boys are playing with a ball which happened to end up in a field and one of them, Gui, is trying to go and fetch it, while the others tell him not to.

(10a)   Léon: … déjala Gui
leave it Gui

         Pedro: ah no puedes dar paso está dentro del campo
ah you can't go there it's in the field

         Léon :   *venga*
come on

         Pedro: está dentro del campo no puedes dar pasos
it's in the field you can't go there

         Sergio: dejarla ya coño
you'll have to leave it stupid

         Pedro: *venga* que no que no puedes dar pasos hijo puta (MASHE3)
come on 'cos no 'cos you can't go there idiot

COLT. Situation: Mark wants to gather some boys for a football match.

(10b)   Mark: Have to get a lot of people.

         Mother: Don't use my telephone.

         Mark: God you're so tight!

         Mother: Come on enough, come and eat [your dinner]

         Mark: [Alright] just gotta get Colin right? (39402)

Notice that Example (10a) like (9a), and more clearly so, illustrates a situation where *venga* objects to a non-verbal action, namely Gui's apparent insistence to go and fetch the ball.

Unlike the above examples, which represent a negative reaction, *okay, right* and *alright* are the best options when the addressee accepts or agrees to what was said, while *come on* is simply impossible. In the examples below, Daniel accepts that there will be three more players (11a), and Aaron accepts willingly to get Susan a drink (11b):

Accept
COLAm. Situation: Pablo and Daniel are playing on the beach.

(11a)   Pablo: bueno es que van a ser tres
                 right there will be three
         Daniel: *bueno venga* tres <bocinazos/> (MAMTE2)
                 fine okay three <signals>

COLT. Situation: Susan and Aaron are chatting about this and that and Susan gets thirsty.

(11b)   Susan: Go and get me a drink Aaron
         Aaron: Alright, hang on (33906)

In (12a), Miguel agrees with Pedro that the third boy is a lousy player since he simply left the ball where it happened to fall. And in (12b) Steve agrees that he laughed at what Peter told him before going on with his own story:

Agree
COLAm. Situation: Pedro and Miguel are playing on the beach.
(12a)   Pedro: mira qué fallos chaval
                 look, what misses, man
         Miguel: *venga* y se deja el balón atrás   (MALCE4)
                  okay and he leaves the ball back there

COLT. Situation: Peter and Steve are discussing injections against malaria when going abroad.

(12b)   Peter: Look, you laughed, I laughed.
         Steve: Right, when I went to Turkey, I had three jabs before I went away (32503)

As reflected in Examples (11) and (12), *venga* has developed pragmatic uses that *come on* has not, despite the fact that the original meaning of both is 'come'; the origin of *venga* is the third person singular subjunctive and imperative of *venir,* and the origin of *come* in *come on* is the imperative use of the verb *come.*

3.3. Evaluative
In the evaluative function, *venga* can involve a shift of topic, or reorientation, as in (13) (cf. Blas Arroyo, 1998: 9), where the most suitable English corre-

sponding marker is *right,* or a follow-up of what was said in the reactive move, as illustrated in (13):

(13) Situation: Rita, José and Inéz have just finished playing a game when Rita realizes that she has to leave.

Rita:	oye pues tía entonces en una hora me tengo que ir de aquí
	listen TÍA[4] in an hour I'll have to leave
José:	[ja ja ja ja]
	ha ha ha ha
Rita:	[y coger el metro]
	and take the metro
José:	soy tía …
	I'm TÍA…
Rita:	sí
	yes
Inéz:	mhm
Rita:	ah … quien lo diría *bueno venga* que me voy tengo un problema de verdad
	ah … who would say well right I'm leaving I've really got a problem
	(MAESB2)

Rita suddenly decides to leave, which leads to an unexpected topic shift. In (14) Juan's *venga* serves both as a confirmation that he heard Ana's answer and his strong reaction to the fact that it was already nine o'clock.

(14) Situation: Juan just wants to know what time it is, and Ana answers emphatically.

Juan:	qué hora es
	what time is it
Ana:	las nueeeveee
	niiiine
Juan:	*venga* ya (MABPE2)
	wow already

3.4. Closing

According to Blas Arroyo (1998), the most recent use of *venga* in its directive and reactive functions is to initiate and close a conversational encounter. But there is variation. Neither the pre-closing (initiating) nor the closing (terminating) marker is exclusively realized by *venga;* rather it is sometimes realized by a different item, often *vale.* In Blas Arroyo's corpus, which consisted of televised dialogues and orderly conversations with the investigator present during the recording, 'prototypical' closing sequences, as in (4) in Section 2 above, were probably quite frequent, unlike in COLAm and COLT, where closing sequences, in the few cases that they occur at all, do not usually resemble the 'model' sequences in his data. The closest example in COLAm is (15), where Inéz's *pues venga* initiates the closing that is 'confirmed' by Ana's *vale*. What happens next is apparently that Inéz, the girl who recorded the conversation, turned off the recording equipment.

(15)   Anita: … pero bueno que no tenemos que pirar *vale*
                  but okay we don't have to run off
        Belén: *vale*
                  okay
        Inéz: pues *venga*
                  okay then
        Ana: vale
                  okay
        María: lo vas a apagar ahora cabrona (MAESB2)
                  you'll have to turn it off now bitch

In Example (16), the directive *venga,* which initiates the closing, triggers *hasta luego* in the reactive turn:

(16)   Alvaro: bueno *venga*
                 right okay
        Pablo: hasta luego (MALCC2)
                 see you later

In Example (17) from COLT, the same item, *alright,* serves as the closing marker in the directive as well as the reactive turn. This sequence occurs at the end of a telephone call, where closing sections are typically initiated by *right, okay* or *alright* with a rising tone, followed by the same item with a falling tone.

(17)   A: Al/right, see you see you, bye. </tel>…
        B: Huh, al\right.40606

'Conventional' conversational closings as well as openings are typically found at the end of telephone calls (see Stenström, 1984, 1999).

3.5. Collocations

An interesting aspect to consider is to what extent *venga* and *come on* collocate with other words and, when they do, what the combined effect is of the collocated elements, that is the combination 'node' plus 'collocate' (cf. Sinclair, 1991: 15). Overall, *venga* occurred less often as a node than *come on*. The most frequent collocations in COLAm consisted of *venga, venga ya* and *venga vamos* and in COLT *come on then, come on* repeated and *come on let's,* in that order.

The repetition of *venga* and *come on* in *venga venga* and *come on come on* does not really need a comment. The repetition obviously has a strengthening effect. But let's consider the other pairs (18a,b) to (19a,b):

COLAm. Situation: Sofía with a baby and Belén have met at a cybercafé.

> (18a) Sofía: conoces a mi hijo?
>   do you know my son
>   Belén: *venga ya*
>   come on
>   Sofía: sí tía es mi hijo
>   yes TÍA it is my son
>   Belán: qué dices
>   what are you talking about
>   Sofía: que no es una broma tía no te has enterado de que estaba embarazada
>   it's not a joke TÍA didn't you realize that I was pregnant
>   Belán: *venga ya* (MABPE2)
>   come on

Sofía is trying to convince Belén that the baby is her own child, but Belén refuses to believe it. It turns out that, when the two girls saw each other about five months ago, Belén had not realized that Sofía was pregnant. Her strong disbelief is reflected in *venga ya,* where *ya* adds emphasis to her incredulity and unwillingness to accept the fact.

COLT. Situation: Some boys and girls are chatting in the street, and a couple of them are on the point of leaving.

> (18b) Mary: Are we going? Are we going?
>   John: Yeah, yeah.
>   Mary: Come on then. See you later you lot!
>   Kent: Where you going? Where you going? (32514)

Mary's *come on then* reflects her reaction, reinforced by *then,* to the fact that the decision to leave has already been made. 'So why wait'?

Finally, (19a) and (19b) show that Spanish *venga vamos* and English *come on let's* function in the same way, though *vamos* is the first person plural present tense of the verb *venir,* while *let's* is the imperative form of the verb *let.*

COLAm. Situation: Elena and Santi are talking about a boy they both find very attractive.

> (19a) Elena: yo creo que va a los jesuitas
>   I think he goes to the Jesuit school
>   Santi: va a Retamar sí porque porque porqueee juega en el equipo de fútbol de
>   Retamar que me dijo que tenía que ir a verles un día

he definitely goes to Retamar cos cos cooos he plays in the Retamar football team and told me that I had to come and see them some day

Elena: ay sí por favor *venga vamos* a verles un día en plan (MAORE2)
oh yes please do let's go and see them some day 'en plan'[5]

COLT. Situation: Paul was planning to call a girlfriend when he broke his phone card by accident.

(19b)   Paul: I've snapped my phone card in half.
         Tom: Yeah why d'ya snap it in half?
         Paul: Cos I didn't know I was doing it?
         Tom: Yeah, kick it up. {nv} sniff {/nv} Elevenses. **Come on let's** go. (39614)

4. Discussion

4.1. Status

As mentioned in Section 1, *venga* is the result of grammaticalization of the imperative use of the verb *venir*, with grammaticalization understood as 'the process whereby lexical items and constructions come in certain linguistic contexts to serve grammatical functions, and, once grammaticalized, continue to develop new grammatical functions' (Hopper and Traugott, 1993: xv). This has led to various uses typical of conversation, such as discourse marker, inter-active marker and interjection, in other words uses that reflect a further process of pragmaticalization (cf. *Gramática Descriptiva de la Lengua Española*, Vol 3. 3993–4050).

While the pragmatic functions of *venga* have been the object of study in quite a few publications in the last decades, the pragmatic functions of *come on* have not been openly referred to. Without mentioning the term 'pragmatic marker' Green (2000: 261) describes *come on* as an 'exclamation' signalling dis-belief, disapproval or irritation, *The New Oxford Dictionary of English* (1998: 365) defines it as an 'imperative' with an encouraging or blaming effect, and *Collins Cobuild English Language Dictionary* (1987: 273) describes its func-tions in a similar vein. The pragmatic functions of *come on* are not mentioned at all in grammar books such as Quirk *et al.* (1985), where it would have fitted in under the label 'reaction signals' (852), or Carter and McCarthy (2006), where *come on* could have been listed as a 'response token' (88f).

Going by their respective definitions, the borderline between pragmatic marker and interjection and between interjection and exclamation seems to be rather fuzzy. Interjections are said to consist of a word or phrase with no particular grammatical relation to a sentence, often an expression of emotion 'a phrase, word or set of sounds used as a sudden remark, usu. expressing a strong feeling such as shock, disapproval, or pleasure' (*Long-man Dictionary of Contemporary English* 1987: 551). And an exclamation is defined in *Merriam-Webster* online as 'a vehement expression of protest or complaint'. Like interjections, pragmatic markers have no particular grammatical relation to the sentence, and like interjections and exclamations, they can express emotional reactions to what is being said or done (cf. Carter and McCarthy (2006: 224)).

According to these definitions, both *venga* and *come on* can be said to serve as interjections with an exclamative effect in examples (20) and (21):

COLAm

(20)   Pablo: olé qué canción más guapa
                  wow what a beautiful song
        Anita: *venga* chaval
                  indeed
        Pablo: me encanta el sonido (MABPE2)
                  I love the sound

COLT

(21)   John: Hi. Where's the French [exchange group?]
        Sue: [I dunno if she's gonna come]
        Jef: Dunno. I think it's in the hall.
        John: Oh.
        Sue: Come on!
        Jef: That's where everyone else seems to have gone. (32503)

In line with Carter and McCarthy (2002: 208), I regard all items that perform pragmatic functions, such as *venga* and *come on* in the above examples, as pragmatic markers, regardless of whether they are referred to elsewhere as interjections, exclamations, or discourse markers.

4.2. Matching items

Come on proved to be the closest equivalent to *venga* in most of its functions, notably the directive functions 'instruct', 'insist', 'encourage' and 'appeal', as well as the reactive functions 'object' and 'reject'. As an evaluative, *venga* might be matched not only by *well,* as in Example (13), but also by *okay, right* or *alright,* depending on the contextual situation. The closing function, realized by Spanich *venga,* was matched by *okay, right* or *alright,* which are the typical closing markers in English conversation, while *come on* is simply not used for this function. As mentioned in Section 3.4, 'proper' conversational closings were very few in COLT, as opposed to COLAm. This is not an indication of impoliteness on the part of the London teenagers, but simply due to the fact that the students in charge of the recordings turned off the recording equipment haphazardly without waiting for a proper ending.

4.3. The sociolinguistic aspect

With particular emphasis on *venga* as a closing marker, Blas Arroyo (1998) observed that *venga* in this new function was most common among young adult urban speakers with a high or middle-class background. Cestero Mancera and Moreno Fernández (2008), who studied adult Madrid speakers, found, like Blas Arroyo (1998), that *venga* was particularly frequent in the younger adults' language, which in their case refers to 25 to 50 year-olds. Their conclusion is that sex and social class are the most significant factors in that the female speakers used *venga* more often than the male speakers, and that it was most often used by middle class speakers.

In the Madrid teenagers' conversations in COLAm, too, the youngest speakers, i.e., the 14 to 16 year-olds, were the most frequent users of *venga,* but unlike the above-mentioned studies, the present study indicates that the boys used *venga* slightly more often than the girls. With regard to social class, it showed that the upper class girls were more frequent users of *venga* than the middle and lower class girls, while the middle class speakers dominated among the boys. Unfortunately, there is not enough statistical information to show whether the use of *venga* is a typical teenage phenomenon or whether the frequency of use is changing as time goes on.

A comparison between the Madrid teenagers' use of *venga* and the London teenagers' use of *come on* pointed to a more frequent use of *venga,* with 1.3 occurrences per thousand words, compared to the London teenagers' 0.9 per thousand words for *come on.* This is despite the fact that all instances of *come on* served as a pragmatic marker, while roughly 10% of the total occurrence of *venga* were used as the third person subjunctive form of the verb *venir* (*Espero que no venga a protestar* 'I hope he won't protest'). With regard to age, gender and social class, the youngest lower class girls used *come on* more often than the other speakers. This shows that *come on* behaves differently from *venga* in terms of gender and social class, but not age.

5. Conclusion

The categorization of the functions of *venga* based on adult conversation proposed by Blas Arroyo (1998), Santos Río (2003) and Cestero Mancera and Moreno Fernández (2008) was matched by exchange patterns in COLAm, with a couple of exceptions among the directives, notably the insisting *venga* in Example (6a) and the strongly objecting *venga* in (9a). I also made a distinction in the reactive category between *venga* as an accept (11a) and an agree (12a), but, admittedly, these uses are very close.

Come on turned out to be the nearest equivalent to *venga* in the majority of cases; that is all the directive functions and the negative reactive functions. As a positive reactive device, signalling acceptance and agreement, *come on* did not fit, however, and was best substituted by *okay, right,* or *alright,* which also correspond to *venga* in conversational closings and in the evaluative function, announcing a change of direction. In the follow-up evaluative function, *come on* had to be substituted, and *well* seemed to be the closest equivalent.

Venga proved to be a more versatile marker than *come on*, since it occurred in all the functions cited, which *come on* did not. Therefore, it should perhaps not come as a surprise that *venga* was used more frequently than *come on* overall. *Come on* cannot be used as an equivalent in a positive reactive utterance (cf. (11b) and (12b)); nor is it used as a closing element (cf. (14)). The study by Cestero Mancera and Moreno Fernández (2008) indicated that the use of *venga* as a pragmatic marker, which was less frequent in their adult corpus than the use of *venga* in COLAm, is spreading from the Madrid area to the periphery. And this is a common phenomenon. Take for instance the marker *en plan*, equivalent to English *like* and *like* used as a 'hedge' (*es en plan psico sabes*), or an 'approximator' (*en plan a las once*) or a 'quotation marker' (*y yo en plan gracias*), which was observed in the Madrid teenagers' talk, but at the time, apparently unknown in the provinces (Stenström, 2008: 214–216), unlike today.

An intriguing question is to what extent pragmatic markers are universal, considering that such items are necessary in order to keep a conversation going. Zimmermann (2002: 150), under the heading *Rasgos universales* ('Universal features'), lists for instance *Señales al interlocutor para llamar la atención* ('attention signals'), *Coletillas* ('tags'), *Particulas discursivas* ('discourse particles') and *Interjecciones* ('interjections'). According to my definition, these are all pragmatic markers, and considering their important functions in spoken interaction, one might suspect that corresponding features exist in most languages. This is what contrastive studies are expected to corroborate.

Notes

1. COLAm is part of the larger COLA corpus, which also contains corpora from Santiago de Chile, Buenos Aires and Costa Rica.

2. This is a reference to one of the texts in COLAm.

3. This is a reference to one of the texts in COLT,

4. *Tía* is a term of endearment that is very common in Spanish girls' conversation but hardly translatable into English, where it would correspond to *girl*.

5. *En plan* in this place indicates 'approximation', which is superfluous to translate, since *some* has the same meaning.

References

Alonso-Cortés. Á. (1999) Las construcciones exclamativas. La interjección y las expresiones vocativas. In I. Bosque and V. Demarte (eds) *Gramática Descriptiva de la Lengua Española, 3. Entre la oración y el discurso/morfología* 3: 3993–4050. Madrid: Espasa Calpe.

Blas Arroyo, J. L. (1998) Un caso de variación pragmatica sobre la ampliación significativa de un marcador discursivo en el español. Aspector estructurales y sociolingüísticos. *Revista de la sección de Filología de la Facultad de Filosofía y Letras* 21 (2): 543–572.

Carter, R. and McCarthy, M. (2006) *Cambridge Grammar of English*. Cambridge: Cambridge University Press.

Casamiglia, H. and Tusón, A. (1999) *Las cosas del decir. Manual de análisis del discurso*, p. 75. Barcelona: Ariel.

Cestero Mancera, A. M. (2005) *Conversación y Enseñanza de Lenguas Extranjeras*. Madrid: Arco/Libros.

Cestero Mancera, A. M and Moreno Fernández, F. (2008) Usos y funciones de vale y venga! En el habla de Madrid. *Boletín Lingüística* 20 (29): 65–84.

Collins Cobuild English Language Dictionary (1987) London: Collins.

Corpus Oral de Lenguaje Adolescente de Madrid. http://www.COLAm.org

Cortés, L. and Camacho, Ma M. (2005) *Unidades de Segmentación y Marcadores del Discurso*. Madrid: Arco/Libros.

Gramática Descriptiva de la Lengua Española (1989) Madrid: Espasa.

Green, J. (2000) *Cassell's Dictionary of Slang*. London: Cassell and Co.

Herrero, G. (2002) Aspectos sintácticos del lenguaje juvenil. In F. Rodríguez (ed.) *El Lenguaje de los Jóvenes*, 67–96. Barcelona: Ariel.

Longman Dictionary of Contemporary English (1987). London: Longman.

Martín Zorraquino, A. A. and Portolés Lázaro, J. (1999) Los marcadores del discurso. In I. Bosque and V. Demonte (eds) *Grámatica Descriptiva de la Lengua Española* 3, 4051–4213. Madrid: Espasa Calpe.

Merriam-Webster Online. http://m-w.com

Moreno Cabrera, J. (1998) On the relationships between grammaticalization and lexicalization. In A. Giacalone Ramat and P. Hopper (eds) *The Limits of Grammaticalization*, 211–227. Amsterdam: Benjamins.

Quirk, R., Greenbaum, S., Leech, G. and Svartvik, J. (1985) *A Comprehensive Grammar of the English Language*. London: Longman.

Santos Río, L. (2003) *Diccionario de Partículas*. Salamanca: Luso Española de Ediciones.

Schourup, L. (1985) *Common Discourse Particles in English Conversation*. New York: Garland Publishing.

Serrano, M.J. (2002) *Aproximación a la gramática del discurso del español.* München: Lincom Europa.

Sinclair, J. (1991) *Corpus. Concordance Collocation.* Oxford: Oxford University Press.

Sinclair, J. and Coulthard, M. (1975) *Towards an Analysis of Discourse. The English Used By Teachers and Pupils.* Oxford: Oxford University Press.

Stenström, A-B. (1984) *Questions and Responses in English Conversation.* Lund: Gleerup.

Stenström, A-B. (1999) *An Introduction to Spoken Interaction.* London: Longman.

Stenström, A-B. (2008.) *Algunos Rasgos Característicos del Habla de Contacto en el Lenguaje de Adolescentes de Madrid.* Oralia: 207–226.

Svartvik, J. and Quirk, R. (1980) *A Corpus of English Conversation.* Lund Studies in English 56. Lund: Lund University Press.

The Bergen Corpus of London Teenage Language. http://www.hit.uib.no/colt

The New Oxford Dictionary of English (1998) Oxford: Oxford University Press.

Vigara Tauste, A. M. (1992) *Morfosintaxis del Español Coloquial.* Madrid: Gredos.

Zimmermann, K.. (2002). La variedad juvenil y la interacción verbal entre jóvenes. In F. Rodríguez (ed.) *El Lenguaje de los Jóvenes,* 137–164. Barcelona: Ariel.

Wiktionary. http://en.wikipedia.org/wiki/Wiktionary

4 Discourse markers in French and German: Reasons for an asymmetry

Séverine Adam and Martine Dalmas

The 'pragmatic movement' at the end of the 1970s, as well as the increasing number of studies on the oral language and the development of phraseology paved the way for descriptions of language and discourse phenomena, which had been neglected until then. Discourse markers are such phenomena: in each language there are units that speakers use to mark certain discourse operations and to convey communicative intentions, feelings and attitudes. Because most of these units are pragmaticalized forms (syntagms), which have undergone a linguistic change, they can't be translated literally, so that they may appear to have no equivalents in other languages. This is the case for German particles, for instance: it would be pointless to look for literal, mono-lexical equivalents for them in French for example. This does not mean, however, that the French language has no specific linguistic means to fulfil similar functions as German particles. On the other hand, the formal similarity of some units in different languages is no guarantee for their functional equivalence. These observations lead to the basic idea of this contribution: if we want to find equivalents in other languages for the units of one language that fulfil pragmatic functions, such as discourse markers, we have to give an accurate formal and functional description of these units first and then to look for possible equivalents in other languages. We want to illustrate this by having a closer look at three French discourse markers (*dis donc, tu vois* and *écoute*) and their possible equivalents in German.

1. Introduction

Forty years ago, the German particle researcher Harald Weydt broke new ground in linguistics with the publication of his book *Abtönungspartikel* (1969). Weydt observed that it would be wrong to consider German particles as unnecessary units, which a speaker could omit without changing the meaning of the sentence: although these units have no literal lexical meaning, they convey communicative intentions, feelings and attitudes.[1] Because they cannot be interpreted literally (no lexical meaning), it would be pointless to look for literal, mono-lexical equivalents for them in other languages – in French for instance. This does not mean, however, that other languages have no specific linguistic means to fulfil similar functions as German particles.

These observations were ground-breaking because before and during Weydt's time, most linguistic researchers considered German particles as 'lice in the fur of language'.[2] German-French cross-linguistic studies did not go much beyond the assertion that such particles were absent in the French language. Additionally, linguists were at the time not aware it is necessary to take into account certain phenomena of morphological and semantic 'rigidity' that affect poly-lexical units; neither did they take the pragmatic dimension of exchanges into account. Because of that, a lot of language – and discourse – phenomena have been neglected (and probably unknown) for a long time. The 'pragmatic movement' at the end of the 1970s, as well as the increasing number of studies on the oral language and the development of phraseology as a specific branch of lexicology paved the way for descriptions of those phenomena (cf. Dalmas, 2009). This explains among other things the significant increase in studies about 'discourse markers'.

We define this rather broad term as follows: discourse markers are (meta) discursive mono- or poly-lexical language units (lexemes or phrasemes), which the speaker or enunciator uses to mark – for the addressee or co-enunciator – certain discourse operations. The speaker or enunciator uses them to structure verbal interactions or to show the connection between the utterance and its utterance context. Unlike units that explicitly link text sequences together ('text organizers'), discourse markers (henceforth: DM) do not operate on the content level, but on the level of enunciation.

Linguists have primarily conducted research on DM within their own language (exceptions include Dalmas, 1989; Métrich and Faucher, 2009). In this study, we look beyond the French language and look for possible equivalents in German. We will situate the French units in their own specific context and look for their German functional equivalents which, most importantly, convey the word's meaning and not their literal translation. Our purpose is to demonstrate that: (a) French speakers use more verbal elements than German speakers do; and (b) the use of the same verbal lexeme in both languages does not necessarily mean that the markers fulfil the same functions. Subsequently, we describe the associated verb types and forms. Finally, we will examine in detail three examples of partial equivalence between French DMs and identify apparently appropriate equivalents in German. At the same time, we will address the problems linked to the corpus constitution in this field of research.

2. Pragmaticalization

2.1. Characteristics

While the process of grammaticalization has been thoroughly documented for lexemes and constructions that have come to fulfil a grammatical function and are admitted as such in grammatical reference books (Meillet, 1912; Marchello-Nizia, 2006), it is only in recent years that the process of pragmaticalization has been described. In the French language, the first traces appeared in the 1980s in the book *Les mots du discours* (Ducrot *et al.*, 1980). The book compiles the results of studies conducted between 1978 and 1979, with a chapter on '*Je trouve que ...*'. As for German, this phenomenon was pointed out in the 1990s and later in studies concerning oral language, e.g., Günthner (1999; 2003; 2004), Gohl and Günthner (1999), Auer and Günthner (2003), Imo (2007) and Dehé and Wichmann (2009). Most of the theoretical work on this matter originates in the 1990s, in particular the often-mentioned works of Traugott (1995) or Lehmann (2002). The debate of the relation between 'grammaticalization' and 'pragmaticalization' is beyond the scope of this paper; we will limit ourselves to a description of the main features of the pragmaticalization process which can be useful for the following analysis (we follow thereby Dostie, 2004). Each feature is illustrated by a few examples in French, restricted to forms including verbs:

- Certain (mono- or poly-lexical) units are no longer used in their referential function; they fulfil a communicative/discursive function. They do not refer to the extra-linguistic world, but they are oriented towards the interlocution partners (speaker/enunciator and/or addressee/co-enunciator) or towards the message itself. These units do not operate on an intra-phrastic level anymore, but rather on the discourse level (in the broad sense of the word discourse):
    - units oriented towards the interaction partners: *tu penses (for sure[3]), tu parles (you bet!), dis donc (oh my!), remarque (mind you), j'te dis pas (I can't tell you), disons (let's say), il faut dire que (indeed), voyons/ voyons voir (let me think), mettons (let's say)* ...
    - units oriented towards the message – and to the speech act performed in it: *il est vrai que (one must admit that), c'est vrai que (it has to be said)* ...

- The shift described above is accompanied by morpho-syntactic modifications and leads to formal frozenness/rigidity. The categorical features of the units are partially neutralized (decategorization):
  - morpho-syntactic modifications and frozenness: *allons/allez/va (come on!), si ça se trouve (maybe), qui sait (who knows), comme qui dirait (sort of), en attendant (in any case), té vé (look)* …
- At the same time, these units shift to another paradigm, depending on the discourse function they serve (reparadigmatization).
  - shift to another paradigm: *si ça se trouve [–> peut-être, sans doute, certainement](maybe)* …
- Units resulting from this process are often stylistically marked; many of them are used in oral language (dialogues) and various forms of speech, which cannot generally be predicted based on their lexical meaning (referential use):
  - various forms of speech: *tu parles (you bet), pensez-vous (some hope!), regarde-moi ça (can you believe it), on sait jamais (one never knows), si vous voulez (one may say), si on peut dire (to put it that way)* …
- In certain cases, the pragmaticalization process is not complete and some forms remain polysemous, conserving their referential meaning, which can sometimes lead to hesitations between the referential and the discursive use:
  - polysemous units: *tiens (well, well), remarquez (mind you), je trouve (I would say), en attendant (in any case)* …
  - ambiguity: *tu vois (you see), si tu veux (to put it that way), je crois (I think), tu remarqueras que (let's note …)* …

Even if we only take into account forms including verbal elements, there is a tremendous number of DMs, many of which are variations of the same verb (*remarque, remarquez, tu remarqueras que* …). The most frequently used verbs are verbs of perception, cognition and speech (Dostie, 2004; Imo, 2007), in most cases in the first person and/or in the imperative form – underlining their interactive dimension. This feature is particularly characteristic of French DMs.

2.2. Equivalents

The question that immediately arises is: what equivalents for those French verbal DMs can be found in German? Starting from the operations performed by means of French verbal DMs, we notice that:

(a) Many French verbal DMs have no German verbal equivalent. However, a good many 'particles' or similar units can be found in the same contexts:

à vrai dire: eigentlich (actually)
il faut dire que: auch (indeed)
tu parles: von wegen, mitnichten (like hell/yeah right…)
allons donc: na so was (come on)
en attendant: jedenfalls, auf jeden Fall ; aber auch; aber (in any case)

(1)   Pendant l'été, j'ai trois articles à rédiger, des copies à corriger …
      Tu parles de vacances!
      … **Vonwegen** Urlaub!
      Over the summer I have three articles to write, correcting to do …Vacation?
      Like hell!

(2)   Si ca se trouve, il a eu un accident!
      Er hat **vielleicht** einen Unfall gehabt!
      Maybe he was in an accident

(3)   'C'est ma mère, annonça-t-il fièrement. Elle est belle ma mère ! …' Il regardait
      Mademoiselle Rakoff avec défi. '**En attendant**, elle n'est pas venue te voir …'
      (Queffélec, 1985: 191)[4]

      'Das ist meine Mutter', verkündete er stolz. 'Meine Mutter ist schön!'. Her-
      ausfordernd sah er Mlle Rakoff an. '**Jedenfalls** hat sie dich nicht besucht …!'
      (Queffélec, 2001: 195)

      'It's my mother', he said proudly, 'She's a beauty'. He threw a challenging look at
      Miss Rakoff. '**Maybe, but** she hasn't stopped by to visit you yet …'

(b) In those cases where a comparable German form with a verbal component
does exist, this form is also pragmaticalized in German; however, it does not
cover all the uses of the corresponding French unit:

tu vois: siehst du, siehste (see?)
écoute: hör mal – naja (listen)
dis donc: sag mal (hey,…)
remarque: wohlgemerkt (mind you)

The fact that some French and German units show certain formal
resemblance does not mean that these units can be considered functional
equivalents. This can be illustrated with a brief comparison of the French
DM *il faut dire (que)* with what seems to be possible German equivalents
at first sight: *man/ich muss sagen (dass)*. Formally, they can indeed be considered similar: they both contain a verb implying, in its literal signification, an obligation for the speaker to say something (or an expression of
the impossibility not to say it), both finite verbs are in present and both
structures can either occur alone (as comment clauses) or introduce a
subordinate:

(4)   Avant j'allais chez le Docteur Lavinié, mon fils ne pouvait pas toujours me conduire, alors je demandais au voisin et j'y payais l'essence, mais c'était toute une affaire. Et puis, il fallait attendre une heure si c'est pas deux, **il faut dire que** le docteur de Lavinié, il a toujours eu une belle clientèle! (Winckler, 1999: 44)

Vorher musste ich nach Lavinié zum Arzt, mein Sohn konnte mich nicht immer hinfahren, also hab ich den Nachbarn gefragt, und ich hab ihm das Benzin bezahlt, aber das war eine Riesenaffäre. Außerdem musste man immer eine, wenn nicht gar zwei Stunden warten, **man muss sagen, dass** Doktor von Lavinié immer einen großen Patientenstamm hatte. (Winckler, 2000: 37)

Dr Lavinié was my doctor in the past, my son couldn't always drive me everywhere, so I had to ask the neighbour, I paid for the fuel but that was always very complicated. And I always had to wait one hour or two sometimes, Dr Lavinié, **it has to be said**, always had a large practice.

(5)   Elle a essayé de se dégager mais j'ai serré de toutes mes forces, je lui ai arraché un petit cri. **Il faut dire** que j'avais pas fait semblant. Si à la place de son bras j'avais cramponné un tube de mayonnaise, la sauce aurait giclé à des kilomètres. (Djian, 1989: 118)

Sie versuchte, sich loszureißen, doch ich drückte mit aller Kraft zu. Ich entlockte ihr einen kleinen Schrei. **Ich muss sagen**, ich tat nicht nur als ob. Wenn ich anstelle dieses Armes eine Tube Mayonnaise zerdrückt hätte, wäre die Soße kilometerweit gespritzt. (Djian, 1990: 125)

She tried to jerk herself free, but I tightened my grip as much as I possibly could, I made her cry out in pain. **I must admit** I wasn't kidding around. If I had held a tube of mayonnaise instead of her arm, the sauce would have squirted out for kilometres.

Upon closer inspection, it is clear that the French and German forms have extremely different functions. Their primary difference lies in their orientation relative to the text: the French marker *il faut dire (que)* is oriented towards the preceding discourse. It allows the speaker to introduce an argument likely to justify a fact that has been mentioned just before. On the contrary, the pseudo-equivalent German form *man/ich muss sagen(, dass)* is oriented towards the following text, and more specifically towards the contents it introduces.

Second, the French and German forms differ as to their signification and discourse function. By introducing its new argument with the DM *il faut dire (que)*, the speaker signals that he concedes, or even admits and accepts the facts which have just been mentioned in the preceding sentence, and/because he acknowledges things must be the way they are considering the argument introduced with the DM *il faut dire (que)*. The primary function of this marker is justification; *il faut dire (que)* thus belongs to the same paradigm as *en effet, parce que, car*, etc. This justification function is totally absent in the case of the

German marker *man/ich muss sagen (dass)*, the function of which consists in underlining the objectivity and irrefutability of the contents it introduces. These contents are seen and presented like something the speaker cannot take the liberty of denying, rejecting or contradicting, nor ignoring or leaving out.

These differences are indicators of different degrees of pragmaticalization for the French and German expressions: the French marker has undergone a change of paradigm – a reparadigmatization; its primary function is at the same time justifying/defensive as well as additive, while the obligation literally expressed by the verb plays only a minor role – and has to be interpreted as part of the concessive move on which the justification is based. Conversely, in the German expression, the notion of obligation deriving from a literal interpretation of the modal verb meaning remains preeminent in the signification and function of the marker *man/ich muss sagen (dass)*. Significant functional asymmetries can thus be observed for forms with striking formal similarities on the other hand.

On the basis of this first example, which reveals an asymmetry of forms and functions in the superficially similar DMs of the two languages, it can be postulated that the comparison of discourse marker use in both languages cannot be based on the forms themselves, but on the functions fulfilled and operations performed by the forms in question.

In the second part of this study, we will take a closer look at three DMs, in order to highlight the role of verbal elements in French discourse, and to show which kind of forms occur in German depending on the degree of pragmaticalization.

3. Three case studies

To begin with, we must first acknowledge the inherent difficulty in compiling a corpus for a comparative study of discourse markers. Characteristically, these units are found in spontaneous oral exchanges, for which very few parallel corpora exist; therefore, the first approach must be made using written texts (fiction or transcripts of spoken exchanges) and their translations. This method establishes the framework of this study, which – for this reason – can only claim to be an exploratory one. We are also very aware that the analytical possibilities are quite limited by the fact that those written texts and their translations at best 'imitate' spontaneous oral exchanges. In order to ensure the authenticity of the material, we augment our data with genuine statements found in the Internet (forums, chats, etc.) and equivalent sentences formulated by native speakers in their mother tongue.

The three markers we selected for a closer contrastive analysis are *dis donc, tu vois,* and *écoute.* From among the numerous markers that exist in French, these were chosen for the following reasons:

(a) These three markers constitute a homogeneous representative sample of the class of verbal French DMs: they are highly addressee-oriented, either because they are in the second person (*tu vois*), or because they are in the imperative form (*dis donc, écoute*). A second similarity is the presence of a verb of perception in two of them (*écoute, tu vois*).

(b) We picked these three DMs, because of the wealth of research that has been specifically done on them (Dostie, 1998; Rodriguez Somolinos, 2003; Dostie, 2004; Bolly, 2010). It is important to note, however, that linguistic researchers have focused on these markers within the French language specifically, and have not conducted any research on possible *dis donc/tu vois/écoute* equivalents in other languages, such as German or English.

(c) As the studies mentioned in (b) show, these markers are characterized by their great polyvalence and discursive poly-functionality: they can be used to accomplish very different discursive operations. This is the sign of their high degree of pragmaticalization and indicates it is appropriate to compare their functions to those of German particles.

(d) Finally, one may be tempted, at first glance, to believe that perfect equivalents actually do exist in German for these three DMs, namely their literal translations (*sag mal, siehst du/ wie du siehst,* and *hör mal*). However, those forms cannot be considered as acceptable equivalents for all instances of use of the French markers, as will be illustrated in the following section.

3.1. Dis donc

The expression *sag mal* can only be considered as a potential equivalent to *dis donc* when the French marker is used by the speaker to invite the addressee to react verbally to what has just been said. This is also the case when *dis donc* serves as a conversation opener (as in example 6); as a signal for a conversational or discourse reorientation (7); or as a way for the speaker to manifest his/her disagreement with or his/her disapproval of facts which imply in the eyes of the speaker the addressee's responsibility; in this last case, the speaker, by using *dis donc*, requests the addressee to explain himself/herself (8):

(6)   Au bout d'un moment, Betty s'est tournée vers l'arrière, ses cheveux devaient lui tenir chaud car elle les soulevait sans arrêt.
– Dis donc, elle a fait, t'imagines jusqu'où on pourrait aller tous les deux avec une bonne bagnole et toute cette bouffe à l'arrière ... (Djian, 1989: 14)

Nach einer Zeit drehte sich Betty nach hinten und anscheinend war es ihr unter ihren Haaren zu heiß, denn sie hob sie pausenlos hoch.

– **Sag mal,** meinte sie, kannste dir vorstellen, wie weit wir zwei es schaffen
könnten mit einer vernünftigen Kiste und dem ganzen Fraß da hinten …
(Djian, 1990: 16)

After a while Betty turned to look behind, apparently she was too warm
because of her hair – she kept on putting it up.
– **Hey,** she said, can you imagine how far we could go with such an awesome
ride and all that food in the back …

(7)   – C'est bien, c'est parfait. Demain, je mets toutes vos affaires dans le train.
– Je compte sur toi. **Dis donc** … Betty et moi on se demandait si on pour-
rait pas mettre un petit coup de peinture dans la cuisine, un de ces quatre …
(Djian, 1989: 162)

– Gut, bestens. Morgen bring ich euer Zeug auf die Bahn.
– Ich verlass mich auf dich … **Sag mal** … Betty und ich, wir haben uns
gedacht, ob wir nicht die Küche ein bisschen anstreichen sollten, irgendwann
mal … (Djian, 1990: 172)

(– Fine, that's perfect. Tomorrow I'll get all your stuff on the train.
– I know I can count on you … **By the way** … Betty and I were wondering if
we should repaint the kitchen sometime …)

(8)   **Dis donc,** t'exagères pas un peu, là?
Sag mal, du übertreibst doch ein wenig, oder?
(**Honestly,** don't you think you're going too far?)

But the marker *dis donc* can also express a speaker's astonishment in an unexpected situation; or, to be more precise, in a situation which does not fit his/
her expectations. In those cases, the use of the marker is essentially expressive and it does not require an answer from the addressee. Therefore, *sag mal,*
which always implies this particular request to the addressee, cannot possibly
be considered as an acceptable equivalent, as examples (9)–(12) show:

(9)   – Ah ! **dis donc,** le mec !
– Jérémy…
– Pardon. (Pennac, 1990:132)
– **Wow,** der Typ!
– Jeremy…
– Tschuldigung. (Pennac, 2003:131)

(– **Oh My!** Can you believe him!
– Jeremy, please…
– Sorry.)

(10)   Ce que tu peux être con, toi, **dis donc!**
Du bist **vielleicht** blöd!
(You know you can be quite the jerk sometimes)

(11)   Qu'est-ce que tu as grandi, **dis donc**!
        Du bist **ja** groß geworden!
        (**Look at you**, all grown up!)

(12)   «J'ai rien compris, dit Micho une fois installé au café. Qu'est-ce qu'il a?
        – Il a qu'il est pas bien.
        – C'est pas ça qui lui coupe l'appétit, **dis donc**!»
        La bouche cernée de chantilly, Ludo venait de finir avant tout le monde son
        café liégeois. (Queffélec, 1985: 91)

        – Ich habe nichts verstanden, sagte Micho, als sie im Café saßen. Was ist mit ihm?
        – Es stimmt eben etwas nicht mit ihm.
        – Das verdirbt ihm **aber** nicht den Appetit!
        Ludo, Schlagsahne um den Mund, war mit seinem Eiskaffee als erster fertig.
        (Queffélec, 2003: 96)

        (– I didn't understand anything, Micho said once he sat in the café. What's
        wrong with him?
         – He's not feeling well.
        – Whatever it is, it doesn't seem to be taking away his appetite!
        Ludo, whipped cream all over his mouth, was the first to finish his *café liégeois*)

3.2. Tu vois

The French markers *tu vois/vous voyez* and the German expressions *siehst du/
du siehst/sehen Sie* can only be considered as synonymous when *tu vois/vous
voyez* are used by the speaker to call the addressee to witness, to invite him to
notice a fact which the speaker considers obvious, or to share his/her point of
view,[5] as in examples (13) to (15):

(13)   – Pierrot, dit à Blandine qu'elle arrête d'embêter le chat, la dernière fois elle l'a
        enfermé dans le cellier, il a pissé sur les patates! Oui! Mets-le dehors. Et fais-la
        sortir, tu vois bien que je téléphone! ... Martine? T'es toujours là? – Oui. – Ah,
        ma pauv'fille, si tu savais, elle me tue! (Winckler, 1999: 305)

        Pierrot, sorg dafür, dass Blandine die Katze nicht ärgert, das letzte Mal hat sie
        sie in den Keller gesperrt, wo sie auf die Kartoffeln gepisst hat! Ja! Schmeiß sie
        raus. Und schick sie aus dem Zimmer, du siehst doch, dass ich telefoniere! ...
        Martine, bist du noch da? – Ja- Ach, mein armes Mädchen, wenn du wüsstest,
        die bringt mich doch um. (Winckler, 2000: 283)

        (–Pierrot, tell Blandine she has to leave the cat alone. Last time she shut him
        in the basement and he pissed all over the potatoes! Yes, put him outside. And
        make her leave too, can't you see I'm on the phone? Martine? Are you still
        there? That girl is really killing me, you can't even imagine!)

(14)   – Ah **tu vois**, j'avais raison!
        – Na **siehst du**, ich hatte doch recht!
        (**See?** I was right!)

(15)   Et où ai-je lu que Virginia Woolf faisait «aussi» des tartes – ce n'est pas incompatible, **tu vois.**
Irgendwo habe ich gelesen, dass Virginia Woolf 'auch' gebackt habe – **siehst du,** das eine schließt das andere nicht aus.
(And I've read somewhere Virginia Woolf also baked pies – **see?** It is not that impossible.)

But the marker *tu vois* can also appeal to the addressee's intellectual faculties and thereby encourage him to try to understand the speaker's point of view; in these cases, adequate German equivalents would rather be expressions containing verbs of cognition such as *wissen* or *verstehen*:

(16)   – Et ça t'arrive souvent? – Non, pas souvent. Huit ou dix fois par jour, mais ça passe très vite, **tu vois,** comme un éclair. C'est ça! J'ai l'impression qu'un éclair me traverse le bras et évidemment ça m'inquiète, à mon âge ... (Winckler, 1999: 334)

– Passiert dir das oft? – Nein, nicht oft, 8 oder 10 mal am Tag, aber es geht schnell vorbei, **weißt du,** wie ein Blitz. Genau das ist es! Ich habe den Eindruck, dass ein Blitz durch meinen Arm fährt, und das beunruhigt mich natürlich, in meinem Alter ... (Winckler, 2000: 309)

(–Does it happen frequently? – No, only eight or ten times a day, but it goes away quickly on its own, **you know,** like a flash. Exactly! It feels like something flashes through my arm, and at my age I'm worried about it, obviously.)

(17)   Mais elle s'intéresse beaucoup à ce que je fais, elle se confie à moi, et moi aussi, je peux enfin lui dire les choses qu'une mère a envie de dire à sa fille, **tu vois,** des trucs de femme ... (Winckler, 1999: 408)

Aber sie interessiert sich sehr für das, was ich tue, sie vertraut sich mir an, und auch ich kann ihr endlich Dinge sagen, die eine Mutter ihrer Tochter gern sagen möchte, **du weißt ja,** Frauengeschichten ... (Winckler, 2000: 378)

(But she's very interested in what I am doing, she confides in me, and now I can finally tell her things a mother wants to tell her daughter, **you know,** girl talk ...)

(18)   L'islam, tout ça. Putain, peuvent bien tous crever! Mais y a des listes de noms, des adresses. Cité après cité. Comme qui dirait un réseau, **tu vois.** Faux papiers. Fric. Dope. Armes. J'te le file, le cahier, et tu t'casses. T'oublies tout. Tu m'oublies. (Izzo, 1996: 236)

Mit Islam und so Geschichten. Von mir aus können sie allesamt verrecken! Aber da sind Listen mit Namen und Adressen. Viertel für Viertel. Wie ein Netz, **verstehst du.** Falsche Papiere. Kohle. Dope. Waffen. Ich geb dir das Heft und du verpisst dich. Warst nie hier. (Izzo, 2002: 402)

(Islam and all that shit. They can all fucking die! But there are lists with names and addresses. For each district. Like a network, **you know.** Counterfeited papers. Dough. Dope. Weapons. I give you the book and you're off then. You forget all about it.)

None of the aforementioned verbal expressions have German equivalency to the function of *tu vois* as a verbal filler[6] (Bolly, 2010) (cf. examples 19–22). In fact, it is very difficult to find adequate German lexical equivalents for the following French examples:[7]

(19)   Faut pas trop attendre, tu sais, un homme ça ne doit pas rester seul. Moi, **tu vois**, je m'y suis pris tard, et je regrette. (Winckler, 1999: 266)

(You shouldn't wait for too long. A man shouldn't ever be alone. Look at me: I waited for too long and now I really regret it.)

(20)   – Ben lui, **tu vois**, il a pas fait payer ... (Winckler, 1999: 386)

(Well, *he* didn't let us pay.)

(21)   Là, **tu vois**, j'avais envie de pleurer, et le médecin l'a bien vu, il m'a donné un mouchoir, et puis il m'a redemandé ce que c'était que cette histoire de fugue. (Winckler, 1999: 402)

(At that moment I barely could hold my tears back and the doctor saw them, so he gave me a tissue and asked again what I meant by 'running away'.)

(22)   – Tu as pris quelque chose, de l'aspirine? – Eh bien, **tu vois**, je n'y ai pas pensé! Le temps que j'y pense ça serait fini, de toute manière! (Winckler, 1999: 333)

(– Did you take something, like an aspirin? – You know what, I didn't even think about it! By the time I'd have thought about it, it would have been over anyway.)

3.3. *Écoute*: An example of a very polysemous discourse marker

This third DM is particularly interesting in the context of the asymmetry of German and French in this domain because of its great polysemy and functional polyvalence. These characteristics will allow us to illustrate the great variety and formal heterogeneity of the German units, which may be considered as adequate equivalents for each of the specific uses of the French marker.

3.3.1. Characteristics of *écoute/écoutez*

The French DM *écoute*, which probably derives from the imperative form of the corresponding verb of perception, still preserves traces of its morphological origins. First, contrary to other markers – including markers which derive from imperatives too, such as *dis donc* or *tiens* – *écoute* can only occur in dialogic contexts, or more precisely, in contexts in which someone is directly addressed by the speaker. Restriction is reflected, among other things, in the persisting opposition of a singular and a non-singular (plural/politeness) form (*écoute/écoutez*). The marker has lost grammatical functionality in that it does not allow the speaker to choose the singular verb form while talking to several addressees or to someone he addresses by using the *vous* form/the politeness pronoun:

(23)   *Écoute, vous avez eu beaucoup de chance.
        Dis donc, vous en avez eu de la chance!

        (Wow, you got very lucky!)

Second, another characteristic the marker *écoute* has in common with its imperative form is its directive dimension, which is often considered as predominant (Dostie, 2009). And all occurrences indeed contain, among other things, an appeal to the addressee's attention.[8] Furthermore, the marker is characterized by its location in discourse: it can only be found in the course of the exchange or in certain circumstances, as we will see, in the exchange's closing utterance. But in its regular, non-marked use, it can never serve as opening mark or occur in the opening utterance of an exchange. This restriction is linked to the essentially reactive nature of the utterances in which it is used: it always introduces a reaction of the speaker to something the addressee said or did, and it is intended to make the speaker's reaction easier to accept for the addressee.

In short, the fundamental and basic meaning of the marker *écoute* can be described as a reactive appeal to reason. When resorting to this DM, the speaker intends to get the addressee to mobilize his/her intellectual and cognitive faculties, his/her reasoning capacity to understand and accept the speaker's message, which expresses in some way his/her reaction to the current situation or discourse. All specific uses of this marker are based on and derived from this common basic signification.

3.3.2. The main uses of the DM *écoute* and its German equivalents

Following Rodriguez Somolinos (2003) and Dostie (1998, 2004, 2009), among others, it can be said that the specific uses of the marker *écoute* fall into two categories. The marker occurs mostly when the speaker wants to make his own point of view easier to accept for the addressee; and reduce the conflict potential of the exchange.

1.1.1.1. Écoute: *Speaker's point of view easier to accept.* First, by opening his/her utterance with *écoute*, the speaker sometimes only intends to make the addressee focus on what he/she is saying and thus to encourage him/her to think about the relevance of what he/she is saying. In such cases, possible German equivalents are expressions such as *hör zu* or *pass auf*, in which the appeal to concentration prevails:

(24)   – Tu crois que c'est faisable …? elle avait demandé. – Ben, je te mentirais si je
        disais le contraire. – Oh … mais alors, pourquoi on le fait pas …? – **Écoute**, si
        tu me dis que t'en as vraiment envie, je veux bien essayer de m'y mettre. (Djian,
        1989: 291)

– Meinst du, das ist machbar ...? hatte sie mich gefragt. – Naja, es wäre gelo-
gen, wenn ich das Gegenteil sagte. – Oh ... ja, aber, warum machen wir's dann
nicht ...? – **Pass auf**, wenn du mir sagst, dass dir was dran liegt, dann will ich's
gern versuchen. (Djian, 1990: 303)

(–Do you really think we can do it? she had asked. – Well, I'd be lying if I said
we can't. – Oh ... Why don't we do it, then? – **Listen,** when you really want
this, I will give it a try.)

(25)   – Écoute, elle a soupiré. Faut qu'il y ait un minimum de justice, tu crois pas? Je
vais pas me laisser emmerder toute ma vie sans rien faire ...! (Djian, 1989: 103)
– **Hör zu**, stöhnte sie. Ein Minimum an Gerechtigkeit muss sein, findste
nicht? Ich lasse mich nicht mein ganzes Leben lang verarschen, ohne was
dagegen zu tun ...! (Djian, 1990: 111)

(– **Listen,** she said with a sigh, there has to be at least some kind of justice,
don't you think? I won't let them fuck around with me all my life and do
nothing...!)

The speaker may also want to convince the addressee that what he/she said
or did was legitimate and appropriate in the context in which he/she said or
did it, by inviting him/her to appeal to his encyclopaedic competence or to
recognize the arguments he/she develops are cogent. By doing so, the speaker
also prevents potential objections from the addressee.

In such cases, the non-accentuated particle *ja*, which presents contents as
well known or obvious, and can be accompanied by the adverb *schließlich*, can
be considered as a possible German equivalent:

(26)   Je lui ai apporté un petit cadeau. **Écoute,** c'était Noël. (cf. Dostie, 2004)
Ich habe ihr ein kleines Geschenk mitgebracht. Es war ja **schließlich**
Weihnachten.

(I brought her a present. It was Christmas and all, **you know.**)

Finally, the speaker may need to ensure his/her words will be accepted,
especially when he/she performs speech acts – such as giving advice, making
demands, forbid, etc – which could be perceived and interpreted by the
addressee as authoritarian, or possibly even aggressive. By introducing such
speech acts with *écoute*, the speaker invites the addressee to think about the
intention underlying them or about the reasons that may have motivated the
speaker to utter them. In such cases, using *hör mal* or *pass auf* to translate
écoute can be problematic, because it tends to reinforce the directive dimension of the utterance instead of lessening it:

(27)   Mince ...! Mais qu'est-ce que c'est que ces trucs? elle a fait. Qui est-ce qui a écrit
ça, c'est toi ...? – **Écoute,** c'est des vieux machins sans intérêt. ***On ferait mieux
de passer à autre chose.*** Je vais les ranger ... (Djian, 1989: 43)

– Mann …! Was ist das für'n Zeug? fragte sie. Wer hat das geschrieben, du etwa …? – **Hör mal**, das ist alter, uninteressanter Kram, *wir sollten besser zu etwas anderem übergehen*. Ich packe sie wieder ein … (Djian, 1990: 47)

(– Gee …! What is this supposed to be? she asked. Did you write this? – That's nothing, just old crap. *Can we please change the subject*. I'll put them away.)

(28) Hé dis donc, c'est vrai que vous allez repeindre tous les trucs? Tu vas t'envoyer tout ça …?? Je me suis arrêté. J'ai posé mon bidon par terre et j'ai regardé Georges dans les yeux. – **écoute**, j'ai dit, je sais pas encore ce que je vais décider mais je veux pas que tu parles de ça à Betty. Est-ce que c'est bien note …? (Djian, 1989: 34)

– He, sag mal, ist das wahr, dass ihr den ganzen Mist anstreichen sollt? Willste dir das antun …?? Ich blieb stehen. Ich setzte meinen Eimer ab und guckte Georges in die Augen. – **Pass auf**, sagte ich, ich weiß noch nicht, wie ich mich entscheide, aber wehe, wenn du Betty was sagst. Ist das klar …? (Djian, 1990: 37)

(– Hey, is it true you will repaint the whole dump here? Do you really want to take that onto yourself? I stopped, put the can on the floor and looked Georges straight in the eyes. – **Listen**, I said, I haven't decided yet but I don't want you to tell Betty. Have I made myself clear?)

But in such cases, on the contrary, the speaker tries to appeal to the addressee's reason and to convince him/her that mutual cooperation is needed. Insofar as the speaker calls upon the addressee's reflection faculties rather than upon his/her attention, one may use German expressions containing a verb of cognition (such as *weißt du*). Perhaps vocatives (*Du*) or verbal fillers such as *tja* or *naja* are also possible: they signal that the speaker wants to pause, and possibly expresses hesitation (*tja, naja*), in order to invite the other participants to take a moment of reflection:

(29) – Tu as des problèmes financiers? Ta femme est au courant?
      – **Écoute**, je préfère que tu la laisses en dehors de tout ça, si tu veux bien.

      – Hast du Geldprobleme ? Weiß deine Frau davon ?
      – **Naja, weißt du**, mir wäre es lieber, wenn du sie daraus halten könntest.

      (– You have money problems? Does your wife know about this?
      – Listen, I'd rather you leave her out of this, if you don't mind.)

(30) – Si je comprends bien le raisonnement de X, seules les victimes ont le droit de débattre sur les sanctions qui doivent être appliquées aux délinquants? Belle logique, quand l'assemblée voudra voter une loi pénale, ne pourront voter que les victimes qui, bien sûr, sont les plus objectives et représentent au mieux le people … Faut réfléchir un peu avant de parler …

      – **Ecoute**, tu ne devrais pas parler comme ca. Essaie de penser au mal qui leur a été fait. (Internet)

– **Du,** du solltest nicht so reden. Denk mal daran, was ihnen angetan wurde.

(– You shouldn't say something like that, you know. Think how much they have been hurt.)

Through the appeal to the addressee's reason made with the marker *écoute*, this last example demonstrates that the speaker seeks conciliation and attempts to build a consensus. This lessening of the conflict potential in the exchange is the main characteristic of the second subtype of this marker.

1.1.1.2. *Reduce the conflict potential of an exchange.* The marker *écoute* can be found in many situations in which the speaker disagrees with the addressee. By using it, the speaker tries to make the addressee consider a point of view that differs from his own, and to think about the reasons which may explain the divergence between the speaker's and the addressee's opinions.

In actuality this DM often appears in exchanges in which the speaker says the opposite of what the addressee says. In such cases, adequate German equivalents could be particles such as *doch*, which underline the gap that may between the representation the addressee seems to have of reality and the speaker's idea of it:

(31)　–Je suis sûre qu'il va revenir
　　　– **Écoute,** je ne voudrais pas te contrarier, mais ca m'étonnerait.

　　　– Er kommt bestimmt zurück.
　　　– Du, ich will dir nicht widersprechen, aber es würde mich **doch** wundern.

　　　(– I'm sure he'll be back soon.
　　　– I'd hate to make you upset, but I really don't think so.)

(32)　– Non, mais c'est pas possible!
　　　– **Écoute,** c'était dans le journal!

　　　– Es kann doch nicht wahr sein!
　　　– So stand es **doch** in der Zeitung!

　　　(–It can't be true!
　　　– It was written in the newspaper, **though**.)

Speakers also use it in exchanges in which they (directly or indirectly) turn down a proposition made by the addressee. In such cases too, German apostrophes would be possible (33), but it can also be omitted (34):

(33)　– Viens tout de suite, il faut absolument qu'on se parle!
　　　– **Écoute,** ca ne va pas être possible, là.

　　　– Komm sofort, wir müssen unbedingt reden !
　　　– **Du,** tut mir leid, ich kann im Moment nicht.

> (– Come over, we really need to talk!
> – Sorry, I can't right now.)

(34)   – Papa, tu me prêtes ta voiture?
      – **Écoute,** ça fait déjà trois fois cette semaine, ca suffit.

      – Papa, darf ich das Auto nehmen ?
      – Das ist schon das dritte Mal in der Woche, jetzt reicht's.

      (– Dad, can I borrow your car?
      – It's already been three times this week, that's enough!)

Finally, *écoute* occurs at the beginning of utterances the speaker produces to close an exchange he/she no longer considers as relevant or adequate, and he/she no longer wants to be involved in. In these cases, *écoute* not only signals the speaker's refusal to cooperate, but also takes on an expressive dimension: it reflects the speaker's exasperation, the exhaustion of his/her patience and resources. The speaker is no longer willing to negotiate, so that his/her only option is to cut the conversation short. This particular discourse function could be fulfilled in German by the modal particle *aber*:

(35)   –**Ecoute,** ca suffit, maintenant!/**Écoute,** ca va bien, maintenant.

      – Jetzt reicht's **aber!**/Jetzt ist **aber** Schluss!

      (– That's enough, now!)

1.1.1.3. *Écoute – other functions.* In order to give a representative, if not exhaustive, account of the polysemy/polyvalence of the marker *écoute*, at least two further uses must be discussed. The first use exhibits some similarities with the use of *écoute* in Example (35): here, the expressive dimension dominates and the purpose of the utterance is to manifest the speaker's virulent disapproval of something the addressee said or did. In this case, the marker does not precede an utterance – the concrete reproach is not explicitly expressed – but builds the core of the message. The marker is also often accompanied by other expressive units and has a particular intonation pattern. The speaker then signals he/she has been pushed to the limits of his patience and now refuses to argue any longer. Possible German equivalents might be units with a primarily expressive dimension in order to underline the speaker's dissatisfaction and signal the speaker wants the situation to be improved:

(36)   – Non, mais **écoute** …
      – Also wirklich/also ich bitte dich …

      (– Oh, please …)

The second use to be mentioned is quite the opposite. It could be described as a mere phatic use of the marker, whose first purpose is to signal the speaker is conserving his/her answering turn or taking the speech turn; to give the speaker time for online discourse planning; to gain or maintain the addressee's attention. In German, corresponding phatic units can be found:

(37)   – Comment ca va?
    – Bah, **écoute,** plutôt bien, ma foi

    – Und? Wie geht's?
    – **Tja,** ziemlich gut, eigentlich.

    (– How are you?
    – **Well, you know,** I'm quite fine.)

(38)   – Et pourquoi êtes-vous plus chère que les autres?
    – **Écoutez,** c'est comme pour les autos, au fond. Il y a les petites voitures, pas chères, mais pas très bien équipées. Et il y a les limousines, plus chères, bien sûr, mais qui présentent certains avantages. (Internet)

    – Und wieso verlangen Sie mehr als die anderen
    – **Naja, wissen Sie,** das ist im Grunde wie beim Auto. Es gibt Kleinwagen, die sind günstig, haben aber natürlich nicht so viel Ausstattung. Und dann gibt es die Limousinen, die kosten natürlich mehr, haben aber auch mehr zu bieten.

    (– And why do you charge a higher price than others?
    – Well, you know, it's like cars. There are compact cars, they're quite cheap, but they don't have many accessories. And then there are limousines, they are more expensive, of course, but they have a lot for them.)

4. Conclusion

The main purpose of this paper is to describe three French discourse markers and to examine their possible German equivalents. We have found the following:

- Similarities can be found between the two languages: since both have pragmaticalized expressions including verbal elements, it is most certainly no accident that those similarities concern the choice and the form of verbs which appear in these expressions. Both French and German preferentially use verbs of perception, verbs of cognition, and verbs of speech as DMs; both languages employ the imperative mood or the first- and second-person forms, which underline the interactive dimension of these units.
- These units are in both languages 'constructs' with a similar fragmentary structure (Imo, 2007).[9]

- The most difficult yet fascinating differences can be observed in the pragmaticalization process: formal similar expressions have by far not reached the same stage of pragmaticalization (cf. *dis donc* vs. *sag mal* for example).
- An interesting observation, promising for future studies, is that, among all parts of speech, verbs have a special status in French; they are more likely than other units to be pragmaticalized and also to reach a high degree of pragmaticalization, which results in a greater poly-functionality of French verbal locutions.

Those results prove once again that a comparison of two languages only makes sense on the functional level. If modal particles, a quantitatively and functionally very important category in German, can be defined as elements with a primarily interactive function,[10] then units fulfilling exactly the same function are to be found in French also. The main difference is that in French they do it more explicitly, because many of the interactive particles contain verbs of perception or cognition through which the speaker and the addressee are directly involved in the verbal interaction.

In this exploratory study, our focus was limited to three French discourse markers: *dis donc, tu vois* and écoute. Specifically, we found the lack of available data to be a large impediment to conducting an in-depth examination of other discourse markers. We hope to continue this exploratory research and we highly encourage others in the field to gather cross-linguistic data, which look at both the French and German functional equivalency, and to compare only their literal translation.

Notes

1.   To that time, there was hardly any systematic study about discourse structuration and specific discourse units like discourse markers; Weydt could not make use of the conceptual apparatus, which will later become established and will be used to describe systematically the discursive functions of those units. He thus speaks of 'politeness/impoliteness' and 'friendliness/ unfriendliness'

2.   Reiners (1959: 183, quoted by Weydt, 1969: 83) coined this expression ('*Läuse im Pelz der Sprache*').

3.   Considering the various meanings the aforementioned units (depending on the context in which they appear), most of the English translations we propose in this section are for comprehension purposes. The proposed phrases represent only *one* of the many possible English translations of French and German discursive markers.

4.   Most often the examples in this paper come from French fiction works and their translation in German. Other examples have been taken from the Internet (chats, forums), and some are self-coined examples, in which case no citation is provided.

5.   Imo (2007: 27–30) describes it as an evidence marker.

6.   Verbal fillers can be defined with Bolly (2010: 682) as units with no or little semantic content that primarily fulfil a pragmatic function: they can either be used interpersonally to

catch or maintain the addressee's attention, or as expressive devices for the speaker to establish his presence in his own discourse and in the speech flow.

7.   For most cases of *tu vois*, no translation could be found. The use of *siehst du*, that occurs in some cases, does not seem to be adequate, because it does not have the same pragmatic function as the French marker: in those examples, *tu vois* has a focalizing function, which is assumed by prosody in German.

8.   Some linguists (Rodriguez Somolinos, 2003, among others) count this marker among what they call the 'attention getters', saying it is part of a strategy of the speaker designed to catch and keep the addressee's attention: 'Il fait partie d'une stratégie de la part du locuteur pour capter et soutenir l'attention de l'allocutaire, il réalise tout d'abord une demande d'attention' (Somolinos, 2003: 72).

9.   Imo uses the term 'construct' to describe actually occurring linguistic expressions of constructions (in analogy to the *type-token* opposition): 'Den Begriff *"construct"* (vs. *"construction"*) verwende ich hier in Analogie zur *type-token* Opposition für sprachlich realisierte Konstruktionen" (Imo, 2007: 6). According to him, many *constructs* have a fragmentary structure: they can vary syntactically, phonetically, functionally depending on the context. But they are only partially fragmentary: in one given context, the addressee is always able to recognize the specific function and meaning of a construct.

10.   These elements are also referred to in research as 'interactive particles' or 'interpretation guides'.

References

Auer, P. and Günthner, S. (2003) Die Entstehung von Diskursmarkern im Deutschen: ein Fall von Grammatikalisierung? In *InLiSt 38*.

Bolly, C. (2010) Pragmaticalisation du marqueur discursif *tu vois*. De la perception à l'évidence et de l'évidence au discours. In F. Neveu, V. Muni Toke, J. Durand, T. Klingler, L. Mondada and S. Prévost (eds) *Discours, pragmatique et interaction*. CMLF 2010. Paris: Institut de Linguistique Française.

Dalmas, M. (1989) Sprechakte vergleichen: ein Beitrag zur deutsch-französischen Partikelforschung. In H. Weydt (ed.) *Sprechen mit Partikeln*, 228–239. Berlin: De Gruyter.

Dalmas, M. (2009) 'Zur Bedeutungsbeschreibung von einigen Pseudokonnektoren. In B. Henn-Memmesheimer and F. Joachim (eds) *Die Ordnung des Standard und die Differenzierung der Diskurse*, 167–178. Frankfurt a.M.: Peter Lang.

Dehé, N. and Wichmann, A. (2009) The multifunctionality of epistemic parentheticals in discourse: Prosodic cues to the semantic-pragmatic boundary. *Functions of Language* 17 (1): 1–28.

Djian, P. (1989) 37,2° le matin. Paris: J'ai lu.

Djian, P. (1990) *Betty Blue. 37,2 Grad am Morgen. Aus dem Französischen von Michael Mosblech*. Zürich: Diogenes Verlag.

Dostie, G. (2009) Discourse markers and regional variation in French. A lexico-semantic approach. In K. Beeching, N. Armstrong and F. Gadet (eds), *Sociolinguistic Variation in Contemporary French*, 201–214. Amsterdam: John Benjamins.

Dostie, G. (2004) *Pragmaticalisation et marqueurs discursifs*. Bruxelles: De Boeck–Duculot.

Dostie, G. (1998) Deux marqueurs discursifs issus de verbes de perception: de écouter/regarder à écoute/regarde. *Cahiers de lexicologie* 73: 125–146.

Ducrot, O. *et al.* (1980). *Les mots du discours.* Paris: Minuit.

Gohl, C. and Günthner, S. (1999) Grammatikalisierung von *weil* als Diskursmarker in der gesprochenen Sprache. *Zeitschrift für Sprachwissenschaft* 18 (1): 39–75. http://dx.doi.org/10.1515/zfsw.1999.18.1.39

Günthner, S. (1993) '*... weil – man kann es ja wissenschaftlich untersuchen*' – Diskurspragmatische Aspekte der Wortstellung in WEIL-Sätzen. *Linguistische Berichte* 143: 37–59.

Günthner, S. (1999) Entwickelt sich der Konzessivkonnektor *obwohl* zum Diskursmarker? Grammatikalisierungstendenzen im gesprochenen Deutsch. *Linguistische Berichte* 180: 409–446.

Günthner, S. (2000) Grammatik im Gespräch: Zur Verwendung von ‚wobei' im gesprochenen Deutsch. *Sprache und Literatur* 85 (31): 57–74.

Günthner, S. and Imo, W. (2003) Die Reanalyse von Matrixsätzen als Diskursmarker: ich mein-Konstruktionen im gesprochenen Deutsch. In M. Orosz and A. Herzog (eds) *Jahrbuch der Ungarischen Germanistik 2003*, 181–216. Budapest/Bonn: DAAD.

Günthner, S. and Mutz, K. (2004) Grammaticalization vs. Pragmaticalization? The development of pragmatic markers in German and Italian. In W. Bisang, N. Himmelmann and B. Wiemer (eds) *What Makes Grammaticalization? A Look from its Fringes and its Components*, 77–107. Berlin/New York: de Gruyter.

Imo, W. (2007) Der Zwang zur Kategorienbildung: Probleme der Anwendung der *Construction Grammar* bei der Analyse der gesprochenen Sprache. *Gesprächsforschung – Online-Zeitschrift zur verbalen Interaktion* 8: 22–45. [www.gespraechsforschung-ozs.de]

Izzo, J-C. (1996) *Chourmo.* Paris: Gallimard.

Izzo, J-C. (2002) *Chourmo. Aus dem Französischen von Katarina Grän und Roland Voullié.* Zürich: Unionsverlag.

Lehmann, C. (2002) *Thoughts on Grammaticalization.* Second revised edition, Arbeitspapiere des Seminars für Sprachwissenschaft der Universität Erfurt, 9. ASSiDUE.

Marchello-Nizia, C. (2006) *Grammaticalisation et changement linguistique*, Bruxelles: De Boeck–Duculot.

Meillet, A. (1912) L'évolution des formes grammaticales. In A. Meillet (1921) *Linguistique historique et linguistique générale*, 2 volumes, 130–149. Paris: Champion.

Métrich, R. and Faucher, E. (2009) *Wörterbuch der Partikeln: unter Berücksichtigung ihrer französischen Äquivalente.* Berlin: De Gruyter.

Pennac, D.l (1990) *La petite marchande de prose.* Paris: Gallimard.

Pennac, D. (2003) *Sündenbock im Bücherdschungel. Aus dem Französischen von Evelyne Passet.* Köln: Kiepenheuer und Witsch.

Queffélec, Y. (1985) *Les noces barbares.* Paris: Gallimard.

Queffélec, Y. (2001) *Barbarische Hochzeit. Aus dem Französichen von Andrea Spingler.* Frankfurt a.M.; Suhrkamp Verlag.

Reiners, L. (1959) *Stilkunst. Ein Lehrbuch deutscher Prosa.* München: C. H. Beck.

Rodríguez Somolinos, A. (2003) Un marqueur discursif du français parlé: *écoute* ou l'appel à la raison. *Thélème* 71: 71–83.

Traugott, E. C. (1995) *The role of the development of discourse markers in a theory of grammaticalization.* Place: Paper presented at the 12th International Conference on Historical Linguistics. [http://www.stanford.edu/~traugott/papers/discourse.pdf]

Weydt, H. (1969) *Abtönungspartikel. Die deutschen Modalwörter und ihre französischen Entsprechungen.* Bad Homburg usw.

Winckler, M. (1999) *La maladie de Sachs.* Paris: J'ai lu.

Winckler, M. (2000) *Doctor Bruno Sachs. Aus dem Französischen von Eugen Helmlé.* München: Carl Hanser Verlag.

5   Thematic Parentheticals in Dutch and English

Mike Hannay and María de los Ángeles Gómez González

Adopting a contrastive-rhetorical stance, this study explores what we call thematic parentheticals in a comparable English-Dutch corpus comprising four written genres. Thematic parentheticals are parenthetical expressions, irrespective of form, which are marked off typographically and occur immediately after, and are triggered by, a thematic element, where the latter is defined in terms of its treatment in Systemic Functional Grammar. Our data suggest that English uses thematic parentheticals much more than Dutch. This quantitative picture is true across the genres studied, but we also see qualitative differences between Dutch and English in the use of parentheticals in news texts and academic texts in particular. In attempting to explain the quantitative difference between the languages, we conclude that an interplay between writing cultures and basic syntactic patterns contrives to facilitate the use of parentheticals in English, which also demonstrates a relatively broad range of discourse functions, whereas for Dutch this interplay leads to a dispreference for certain kinds of thematic parentheticals.

1. Introduction[1]

This contribution examines how written Dutch and written English make use of what we call 'thematic parentheticals' (henceforth TPs). These constructions occur in sentence positions which may be seen as part of the 'multiple theme' (cf. Halliday and Matthiessen, 2004: 81) or 'extended multiple theme' (Gómez González, 1998, 2001: 329ff.). Examples of English TPs are given in (1–2), with the TPs in bold print:

(1)　Back in the 1640s advocates of the Solemn League and Covenant, **New Englanders and Scots alike**, had emphasized that it could only be kept through the efforts of the individual covenanters to lead pious and penitent lives. [sn 4126 ac][2]

(2)　Recently, **particularly with respect to the Internet**, research into the possibility that some people are spending excessive amounts of time, and sometimes money, on computing activities has increased. [sn 5876 ac]

Our interest is of a contrastive-rhetorical nature. The primary motivation for the analysis comes from Tavecchio (2010), who, in a corpus study of sentence patterns in English and Dutch, found that English text sentences are significantly more interruptive in nature than their Dutch counterparts; that is to say, English uses more parenthetical devices of various types. This difference prevails across a range of genres and can arguably be explained in terms of a general rhetorical preference in Dutch for less structurally complex sentences. For instance, Tavecchio (2010: 458) found that Dutch style guides were more prescriptive than English ones when it came to promoting readability by means of relatively short sentences. For the present study we were interested in establishing whether TPs, as a particular kind of parenthetical, also differed in frequency in the two languages, and in addition how they can further be characterized in terms of syntactic features and the semantic and discourse functions which they perform. While written Dutch and English may indeed differ with regard to rhetorical style in terms of sentence complexity, we are specifically interested in looking for other, possibly genre-related explanations for any frequency differences that might emerge.

Seen in broader terms, this study has an exploratory character in terms of its focus on the structure of the text sentence in different languages. Text sentences are important rhetorical-orthographical units of written discourse (cf. Downing and Locke, 2004: 274; Siepmann *et al.*, 2011: 92ff), and form the building blocks of paragraphs. As such, understanding the ways in which the grammatical repertoire of a language is used to construct potentially complex sentences can provide a substantial contribution to a contrastive-rhetorical analysis of in this case Dutch and English. Insight into how text sentences in different languages are structured can provide valuable input to the development of advanced writing skills materials, a traditional application of contrastive studies (cf. Hannay, 2007).

In this context yet another motivation for our concern for TPs stems from a special interest in the notion of theme, or the initial slot in discourse units, which we believe plays a crucial role in the information management required for human serial processing (Clark and Haviland, 1977). There is a considerable amount of literature on the ways in which different kinds of theme are used to organize the message and stage the text in different genres (see e.g., Nwogu,

1990; Ghadessy, 1995; Hasan and Fries, 1995; Gómez González, 2001; Rav-elli, 2003; Halliday and Matthiessen, 2004; Fetzer, 2008; Martínez Lirola, 2009; Jalilifar, 2010). However, despite Thompson (1996: 139) drawing attention to the importance of interpolation in the theme – our subject here – the com-bination of thematic elements with parenthetical material has only received little attention (notable exceptions being Hartnett (1995) and Smits (2002)). With this study investigating the discourse functions performed by TPs with a range of syntactic realizations, we hope to gain insight into how writers build up different kinds of complex orientational frameworks (schemas or frames) for selectively attending to and interpreting the subsequent message in a spe-cific way.

The text is organized as follows. In Section 2 we define the class of the-matic parentheticals and go on in Section 3 to briefly outline the relevant structural differences between English and Dutch clause construction. Section 4 describes how we compiled and analysed the data, after which Section 5 presents the most prominent findings with regard to syntactic characteristics, semantic relations, and punctuational features. Section 6 pays separate attention to the discourse functions performed by TPs in the two languages. We discuss the contribution of parentheticals to the crea-tion of complex orientational frames for text sentences, and reflect on the extent to which grammatical and rhetorical aspects might be responsible for the differences that we see in the behaviour of thematic parentheticals in Dutch and English.

2. Thematic parentheticals

With regard to written language we take the notion 'parenthetical' to refer to any linguistic expression which can be said to provide additional infor-mation to the main message of the sentence, and which is marked off typo-graphically from the rest of the sentence. Moreover, following the principle applied in accounting for the positional constraints on parenthesized units by Nunberg *et al.* (2002: 1749), we do not consider elements which occur sentence-initially as parenthetical; in other words, in order to be parenthet-ical, a linguistic expression must be positioned in the sentence following some other element, which – again following Nunberg *et al.* (2002: 1749) – we will call the anchor. Significantly, parentheticals constitute a specific dis-course act, which we take to subsume both substantive and regulatory acts as described by Chafe (1994).

Much recent work on parenthetical expressions has focused on formal syntactic issues (e.g. Burton-Roberts (2005) and the contributions to Dehé and Kavalova (2007)), while more pragmatically oriented studies have usually been restricted to individual parenthetical constructions (e.g. Blakemore, 2005; Hannay and Keizer, 2005). However, little work has been done on the functioning of parenthetical expressions defined in terms of their position, despite the clear relevance of position for determining their appropriateness (cf. Blakemore, 2005, 2006). A basic assumption in this study is that parentheticals relate in a specific way to their anchor. Blakemore (2006: 1685–1686) demonstrates the relevance of position by comparing (3a) with (3b):

(3)   a.   The ambulance driver refused to drive the only remaining ambulance –
            the other three had been stolen – and disappeared into the night.
      b.   The ambulance driver – ?**the other three had been stolen** – refused to
            drive the only remaining ambulance and disappeared into the night.

The appropriateness of (3a) is partly due to the ready interpretation of the parenthetical as adding a relevant contribution to the meaning of the sentence; more precisely, the expression *the only remaining ambulance* suggests that there was once more than one, and the parenthetical expression explains how this had come about. By contrast, (3b) is inappropriate because, in relevance-theoretic terms, the interpretation of the anchor does not give access to a context which would allow the parenthetical to be seen as relevant.

For many parentheticals the relationship with the anchor is loosely one of postmodification, even though as non-restrictive elements they do not technically belong to the anchor phrase, but are supplements to it. In functionally oriented grammars such as Downing and Locke (2006: 446f) this relation is described in terms of identification and further elaboration of the referent of the anchor. Typically, the parenthetical is realized as a prepositional phrase, a relative clause, a participial clause, or an appositive noun phrase. However, our data also show that there are different types of parenthetical which do not belong to the standard set of postmodificational structures, but which might nevertheless be said to be triggered by their thematic anchor. We will come back to these parenthetical expressions, and the matter of their interpretation, in Section 6.

We now turn to the matter of defining parentheticals which are thematic. The scope of the theme as applied in Systemic Functional Grammar is not uncontroversial (cf. Downing, 1991; Berry, 1992; Gómez González, 1998, 2001: 130–137; Fawcett, 2003). The standard position is set out by Halliday and Matthiessen (2004: 79), who state that for English, the first experiential element of the clause, typically a subject phrase or a circumstantial adverbial, will be seen as the topical theme. In addition, speakers can add textual and interpersonal perspectives on the content of the utterance by constructing a multiple theme (when textual and/or interpersonal items precede a topical theme) (for an overview of theme types see Gómez González, 2001: 180–358; Downing and Locke, 2002: 222–237). An example of a multiple theme is given in (4), where *alternatively* is a textual theme and *at the older age* is a topical marked theme:

> (4)   Alternatively, at the older age (**33 months**) the children were less likely to point on the sham hiding trials.

Because textual and interpersonal themes provide additional kinds of framework for interpreting the message to come, they do not exhaust the thematic potential of the clause, and the speaker can still make a thematic choice in the experiential domain. By contrast, in a sentence like (5), the choice of a circumstantial element in initial position means, according to the standard view, that no other experiential thematic choices can be made. In other words, the subject phrase in (5) is not regarded as thematic. However, Downing (1991: 125) argues against this view, demonstrating that circumstantial adverbials used thematically set up separate circumstantial frameworks for the interpretation of the utterance, while subject noun phrases set up participant frameworks (see Butler, 2003: 129ff, for an overview of the issues involved). For our study we followed Downing's proposals, which means that in (5) both *at the start of the week* and *Oliver Letwin* are seen as thematic, as indeed would *at the older age* and *the children* in (4) above:

> (5)   At the start of the week Oliver Letwin, the shadow chancellor, was suggesting the vouchers would be available to help subsidise private schools were the fees cost 'slightly more than the maintained sector'. [sn 1303 na]

A further expansion of the theme then involves including those parentheticals which have any kind of thematic element, including topical themes, as their anchor (cf. Gomez-Gonzalez, 2001: 330). The theme in (5) and in (6) below thus extends up to the finite verb of the main clause.

> (6)   In the second section the other patriotisms of the British Isles – **loyalty to Wales, Scotland, Ireland and England** – are considered in much the same way. [sn 4176 ac]

Here *in the second section* is a circumstantial theme, and the subject phrase *the other patriotisms of the British Isles* together with the parenthetical which it anchors is a topical theme.

Accordingly, we can now define a TP as any parenthetical element which occurs immediately after an element of the theme and is anchored by that element. Importantly, the anchoring requirement means that certain expressions which are separated by punctuation nevertheless do not count as TPs. Consider the following pair of sentences from Smits (2002: 76):

(7) a. By the early 1970s, **however**, this attitude was changing and Sir Robert Mark, who took over as Metropolitan Police Commissioner, promised to do away with corruption within the force.

  b. However, by the early 1970s this attitude was changing and Sir Robert Mark, who took over as Metropolitan Police Commissioner, promised to do away with corruption within the force.

In (7a) the initial circumstantial element, *by the early 1970s*, provides a temporal setting for the whole sentence. The second element, *however*, relates the whole sentence to the preceding discourse by signalling a contrast, but the initial element functions as a trigger for that contrast, so that *however* is analysed as a TP. In (7b), by contrast, the initial textual theme provides a frame for all that is to come and the circumstantial adverbial in second position sets the scene for the rest of the clause, but is not as a separate element triggered by *however*. The comma after *by the early 1970s* is optional here, and does not mark the end of a parenthetically inserted element. This pattern is accordingly labelled a 'stepwise complex beginning' since the writer orients his reader to the content of the message in two unrelated steps, one within the scope of the other. Smits's analysis of the orientational patterns in (7a-b) also reveals that the choice of pattern is strongly governed by contextual factors: the (a) pattern tends to be used where the discourse is progressing by chronological development, whereas the (b) pattern tends to be used in an argument-based context.

3. English vs Dutch

Extending the theme to include the preverbal grammatical subject in English presents a problem for a contrastive analysis, given that Dutch is a verb-second language. Compare (8) and (9):

(8) A week later, the minister handed in his resignation.

(9) Een week later heeft de minister zijn ontslag ingediend.
  A week later has the minister his resignation handed in
  ('A week later the minister handed in his resignation.')

In a standard Dutch declarative clause, an initial circumstantial adverbial, for example, will be followed by the finite verb, with the subject occurring postverbally. The initial preverbal element is seen as occupying the one single theme slot in the Dutch clause (Onrust *et al.*, 1993: 13). This does not, of course, prevent Dutch from having parenthetical items between the clause-initial element and the finite verb, since parentheticals are in principle outside the scope of syntactic operations within the clause. Indeed, Schelfhout *et al.* (2004: 331) note that elements belonging to a host of grammatical categories can be found in the position between an initial subject and the finite verb, and this also easily extends to initial elements other than the grammatical subject. The consequence of the single theme slot is that Dutch may be seen as having less thematic potential than English, which has at least two thematic slots before the finite verb. Consequently, in order to develop a balanced view at least in quantitative terms, we decided to include cases like (10) in our analysis, which allows us to look separately at parentheticals which occur following non-initial subjects.

> (10)　Volgens de minister　　　is de huidige geweldsinstructie,
> 　　　　According to the minister　is the current force instruction
>
> 　　　　**die in grote trekken overgenomen werd**　**van de Britten,**
> 　　　　which to a large extent adopted was　　　from the British
>
> 　　　　'helder en werkbaar' <sn 3216 na>
> 　　　　'clear and practicable'.
>
> 　　　　('According to the minister, the current instruction on the use of force, which to a large extent was adopted from the British, is "clear and practicable".')

However, there may still be an imbalance in thematic potential, relating to the kinds of thematic patterns which Dutch and English facilitate when combining anchor and parenthetical. Whereas the complex pattern given in (7a) above is common in English, and technically possible in Dutch, it is by no means common in Dutch (cf. Haeseryn *et al.*, 1997: 1297; Smits, 2002, Chapter 7). The Dutch sentence in (11) follows the same pattern as (7a):

> (11)　Gisteren echter was het weer heel wat mooier (Haeseryn *et al.*, 1997: 1297)
> 　　　　Yesterday however was the weather a lot better
> 　　　　('Yesterday, however, the weather was a lot better.')

The reason for this structure being highly infrequent, at least in written Dutch (cf. Smits, 2002: 174), may arguably be found in the fact that the two preverbal constituents, even though in the spoken language they are often integrated into one intonation unit (cf. Goméz-González, 1998: 98; Smits, 2002), do not easily combine to form one complex postmodified unit in the same way that relative clauses, prepositional phrases and appositional noun phrases do: in (11), the TP does not provide a particular attribute of 'yesterday'. A sentence like (11) thus goes against the basic principle of a single thematic element for Dutch. English, on the other hand, has no problem with two different separate elements presenting separate information being placed in a thematic preverbal position. We will come back to this in Section 6.

4. Data collection and annotation

The data for the analysis were extracted from the corpus compiled by Tavecchio (2010; see esp. Chapters 2–4). This is a contrastive corpus of 214 English and

209 Dutch texts totalling approximately 146,000 and 141,000 words respectively and drawn from four genres: academic texts, newspaper texts, short stories and public information leaflets. The corpus was annotated using what Tavecchio calls sentence information units, which correspond to a considerable extent with punctuation units. For the purposes of our study, all those parenthetical units were extracted from the corpus which satisfied the following conditions:

(a) The main clause should be a declarative and should not involve a presentational construction with sentence-final subject, which meant excluding parentheticals in interrogatives like (12):

   (12) How, **then**, should the histories of these diverse nation-states be reconnected with the history of empire? [sn 4362 ac]

(b) The parenthetical unit should follow a complete constituent, and not interrupt one. We thus excluded cases like (13):

   (13) Many, **if not most**, Iranians have already written off the elections as rigged beyond repair. [sn 1335 na]

(c) The parenthetical unit should not immediately follow a conjunction. We thus excluded cases like (14), because it was not clear in what way the parenthetical could be understood as triggered by the conjunction:

   (14) And, **so Greenberg understood,** there were some pioneers who had gone even farther afield: to the comets out in the Oort Cloud and the Kuiper Belt, where billions of ice moons the size of Ganymede swam through the darkness. [sn 10940 ss]

Note, however, that it could be argued here that the parenthetical must in some sense be triggered by the initial conjunction, otherwise it would be difficult to explain the use of the anaphoric pronoun in *so Greenberg understood*.

After filtering, we stored the remaining data in a separate database and provided annotations for syntactic status (including whether the parenthetical was appositional or not), semantic relation with the anchor, punctuational format and discourse function.

5. Analysis

In this section we first look at the frequency of TPs in the two subcorpora and consider the extent to which syntactic distinctions between the two languages as well as genre features might account for the differences found.

5.1. General frequencies

We encountered a total of 605 thematic parentheticals in the two subcorpora which fulfilled the conditions set out in the previous section. Table 1 gives an overview.

Table 1: Distribution of thematic parentheticals in the English and Dutch subcorpora

Language	Thematic parentheticals	Sentences without thematic parentheticals	Total
Dutch	243 (40.2%)	8465 (52.4%)	8708 (52.0%)
English	362 (59.8%)	7678 (47.6%)	8040 (48.0%)
Total	605 (100%)	16143 (100%)	16748 (100%)

The distribution is significant: in other words, for any parenthetical found in the corpus, there is a statistically significant greater chance that it will be in the English data than in the Dutch data ($p < 0.001$). On the assumption that the text and genre sample is representative, we may thus conclude that thematic parentheticals occur more in English than in Dutch, which is in line with Tavecchio's (2010) findings for parenthetical expressions in general.

We now turn to the frequency of TPs in the four genres. These figures are given in Table 2.

Table 2: Distribution of thematic parentheticals over the four genres in English and Dutch.

Language	Academic	Leaflet	News	Short story	Total
Dutch	93 (38.3%)	35 (14.4%)	67 (27.6%)	48 (19.8%)	243 (100%)
English	117 (32.4%)	54 (15.0%)	131 (36.3%)	60 (16.3%)	362 (100%)
Total	210 (34/8%)	89 (14.7%)	198 (32.8%)	108 (17.7%)	605 (100%)

The distribution across the four genres is not significant ($p = 0.12$). That is to say, the distribution in both languages follows much the same pattern, even though English does appear to slightly favour the use of parentheticals in news discourse and Dutch uses most TPs in academic discourse. The basic conclusion here is that the frequency differences between the two languages cannot be attributed to one or more specific genre.

Another area where we might look for an explanation for the frequency differences is the status and position of the anchor expression. If English were to have significantly more TPs following non-initial subjects, with such TPs in Dutch being postverbal and hence not thematic, then this might be seen as evidence of English indeed having greater thematic potential than Dutch. Table 3 shows the distribution of TPs according to whether they follow an initial grammatical subject, a non-initial grammatical subject, or an initial adverbial expression. Again, however, the distribution of TPs per genre according to host does not differ significantly ($p = 0.316$).

Table 3: The distribution of parentheticals in the English and Dutch subcorpora according to the status of the host

Language	Initial adverbial	Initial subject	Non-initial subject	Total
Dutch	74 (30.5%)	132 (54.3%)	37 (15.2%)	243
English	100 (27.6%)	218 (60.2%)	44 (12.2%)	362
Total	174	350	81	605

Given that the genre distribution as a whole and the thematic potential afforded by structural differences do not seem to provide an explanation for the significant differences in frequency between Dutch and English, we looked in more detail at a number of other features, starting with the grammatical categories found in TPs.

5.2. Grammatical categories and relations

The distribution of TPs according to grammatical category is given in Table 4.

Table 4: The distribution of thematic parentheticals in the Dutch and English subcorpora according to grammatical category

Grammatical category	Dutch	English	Total
Noun phrase	92 (37.9%)	129 (35.6%)	221 (36.5%)
Prep phrase	41 (16.9%)	43 (11.9%)	84 (13.9%)
Adjective phrase	1 (0,4%)	8 (2.2%)	9 (1.5%)
Coordinated phrase	9 (3.7%)	13 (3.6%)	22 (3.6%)
Adverb	2 (0,8%)	42 (11.6%)	44 (7.3%)
Adverbial clause	11 (4.6%)	22 (6.1%)	33 (5.4%)
Comment/reporting clause	4 (1.6%)	9 (2.5%)	13 (2.1%)
Independent clause	11 (4.6%)	5 (1.4%)	16 (2.6%)
Minor clause	8 (3.2%)	2 (0.5%)	10 (1.6%)
Participial clause	21 (8.6%)	49 (13.5%)	70 (11.6%)
Relative clause	43 (17.7%)	40 (11.1%)	83 (13.7%)
Total	243 (100%)	362 (100%)	605 (100%)

Because of low cell counts, the data here are not amenable to statistical testing, but two points are worth making. First of all, there are sizeable cross-language differences between the contribution of prepositional phrases, participial clauses and relative clauses – categories typically associated with providing postnominal modification (cf. Downing and Locke, 2006: 448). Despite the English corpus having 50% more TPs than the Dutch corpus, prepositional phrases and relative clauses occur equally often in the two languages, and are hence overused in Dutch (34% of all TPs vs 23% in English), whereas the English data contain more than twice as many participial clauses. While

Dutch allows all these categories as postnominal modifiers, English typically uses more non-finite clausal structures than Dutch (Aarts and Wekker, 1993: 148–149), and it is therefore not surprising that the English data has more participial clauses.

One possible explanation for the overuse of prepositional phrases and relative clauses in Dutch is thus that these two constructions can compensate for the restricted usability of the participial clause. Dutch is indeed more likely to express the content of (15) by using the relative clause structure in (15b) rather than the non-finite construction in (15a). We therefore tentatively conclude that the expressive power of the two languages is not significantly constrained by the differences in syntactic options in this particular area.

> (15a) But Ms Abbott, sitting next to former Labour minister Keith Vaz, added in the minute and a half address: … [sn 1032 na]
> (15b) But Ms Abbott, who was sitting next to former Labour minister Keith Vaz, added in the minute and a half address: …

The second point worth mentioning about Table 4 is that while the English data contain 42 cases of an adverb as TP, Dutch only has two cases. This can be seen as related to the preference in Dutch for a single thematic element, as mentioned in section 3 above. The two adverbs in Dutch are given below:

> (16) Toen we elkaar weer tegenkwamen, **toevallig,** hielp hij me aan dit baantje
> When we each other again ran into, by chance, helped he me to this job
>
> 'When we ran into each other again, by chance, he got this job for me'
> [sn 16230]

> (17) Horende kinderen,   **daarentegen,**   dachten vaker dat de
> Children with normal hearing,   on the other hand,   thought more often that the
>
> Protagonist bereid zou zijn   om een confrontatie met de omgeving aan te gaan.
> protagonist prepared would be a confrontation with the environment to accept
>
> 'Hearing children, on the other hand, thought more often that the protagonist would be prepared to accept a confrontation with the environment'
> [sn 6195]

The first example involves *toevallig* ('by chance') as an appended phrase to the initial adverbial clause. As such, this does not cause any problem for the Dutch verb-second rule, since the adverbial clause and the TP in content terms together form a kind of complex initial constituent. The second example is different, and is similar to (7a) above. In this case, the parenthetical tells us that there is a contrastive relationship between this sentence and the previous one, and in addition that this contrast relates to children with normal hearing versus children with some contrasting characteristic that has been detailed in the previous sentence.

What is of interest here is that there is only one such case in the Dutch data, whereas the vast majority of the English examples of adverb TPs are of this kind. Consequently, we might conclude that this parenthetical option in English contributes to the distributional pattern observed for English and Dutch in Table 1 above. It should be noted, however, that even if TPs in the adverb category were to be discounted, the basic distribution of TPs in the Dutch and English subcorpora would still be significant. In Section 6 below we will present an analysis of such constructions in the light of other types of TP that occur more often in the English data and which seem to function in a similar way to the adverb TPs but do not comprise conjunctive or stance adverbs.

Another feature worth looking at from a structural point of view is apposition. Appositions do not constitute a clear grammatical category but rather involve a relationship between elements usually belonging to the same grammatical category. We annotated all parenthetical noun phrases, prepositional phrases and adverbial clauses as either appositional or non-appositional. Appositional TPs are prevalent in both subcorpora, constituting 36.2% of the Dutch TPs and 36.5% of the English TPs. English examples are given in (18–20) for the three grammatical categories involved – appositional noun phrases, prepositional phrases and adverbial clauses respectively:

(18) Similarly, the graduates who command the really big salaries – City bankers, lawyers **and accountants** – could afford to pay back more after university than those in public services. [sn 701 na]

(19) But for all the republics, **even for Venice and Florence**, much work remains to be done before a proper understanding of the role and significance of the councils can be reached. [sn 4136 ac]

(20) In some circumstances, therefore (**for example where children in the same class differ widely in reading levels**), getting children to read on their own may be more effective for some than is direct instruction. [sn 5763 ac]

The distribution of appositive TPs across the genres is given in Table 5.

Table 5: Distribution of appositional thematic parentheticals across four genres in English and Dutch

Language	Academic	Leaflets	News stories	Short stories	Total
Dutch	38 (43.2%)	20 (22.7%)	21 (23.9%)	9 (10.2%)	88 (100%)
English	29 (22.0%)	27 (20.5%)	61 (46.2%)	15 (11.4%)	132 (100%)
Total	67 (30.5%)	47 (21.4%)	82 (37.3%)	24 (10.9%)	220 (100%)

The distribution across the genres differs significantly (Chi-Square, $p<0.002$), with a medium effect in terms of effect size (Cramer's V=0.262). The relevant genres are academic and news. While appositions are more likely to occur in Dutch academic texts than in English ones, they are more likely to occur in English news stories than in Dutch ones. Overall, English has approximately 50% more appositions, which is in line with the basic overall frequency for the two languages, but this hides the fact that English news stories have three times as many appositional TPs as Dutch.

We also considered whether the semantic relation between the anchor and the apposition might differ between the two languages. Because the categorization of appositional relations is complex (cf. Quirk *et al.*, 1985: 1308ff; Meyer, 1992: 74ff), we only considered a basic distinction between an identifying or specifying relation, where a value is given for a presupposed variable, as in (18) above, and a classifying relation, where the appositional element assigns a property to the host element, as in (19–20) (cf. Hannay and Keizer, 2005: 167). However, the distributional pattern did not differ between the identifying and classifying functions ($p=0.8$). We therefore have no reason to believe that differences have to do with the kind of job that appositions can perform. One tentative explanation for the difference might be related to a more general rhetorical difference between news language in Dutch and English (see also Section 5.3 below), but this would require further investigation and is beyond the scope of this article.

5.3. Punctuational style

A specific feature of parentheticals is that they are punctuationally separated from the host clause. The default form of separation is the comma, but the bracket and the dash can also be used, and these are associated with different rhetorical effects. Brackets signal the inessential, background status of the parenthetical information, and hide it away from the rest of the sentence, as it were (cf. Nunberg *et al.*, 2002: 1748). Dashes, by contrast, signal that writer wishes to draw the reader's attention to the parenthetical information, for instance for dramatic effect (cf. Kane, 1988: 299; Quirk *et al.*, 1985: 1629). With regard to our data, there is a three-way interaction between form of punctuation, genre and language. That is to say, every difference is dependent on the other two factors. We can see what is involved here by considering Table 6.

Table 6: The distribution of punctuation forms across four genres in the Dutch and English subcorpora

Genre	Language	Form of punctuation			Total
		bracket	comma	dash	
Academic	Dutch	22 (23.7%)	62 (66.7%)	9 (9.7%)	93 (100%)
	English	12 (10.3%)	95 (81.2%)	10 (8.5%)	117 (100%)
Leaflet	Dutch	16 (45.7%)	17 (48.6%)	2 (5.7%)	35 (100%)
	English	18 (33.3%)	32 (59.3%)	4 (7.4%)	54 (100%)
News	Dutch	24 (35.8%)	39 (58.2%)	4 (6.0%)	67 (100%)
	English	2 (1.5%)	112 (85.5%)	17 (13.0%)	131 (100%)
Short story	Dutch	1 (2.1%)	47 (97.9%)	0 (0%)	48 (100%)
	English	1 (1.7%)	55 (91.7%)	4 (6.7%)	60 (100%)
All	Dutch	63 (25.9%)	165 (67.9%)	15 (6.2%)	243 (100%)
	English	33 (9.1%)	294 (81.2%)	35 (9.7%)	362 (100%)
	Total	96 (15.9%)	459 (75.8%)	50 (8.3%)	605 (100%)

A Chi-Square test showed a significant difference between English and Dutch for the academic ($p<0.03$) and news genres ($p<0.001$), with a small to medium effect for the academic genre (Cramer's V=0.196) and a large effect (Cramer's V=0.482) for the news genre. The first striking difference here concerns the use of brackets in Dutch academic and news texts. While commas may be seen as the rhetorical default for parenthetical information in the broad definition that we have adopted here, dashes and brackets are clearly marked options, used for rhetorical purposes. Example (21) is an instance of a very specific way that Dutch news texts use brackets, while (22) illustrates the use of dashes in English news texts.

(21)   Liesbeth Spies **(CDA)** vond dat Van der Horst een beetje overdrijft. [sn 3462 na]
       Liesbeth Spies (CDA)   found   that Van der Horst a little exaggerates
       'Liesbeth Spies (CDA) thought that Van der Horst was exaggerating a little.'

(22)   His refusal to accept a share of responsibility for the death of Sgt Steve Roberts **– killed because he had to give up his body armour** – was disgraceful. [sn 304 na]

The bracketed information in (21) exemplifies a basic convention in Dutch journalistic writing whereby a politician's party affiliation is specified by naming the party between brackets. By contrast, the writer of (22) adds an extra dramatic layer to his judgement that the refusal concerned was 'disgraceful' by using the parenthetical to emphasize the particular nature of the soldier's death.

As with other features discussed in this section, it is the academic and news genres that stand out as being different between the two languages.

6. Discourse functions

In order to determine the contribution of the TP to the understanding of the utterance, we analysed each TP in its sentential and, where relevant, wider context. The analysis revealed a basic distinction between two different kinds of discourse function performed by the TP, and this turns out to be useful when comparing the two languages. The vast majority of TPs provide additional information about the anchor expression itself, and we label such TPs 'theme-oriented'. However, a minority appear to be clearly 'rheme-oriented', or to relate to the utterance as a whole. This is despite their position immediately following the theme and despite the fact that they in some sense are dependent for their interpretation on the initial thematic expression. To illustrate the two types of TP, consider (23–24), which are theme-oriented TPs, and (25–26), which are rheme-oriented.

> (23) De BMI-test (**Body Mass Index**) is de beste test om de juistheid
>   The BMI-test (Body Mass Index) is the best test in order the correctness
>   van je gewicht te bepalen. [sn 9493 lf]
>   of your weight to determine
>
>   'The BMI-test (Body Mass Index) is the best test for accurately determining your weight.'

> (24) In many situations (**e.g. a noisy room full of people**), many sounds enter our ears at once. [sn 5588] ac

> (25) De inbreng van de persona, zoals Frijhoff in zijn afsluitende essay signaleert,
>   The contribution of the persona, as Frijhoff in his final essay signals,
>
>   is een ander verhaal: ze is eerder impliciet gebleven. [sn 5221 ac]
>   is a different story: it has actually implicit remained.
>
>   'The contribution of the persona, as Frijhoff signals in his final essay, is a different story: it has actually remained implicit.'

> (26) Industry, **aside from its economic importance**, was also of course a bourgeois virtue. [sn 4608 ac]

In (23–24), the TPs serve to exemplify and explain the theme. By contrast, the reporting clause in (25) and the prepositional phrase in (26) do not characterize the theme as such. Rather, they appear to combine more loosely with the theme to give the reader an additional piece of information before coming to the core of the message in the rheme. The syntactic devices that we come across in this latter category are also not typically associated with nominal postmodification. Kaltenböck (2007b: 11), for instance, notes a 'semantic-pragmatic mismatch' between parenthetical and anchor in the case of comment clauses.

The distribution of theme-oriented and rheme-oriented TPs is markedly different in Dutch and English, as shown in Table 7.

Table 7: Discourse functions of thematic parentheticals in the Dutch and English subcorpora

Language	Theme-oriented	Rheme-oriented	Total
Dutch	235 (96.7%)	8 (3.3%)	243 (100%)
English	301 (83.1%)	61 (16.9%)	362 (100%)
Total	536 (88.6%)	69 (11.4%)	605 (100%)

A Chi-Square test showed a significant difference between English and Dutch ($p < 0.001$). We will now look at theme-oriented and rheme-oriented TPs in more detail.

6.1. Theme oriented TPs

The theme-oriented parentheticals in our data perform a set of well-established functions relating to the use of appositions (e.g. Meyer, 1992; Hannay and Keizer, 2005) and postmodifiers such as relative clauses and participial clauses (Halliday and Matthiessen, 2004: 399–400; Downing and Locke, 2006: 447–451). For instance, appositional structures are used for purposes of identification, particularization, reformulation and exemplification, amongst other things (cf. Quirk *et al.*, 1985: 1308). In some cases the TP contributes increased recognizability to the anchor expression in the context: if the writer's first attempt to identify the intended referent is unsuccessful, the second attempt may increase the chance of success. Relative clause TPs, too, typically provide background information which gives the reader a fuller understanding of the anchor expression. Examples of theme-oriented TPs, with different syntactic realizations and different theme-enriching functions, are given in (27–31):

(27)   Of anders gezegd, de buitenlandse politiek– **en de Vietnamoorlog in het bijzonder –**
       Or otherwise said the foreign policy – and the Vietnam war in particular –

       bleek uitermate geschikt om van een progressieve grondhouding te getuigen. [sn 3786 ac]
       appeared particularly appropriate a basic progressive attitude to promote

       'Or to put it differently, foreign policy – and the Vietnam war in particular – turned out to be particularly appropriate for promoting a basic progressive attitude'

(28)   But all the envelopes, **of which there were a great many**, proved to be brown, windowed, and registered. [sn 10529 ss]

> (29) Yesterday the Shadow Chancellor, **Oliver Letwin,** tried the old con trick
> again. [sn 286 na]
>
> (30) All but one of those notes which were published – **and about half of the
> notes were never published** – first appeared in the second edition of the
> Act and monuments, printed in 1570. [sn 4204-7 ac]
>
> (31) Studies of the development of artistic understanding, **such as those car-
> ried out by Gardner *et al.* (1975) and Parsons (1987),** have indicated that
> children at this age have broad tastes and will consider as good or pleasing a
> rich diversity of abstract and non-figurative art. [sn 5530 ac]

In most cases, the information added in the TP has only the local function
of adding to the appreciation of the theme. In (30), for example, the notes
referred to are the central discourse topic of the segment in which the relevant
sentence occurs. The expression *all but one of those notes which were published*
– even though there is nothing in the preceding context to suggest that the
finite verb should be read with contrastive stress – serves as a trigger for the
writer to add the information in the TP, perhaps in order to stress the importance of the notes in the given context. However, the TP is not at all relevant to
an understanding of the new information provided in the rheme.

However, the data also include cases where the TP clearly does more than
simply provide a further description of the theme for a fuller understanding of
the referent. Consider first (32):

> (32) Professor Anne Power and Sir Richard Rogers, **who spearheaded the govern-
> ment's urban taskforce,** have both spoken out against the plan. [sn 1168 na]

Here the topical theme introduces two people into the discourse for the first
time, and the writer needs to provide a grounding for them (cf. Smits, 2002:
84), so that the reader can not only identify them in the context of the discourse, but also see that the choice of theme is justified. Consequently the TP
provides a justification for the choice of theme, or in other words a justification of the decision to compose an utterance about the theme in question.

A particular kind of grounding involves a circumstantial theme indicating
a general expression of time followed by a TP which describes an event or situation. Consider the example with *later* in (33):

> (33) A few years later, **when successive British ministries were asserting the
> imperial authority of the British Parliament and looking to extract a
> revenue from the North Americans,** the old colonies were often concep-
> tualized not simply as part of the British dominions but as outposts of the
> extended British nation. [sn 4183 ac]

In this type of complex theme expression, the initial thematic element
moves the narrative along and sets it at a more or less specific moment in
time, while the second grounds that moment in the discourse and by so doing

provides a relevant orientation by specifying features which make it relevant to take that moment as an orientation for the message to follow. Thus (33) can be read as (33') (see Hannay, 2007, for further discussion of cases like this):

> (33')   A few years later successive British ministries were asserting the imperial authority of the British Parliament and looking to extract a revenue from the North Americans. In this context the old colonies were often conceptualized not simply as part of the British dominions but as outposts of the extended British nation.

With cases like (32–33) we see that the TP provides a second and essential step in the construction of a thematic framework; without the TP the sentence loses relevance.

A final set of examples involve TPs which not only give background information for an enriched understanding of the theme but also prepare the way for the information in the rheme to be presented as particularly newsworthy. In our sample, these are most common in English news texts. Examples are given in (34) and (35), both including the wider context:

> (34)   Disgraced former minister Jonathan Aitken has been knocked back by his friend Michael Howard in his bid for a comeback. Aitken – **jailed for perjury after a sensational libel trial** – announced yesterday his desire to get back into front-line politics as an MP. He applied to become the Conservative candidate for his former seat of South Thanet, now held by Labour. [sn 624–626 na]

> (35)   Yet the most important news on this front is that the Conservatives signalled this week they were anxious not to be portrayed as hard-faced policy-makers. Compassionate conservatism, **which until now has been ignored by Michael Howard**, has been placed back on the agenda. Tax credits would not be axed by a Conservative administration. The education passport – the old voucher policy with a new name – has also been trimmed. [sn 1299–1302 na]

In (34) a contrast set up by *jailed for perjury* vs *back into front-line politics*. Similarly, in (35) there is a contrast between *ignored* and *placed back on the agenda*. This rhetorical design, of using the first part of a complex sentence to provide information which – sometimes dramatically – paves the way for the new information at the end of the sentence, is a recognized stylistic feature of English, as we will see below.

To summarize, the theme-oriented TPs in both Dutch and English serve a variety of functions. Not only are we dealing with information which provides a fuller appreciation of the thematic anchor expression, which may for instance aid its recognizability, but we have also seen that in both languages the relevance of the theme in the context is supported in different ways. A particular case is where the TP provides background information which seems specifically designed to promote the newsworthiness of the rheme.

6.2. Rheme-oriented TPs

Accordingly, we now turn to rheme orientation. Here we found that three different types could be distinguished, along structural lines. The three types involve comment and reporting clauses, focusing adverbs and framing adverbials. The distribution of rheme-oriented TPs is given in Table 8.

Table 8: Types of rheme-oriented TP in the Dutch and English subcorpora

Language	Comment/reporting clause	Focus adverbials	Framing adverbials	Total
Dutch	6	1	1	9
English	9	42	10	61
Total	15	43	13	70

We provide a description of each type below, paying most attention to what we have called framing adverbials. We will then consider the implications for a broader understanding of how TPs are used in Dutch and English.

Comment and reporting clauses

This category includes main clause forms and adverbial finite clauses introduced by *as* and *so* (Quirk *et al.*, 1985: 1115–1116) and their Dutch equivalents *zoals* and *zo*:

(36) De inbreng van de persona, zoals Frijhoff in zijn afsluitende essay signaleert,
      The contribution of the persona, as Frijhoff in his final essay signals,

      is een ander verhaal: ze is eerder impliciet gebleven. [= (25)]
      is a different story: it has actually implicit remained.

      'The contribution of the persona, as Frijhoff signals in his final essay, is a different story: it has actually remained implicit.'

(37) Het hoogtepunt van het feest, memoreerde ik, was een bal in een hotel aan zee.
      The highlight of the party noted I,   was a ball in a hotel at sea

      'The highlight of the party, I noted, was a ball in a seaside hotel.'

(38) The alternative, Mr Hoon admitted, is for the present situation to go on and on – with British troops bogged down, facing an increasingly hostile population. [sn 26 na]

The reporting clause in (38), for example, tells us that the message to be delivered about the alternative should be interpreted as an admission. The position of the TP following the topical theme *the alternative* is also relevant. Compare in this context examples (39a–b), the first of which is discussed by Blakemore (2006: 1683):

(39a)   My paper will, I promise you, be very short. [= Blakemore's (49)]

(39b)   My paper, I promise you, will be very short.

While the effect of the positioning of the parenthetical in (39a) is to add emphasis to the belief of the speaker that the paper will indeed have a certain quality, the effect of the positioning in (39b) is to highlight the idea that the message concerning the paper constitutes a promise. The illocutionary status of the whole utterance is thus more strongly presented in (39b) than (39a).

Focusing adverbs

The next category of rheme-oriented TPs consists of focusing adverbs such as *however, of course,* and *for example,* as in (41). There is only one example of this kind in the Dutch data, given in (40):

(40)   Horende kinderen, *daarentegen*, dachten vaker dat   de protagonist
       Hearing children, on the other hand, thought more often that the protagonist

       bereid zou zijn   om een confrontatie met de omgeving aan te gaan.
       prepared would be a confrontation with the environment to accept

       'Children with normal hearing, on the other hand, thought more often
       that the protagonist would be prepared to accept a confrontation with the
       environment'
       [sn 6195 ac]

(41)   Poets, of course, seldom had that kind of clout. [sn 10491 ss]

These were discussed above briefly in Section 5.2. The value of placing the adverb immediately following the theme is that it focuses the reader's attention on how the theme relates to what is to come. In (40), for instance, the previous context mentions both children with hearing difficulties and children with normal hearing. By choosing the theme *horende kinderen* and using the adverb *daarentegen* as a TP, the writer makes clear that there is going to be a message about children with normal hearing, that the message is to be seen as presenting a contrast with respect to the previous sentence, and crucially that the base for this contrast lies in the children with normal hearing as against another group. Similarly, in (41) a message is conveyed about poets which the writer wishes to present as being obviously the case, namely that they have a lack of clout; but more specifically, the idea is that it is precisely with regard to poets that a lack of clout holds true.

Framing adverbials

The final category involves a pattern which is found almost exclusively in the English data, the only Dutch example in the data being (45):

(42)   On occasion, **though without ever condoning the killing**, it is even possible to sympathize with what drove them to it. [sn 1400 na]

(43)   Generally, this inconsistency – **though it does not assist in establishing the potential reliability of participants' memories** – suggests that when questionnaires are developed there is a need to define conceptually the meanings underpinning items. [sn 5438 ac]

(44)   This broadside takes the long-running struggle between conservative and reformist factions to a new level. Many, if not most, Iranians have already written off the elections as rigged beyond repair. Leading parties and politicians, **even if they have not been disqualified**, are boycotting the polls. Turnout, especially in the cities, is expected to be poor. [sn 1334-6 na]

(45)   Ongeveer 65% van alle ouders, **ongeacht de leeftijd van hun eigen kinderen**,
       approx. 65% of all parents,   regardless of the age of their own children

       verwacht het moeilijk te krijgen als het kind de adolescentie bereikt. [sn 6027 ac]
       expects to have it difficult when the child adolescence reaches

       'Approximately 65% of all parents, regardless of the age of their own children, expect to have problems when their child reaches adolescence.'

Let us look at two of these examples more closely. What the reader can conclude after the TP in (45) is that something is going to be said about 65% of all parents, and what is going to be said is relevant irrespective of the age of their children. From the writer's point of view there has been cause to construct the utterance from the point of view of the parents, but it would appear that the writer wishes to nip in the bud a possible misinterpretation of what is to come by stressing in advance that the rheme of the utterance has to be understood as being irrespective of the age of the child (Lachlan Mackenzie, p.c.).

In (44), it tells the reader that he can expect to be told something about the leading parties and politicians which one would not really expect if they have been allowed to participate in the elections. In other words, the addition of the TP after the topical theme of the sentence appears to invite the reader to create a kind of complex utterance frame which involves an unexpected statement about the topic. The rhetorical design followed by the writer here is very similar to that discussed for the preceding two types.

Given that the TP in these cases consists of an adverbial expression, it is worth looking at the relative position of the theme and its associated TP, since the adverbial might alternatively occur as an initial theme in its own right. Consider (44) in its wider context. The first sentence establishes the intensity of the struggle between different political factions in Iran ahead of elections.

The next two sentences then detail the intensity by stating the standpoint of groups involved. This involves introducing 'leading parties and politicians'. By contrast, the following, alternative formulation yields a text with questionable coherence:

> (44') This broadside takes the long-running struggle between conservative and reformist factions to a new level. Many, if not most, Iranians have already written off the elections as rigged beyond repair. **Even if they have not been disqualified**, leading parties and politicians are boycotting the polls. Turnout, especially in the cities, is expected to be poor.

First of all, what is lost in this re-ordering is the presentation of two topical themes – *many Iranians* and *leading parties and politicians* – in the same sentence-initial position, instead of which we have an intervening adverbial clause as a circumstantial theme. Second, the initial position of this adverbial clause now suggests, particularly given the choice of *even if*, that there has already been a discussion about the possible disqualification of the parties concerned, but that is not the case. In other words, the two different orderings in (44) and (44') reflect two different rhetorical designs, whose appropriateness is dependent on the specific context. This is very similar to the situation with focusing adverbials discussed briefly in Section 3 concerning (7a–b), where the appropriateness of a particular order is strongly determined by the context (cf. Smits, 2002: 76).

An important characteristic of our analysis here is the assumption that the reader will be decoding the message incrementally, and that the writer is sensitive to this. Specifically, what we suggest that with rheme-oriented TPs it is not so much the anchor itself which triggers the parenthetical but rather the initial communicative frame which is set up by the choice of the thematic anchor (cf. Downing and Locke, 2006: 223). Indeed, while the choice of theme is traditionally held to be strongly speaker/writer-oriented, expressing what is in the speaker/writer's point of departure for the message (Halliday and Matthiessen, 2004: 64), we see in all rheme-oriented TPs, as well as in some theme-oriented TPs, that the use of these parentheticals is a reflection of the writer's interaction with the reader in the course of sentence construction, preparing the way for optimal understanding of the rheme.

To summarize, TPs with rheme orientation give information which in combination with the anchor provide a complex framework for the understanding of the utterance as a whole. The main characteristic of this rhetorical design is that a writer first selects a – usually experiential – theme but before moving on to the rheme presents extra information about how the newsworthy information in the rheme is to be interpreted. This is a two-step process, performed using parenthetical structures which are not typically seen as postmodifiers. As such, one might expect that Dutch would make less use of such structures, given that the verb-second nature of Dutch promotes a single theme.

More generally, the analysis of discourse functions in this section has revealed that parentheticals contribute in different ways to the understanding of the host utterance: they may simply further specify the thematic element; they may ground the theme so that it can function as a relevant starting point in the given context for the host utterance; they may provide background information about the theme in such a way that the rheme can appear in a form of distinct relief as particularly newsworthy, or they may contribute to the relevance of the utterance as a whole by forming together with their anchor a complex orientation frame which is distinctly different in rhetorical terms from the frame provided by initial adverbials followed by a topical subject.

6.3. Structural features and effective writing guides

Given what we have seen when looking at rheme-oriented TPs, it may be useful to consider what usage and effective writing guides for Dutch and English have to say about the complexity of the written sentence, particularly concerning the beginning of the sentence. What we see is that this body of literature reflects two markedly different approaches to sentence construction.

Dutch writing guides place considerable emphasis on readability. Essentially, there are two traps that the writer is advised to avoid at his peril. The first is the so-called subject-finite verb 'pincer' construction (Renkema, 2002: 82), whereby the subject and the verb of the main clause are separated by too much information. Put simply, it would seem that all longer TPs, clausal rather than phrasal and appositional, potentially run the risk of being seen as pincer constructions to be avoided. The second risky construction is what is called a 'long run-up'. Tiggeler (2005: 192), for instance, stresses that the first constituent in the sentence should not be kept too long; otherwise the reader will have to work his way through a lot of words and remember a lot of information, before eventually landing at the next constituents. Onrust *et al.* (1993: 166) also point out the danger of a single thematic element that is too long: the core of the sentence is formed by the subject and verb of the main clause, and one should not have to wait too long for this information, because it is important to know what the thematic background is presented in service of.

In stark contrast, the relevant literature for English takes a predominantly form-function approach, concentrating on the rhetorical effects that can be created by adopting different sentence patterns. The use of a complex theme, with parenthetical information between the initial theme and the verb of the main clause, is presented as having a clear effect. Nash (1986: 38), for instance, contrasts (46) with (47), where (46) contains an initial clausal theme followed by a TP:

> (46) Although he had come very early, in the compulsive way of one who frets about punctuality and consults his watch ever minute, he almost missed the interview.

> (47) He almost missed the interview, although he was one of those people who go very early to any appointment, consulting their watches every minute, so fretful are they about punctuality.

He notes that both forms are 'important possibilities in the repertoire of stylistic choice' and that the form in (46) is used 'to hold attention, create suspense, or delay the giving of information'. We saw a specific application of this stylistic principle in some of the TPs in English news texts, where the parenthetical provides a particular kind of background information which allows the newsworthy information in the rheme to stand out more prominently.

In a similar vein, Kane (1988: 135) gives (48) as an example of what he calls a periodic sentence. Here there is a rather long initial adverbial theme, itself interrupted by a parenthetical relative clause:

> Given a moist planet with methane, formaldehyde, ammonia, and some usable minerals, all of which abound, exposed to lightning or ultraviolet radiation at the right temperature, life might start almost anywhere.

He notes that the periodic style is emphatic and that 'delaying the principal thought increases its importance'. Furthermore, 'to the degree that more and more subordinate clauses and phrases are accumulated at the beginning, further postponing the main clause, the sense of climax increases'. Admittedly, Kane adds that there are limits to such accumulation, since it can lead to confusion, but the difference between the advice given in the two languages is still very marked. Dutch sentences with the structure of (46) and (48) would be strongly dispreferred for having an overly long 'run-up'.

What this sketch suggests is that structural features may in a sense go hand in hand with stylistic options and constraints. The essential structural characteristic for Dutch is that there is a single theme slot before the verb, with a usage constraint stating that writers should get to the verb as soon as possible. By contrast, the relevant feature of English is that two or more constituents may occur before the subject, and there is a dominant approach to sentence construction which highlights the rhetorical effects that can be achieved by making use of complex themes, including the use of TPs.

7. Conclusions

This paper set out to characterize thematic parentheticals along syntactic, semantic and rhetorical lines, in order to gain insight into how Dutch and English go about using the grammatical repertoire at their disposal to create complex thematic frameworks for the interpretation of text sentences.

The contrastive analysis first of all revealed a difference in frequency: we found that English uses TPs significantly more than Dutch does. In an attempt to find possible explanations for this difference, we first looked at the distribution of TPs across the four genres studied, but the distribution was not significant. However, when we looked in greater detail we found that there are significant differences between the two languages when it comes to the news and academic genres. In particular, these genres differ with regard to appositional and punctuational style. Further research is needed to ascertain whether these features are part of a more general difference in rhetorical style between these two genres in English and Dutch. The most pertinent conclusion in this respect, however, might be that the analysis of sentence patterning from a contrastive-rhetorical point of view should in principle adopt a genre-specific approach (cf. Tavecchio, 2010: 470–471).

We also sought an explanation for the distributional data in terms of syntactic features. Given its verb-second nature, Dutch only has one thematic slot, whereas English, on the definition of theme adopted here, has two. This greater thematic potential might also be utilized for adding extra, parenthetical information to enrich the orientational function of the theme. There are two points to be made in this context. First, our quantitative analysis also included Dutch parentheticals following non-initial subjects, which are strictly speaking not thematic, but even with these included in the data, the distribution of parentheticals was still significant. Second, and most importantly, we saw that rheme-oriented TPs, which typically have a different syntactic make-up than theme-oriented TPs, occur much more frequently in English than in Dutch in our data. The distribution of rheme-oriented TPs helps us account for a substantial part of the distributional data. Furthermore, by considering the nature of rheme-oriented TPs in the context of structural features of Dutch and English, as well as in terms of differences in writing culture, we can begin to see how a combination of forces may be at work in determining the overall differences we have seen in the two languages.

Dutch is structured in such a way that there is a preference for single themes, while the structure of English promotes multiple themes. The single theme notion in Dutch may well interact with more general advice given in Dutch style guides relating to sentence construction, and the beginning of the sentence in particular. Similarly, one might speculate that guidelines in texts on English usage are at least partly predicated on the structural possibilities of the language. In terms of thematic patterning, this view permits the conclusion that the rhetorical patterns of Dutch and English are co-determined by the interplay between basic structural features and fundamental elements of writing culture. In Dutch, the combination of a structurally determined single theme, a clear preference for a relatively short theme, as well as an aversion to so-called pincer constructions, may contribute to the relatively limited use of thematic parentheticals in that language. And significantly, to the extent that Dutch does use thematic parentheticals, their grammatical realization and the discourse functions that they may serve are consequently constrained by the preference for a notionally singular theme, even though it may be structurally complex. In English, by contrast, the combination of multiple theme options and a greater tolerance of relatively long sentence openings may contribute to the relatively frequent use of thematic parentheticals. And equally significantly, this greater thematic potential may well be a reason why English makes greater use of complex themes with a rhetorical patterning characterized by two orientational steps, which we have seen to be the case with rheme-oriented TPs.

Notes

1. The research conducted for this paper has benefited from support from the Spanish Ministry of Education and Science (MICINN, FFI2010-19380) and the Autonomous Government of Galicia (XUGA, INCITE09 204 155PR). Many thanks are due to Lotte Tavecchio for making her corpus available, to Gerben Mulder for much more than assistance with the statistical treatment of the data, to Eric Akkerman for invaluable help with organizing the database, and last but not least to Lachlan Mackenzie for comments on an earlier version of the paper.

2. The codes starting with 'sn' (standing for 'sentence') at the end of example sentences are those used in Tavecchio's (2010) contrastive corpus. We have added further abbreviations to show the genre: 'ac' stands for 'academic text', 'na' for 'news article', 'ss' for 'short story', and 'If' for 'public information leaflet'. If examples are not coded, then they have not been taken from the corpus.

References

Aarts, F. and Wekker, H. (1993) *A Contrastive Grammar of English and Dutch*. Groningen: Martinus Nijhoff.

Berry, Margaret (1996) What is Theme? A(nother) personal view. In M. Berry, C. S. Butler, R. Fawcett and G. Huang (eds), *Meaning and Form: Systemic Functional Interpretations. Meaning and Choice in Language: Studies for Michael Halliday*. Norwood, NJ: Ablex, 1–64.

Biber, D., Johansson, S., Leech, G., Conrad, S. and Finnegan, F. (1999) *Longman Grammar of Spoken and Written English*. London: Longman.

Blakemore, D. (2005) *And*-parentheticals. *Journal of Pragmatics* 37 (8): 1165–1181. http://dx.doi.org/10.1016/j.pragma.2005.04.003

Blakemore, D. (2006) Divisions of labour: The analysis of parentheticals. *Lingua* 116 (10): 1670–1687. http://dx.doi.org/10.1016/j.lingua.2005.04.007

Burton-Roberts, N. (2005) Parentheticals. In E. K. Brown (ed.) *Encyclopedia of Language and Linguistics,* 2nd edition, 179–182. Oxford: Elsevier.

Butler, C. (2003) *Structure and Function. A Guide to Three Major Structural Functional Theories. Part 2: From Clause to Discourse and Beyond.* Amsterdam and Philadelphia, PA: Benjamins.

Chafe, W. L. (1994) *Discourse, Consciousness and Time.* Chicago, IL: Chicago University Press.

Clark, H. H. and Haviland, S. E. (1977) Comprehension and the given-new contract. In R. O. Freddle (ed.) *Discourse Production and Comprehension,* 1–40. Norwood, NJ: Ablex.

Dehé, N. and Kavalova, Y. (eds) (2007) *Parentheticals.* Amsterdam and Philadelphia PA: Benjamins.

Downing, A. (1991) An alternative approach to theme: a systemic-functional perspective. *Word* 42 (2): 119–143.

Downing, A. and Locke, P. (2006) *English Grammar: A University Course* (2nd edn). London and New York: Routledge.

Fawcett, R. (2003) The many types of 'theme' in English: Their semantic systems and their functional syntax. Unpublished manuscript, available from the Systemic Paper Archive at http://www.wagsoft.com/Systemics/Archive/Fawcett-ThemePaperv3.pdf.

Fetzer, A. (2008) Theme zones in contrast: An analysis of their linguistic realization in the communicative act of a non-acceptance. In G. González, M. de los Ángeles, J. L. Mackenzie and E. M. González Álvarez (eds), *Languages and Cultures in Contrast and Comparison,* 3–31. Amsterdam and Philadelphia, PA: John Benjamins.

Ghadessy, M. (ed.) (1995) *Thematic Development in English Texts.* London and New York: Pinter.

Gómez-González, M. de los Ángeles (1998) A corpus-based analysis of Extended Multiple Themes in PresE. *International Journal of Corpus Linguistics* 3 (1): 81–113. http://dx.doi.org/10.1075/ijcl.3.1.05gom

Gómez-González, M de los Ángeles (2001) *The Theme-topic Interface. Evidence from English.* Amsterdam and Philadelphia, PA: John Benjamins.

Haeseryn, W., Romijn, K., Geerts, G., de Rooij, J. and van den Toorn, M. C. (1997) *Algemene Nederlandse Spraakkunst* [= 'General Dutch Grammar']. 2nd edition. Groningen and Deurne: Martinus Nijhoff /Wolters Plantyn.

Halliday, M. A. K. and Matthiessen, C. M. I. M. (2004) *Introduction to Functional Grammar,* 3rd edition. London: Edward Arnold.

Hannay, M. (2007) Patterns of multiple theme and their role in developing English writing skills. In C. Butler, R. Hidalgo and J. Lavid (eds), *Functional Perspectives in Grammar and Discourse*, 257–278. Amsterdam and Philadelphia PA: Benjamins.

Hannay, M. and Keizer, M. E. (2005) A discourse treatment of English non-restrictive nominal appositions in Functional Discourse Grammar. In J. L. Mackenzie and M. L. Á. Gómez-González (eds) *Studies in Functional Discourse Grammar*, 159–194. Bern: Peter Lang.

Hartnett, C. G. (1995) The pit after the theme. In M. Ghadessy (ed.) *Thematic Development in English Texts*, 198–212. London and New York: Pinter.

Hasan, R. and Fries, P. (eds) (1995) *On Subject and Theme: A Discourse Functional Perspective*. Amsterdam: John Benjamins.

Jalilifar, A. R. (2010) The status of theme in applied linguistics articles. *Asian ESP Journal* 6 (2): 7–39.

Kaltenböck, G. (2007) Position, prosody and scope: The case of English comment clauses. *Vienna English Working Papers*, 16 (1): 3–38.

Kane, T. S. (1988) *The New Oxford Guide to Writing*. New York and Oxford: Oxford University Press.

Martinez Lirola, M. (2009) *Main Processes of Thematization and Postponement in English* (European University Studies: Series 21, Linguistics. Vol. 347). Bern: Peter Lang.

Nash, W. (1986) *English Usage: A Guide to First Principles*. London: Routledge and Kegan Paul.

Nunberg, G., Briscoe, T. and Huddleston, R. (2002) Punctuation. In R. Huddleston and G. K. Pullum (eds) *The Cambridge Grammar of the English Language*, 1723–1764. Cambridge: Cambridge University Press.

Nwogu, K. N. (1990) *Discourse Variation in Medical Texts: Schema, Theme and Cohesion in Professional and Journalistic Accounts* (Monographs in Systemic Linguistics, 2) Dept. of English Studies, University of Nottingham.

Onrust, M., Verhagen, A. and Doeve, R. (1993) *Formuleren* [= 'Formulating']. Houten and Zaventem: Bohn Stafleu Van Loghum.

Quirk, R., Greenbaum, S., Leech, G. and Svartvik, J. (1985) *A Comprehensive Grammar of the English Language*. London: Longman.

Ravelli, L. (2003) A dynamic perspective: implications for metafunctional interaction and an understanding of theme. In A. Simon-Vandenbergen, M. Taverniers and L. Ravelli (eds), *Grammatical Metaphor*, 187–234. Amsterdam and Philadelphia PA: Benjamins.

Renkema, J. (2002) *Schrijfwijzer* [= 'Writing guide']. 4th edition. The Hague: Sdu.

Schelfhout, C., Coppen, P-A. and Oostdijk, N. (2004) Finite comment clauses in Dutch: A corpus-based approach. *Journal of Germanic Linguistics* 16 (4): 331–349. http://dx.doi.org/10.1017/S1470542704040437

Siepmann, D., Gallagher, J. D., Hannay, M. and Mackenzie, J. L. (2011) *Writing in English: A Guide for Advanced Learners*, 2nd edition. Tübingen and Basel: Francke.

Smits, A. (2002) *How Writers Begin their Sentences. Complex Beginnings in Native and Learner English*. LOT dissertation series 67. Utrecht: LOT.

Tavecchio, L. M. (2010) *Sentence Patterns in English and Dutch: A Contrastive Corpus Analysis*. LOT dissertation series 248. Utrecht: LOT.

Thompson, G. (1996) *Introducing Functional Grammar*. London: Edward Arnold.

Tiggeler, E. (2005) *Vraagbaak Nederlands* [= Handbook for Dutch], 5th edition. The Hague: Sdu.

6 Word order and information structure in English and Swedish

Jennifer Herriman

Both English and Swedish follow the principles of information and end-weight when ordering the elements of the clause and both languages have translationally equivalent means of re-ordering clause elements to follow these principles, i.e., fronting, postponement by extraposition, existential constructions and cleft sentences. This chapter compares these word order changes in English and Swedish and shows that Swedish follows the principles of information and end-weight more strictly than English. This is supported by empirical evidence from comparisons of original texts in English and Swedish and their translations, and comparisons of writing in English by Swedish advanced learners and native speaker students, where an overuse of certain re-ordering reflects the transfer of a different usage in Swedish.

1. Introduction

The concept of word order can be approached on a number of levels (Hasselgård, 1996: 115). On the word level, it can be defined as the order of individual words. Prepositions in English and Swedish, for instance, are normally placed before their complements. On the phrase level, it can be defined as the order of clause elements. In English and Swedish, subjects and objects in declarative clauses, for instance, are normally placed before and after the verb, respectively, whereas adverbials are more mobile. Finally, on the discourse level word order can be defined as the ordering of information units. It is this third level of word order, the ordering of the information in a message that this paper is concerned with. Seen from a Hallidayan approach (Halliday and Matthiessen, 2004: 60–105), this is the usage of word order to create what is regarded as textual meaning, i.e., to create a coherent message which fits in with the other information surrounding it and with the wider context in which talking or writing takes place. As this eases communication, the textual function of language is referred to as the 'enabling' function (Halliday and Matthiessen, 2004: 30).

Both English and Swedish follow similar principles for ordering information units in the message (Altenberg, 1998: 117). Initial position, which is usually labelled the Theme (Halliday and Matthiessen, 2004: 64) is the normal position for short, familiar information that forms the point of departure for what follows. In both English and Swedish, it is, in the unmarked case, the subject of the clause.[1] Heavy, more newsworthy information is normally placed later in the remainder of the message, which is generally labelled the Rheme (Halliday and Matthiessen, 2004: 64). Both English and Swedish have similar means of changing the order of the information in the clause in order to follow the information principle. This includes the fronting of non-subject clause elements, such as adverbials, objects and complements, thereby creating marked Themes, and the postponement of new and heavy information to the Rheme by special constructions such as extraposition, and existential *there/det* sentences.[2] Both languages also have cleft sentences, which split the content of the clause into a Theme and Rheme structure in order to give prominence to a part of its informational content.

However, although English and Swedish both follow similar principles of ordering information, there is a crucial difference in the syntactic order of the clause elements on to which this information is mapped. English has a SV constraint, which requires the subject to precede the verb in declarative clauses, and as a result allows a clustering of adverbials in initial position before the subject and verb. Swedish, in contrast, is a V2 language, i.e., it has a verb second constraint, which means that if there is an adverbial in initial position, the subject and verb are inverted. According to Erman (1998: 130), these syntactic constraints have consequences for the information structure of Swedish and English. As it only allows one clause element before the verb, Swedish tends to have shorter, more 'backward oriented' Themes in order to ensure topical coherence. English, on the other hand, allows a greater information load to be placed in the Theme (Bäckström, 2004: 94). Thus Swedish appears to follow the information and end-weight principles more strictly than English. This paper investigates what empirical evidence there is to support this claim. It focuses on fronting, postponement by extraposition and existential *there/det* sentences, and clefting, and discusses findings from comparisons (Johansson, 1996a, 1996b, 2002; Altenberg, 1998; Svensson, 2000a, 2000b; Herriman, 2008) of original texts and translations in the English-Swedish parallel corpus (see Aijmer and Johansson, 1996)[3] as well as a comparison of Swedish translations of English EU texts by Bäckström (2004). As over- and underuse of a certain word order in learners' writing may be the result of transfer of a different usage, it will also consider findings from studies that have compared Swedish advanced learners' writing in English in the International Corpus of Learner English project (SWICLE) with native speaker students' writing in the Louvain Corpus of Native English Essays (LOCNESS) (see Granger, 1998) (e.g., Boström Aronsson, 2005; Herriman and Boström Aronsson, 2009; Herriman, 2011b, 2011c).[4]

The chapter is organized as follows: Section 2 examines fronting in English and Swedish. Section 3 examines postponement, and Section 4 examines clefting.

2. Fronting in English and Swedish

Both Swedish and English allow other constituents than the subject to be fronted to initial position, where they become Themes, i.e., the starting point of the message. This deviation from the normal sentence sequence occurs when contextual reasons overrule the unmarked choice of subject as Theme (Thompson, 2004: 145). As Kong (2004: 347) notes, it is therefore 'an exceptional option, which somehow indicates what the writer/speaker is aware of and has in his mind as a priority'.

Adverbials are the most mobile clause elements and are therefore the clause elements that are most frequently fronted in both languages. Altenberg (1998: 124) and Svensson (2000b: 358), for instance, found that approximately one quarter of the Themes in a sample of English and Swedish original texts (both fiction and nonfiction) from the English-Swedish parallel corpus were adverbials. In (1) and (2), the locative adverbials (*On the streetcars, På spårvagnarna*) and temporal adverbials (*På hösten 1920 In the autumn of 1920*) are fronted.

(1) On the streetcars there are always old ladies, or we think of them as old.

På spårvagnarna finns det alltid gamla tanter, åtminstone uppfattar vi dem som gamla. (AT1)5

On the trams are there always old ladies, at least consider we them as old

(2) På hösten 1920 flyttade vi till Villagatan 22 på Östermalm.
In the autumn 1920 moved we to Villagatan 22 on Östermalm

In the autumn of 1920, we moved to Villagatan 22 in the Östermalm district of Stockholm. (IB1)

Fronted locatives and temporal adverbials such as these are typically used to establish a time or place frame for the rest of the message (Enkvist, 1991: 9; Downing and Locke, 2006: 228). As these time or place frames can hold over long stretches of discourse, these adverbials may also be associated with major textual transitions (Thompson and Thompson, 2009: 63). The adverbials in (1) and (2) both occur at the beginning of new paragraphs. In other positions in the clause, in contrast, locative and temporal adverbials do not have this scene-setting effect (Downing and Locke, 2006: 228).[6]

In their comparisons of different samples of original texts in the English-Swedish parallel corpus, both Johansson (1996b: 34) and Svensson (2000a: 116b) found greater proportions of fronted locative and temporal adverbials in Swedish than in English. Johansson (1996b: 34) also found more fronted temporal adverbials. In the translations in (3) and (4), the Swedish originals with locative adverbial Themes have been translated into sentences where the subject is the Theme in English. In (3) the locative adverbial (*Under kriget, during the war*) has been moved to the Rheme in English, and in (4) the locative adverbial (*I sina dynamiska illustrationer*) has been restructured as a separate clause.

(3) ... som gammal elev i en kväkarskola inneslöts Erskine i deras nätverk under sin arkitektutbildning. Under kriget blev dessa kontakter naturligtvis inte lika täta, särskilt som Erskine betraktade sig som socialist och icke religiös.
During the war became these contacts ...

... Ralph, being a former pupil of a Quaker school, was embraced in the Quaker network. This contact was naturally less close during the war, especially as Erskine regarded himself as unreligious and a socialist. (CE1)

(4) I sina dynamiska illustrationer propagerade Cullen för en levande stadsmiljö.
In his dynamic illustrations campaigned Cullen for ...

Cullen spoke out for a living urban environment, drew dynamic illustrations to make his point, ... (CE1)

Altenberg (1998: 125–128) found that when there are one or more adverbials and a conjunct in initial position before the subject in English, Swedish translations tend to retain the adverbial in initial position, in particular if it is a temporal or locative adverbial which indicates a shift in the perspective of the text. The subject and conjunct are then moved to medial position, as in (5).

(5) Further east, on the other hand, the Thracians (in what is today Bulgaria) and the Scythians north of the Black Sea buried their princes under richly furnished mounds.

Längre österut begravde å andra sidan trakterna (i det som nu är Bulgarien) och skyterna norr om Svarta Havet sina furstar i rikt försedda gravhögar.
Further eastwards buried on other hand the Thracians...

Thus there appears to be a tendency for locative and temporal adverbials to be fronted more frequently in Swedish. Further evidence for this can be found in Swedish learners' writing in English. In a comparison of two samples of problem-solution texts from the SWICLE and LOCNESS corpora (Herriman, 2011: 11), there were twice as many initial locative and temporal adverbials in the writing by the Swedish advanced learner as in the native speaker students' writing.

The higher frequency of fronted locative and temporal adverbials may to some extent be explained by differences in preferences for the assignment of subject status in English and Swedish. According to the semantic function hierarchy (Dik, 1997: 266), the semantic roles which may most easily be assigned subject status in a language form the following hierarchy:

agent>goal>recipient>beneficiary>instrument>locative> temporal

The most central semantic role of the subject is the agent. As we move away from the most central role, subject assignment becomes more difficult and marked. Languages are characterized by cut-off points on this hierarchy. If they allow one semantic role as the subject, they allow all the others to the left of this in the semantic function hierarchy. In active clauses, both in English and Swedish, it is possible for all the semantic roles on the hierarchy to be assigned subject status, even the semantic roles which are at lower end of the hierarchy: the locative and temporal roles, as in (6).

> (6) a. Athens (locative) is hot in summer.
>   b. Staden (locative) vimlar av turister.
>   The town is teeming with tourists.
>   c. Tomorrow (temporal) is a good day for the meeting. (Johansson and Lysvåg, 1986: 73)
>   d. Vi måste göra det idag. Nästa vecka (temporal) blir för sent.
>   We must do it today. Next week becomes too late.

In passive clauses, the cut-off point for the subject of the clause is between the recipient and the beneficiary in English, as in (7) and the same is true of Swedish as in (8).

> (7) a. Mary (Recipient) was given a large sum of money.
>   b. *Mary (Beneficiary) was baked a cake for her birthday.
> (8) a. ?Maria (Recipient) skänktes en stor summa pengar.
>   b. *Mary (Beneficiary) bakades en tårta på sin födelsedag.

There is, however, as Teleman *et al.* (1999: 65) point out, a general tendency for Swedish to prioritize animate semantic roles as subjects and to avoid inanimate subjects with active verbs that would normally take an animate, conscious subject (Bäckström, 2004: 93). English, on the other hand, tends to be more tolerant of inanimate subjects and is less restrictive when it comes to assigning them subject status. In his study of translations of EU pamphlets from English to Swedish, Bäckström found that when inanimate subjects in English (e.g., *A decision by the Council* in (9) and *This booklet* in (10)) occur with active verbs that normally take an animate, conscious subject, they were often translated into adverbials in Swedish (*Vid ett beslut i rådet, I denna broschyr*).

(9)   A decision by the Council often requires that countries representing about 72% of the votes are in favour.

Vid ett beslut i rådet krävs ofta att landet som representerar 72% av rösterna är för.

At a decision in the council is required often that …

(10) This booklet describes how EU trade policy works.

I denna broschyr ges en förklaring av Eu:s handelspolitik.

In this booklet is given an explanation of EUs trade policy.

Swedish appears thus to prefer adverbials for locative and temporal meanings. This tendency is also reflected, for instance, in the following examples from the SWICLE and LOCNESS corpora, where the locative meanings in initial position are adverbials and subjects, respectively.

(11) a. In the west we are obsessed with things. (SWICLE-UG-0037.2)
      b. But even in today's highly urbanised industrial countries we eat, drink and breathe and are likely to continue having to do so in the future. (SWICLE-LND-0008.1)
      c. In this essay I intend to give a few examples of why the earth is in this mess and also point out what we as 'borrowers' can do to make this planet of ours a better place to live in. (SWICLE-LND-0015.1)
(12) a. Britain now has the most cars per mile of road anywhere in the world. (LOCNESS Transport 08)
      b. Most of the world besides Britain seems to run a reliable service even developing countries. (LOCNESS Transport 08)
      c. Rivers need bridges to cross them costing more money which is not already there. (LOCNESS Transport 09)

A further explanation for the higher frequency of fronted locative and temporal adverbials is that Swedish is more restrictive than English when it comes to placing new information in the Theme. Adverbials are therefore fronted more often in Swedish in order to create a cohesive link to the preceding discourse and to keep new information out of the Theme. English, in contrast, allows Themes to present or identify new entities when they are subjects in clauses with intransitive verbs (Downing and Locke, 2006: 228). This is illustrated by (13) (from Johansson, 1996: 37), where the locative adverbials in Swedish (*På den bukiga byrån med guldbeslagen och guldfötterna* and *Mot urtavlan*) have been fronted and the new entities in the subjects (*en förgylld klocka under en glaskupa* and *en ung man som spelar flöjt*) have been postponed to the Rheme. Because of their typical scene-setting function, these locative adverbials create a place frame linking one utterance to the other. In the English translation, in contrast, the locatives have been postponed to the Rhemes and the new entities are in the Themes.

(13) På den bukiga byrån med guldbeslagen och guldfötterna star en förgylld klocka under en glaskupa. Mot urtavlan stöder sig en ung man som spelar flöjt. Tätt intill honom står en liten dam med stor hatt och vid kort kjol.
On the bulging bureau with its gold fittings and gold feet stands a gilt clock under a glass dome. Against the clock-face leans himself a young man...

A gilt clock under a glass dome stands on the bulging bureau with its gold fittings and feet; a young man leans against the clockface, playing a flute; close to him is a little lady in a big hat and a short wide skirt. (IB1)

In contrast to adverbials, other constituents such as objects and complements are fronted much less frequently in both languages, and are therefore the most unusual type of Theme. As Thompson (2004: 145) points out, this kind of fronting 'usually needs a particular kind of context for example when the constituent in Theme position is being contrasted with something else in the text.' As well as having this contrastive function, fronted objects and complements are also used to link to something in the preceding context (Downing, 2006: 229). Fronted direct objects and complements in English and Swedish are exemplified in (14) and (15), respectively.

(14) a. All the rest we'll do for you. (Thompson, 2004: 145)
      b. Den boken har jag inte läst. (Holmes and Hinchcliffe, 2003: 470)
          That book have I not read
(15) a. [How did the meeting go?] – A complete waste of time it was. (Downing, 2006: 229).
      c. Hemskt var det. (Holmes and Hinchcliffe, 2003: 471)
          Awful was it.

There is, however, as is the case with adverbials, also a difference in the frequency in which objects and complements are fronted in Swedish and English. Studies by Johansson (1996b: 32), Svensson (2000a, 2000b) and Erman (1998: 128) have found a much higher frequency of non-adverbial clause elements in initial position in Swedish than in English, in particular direct objects. It was also found that fronted objects in Swedish were rarely translated into fronted objects in English (Johansson, 1996b: 33; Svensson, 2000a: 113). Initial position is, in fact, the normal word order in Swedish for the object proform *det* ('it/that/so') in short answers when it is the direct object of verbs representing mental and verbal processes, such as *tro* ('believe') and *säga* ('say') as in (16a), or the subject complement of copula verbs, such as *vara* ('be'), in short answers such as (16b).

> (16) a.   Har han åkt hem? / Det tror jag / Det sa han
>   Has he gone home? / That I think / That he said
>   b.   Är du rik? Ja, det är jag.
>   Are you rich. Yes, that I am.
>   (Holmes and Hinchcliffe, 2003: 125)

In (16) the fronted proforms link answers to the preceding questions. In English, in contrast, placing a non-subject pronoun in the Theme would be highly marked and therefore emphatically contrastive (e.g., *This I do know, This I am*). Instead, the direct object pronoun would normally be placed in the Rheme, e.g., *Has he gone home. Yes, I think so* and the subject complement pronoun would normally have no equivalent, e.g., *Are you rich. Yes I am*. In the following translations from Swedish to English, the translator has moved the direct object pronoun from the Theme to the Rheme in order to avoid too much contrastive emphasis.

> (17) Den ungen vet och förstår redan lite av   That child understands just about
>   varje, det ser man, sa Mattis.   everything already – you can see
>   That child knows and understands already   that, said Matt. (AL1)
>   a little about everything, that sees one.
>
> (18) Allt detta kan jag erinra mig men jag   I can recall it all, but I do not
>   minns ingen rädsla. Den kom senare.   remember any fear. That came
>   all this can I remind me ....   later. (IB1)

In sum, fronted adverbials, objects and complements are somewhat more usual in Swedish than in English. In Swedish, this kind of fronting is typically used as a cohesive device and it is often a proform linking to the preceding clause. In English, in contrast, fronting is more marked and therefore more contrastive. A higher frequency of fronted adverbials has also been found in contrastive studies of other Scandinavian languages (which like Swedish also have a V2 constraint) and English, i.e., in Norwegian (Hasselgård, 1998, 2004) and in Danish academic writing (Shaw, 2004).

I will now go on to examine how special constructions in English and Swedish are used to vary what is placed in the Theme and Rheme positions, looking first at postponement by extraposition and existential constructions.

3. Postponement

Extraposition and existential constructions both postpone newsworthy and heavy information from initial position to the Rheme and have the proform *det* as 'dummy' subjects. A high frequency of the dummy subject *det* as the Theme has been found in the studies of Swedish by Bäckström (2004: 91) and Koskela (1996: 211). Sections 3.1 and 3.2 examine extraposition and existential constructions, respectively.

3.1. Existential constructions

Existential constructions (Biber *et al.*, 1999: 943–954; Holmes and Hinchcliffe, 2003: 480, 503–505; Downing and Locke, 2006: 257; Holmberg and Karlsson, 2006: 153) use the pronouns *there/det* as the dummy subject and typically occur with intransitive verbs of existence or appearance, an indefinite NP and an optional adverbial of space or time. Their main function is to present and assert the existence of new information in the discourse. For instance, in contrast to (19a), which implies that any three people 'can sign this application', the existential construction in (19b) asserts the existence of three people who *can sign this application* and thereby implies that only three such people exist (Huckin and Hutz Pesante, 1988: 378).

> (19) a. Three people can sign this application
>   b. There are three people who can sign this application

Existential constructions are translationally equivalent in English and Swedish as illustrated by the translation in (20).

> (20) Men det finns bara en tjänstgörande kammarherre, anställd på heltid och utnämnd av kungen.
>
> But there is only one serving Chamberlain, employed full time and appointed by the king
>
> But there is only one Chamberlain on duty, working full time and who has been appointed by the King. (GAPG1)

There appear however, to be differences in the usage of existential constructions in Swedish and English. In Bäckström's study (2004: 94), it was found that plain sentences with content Themes in English, i.e., Themes concerned with the topic of their texts, were translated into sentences with existential constructions in Swedish, as in (21), thereby postponing new information to the Rheme.

> (21) a. Negotiations are going on in Syria.
>
> a. Det pågår förhandlingar i Syria.
>
> There go on negotiations …
>
> b. But a wide range of players are involved in drawing up the EU's trade policy
>
> b. Det är dock många aktörer som deltar i utformingen av EU:s handelspolitik.
>
> There are however many actors …

Similarly, in a comparison of existential constructions in original texts and their translations, Herriman (forthcoming) found that existential constructions occurred somewhat more frequently in the Swedish samples, and about a third of the existential constructions in one language were not matched by existential constructions in the other. Many plain sentences in the English originals have been translated into Swedish existential constructions, as in (22) and (23).

(22) Certain aspects of heroism baffled Henry though.

Men det fanns vissa sidor av heroismen som förbryllade Henry. (RF1)

But there were certain sides of the heroism that …

(23) Other aspects of the relationship disturbed him.

Det fanns också andra aspekter på förhållandet som oroade honom. (RF1)

There were also other aspects of the relationship that …

Conversely, many of the English existential constructions in the sample have been translated into non-existential constructions with fronted locative adverbials in Swedish, as in (24).

(24) There was a big municipal clock outside the town hall, and we took some photographs underneath it.

På rådhusfasaden satt en stor klocka, och när vi kom ut vidtog fotografering under den. (JB1)

On the townhall façade sat a big clock and when we came out followed photographing under it

Many of these fronted adverbials represent given information which connects to the preceding message, such as the anaphoric *därmed* ('therewith') in (25).

(25) Den här gången kunde han se budskapets överbringare i ögonen, men därmed var egentligen inget vunnet.

but therewith was really nothing gained

This time, he was able to look the messenger in the eye, but there was nothing to be gained by doing so. (KOB1)

In sum, existential constructions are somewhat more usual in Swedish than English. Furthermore, English existential constructions often correspond to plain clauses with fronted adverbials in Swedish, which not only postpone new information to the Rheme but also link to the preceding utterance. Similar differences were found in a comparison of existential constructions in Norwegian and English (Ebeling, 1999).

3.2. Extraposition

Extraposition (Biber *et al.*, 1999: 660; Holmes and Hinchcliffe, 2003: 480; Downing and Locke, 2006: 260; Holmberg and Karlsson, 2006: 153) has *it/det* as the dummy subject and it postpones a finite or nonfinite clause to the Rheme, as in (26) and (27).

> (26) a. Det är mycket troligt att han vinner.
>   b. Det är roligt att vinna.
>   (Sundman, 1987: 112–113)
> (27) a. It's a nuisance that the banks are closed on Saturday.
>   b. It would be unwise to interfere.
>   (Downing and Locke, 2006: 260).

The matrix clause usually expresses some kind of attitudinal meaning: epistemic modality, (e.g., *It is true*) deontic modality (e.g., *it is necessary*) dynamic modality (e.g., *it is possible/easy*) or general evaluations (e.g., *it is good*) (Herriman, 2000a, 2000b).

Extraposition is translationally equivalent in English and Swedish, as illustrated by the translations in (28) and (29).

> (28) Det var konstigare att han inte kommit   In fact, it was strange that he
>   på den på en gång.   hadn't thought of it at once.
>   (KE2)
>   It was stranger that …
>
> (29) Det var faktiskt litet svårt att ta det hela   It was hard to take Dag's dream
>   riktigt på allvar.   seriously. (MG1)
>
>   It was in fact a little hard to …

Again, however, there appear to be differences in how this construction is used in English and Swedish. English has an alternative non-finite construction, the gerund *-ing* form, which is much less frequently extraposed than non-finite clauses with *to*-infinitives (Herriman, 2000a; Downing and Locke, 2006: 261), as in (30) and (31).

> (30) Doing this won't be easy *vs.* ?It won't be easy, doing this.
> (31) ?To do this won't be easy *vs.* It won't be easy to do this.

As the gerund has no direct translational equivalent in Swedish, it has to be translated into another form. In the following example from Bäckström (2004: 94), for instance, the gerund, *improving*, is translated into a finite verb and the clause is then extraposed to achieve end-weight.

> (32) Improving their access to global markets for agricultural and industrial goods and services is crucial.
>
> Det är av avgörande betydelse att deras jordbruks- och industrivaror och deras tjänster får bättre tillträde till de globala marknaderna.
>
> It is of crucial significance that their industrial goods and services get better access to …

Similarly, the infinitives in extraposed infinitival clauses in Swedish may be translated into gerunds in initial position in English, as the following examples with gerunds (*going on* and *talking*) from the English-Swedish Parallel corpus illustrate:

> (33) Det var mycket lätt att fortsätta det jobbet.
>
> Going on with that job was very easy. (CE1)
>
> It was very easy to continue that job.
>
> (34) Det skulle bryta den overkliga stämningen att få prata ett tag.
>
> Talking to someone would break the unreal atmosphere. (MG1)
>
> It would break the unreal atmosphere to talk for a while.

Gerunds in English may, therefore, take on some of the functions of *att*-infinitive clauses in Swedish and, as they are more easily retained in initial position as Theme, this may result in an overall less frequent usage of extraposition in English. As gerunds have more informational content than the dummy subject *it/det* (as in 32–34 above), this also indicates that there is the tendency for English to allow a greater informational load in the Theme, whereas Swedish tends to avoid top heavy sentences with long Themes. Further evidence may again be found in advanced learners' writing. Boström Aronsson (2005: 88) found that SWICLE writers use extraposition twice as frequently as the LOCNESS British and American writers. In particular there is a somewhat higher frequency of extraposition with attributes expressing dynamic modality (e.g., *it is hard, easy, possible*) as in (35a) and evaluative attributes, such as *cruel*, as in (35b).

> (35) a. It is not easy to change people's attitudes. (SWICLE-LND-017)
>
> b. In fact, I think it would be cruel to ask them to do so. (SWICLE-LND-091)
> (Boström Aronsson, 2005: 91)

These may easily occur with gerunds in English, where the 'unextraposed' alternative is also quite natural (Herriman, 2000a) (cf. *Changing people's attitudes is not easy. In fact, I think asking them to do so would be cruel*). The lower frequency of extraposition in the LOCNESS corpus may therefore be partly due to the fact that the native speakers use the gerund more often whereas the learners are less familiar with this construction.

In sum, there are factors which suggest that extraposition is used more often to postpone information in Swedish than in English. More empirical evidence is, of course, needed to support this claim.

4. Clefting

Cleft sentences (Biber *et al.*, 1999: 958–963; Holmes and Hinchcliffe, 2003: 503–505; Downing, 2006: 249–252; Holmberg and Karlsson, 2006: 154) are sentence constructions which re-organize the content of a single clause into two parts in order to give prominence to one of its elements. A simple clause, such as *We need more money/Vi behöver mer pengar,* is thus re-organized into a cleft clause, e.g., *what we need,* or *that we need,/vad vi behover/som vi behöver* and a clefted constituent, e.g., *more money/mer pengar,* and these two parts are linked to each other by the copula verb *be/vara.*[7] There are three chief types of cleft sentences, *it*-clefts, and two types of *wh*-clefts, basic or reversed.[8] All of these three cleft types are translationally equivalent in English and Swedish, as examples (36)–(38) illustrate.

(36) Det är framförallt det ökade antalet långtidssjukskrivningar som medför denna effekt.

It is chiefly the increase in the amount of long-term sickness absence which lies behind this effect. (ARB1)

It is above all the increased number of long-term sickness absences that brings this effect.

(37) What is important to grasp is that these activities do not consume simply money as such …

Vad som är angeläget att få ett grepp om är emellertid det faktum att militära aktiviteter inte bara slukar pengar…

What that is important to get a grip of is however the fact that military activities not only consume money … (CS1)

(38) Anyway, I'm sure you're going to cheer up again one of these days. You're bound to. You can't not.

Dessutom är jag säker på att du snart får ditt glada humör tillbaka. Det är säkert. Lita på mig.

That's what I tell myself.

Det är vad jag försöker intala mig. (MD1)

That is what I try tell myself

This division of the content of the message into a cleft clause and clefted constituent is a heteroglossic rhetorical strategy for negotiating an authorial position, i.e., it positions the utterance in a dialogic context where other utterances have been or could have been expressed (Herriman, 2005; 2008). The cleft clause represents a variable and the superordinate clause identifies the one specific item which satisfies the definition in the variable, i.e., the clefted constituent, in this case *money*. In this way, cleft constructions acknowledge the potential existence of alternative positions but assert the speaker's alternative in contrast to all others, i.e., they add more argumentative force to the authorial position that 'we need more money' by asserting that 'more money' is what we need in contrast to all the other things that we might need.

In *it*-clefts, such as (36), the clefted constituent is predicated as the complement of *it/det* and the copula. This draws attention to its status as the Theme of the message and therefore gives it prominence of a textual nature. *It*-clefts are often used to express a contrast (Collins, 1991: 182; Johansson, 2002: 79; Biber *et al.*, 1999: 962). Further, as the clefted constituent is placed early in the clause, *it*-clefts may also have a cohesive function, making a connection with the preceding text and thereby marking a transition from this to the following segment of discourse (Biber *et al.*, 1999: 962; Johansson, 2002: 155).

In *wh*-clefts, as in (37) and (38), the clefted constituent is placed in an identifying relationship with the cleft clause. This draws attention to its content by equating it with a definition of its content and therefore gives the clefted constituent prominence of an ideational nature (Halliday, 1967). Basic *wh*-clefts, where the cleft clause is in initial position as the Theme, as in (33), are typically used to highlight newsworthy information (Collins, 1991: 213; Biber *et al.*, 1999: 963; Johansson, 2002: 203). Reversed *wh*-clefts, where the cleft clause is in the Rheme, such as (38), frequently have anaphoric pronouns *det/it* as their clefted constituents and are typically used to either comment on, draw conclusions from or merely repeat or summarize information which has already been conveyed by the text or which may be inferred by its context (Collins, 1991: 117; Biber *et al.*, 1999: 962; Johansson, 2002: 185–203).

Differences, however, have been found in the usage of these three types of clefts in English and Swedish. In his study of clefts in the English-Swedish parallel corpus, Johansson (2002: 111) found that *it*-clefts were used twice as frequently in the Swedish original texts. In the English original texts, on the other hand, basic *wh*-clefts were used twice as frequently and reversed *wh*-clefts were used seven times more frequently (Johansson, 2002: 111). Similarly, in her comparison of argumentative writing by Swedish advanced learners of English and native speaker students, Boström Aronsson (2005: 97) found that the Swedish advanced learners used *it*-clefts more than twice as frequently as native speaker student writers, as in (39), for instance.

(39)   It is science that helps widen our horizons, but it is also science that
       pushes the limits and often neglects side effects. (SWICLE LND 018).

The lower frequency of basic *wh*-clefts in Swedish may be explained by the fact
that Swedish favours the construction with *det* (*that*), and a relative clause, *Det
(som) vi behöver är mer pengar* ('that (which) we need is more money'), which
has a similar function to the basic *wh*-cleft[9] and is therefore often used where
English has a *wh*-cleft, as illustrated by translations such as (40).

(40) What he missed above all was a sense of   Det han framför allt saknade var en
     connection, some suggestion that every-   känsla av samband, en antydan om
     thing hung together.   att allting hängde ihop. (RF1)

                                                   That he above all missed was …

The different frequencies of *it*-clefts in Swedish and reversed *wh*-clefts in English can be partly explained by constraints on clefting possibilities in Swedish (Johansson, 2002: 85–109). Reversed *wh*-clefts in Swedish only allow *vad*
('what') as the pronoun in their cleft clauses, and therefore only have inanimate NPs as their clefted constituents. English reversed *wh*-clefts, in contrast,
also allow *why, where, how, when* and *who* in their cleft clauses and may therefore also have adverbials and animate NPs as their clefted constituents. As
a result, Swedish *it*-clefts are often used where reversed *wh*-clefts would be
used in English, and many of the English reversed *wh*-clefts with adverbials
as their clefted constituents in the corpus are translated into Swedish *it*-clefts,
as in (41), and some Swedish *it*-clefts with adverbials as their clefted constituents are translated into English reversed *wh*-clefts (Johansson, 2002: 131), as
in (42).

(41) Yes I *do* know it's bad for my health   Visst, jag vet att det inte är bra för min
     as a matter of fact, that's why I like it.   hälsa; det är därför jag gillar att röka.
                                                   (JB1)

                                                   … it is therefore I like to smoke

(42) Om du är rädd, känner di det på   If you're frightened, they can feel it
     långt håll, det är då di blir farliga.   a long way off. That's when they get
                                                  dangerous. (AL1)
     …it is then they get dangerous

Furthermore, Johansson (2002: 171) notes that when the clefted constituents
in Swedish *it*-clefts have a cohesive function, i.e., they are anaphors such as *så*
('thus'), they are also frequently translated into reversed *wh*-clefts in English,
as in (43).

> (43) Det var verkligen inte så hon menade.   That's not what I mean. (GT1)
> It was really not thus she meant

However, as Johansson (2002: 168) points out, the higher frequency of *it*-clefts in Swedish texts cannot be entirely explained by the fact that reversed *wh*-clefts take over some of the functions of English reversed *wh*-clefts. About half of the Swedish *it*-clefts in the translations in the parallel corpus were translated into non-clefts in English, as in (44), and some non-clefts in English were translated into *it*-clefts in Swedish, as in (45).

> (44) Men det är bara hans mamma Gudrun   But his mother Gudrun is the only one
> som tycker att han ska fortsätta.   who thinks he should go on. (KE2)
>
> But it is only his mama Gudrun who
>
> …

> (45) 'Johnny Paul opened my eyes,' he once   'Det var Johnny Paul som öppnade
> wrote. 'Not Jesus, not Socrates, not the   mina ögon', skrev han vid ett tillfälle.
> Buddha.'   'Inte Jesus, inte Sokrates, inte Buddha.'
>   (RF1)
>
>   'It was Johnny Paul who opened my
>   eyes …'

Furthermore, some of the Swedish *it*-clefts which are translated into non-clefts in English have pronouns as their clefted constituents, as in (46).

> (46) Han var någon slags kontorschef. Det   He was a kind of office manager. He
> var han som satte ihop vad grabbarna   would put together what the boys
> gjort och sedan diskuterade det med   had done and then talk it over with
> Asplund.   Asplund. (CE1)
>
> It was he who put together …

As English *it*-clefts, in contrast to Swedish, rarely have pronouns as their clefted constituents, this suggests that Swedish *it*-clefts are used more often to provide a cohesive link to the preceding discourse (Johansson, 2002: 145).

In sum, there are a number of differences in the ways in which clefts are used to structure information in English and Swedish. In particular *it*-clefts are used more often in Swedish. As this type of cleft has the proform *det* in initial position, this reflects the tendency for Themes in Swedish to be short and 'light'. A higher frequency of *it*-clefts has also been found in Norwegian (Gundel, 2002).

5. Conclusion

Corpus studies have shown, thus, that there are differences in the extent in which the canonical order of clause elements is re-ordered in English and Swedish. To some extent this can be explained by semantic-syntactic constraints in one language, which result in an alternative construction which has similar functions being used to carry out these functions in the other. Swedish, for instance, is less tolerant of inanimate subjects than English and therefore prefers fronted adverbials for locative and temporal meanings, for example. It is also more restrictive than English in what may be clefted in reversed *wh*-clefts and therefore uses *it*-clefts for some of the functions carried out by *wh*-clefts in English. Similarly, Swedish has no non-finite verb form which corresponds to the gerund -*ing* form in English and therefore uses other forms, e.g., finite or *att*-infinitive clauses, instead. This, in turn, may contribute to a higher frequency of certain kinds of extraposition in Swedish.

There is, however, considerable empirical evidence that the word order of Swedish is changed more frequently in order to follow the information and end-weight principles, i.e., to keep new information out of the Theme. Non-subject clause elements, such as adverbials, objects, and complements, which represent given information are fronted to the Theme more often, and new and heavy information is postponed more often to the Rheme by special constructions such as extraposition, and existential there/*det* sentences. English, in contrast, has a greater tolerance of new information in the Theme. There is thus a difference in the markedness of these translationally equivalent constructions in the two languages. Similar differences have also been found in contrastive studies of English with other Scandinavian languages, which, like Swedish, also have a V2 constraint.

Transfer of a more frequent usage of word order changes from Swedish to English may have the effect of making a text somewhat contrastive and over-emphatic (Boström Aronsson, 2005: 97). This difference in the markedness of word order changes in Swedish and English has, therefore, important pedagogical implications for Swedish learners. It also gives rise to a number of questions which call for further contrastive studies. For instance, under what conditions does English allow new information in Themes? If there are differences in what is placed in the Theme in English and Swedish, how does this affect the informational load placed in the Rheme? The answers to these and other related questions are of significance for translators and teachers alike.

Notes

1.   See Fredriksson (2004) for a discussion of contrastive analysis of Themes in English and Swedish.

2.   Both English and Swedish also have dislocations, e.g., *This girl this morning threw a wobbly* (Biber *et al.*, 1999: 956), *Eva, henne tycker jag inte om* (Holmes and Hinchcliffe, 2003: 502).

3.   The English-Swedish parallel corpus contains 2.8 million words of fiction and non-fiction texts. There are 64 English original texts and their translations into Swedish and 72 Swedish original texts and their translations into English.

4.   The Swedish component of the *International Corpus of Learner English* project (ICLE, 2002) consists of 350 essays written by Swedish students in the second year of university studies of English. The *Louvain Corpus of Native English Essays* (LOCNESS) consists of 293 essays by American and British university students and some British A-level students.

5.   Unless otherwise indicated, all the examples are from the English-Swedish Parallel Corpus and the codes following examples refer to the text in the corpus. See http://www.englund.lu.se/content/view/65/125/

6.   Fries (2002: 141) found that similar temporal adverbials have different effects depending on whether they are placed in the Theme or Rheme.

7.   Swedish may have the copula *bliva* ('become') as well as *vara* ('be').

8.   Halliday (2004: 68, 95) calls these thematic equatives and Theme predications, respectively. Other types of clefts such as *all*-clefts, *th*-clefts (see Collins, 1991) are not considered here.

9.   This type of construction was not, however, included in Johansson's study..

References

Aijmer, K., Altenberg, B. and Johansson, M. (1996) Text-based contrastive studies in English. Presentation of a project. In K. Aijmer, B. Altenberg and S. Johansson (eds) *Languages in Contrast. Papers From a Symposium on Text-based Cross-linguistic Studies in Lund, 4-5 March 1994*, 73–85. Lund: Lund University Press.

Altenberg, B (1998) Connectors and sentence openings in English and Swedish. In S. Johansson and S. Oksefjell (eds) *Corpora and Cross-Linguistic Research*. Amsterdam, Atlanta: Rodopi.

Bäckström, J. (2004) Tema och rema i översättning. En komparativ undersökning av informationsstrukturen i engelska och svenska. *Texter Emellan* 6: 81–100. Översättningstudier vid Göteborgs Universitet.

Biber, D., Johansson, S., Leech, G., Conrad, S. and Finnegan, E. (1999) *Longman Grammar of Written and Spoken English*. Longman: London.

Boström Aronsson, M. (2005) *Themes in Swedish Advanced Learners' Written English*. Unpublished PhD thesis: University of Gothenburg.

Collins, P. C. (1991) *Cleft and Pseudo-cleft Constructions in English*. London and New York: Routledge. http://dx.doi.org/10.4324/9780203202463

Dik, S. (1997) *The Theory of Functional Grammar. Part I: The Structure of the Clause*. 2nd edn. by K. Hengeveld. New York: Mouton de Gruyter.

Downing A. and Locke, P. (2006) *English Grammar. A University Course*. 2nd edn. London and New York: Routledge.

Ebeling, J. (1999) *Presentative Constructions in English and Norwegian. A Corpus-based Study*. Oslo: Acta Humaniora, Faculty of Arts, University of Oslo.

Enkvist, N. E. (1991) Discourse strategies and discourse types. In E. Ventola (ed.) *Functional and Systemic Linguistics: Approaches and Uses*, 3–22. Berlin: Mouton de Gruyter.

Erman, B. (1998) Information structure in Swedish and English. *Översättning och tolkning*. Rapport från ASLA:s höstsymposium Stockholm 5-5 November 1998.

Fredriksson, A. L. (2002) Exploring Theme contrastively: The choice of model. In K. Aijmer and B. Altenberg (eds) *Advances in Corpus Linguistics; Papers from the 23rd International Conference on English Language Research on Computerized Corpora* (ICAME 23), 353–370. Amsterdam, New York: Rodopi.

Fries, P. H. (2002) The flow of information in a written English text. In P. Fries, M. Cummings, D. Lockwood and W. Spruiell (eds) *Relations and Functions within and around Language,* 117–155. London and New York: Continuum.

Granger, S. (1998) The computer learner corpus: A versatile new source of data for SLA research. In S. Granger (ed.) *Learner English on Computer,* 3–18. Longman: London.

Gundel, J. J. (2002) Information structure and the use of cleft sentences in English and Norwegian. *Language and Computers* 39: 113–128.

Halliday, M. A. K. (1967) Notes on Transitivity and Theme in English. 2. *Journal of Linguistics* 3 (2): 177–244. http://dx.doi.org/10.1017/S0022226700016613

Halliday M. A. K. and Matthiessen, C. M. I. M. (2004) *An Introduction to Functional Grammar,* 3rd edn. London: Arnold.

Hasselgård, H. (1996) Some methodological issues in a contrastive study of word order in English and Norwegian. In K. Aijmer, B. Altenberg and M. Johansson (eds) *Languages in Contrast. Papers from a Symposium on Text-based Cross-linguistic Studies,* 113–126. Lund: Lund University Press.

Hasselgård, H. (1998) Thematic structure in translation between English and Norwegian. In S. Johansson and S. Oksefjell (eds) *Corpora and Cross-Linguistic Research,* 145–167. Amsterdam and Atlanta, GA: Rodopi.

Hasselgård, H. (2004) Spatial linking in English and Norwegian. In K. Aimer and H. Hasselgård. *Translation and Corpora,* 163–188. Göteborg: Acta Universitatis Gothoburgenis.

Herriman, J. (2000a) Extraposition in English: A study of the interaction between the matrix predicate and the type of extraposed clause. *English Studies* 81 (6): 582–599. http://dx.doi.org/10.1076/enst.81.6.582.9180

Herriman, J. (2000b) The functions of extraposition in English. *Functions of Language* 7 (2): 203–230.

Herriman, J. (2005) Negotiating a position within heteroglossic diversity: *Wh*-clefts and *it*-clefts in written discourse. *Word* 56 (2): 223–248.

Herriman, J. (2008) The interpersonal function of clefts in English and Swedish. *Languages in Contrast* 8 (2): 143–160. http://dx.doi.org/10.1075/lic.8.2.02her

Herriman, J. (2011a) N-Rhemes in English problem-solution texts. *English Text Construction* 4 (1): 29–53. http://dx.doi.org/10.1075/etc.4.1.03her

Herriman, J. (2011b) Themes and Theme progressions in Swedish advanced learners' writing in English. *Nordic Journal of English Studies* 10 (1): 1–28.

Herriman, J. (to appear) Existential *there/det* constructions in English and Swedish. *Languages in Contrast.*

Herriman, J. and Boström Aronsson, M. (2009) Themes in Swedish advanced learners' writing in English. In Aijmer, K. (ed.) *Corpora and Language Teaching*, 101–120. Amsterdam: John Benjamins.

Holmberg, P. and Karlsson, A. M. (2006) *Grammatik med betydelse. En introduktion till funktionell grammatik*. Uppsala: Hallgren and Fallgren.

Holmes, P. and Hinchcliffe, I. (2003) *Swedish: A Comprehensive Grammar* (2nd edn.) London and New York: Routledge.

Huckin, T. and Pesante, L. Hutz (1988) Existential *there. Written Communication* 5: 368–391. http://dx.doi.org/10.1177/0741088388005003006

Johansson, M. (1996a) Contrastive data as a resource in the study of English clefts. In K. Aijmer, B. Altenberg and M. Johansson (eds) *Languages in Contrast*, 127–150. Papers from a Symposium on Text-based Cross-linguistic Studies, Lund University Press.

Johansson, M. (1996b) Fronting in English and Swedish: A text-based contrastive analysis. In C. E. Percy, C. F. Meyer and I. Lancashire (eds) *Synchronic Corpus Linguistics*, 29–39. Amsterdam and Atlanta, GA: Rodopi.

Johansson, M. (2002) *Clefts in English and Swedish: A Contrastive Study of IT-clefts and WH-clefts in Original Texts and Translations*. Unpublished Doctoral Dissertation, Lund University.

Kong, K. (2004) Marked Themes and thematic patterns in abstracts, advertisements and administrative documents. *Word* 55 (3): 343–362.

Koskela, M. (1996) *Tema och rema i vetenskaplig och populärvetenskaplig text*. Universitas Wasagensis Vasa.

Shaw, P. (2004) Sentence openings in academic economics articles in English and Danish. *Nordic Journal of English Studies* 2 (3): 67–84.

Sundman, M. (1987) *Subjektval och diates i svenskan*. Åbo: Åbo Akademis förlag.

Svensson, M. (2000a) Sentence openings in English and Swedish. A contrastive pilot study. In T. Virtanen, and I. Maricic (eds) *Perspectives on Discourse*, 103–122. Växjö: Växjö University Press.

Svensson, M. (2000b) Sentence openings and textual progression in English and Swedish. In C. Mair and M. Hundt (eds) *Corpus Linguistics and Linguistic Theory. Papers from the Twentieth International Conference on English Language Research on Computerized Corpora (ICAME 20)*, Freiburg im Breisgau, 1999, 355–370. Amsterdam and Atlanta, GA: Rodopi.

Teleman, U., Hellberg, S. and Andersson, E. (1999) *Svenska Akademiens grammatik*. Norstedts: Stockholm.

Thompson, G. (2004) *Introducing Functional Grammar* 2nd edn. London: Arnold.

Thompson, G., and Thompson, S. (2009) Theme, subject and the unfolding of text. In G. Forey and G. Thompson (eds) *Text Type and Texture*, 45–69. London: Equinox.

7 The use of it-clefts in the written production of Spanish advanced learners of English

Susana Doval Suárez and Elsa González Álvarez

Learner writing has been shown to differ from native speakers' (NS) writing in terms of frequency of certain words or structures (Granger *et al.*, 2002). On the basis of data obtained from two comparable corpora, the Spanish component of the ICLE (International Corpus of Learner English) and the LOCNESS (Louvain Corpus of Native English Essays), the present study explores the use of it-cleft constructions, a type of focusing device that has been claimed to be over-represented in the written production of advanced learners with different L1 backgrounds (Böstrom Aronsson, 2003; Callies, 2009). Its objective is threefold: first of all, to investigate how Spanish advanced EFL learners compare with NSs from the point of view of their use of it-clefts, thereby contributing to the characterization of advanced learner variety (ALV). Second, it addresses the issue of how NNSs and NSs compare regarding their use of the different discourse functions of it-clefts (i.e. identification and contrast), and also regarding the selection of the highlighted element. Finally, the study investigates whether the differences between the two groups may be attributed to influence of the L1. The Independent Samples *t*-test indicates that Spanish EFL learners significantly underuse it-clefts ($t = 2.100$; $p \leq 0.05$). It is suggested that this underuse cannot be ascribed to L1 transfer but to the learners' preference for other types of clefting, which points to the need for further research on the use of clefts in Spanish texts and in English texts written by Spanish learners. The results also indicate statistically significant differences between the two groups in the discourse functions assigned to it-clefts. It is suggested that the Spanish advanced learners' underuse of contrast may also indicate that they prefer to use pseudoclefts and other lexical or syntactic means for this purpose. As regards the length and syntactic features (category and function) of the highlighted element and the use of the relative pronoun, our results confirm that Spanish learners have generally acquired the English pattern, even though more qualitative analysis is needed to provide a detailed description of this component of the learners' pragmatic abilities.

1. Introduction

In the last decade we have witnessed a growing interest in the advanced learner and in questions of native-like proficiency, which contrasts with the relative scarcity of studies focusing on this stage of acquisition (Carroll *et al.*, 2000; Callies, 2009). The difference between advanced learners and native speakers (NS) was expressed in the past in terms of the mistakes these speakers continue to make (Singleton and Lengyel, 1995; White and Genesee, 1996). Recent research, however, has pointed out that the main differences between the advanced learner variety (ALV) and the target language (TL) have to do with questions of unidiomaticity or style, not with violations of frequently taught rules (Lube, 2000: 2). Carroll *et al.* (2000) remark that 'it is necessary to account for the fact that ALVs show a high degree of compatibility with the target language with respect to the forms acquired, but that the functions that those forms serve in context differ in the interlanguage (IL) and TL' (2000: 442).

In this regard we should emphasize the contribution of corpus-based research (Granger *et al.*, 2002; Hinkel, 2002), which has shown that the differences between the TL and the ALV can be expressed in terms of frequencies (i.e. overuse and/or underuse) of certain words, phrases and syntactic structures, both at a lexico-grammatical and syntactic level. The application of corpus analysis to learner language has resulted in a number of studies oriented at discourse aspects of learner writing. Although there is evidence that Information Structure (IS) is a learning problem even for advanced second-language (L2) learners, it nevertheless constitutes an underexplored area in the field of Second Language Acquisition (SLA) research (see Schachter and Rutherford, 1979; Carroll *et al.*, 2000; Von Stutterheim, 2003; Callies, 2009), and there are virtually no studies on the use of cleft constructions by Spanish learners of English. This study is intended to fill this explicit research gap by addressing the issue of how learners deal with *it*-clefts.[1]

The purpose of the study is threefold. It aims, first of all, to investigate how Spanish advanced EFL learners compare with NSs from the point of view of their use of *it*-clefts, and, therefore, it intends to contribute to the characterization of the ALV. This will allow us to compare our results with those obtained in previous studies (cf. Böstrom-Aronsson (2001a, 2003), Hinkel (2002) and Callies (2009)) that suggest that clefts are generally overused in writing by learners (cf. Section 2). Second, we seek to address the issue of how NNSs and NSs compare regarding their use of the different types and discourse functions of clefts, and also regarding the selection of the highlighted element. Finally, the study will investigate whether the differences between the two groups may be attributed to influence of the L1.

Our interest in the developing discourse competence of these learners is geared first towards determining the extent to which the Spanish learners have acquired the specific structures available in English and their functions, considering the differences between the two languages in word order and the information-structural constraints on clefts. Therefore, the study may have important implications related to SLA and general linguistic theory by exploring the interrelationship of grammatical and pragmalinguistic ability in an L2, and the impact of the principles of Information Structure (IS) of the learner's L1 on the acquisition of L2-English.

A comment here is in order regarding terminology. The term *Information Structure* (Halliday, 1967) (see also *Information Packaging*, cf. Chafe, 1976) is used to refer to the strategies deployed by speakers to present information in a certain way (Prince, 1978; Collins, 1991; Biber *et al.*, 1999; Gómez-González, 2001; Ward *et al.*, 2002; Gómez-González and Gonzálvez-García, 2005). While *marked* Information Structure (IS) constructions (such as *clefting, extraposition, inversion* or *fronting*) may have the same propositional content as their canonical counterparts, they differ from them syntactically and semantically, and also convey different pragmatic functions. One of the most important concepts of IS theory is that of *focus*, which is associated with the idea that one particular discourse element is highlighted, foregrounded, or simply given more prominence than other elements (Callies, 2009: 20). Although focus can be also seen as independent from information status, since both new and given information can be highlighted, there is a strong correlation between focus, sentence position and information status. In English, the general principle is that of *end-focus*: new information at the end of a sentence is in focus and thus receives prominence (Biber *et al.*, 1999: 896). This principle often combines with that of *end-weight* (the principle by which longer and more complex constituents of the clause tend to occur late in clause), so that *heavy* tends to correlate with *new* (Ward *et al.*, 2002: 1371).

This study focuses on *it-cleft* constructions, as in (1); we therefore exclude from our analysis *basic* pseudo-clefts, as in (2), and *reversed* pseudo-clefts, as in (3):

(1)   What I saw.
(2)   Was **a spider**.
(3)   <u>**A spider**</u> is what I saw.

The different types of clefts (1–3) establish an identity relationship between two propositions and/or referents codified as *Theme* (the <u>underlined</u> part in 1–3 above) and *Rheme* (or final clause/phrase). However, the three types differ in the following aspects: (a) the position of focus (in **bold** type) either in the Theme or in the Rheme; (b) the syntactic function and weight of the focus: in *it*-clefts, subject and object NPs and PPs occur most frequently, while VP focusing is ungrammatical and the focusing of full clauses is possible but not preferred; the focused part in pseudo-clefts is significantly longer than in *it*-clefts; (c) their frequency in different registers.

Following Callies (2009), we will distinguish two types of focus: *contrast* (Example 4) and *intensification* (Example 5).

(4)   a.   My brother helped a lot with the party, but <u>it was my mother</u> who did
           most of the work.
      b.   I didn't say that. <u>What I said</u> was **that you should not have come alone**.
(5)   In 1992 they moved to Rome. <u>It was at this time</u> that they started to
           have serious economic problems.

The terms were first used by Biber *et al.* (1999: 897; quoted by Callies, 2002: 22) to apply to 'special cases of emphasis arising when elements are in focus'. Different definitions and taxonomies of *contrast* are found in Halliday (1967: 206), Chafe (1976), Givon (2001: 224), and Dik *et al.* (1981: 59–68), among others. Following Halliday (1967), Chafe (1976) and Callies (2009: 23) we will consider *contrast* as 'contrary to some predicted or stated alternative'; while *intensification* will be defined as 'adding importance to a certain piece of information without explicit or implicit contrast, involving an open set of possible alternatives' (Callies, 2009: 23).

2. Clefts in English and Spanish: Acquisitional aspects

2.1. The use of clefts in English and in Spanish

An important typological question that has often been addressed in the literature is whether there is any relationship between word order and information structure. According to Siewierska (1994: 4994ff), the interaction between word order and information structure is relevant for the degree of markedness of a given focusing device.

Typologically, both English and Spanish are SVO languages (Greenberg, 1966). Thompson (1978: 20) further distinguishes between languages with Pragmatic Word Order (PWO), i.e. languages that can use word order to signal information status of sentence constituents (*given* vs. *new*), and languages with Grammatical Word Order (GWO), i.e. languages that use word order to encode the grammatical relations (subject vs. object). English, with its rather fixed SVO, is positioned towards the grammatical end of the continuum, as is shown by the occurrence of dummy subjects, and structure preserving operations such as the passive, raising constructions and clefting. Spanish, on the contrary, comes closer to the pragmatic type, with its greater word order flexibility and its richer morphological system. Typically, Spanish does not have a dummy subject and does not always require the understood subject to be specified ((S)VO).

What are the implications of word order for IS? The existence of clefts has been attested to in different languages in a number of cross-linguistic studies (Dik, 1980; Sornicola, 1994), but Jespersen (1949) attributes differences in the frequency of use of clefts across languages to differences in word order flexibility. Thus, clefting seems to be frequent in relatively rigid word order languages like English, the Scandinavian languages, and French, and less frequent in languages with more flexible word order such as Spanish, German, and Russian (Gundel, 2008: 70).

The few studies comparing the use of clefts in English and Spanish (Pinedo, 2000; Gómez-González and Gonzálvez-García, 2005; Gundel, 2008) have yielded the following findings:

1. Clefting is less frequent and more marked in Spanish than in English for the following reasons: (a) Spanish has greater word order flexibility: 'rigid word order languages like English need to make use of marked syntactic constructions in order to convey some of the pragmatic emphases which more flexible word order languages like Spanish can achieve via word order alone' (Pinedo, 2000: 127); (b) the same function can be performed by verb-subject inversion (intransitive VS clauses with a focal contrastive subject, OVS with a focal object (frontings), OVS with a topical object or a clitic object (left-dislocations) and VS constructions with initial topical adverbials (AVS)); (c) Van Valin and La Polla (1997) and Lambrecht (1994) refer to restrictions against preverbal focus in Spanish, since in this language the sentence initial position is often associated with the topic function (see also Martínez-Caro, 2007).

However, Gundel (2008: 30) in a study comparing the use of it-clefts in Spanish, Norwegian and English, concludes that 'none of the proposed structural/typological explanations for frequency differences in cleft usage is completely satisfactory' (2008: 84) and makes the interesting suggestion that the higher number of clefts in English than in Spanish might be 'attributable to a stronger preference for pseudo-clefts and reverse pseudo-clefts over clefts in Spanish, rather than a general weaker tendency to use syntactic structure to encode information structure' (2008: 84).

2. In Spanish, the range of morphosyntactic realisations and syntactic functions of the highlighted elements, as well as their frequencies, reproduce (at

least formally) the English pattern of *it*-clefts, except for the zero realization of the relative (Gómez-González and Gonzálvez-García, 2005: 166).

3. Structural differences between Spanish and English clefts are especially evident in the case of *it*-clefts, which differ from their English counterparts in three respects (Gómez-González and Gonzálvez-García, 2005: 160–170): (a) they lack a pronominal subject; (b) the copula typically agrees with a nominal cleft constituent and is plural if the nominal is plural; (c) the relative pronoun cannot be omitted under any circumstances.

Because of these differences, some authors (Barcelona-Sánchez, 1983; Martínez-Caro, 1999: 132) maintain that Spanish does not have *it*-clefts. As we do not consider overt pronominal subject to be a crucial component of the cleft structure, we will follow Gómez-González and Gonzálvez-García (2005: 160) (in line with Moreno-Cabrera, 1999: 42–48), and Gundel (2008: 70ff) in assuming the existence of *it*-clefts in Spanish.

2.2. Clefts and other focus constructions: Second Language Acquisition (SLA) research

There is evidence that IS management is an important but problematic part of L2 knowledge, and that learners may have difficulties with the placing of focus (Bülow-Møller, 1996). One of the reasons for this seems to be that the discourse structure and the pragmatic principles of information organization in the L1 may influence L2 acquisition in terms of transfer or overproduction (Schachter and Rutherford, 1979; Rutherford, 1983) or avoidance (Plag, 1994).

Other causes of difficulty have been identified, such as teaching-induced factors, i.e., the strong SV orientation of EFL teaching (Hannay and Martínez-Caro, 2008: 233), or typological factors connected with the difficulty to acquire or transfer marked focusing devices. Thus, the basic assumptions of the functional-typological approach to SLA (Eckman 1977, 1996; Trévise, 1986; Callies, 2009) are that less marked structures will be acquired first or more easily than more marked structures, and that learners do not seem to transfer what they feel to be an L1-specific device and resort to more neutral constructions with the feeling that there is a hierarchy in the transferability of various constructions, in terms of L1-specificity, or neutrality.

An interesting distinction is the one made by Callies (2009: 54) between *structural* and *pragmatic markedness*: the former refers to the ordering of sentence constituents in comparison to the basic, unmarked word order; the latter is associated with the presentation and ordering of information within a sentence or utterance compared to the unmarked distribution according to the information and the principles of end-focus and end-weight. In line with Dryer (1995), Callies (2009) considers that a pragmatically marked construction is characterized by a break of a communicative norm 'in that it involves some sort of surprise or unexpectedness, either by a change in the direction of the flow of information or the introduction of (a) information that is counter to expectation or (b) a brand-new discourse entity' (Callies, 2009: 55). A pragmatically marked construction also has additional pragmatic meaning, for example, expressing contrast.

Furthermore, different focus constructions exhibit different degrees of structural markedness. This means that, although *it*-clefts and pseudo-clefts may be considered *structurally marked* constructions in comparison to their corresponding non-cleft counterparts (i.e. they split the declarative clause into two different clauses), they can be said to be structure-preserving constructions (in comparison with, for instance, *inversion*), since they generally retain the canonical SVO/SVC word order (Callies, 2009: 60). In a similar way, there exist different degrees of pragmatic markedness: *it*-clefts and reversed pseudo-clefts, which place new information in initial position in opposition to the information principle, may be considered as more *pragmatically marked* than pseudoclefts, which place new information in final position (Gómez-González, 2001: 324ff; Callies, 2009: 58–60).[2]

Empirical research on specific focus constructions in advanced learner English is scarce, and in the case of Spanish learners, virtually non-existent. Among the studies carried out on the acquisition of English *it*-clefts by L2 learners, the following deserve mention: Klein (1988) and Boström Aronsson (2001, 2003) on cleft constructions; and Hinkel (2002), Rowley-Jolivet and Carter-Thomas (2005), Callies and Keller (2008) and, especially, Callies (2009) on the use of the full range of focus devices in the IL of advanced German learners. The results yielded by the studies focusing on the use of clefts suggest that (cf. Callies, 2009: 105):

(a) Learners have a limited knowledge of the appropriate use of clefts in formal and informal registers in the spoken and written mode.

(b) Learners tend to overuse *it*-clefts (Boström Aronsson, 2001, 2003; Hinkel, 2002; Callies, 2009) and other sentence types headed by the dummy subjects *it* and *there*, i.e. preserving canonical SVO.

(c) Advanced learners have a limited knowledge of their contextual use and discourse functions (syntactic weight and information highlighting).

3. Research questions

Drawing on the contrastive analysis of English and Spanish and on the review of previous studies on clefting in SLA, the following research questions (RQ) can be formulated:

Evidence 1:   Previous research has shown that the ALV is characterized by the learners' *overuse* and *underuse* of specific structures, and that clefts and other focus constructions are an explicit learning difficulty.

RQ 1:   Are there any differences between NNS and NS in the frequency of use of *it*-clefts?

Evidence 2:   It has been noted that learning difficulties may be ascribed to the existence of differences between the L1 and the L2, and there is evidence which suggests that *it*-clefting is not as frequent in Spanish as in English due to the word order features of Spanish or to the Spanish preference for pseudo-clefts. Furthermore, functional-typological approaches to clefts predict that canonical pseudo-clefts will be acquired first or more easily than the other two types, due to their lower degree of pragmatic markedness. Consequently, we might expect *it*-clefts to be underused by learners. However, previous studies on other learner varieties have shown that learners generally avoid structurally marked structures to a significant extent, and tend to rely on the safe canonical SVO word order in English due to the combined effects of training and typological (un)markedness. This often leads to the overuse of structure-preserving constructions such as clefts (and extrapositions).

RQ 2:   What are the causes for the differences in frequency of *it*-clefts in the two corpora?

Evidence 3:   It has been noted that learners differ from NSs in the discourse functions assigned to clefts, which sometimes leads to unmotivated or untypical uses, and generates style problems.

RQ 3:   Do NSs and NNSs differ in the frequency of the discourse functions (intensification and contrast) assigned to the different types of clefts?

Evidence 4:   Contrastive studies of the use of clefts in English and Spanish have shown that the two languages do not show substantial differences regarding the range of morphosyntactic realizations and syntactic functions of the highlighted elements, as well as their frequencies.

RQ 4:   Are there any differences between NS and NNS in the length and syntactic features (category and function) of the highlighted element, and in the use of the relative pronoun?

4. Methodology

The methodology adopted to describe quantitative differences between NSs and NNSs is *Contrastive Interlanguage Analysis* or CIA (Granger, 1996; Granger *et al.*, 2002), which involves two major types of comparison: Native Language vs. Interlanguage (IL) comparisons, and IL vs. IL. This study focuses on the first type of comparison.

The study presents a contrastive, corpus-based analysis of argumentative essay *writing* based on material from two comparable corpora. The NNS corpus is the Spanish component of the *International Corpus of Learner English* (ICLE). The Spanish subcorpus (SPICLE) comprises 251 essays with a total of 200,376 words written by L1-Spanish university students. The NS control corpus is the LOCNESS (the Louvain Corpus of Native English Essays), which comprises essays written by American and British university students, and essays written by British A-level students. It has the advantage of being directly comparable to the ICLE, but, in order to make it comparable to the Spanish subsection of the ICLE, we limited our study to a subsection of the LOCNESS, a sample of 322 essays (totalling 227,968 words) which excludes essays produced by A-level students.

As regards data analysis, cleft constructions were first retrieved from the learner and the native speaker corpora by means of the software package *Wordsmith Tools 3.0*. Since the corpora are not annotated, the cleft structures had to be detected by extracting lexical patterns, keywords and triggering elements (for example, the dummy subject *it*). These were automatically retrieved from the corpora, and then analysed manually.

Second, the data extracted from both corpora were stored in an ACCESS database coded for the following variables: an independent variable, i.e. the subject's L1; and a number of dependent variables, namely, the type of focus (basically *intensification* and *contrast*); and the category, function and weight (expressed in number of words) of the highlighted element.

The last step involved carrying out statistical analyses in order to determine what combinations the learner uses significantly more or significantly less than a NS. For the quantitative analysis, we used the PASW Statistics for Windows. Frequencies of occurrence of the relevant structures were compared for NSs and NNSs using the Independent Samples *t*-test. Although the study presented here is predominantly quantitative, some qualitative insights into the use of clefts were performed in order to provide explanations for the numerical data obtained.

5. Results

5.1. Total frequency of *it*-clefts

The first objective of this study was to check whether Spanish advanced writers use *it*-clefts to the same extent as native writers. Since the two corpora are not equal in length (i.e. in number of words), we normalized the frequency of clefts to presence per thousand words. As is shown in Table 1, the frequency is higher for the NSs.

The Independent Samples *t*-test indicates that this difference is statistically significant ($t = 2.100$; $p \leq 0.05$). This result seems to contradict findings of previous studies which pointed to a general overuse of *it*-clefts by learners. It has to be mentioned that none of these was conducted with Spanish learners, but with German and Swedish learners. However, it does not seem possible to ascribe these differences to L1 transfer of word order features, since the predictions based on previous typological research would classify Spanish with German and Swedish with English as regards word order restrictions. We claim that the differences could be explained by suggesting that the learners may be using a different type of cleft or a different focus construction (cf. the Spanish preference for pseudoclefts pointed out by Gundel (2008)).

Table 1: Frequency of *it*-clefts in the NS and NNS[3] corpora

Group	N subjects	N clefts	Frequency per thousand words	Standard Dev.
NS	322	103	0.45	1.047
NNS	251	42-**	0.20	0.540
BOTH	573	145		

5.2. Discourse functions of it-clefts: intensification vs. contrast

As is shown in Table 2, the inter-group analysis reveals that NNSs underuse both types, but the difference is only statistically significant for *contrast*. This might be an indication that learners use other devices to express contrast (a different type of cleft, lexical means, etc.), which needs to be fully confirmed by further research. The intra-group comparison shows that both groups use *it*-clefts to carry different types of focus. Furthermore, although *intensification* is the most frequent function for both NSs and NNSs, it represents a higher percentage of occurrences in the case of NNSs.

Table 2: Discourse functions of *it*-clefts

	NS		NNS	
	n	%	*n*	%
Contrast	30	29	10-**	24
Intensification	73	71	32	76
Total clefts	103	100	42	100

The fact that the *intensification* uses predominate in both corpora points to the necessity to revise the view of *it*-clefts as 'markers of contrastiveness par excellence' (Biber *et al.*, 1999; Jespersen, 1949; Ward *et al.*, 2002). Examples of the use of *contrast* and *intensification* taken from both corpora are given in (6) and (7) respectively:[4]

(6) a. Until the last 30 years religion was the institution which moved the masses; it was compulsory to go to church, pray and do one's duty to God, but now, it is the television which moves the society to accept the established systems. (ICLE: SPM03024)

 b. At the higher education level, there are universities and *grands-écoles* in France. It is the *grands-écoles* which are seen as elitist and since two years studying needs to be done before you even take the entrance exam, once again, those with less financial resources will be discouraged from taking this route. (LOCNESS: 350BRSUR1)

(7) a. All this is completely anecdotal, but it could raise many considerations to be borne in mind. In mankind relationships love is the essential element, but sometimes money regulates social passions as well as love does, and sometimes even above it. It is in this opposition that the society is based, love-money. (ICLE: SPM04053)

 b. In the 'comte' 'Candide' we see Candide, the principal character on a journey of discovery filled with strange episodes. It is in the course of this journey that Voltaire shows us how abhorrent the climate of optimism was to him, an optimism which often was simply an excuse for the lethargy of contemporary society. (LOCNESS: 372BRSUR2)

5.3. Structural features

The relative word

According to Gómez-González (2000: 305–30) 'unlike in standard relatives, *wh*-forms are relatively rare except where the *wh*-word is *who, whom* and *whose* (although less so than Quirk *et al.*, (1985: 1397) claim), in comparison with the higher frequency of *that-* and zero realisations'. This means that Examples (8)–(10) are grammatically wrong while Examples (11)–(13) are at least 'questionable'.[5]

(8) These critics were extremely attracted by that age in which poetry was a spontaneous expression of the people and played an important role in society. **It is not <u>that Golden Age</u> *what interest* us now, but the preoccupation that underlied the critics' admiration:** (ICLE: SPM04019).

(9) If they sued their superiors there would be more problems for them. This would not happen with a professional army, at least not as frequently. In other words, **it is the <u>lack of respect</u> *what* differences (in this point) both systems.** (ICLE: SPM04028)

(10) As in many other plays of this 17th century, appearances and reality turn to be the thematical center of most of them. Middleton and Rowley's 'The changeling' is also another example of this contrast. Perhaps, **it is <u>this play</u> *the one which* shows more visibly this opposition.** (ICLE: SPAL1005)

(11) **Some years later, a similar uneasiness led Dickens to attack the utili-
      tarian educational system in *Hard Times*. Significantly,** it was <u>in that
      time</u> *when* the utopian societies created by the early socialists appeared.
      (ICLE: SPM04019)

(12) The answer for this question is something open, anybody may have an
      opinion about it, and **it is precisely in** <u>this diversity</u> *where* **it falls the
      richness of freedom, a freedom, which should never be threatened by
      an intelligent use of censorship.** (ICLE: SPM10013)

(13) Until the last 30 years religion was the institution which moved the
      masses; it was compulsory to go to church, pray and do one's duty to
      God, but now, **it is** <u>the television</u> *which* **moves the society to accept the
      established systems.** (ICLE: SPM03024)

However, as can be seen in Table 3, both NSs and NNSs use some of the 'rare'
relatives (although the clearly wrong ones are exclusive to the NNSs). *That* and
which are the most frequently used pronouns, with a similar distribution in both
groups, and NNSs use *when* and *where* much more frequently than NSs. In addition, whereas only learners use *what*, the *zero pronoun* is only found in NS examples. Furthermore, NSs also show a more frequent use of *which*. Another 'rare'
example' found in the NS corpus is *upon which*, despite the fact that, according
to different standard descriptions such as Gómez-González (2000: 306) 'the *wh*
word cannot, or can scarcely, follow a preposition or longer sequence'.

Table 3: Relative pronouns used by NSs and NNs

	That	*Which*	*Who*	*When*	*Where*	*Zero*	*what*
NS %	54	22	18	1	1	5	0
NNS %	43	10	14	17	10	0	7

The Element In Focus (EIF)

Syntactic category. The highlighted element is realized by the same range of
categories in both corpora, namely, NP, PP, AdvP and Adverbial Clause of
time, as can be seen in Examples (14)–(17) below:

(14) a. Some months later they had to close the business as no bank would
          grant them any credit. Governmental institutions completely boycotted
          them by not giving them public advertising; let me remind you [that] **it
          is** <u>the advertising</u> **that enables newspapers to survive economically.**
          (ICLE: SPM04009)

      b. Scipion also shows understanding of Caligula and even goes out on
          behalf of the latter's quest. Caligula believes that. To make his people
          aware of this he decides to make them die and unhappy. **It is** <u>Cherea
          and Caesonia</u> **who show that the Emperor's logic is morally wrong.**
          (LOCNESS: 341BRSUR1)

(15) a. The sea was the birthplace of the first primitive organism, where all the organisms were descended from; and it is the main factor in climatic evolution. **It is <u>by sewage and petroliferous remains</u> from accidents that a lot of sea animals are dying.** (ICLE: SPM05009)

  b. It has the capabilities of being unsafe and expensive in the beginning, but once it is used, nuclear power is much better for the environment, for people's lives, and better for the economic gain of the United States. **It is <u>with innovations like this</u> that we move ahead in the world of energy.** (LOCNESS: 424USARGmrq)

(16) a. Edward II is immature, he learns about himself along the play. He goes from a childish way of acting to a more mature one when he is running to his destruction and **it is <u>then</u> when the audience begins to identify and understand.** (ICLE: SPM01020)

  b. It is shown that Clemanceau used to like defending widowers(???) and orphans, but **it is <u>only later</u> that he realizes he did not really care for these people but simply wanted to remain on the right side of the law.** (LOCNESS: 332BRSUR1)

(17) a. First of all, it is necessary this affirmation to be very clear: money is something more than a piece of paper. This is true from two points of view: Money in itself could never make men happy. **It is only <u>when man change it for material things, when he buys things</u>, when it has its real value.** (ICLE: SPM03042)

  b. Through the course of the play he is seen to turn away from religion as a way out and decides his actions for himself. **It is <u>when he decides the murder [of] the present king and queen (his mother)</u> that he seems most sure of himself.** (LOCNESS: 332BRSUR1)

Table 4 shows the frequency of the different categories that may realize the highlighted element in each corpus. The inter-group analysis reveals that NNSs underuse Adverbial Clauses of time, NPs and PPs, but overuse AdvPs. Nevertheless, the Independent Samples *t*-test reveals that the differences are statistically significant only in the case of NNSs' underuse of Adverbial Clauses ($t = 1.983$; $p \leq 0.05$) and NPs ($t = 2.658$; $p \leq 0.05$).

Table 4: EIF syntactic category in the NSs and NNSs corpora

EIF Category	Group	N Clefts	% clefts	Mean	Standard Dev.
Adverbial Clause of Time	NS	8	7.8%	0.02	0.175
	NNS	1-**	2.4%	0.00	0.063
AdvP	NS	4	3.9%	0.01	0.136
	NNS	9	21.4%	0.04	0.242
NP	NS	61	59.2%	0.19	0.696
	NNS	18-**	42.9%	0.07	0.339
PP	NS	30	29.1%	0.09	0.327
	NNS	14	33.3%	0.05	0.214

The intra-group analysis (Table 5) shows that NPs are the most frequent category in both groups, followed by PPs. However, the next in frequency are Adverbial Clauses of time followed by AdvPs in the case of NSs, while this order is reversed in the case of NNSs. Even though NSs and NNSs use the different categories with quite similar frequency, it seems that NNS use comes closer to the NS tendencies described in the literature (cf. Gómez González, 2000: 309).

Table 5: Frequency order of EIF syntactic category

	NS	NNS
1	NP (59.2%)	NP (42.9%)
2	PP (29.1%)	PP (33.3%)
3	Adverbial Cl. of time (7.8%)	AdvP (21.4%)
4	AdvP (3.9%)	Adverbial Cl. of time (2.4%)

Syntactic Function. The intergroup analysis (Table 6) shows that NNSs underuse all EIF functions. The Independent Samples *t*-test reveals that NNSs only underuse significantly those highlighted elements functioning as subjects ($t = 2.681$; $p \leq 0.05$). This result parallels their significant underuse of NPs.

Table 6: EIF syntactic category in the NSs and NNSs corpora

EIF function	Group	N clefts	Mean	Standard Deviation
Adjunct	NS	41 (39.8%)	0.13	0.486
	NNS	25 (59.5%)	0.10	0.403
Direct Obj.	NS	2 (1.9%)	0.00	0.056
	NNS	0 (0%)	0.00	0.000
Prepositional Compl.	NS	2 (1.9%)	0.01	0.079
	NNS	1 (2.4%)	0.00	0.063
Subject	NS	58-** (56.4%)	0.18	0.692
	NNS	16 (38.1%)	0.06	0.316

The intragroup analysis (Table 7) shows different frequency orders in the native and learner corpora. The subject function has been described as the most frequent function realized by the EIF (Collins, 1991: 56; Ward *et al.*, 2002: 1418) and the NSs results are in accordance with these descriptions. However, the NS corpus contains a very low number of EIFs functioning as DO (only a 1.9% of the total number), and the NNSs never highlight elements with this function, which is surprising since it appears as one of the most frequent functions of the EIF in the literature (Collins, 1991: 56; Ward *et al.*, 2002: 1418). Further research is needed to find out whether this particular outcome can be linked to the peculiarities of the use of *it*-clefts in a particular genre.

Table 7: Frequency order of EIF syntactic functions in the NS and NNS corpora

	NS	%	NNSs	%
1	Subject	56.4	Adjunct	59.5
2	Adjunct	39.8	Subject	38.1
3	Prep. Comp.	1.9	Prep. Comp.	2.4
4	Direct Object	1.9	Direct Object	0

Weight (expressed in number of words). The principle of end-weight establishes that longer and more complex constituents tend to occur late in the clause. This means that *it*-clefts are often used when the EIF is not especially heavy, while pseudo-clefts are generally chosen when the focused part is significantly long, i.e. they typically serve to highlight full VPs, finite content clauses and non-finite clauses (cf. Prince, 1978; Collins, 1991; Gómez-González, 2001; Lambrecht, 2001). Table 8 compares the weight of the EIF in the two corpora. Despite the fact that the weight principle is at work in the English language, the mean length of the focused element is higher in the NS group. The *t*-test reveals that this difference is statistically significant ($t = 2.411$; $p = 0.018$).

Table 8: EIF Mean Length (number of words) in the NS and NNS corpora

	EIF Mean Length	Standard Deviation
NS	4.660	4.0573
NNS	3.262	2.7235

This result is related to the fact that NSs highlight significantly more clauses than NNSs (Example 18, with 21 words), and use quite complex NPs and PPs as focused elements (Examples 19 and 20, with 16 and 11 words respectively):

(18)   When he was alone and dependent upon no one he was equal to his fellow man, **it was only <u>when man discovered the ability to co-operate with other men, to work together and thus found the basis of a civilization</u> did [that?] man's corruption begin, leading to social inequalities.** (LOCNESS: 369BRSUR2)

(19)   With time, politically, there is no segregation of races, or differences in the color of skin. **<u>It is only the remainder of a racist culture and the effects it has had on the black community</u> that linger on to keep the stereotypes alive.** (LOCNESS: 426USARG)

> (20)   We all judge each other and punish each other, after all it was man who
> invented [?] **It is because of this realization that we are always judg-
> ing each other that Clamence accepts absolute guilt.** (LOCNESS:
> 344BRSUR1)

The fact that the EIF is shorter in the learner corpus can be related to the claim made earlier that pseudoclefts (which are normally used when the EIF is especially long) are much more frequent than *it*-clefts in Spanish. However, there is no pseudocleft counterpart for examples such as the ones in (18) and (20), and, in many cases, the differences could be ascribed to the fact that learner language tends to be stylistically and syntactically less complex than native language.

6. Conclusion

Previous research has shown that the ALV is characterized by the learners' *overuse* and *underuse* of specific structures, and that clefts and other focus constructions are an explicit learning difficulty. The study of different learner varieties has shown that learners generally avoid marked structures to a significant extent, and tend to rely on the *safe* canonical SVO word order in English due to the combined effects of training and typological (un)markedness. This often leads to the overuse of structure-preserving constructions such as *it*-clefts (and extrapositions). While *it*-clefts have been claimed to be overused by German and Swedish learners, the present study shows that they are underrepresented in Spanish advanced learner writing.

Since our results indicate that Spanish learners underuse *it*-clefts, we could postulate that this might be due to the effects of transfer. It has been noted that learning difficulties may be ascribed to the existence of differences between the L1 and the L2, and there is evidence which suggests that clefting is not as frequent in Spanish as in English due to the word order features of Spanish. However, previous studies carried out with L2-German learners report that they tend to overuse these constructions, which seems to suggest that the differences between NS and NNSs in our study cannot be ascribed to the different syntactic structures of English and Spanish.

Previous research has also reported the existence of important differences in the frequency of use of the different types of clefts in English and Spanish, with a notable predominance of *it*-clefts and reversed pseudo-clefts in native English writing, in contrast with a predominance of pseudoclefts in Spanish, which might also explain learners' non-native use. Furthermore, functional-typological approaches to clefts predict that canonical pseudo-clefts will be acquired first or more easily than the other two types, due to their lower degree of pragmatic markedness. This might imply that the underuse of *it*-clefts by

Spanish learners might be ascribed to their preference for other types of clefting. However, more research is obviously needed here, specifically the use of clefts in Spanish texts and in English texts written by Spanish learners.

It has been also noted that learners differ from NSs in the discourse functions assigned to *it*-clefts, which sometimes leads to unmotivated or untypical uses, and generates style problems. Spanish advanced learners' underuse of *contrast* may indicate that they prefer to use pseudoclefts and other lexical or syntactic means for this purpose. Furthermore, the predominance of *intensification* in both the native and the learner group might reject the idea that *it*-clefts are used exclusively to express contrast.

Another question has to do with the existence of differences between NSs and NNs in the length and syntactic features (category and function) of the highlighted element and in the use of the relative pronoun. Contrastive studies of the use of clefts in English and Spanish have shown that the two languages do not exhibit substantial differences regarding the range of morphosyntactic realizations and syntactic functions of the highlighted elements, as well as their frequencies. Our results confirm that Spanish learners have generally acquired the English pattern with the following exceptions: (1) they underuse NPs; (2) their writing shows differences in the use of relatives which sometimes lead to wrong or questionable clefts; (3) they underuse the Subject function; and (4) they use shorter EIFs.

The analysis we have carried out is only a first step, and the picture emerging can be expanded by studying other types of clefts as well as additional lexical and syntactic means of conveying focus. More qualitative analysis of learner text may also be fruitful with regard to understanding how learners cope with the different discourse functions of clefts. By taking these elements into account it should be possible to provide a detailed description of one important component of the learners' pragmatic abilities.

Notes

1.   This work is part of a wider project on Information Structure and other aspects of the Grammar-Discourse interface (grant numbers INCITE09 204 155 PR; FFI2010-19380), carried out within the framework of the international research group *SCIMITAR* (Santiago-Centred International Milieu for Interactional, Typological and Acquisitional Research) based at the University of Santiago de Compostela (Spain). Further research will focus on the other types of clefts and the full range of focus constructions.

2.   These are the main tendencies but there may be exceptions to the neat analysis proposed by Callies. In fact, Gómez-González (2001) found non-reversed pseudoclefts which have intonational prominence in initial position, and from that point of view could also be regarded to encode new information in initial and final position. Likewise, sometimes the syntactically highlighted element does not get intonational prominence, and therefore could be regarded as given information.

3.   Significant levels of overuse or underuse on the part of the learners are indicated by a plus or a minus sign followed by a double asterisk.

4.   In the following examples, bold type will be used to mark *It*-clefts and underlining will be used for the focused element.

5.   Wrong and questionable elements appear in italics.

References

Aston, G. (1995) Corpus evidence for norms of lexical collocation. In G. Cook and B. Seidl-hofer (eds), *Principle and Practice in Applied Linguistics: Studies in Honour of H. G. Widdowson*, 257–270. Oxford: Oxford University Press.

Barcelona-Sánchez, A. (1983) *El Orden de los Constituyentes en Inglés y Español.* Unpublished Ph.D. thesis, University of Granada.

Biber, D., Johansson, S., Leech, G., Conrad, S. and Finegan, E. (1999) *Longman Grammar of Spoken and Written English.* Harlow: Longman.

Boström Aronsson, M. (2001) *It*-clefts and pseudo-clefts in Swedish advanced learner English. *Moderna Språk*, 95 (1): 16–23.

Boström Aronsson, M. (2003) On clefts and information structure in Swedish EFL writing. In S. Granger and S. Petch-Tyson (eds), *Extending the Scope of Corpus-Based Research. New Applications, New Challenges*, 197–210. Amsterdam: Rodopi.

Bülow-Møller, A. (1996) Control from the background: A study of information structure in native and non-native discourse. *International Journal of Applied Linguistics* 6 (1): 21–42. http://dx.doi.org/10.1111/j.1473-4192.1996.tb00087.x

Butler, C. S. and Gonzálvez-García, F. (2005) Situating FDG in functional-cognitive space: an initial study. In J. L. Mackenzie and M. D. L. Á. Gómez-González (eds) *Studies in Functional Discourse Grammar* (Linguistic Insights, 26), 109–158. Berne: Peter Lang.

Callies, M. (2009) *Information Highlighting in Advanced Learner English.* Amsterdam: John Benjamins.

Callies, M. and Keller, W. (2008) The teaching and acquisition of focus constructions: An integrated approach to language awareness across the curriculum. *Language Awareness* 17 (3): 249–266.

Carroll, M., Murcia-Serra, J., Matorek, M. and Bendiscioli, A. (2000) The relevance of information organization to second language acquisition studies. The descriptive discourse of advanced adult learners of German. *Studies in Second Language Acquisition* 22 (3): 441–466. http://dx.doi.org/10.1017/S0272263100003065

Chafe, W. (1976) Givenness, contrastiveness, definiteness, subjects, topics and point of view. In C. Li (ed.) *Subject and Topic*, 25–56. New York: Academic Press.

Cobb, T. (2003) Analyzing late interlanguage with learner corpora: Québec replications of three European studies. *The Canadian Modern Language Review/La Revue canadienne des langues vivantes* 59 (3): 393–423.

Collins, P. C. (1991) *Cleft and Pseudo-Cleft Constructions in English.* London: Routledge. http://dx.doi.org/10.4324/9780203202463

Council of Europe (2001) *Common European Framework of Reference for Languages. Learning, Teaching, Assessment.* Cambridge: Cambridge University Press.

Di Tulio, Á. (1990) Sobre hendidas y pseudohendidas. *Revista de Lengua y Literatura 7*: 3–16.

Dik, S. (1980) Cleft and pseudo-cleft in functional grammar. In W. Zonneveld (ed.) *Linguistics in the Netherlands 1977–1979,* 26–43.Dordrecht: Foris.

Dryer, M. S. (1995) Frequency and pragmatically unmarked word order. In P. Downing and M. Noonan (eds) *Word Order in Discourse,* 105–135. Amsterdam: Benjamins.

Eckman, F. (1977) Markedness and the contrastive analysis hypothesis. *Language Learning* 27 (2): 315–330. http://dx.doi.org/10.1111/j.1467-1770.1977.tb00124.x

Eckman, F. (1996) A functional-typological approach to second language acquisition theory. In W. Ritchie and T. Bhatia (eds) *Handbook of Second Language Acquisition,* 195–211. San Diego, CA: Academic Press.

Gómez-González, M. D. L. Á. (2001) *The Theme–Topic Interface: Evidence from English.* Amsterdam: John Benjamins.

Gómez-González, M. D. L. Á. and Gonzálvez-García, F. (2005) On clefting in English and Spanish. In C. S. Butler, M. D. L. Á Gómez-González and S. M. Doval-Suárez (eds) *The Dynamics of Language Use,* 155–196. Amsterdam: Benjamins.

Gonzálvez-García, F. and Butler, C. S. (2006) Mapping functional-cognitive space. *Annual Review of Cognitive Linguistics* 4 (1): 39–96. http://dx.doi.org/10.1075/arcl.4.04gon

Granger, S. (1996) From CA to CIA and back: An integrated approach to computerized bilingual and learner corpora. In K. Aijmer, B. Altenberg and M. Johansson (eds) *Languages in Contrast. Text-based Cross-linguistic Studies. Lund Studies in English 88,* 37–51. Lund: Lund University Press.

Granger, S., Dagneaux, E. and Meunier. F. (2002) *The International Corpus of Learner English. Handbook and CD-ROM.* Louvain-la-Neuve: Presses Universitaires de Louvain.

Greenberg, J. H. (1966) Some universals of grammar with particular reference to the order of meaningful elements. In J. H. Greenberg (ed.) *Universals of Language* (2nd edn), 73–113. Cambridge, MA: MIT Press.

Gundel, J. K. (2008) Contrastive perspectives on cleft sentences. In M. D. L. Á. Gómez-González, J. L. Mackenzie and E. M. González Álvarez (eds) *Languages and Cultures in Contrast and Comparison,* 69–87. Amsterdam: Benjamins,

Halliday, M. A. K. (1967) Notes on transitivity and theme in English. *Journal of Linguistics* 3 (1): 37–81; 199–244.

Hannay, M. and Martínez-Caro, E. (2008) Thematic choice in the written English of advanced Spanish and Dutch learners. In G. Gilquin, S. Papp and B. Diez (eds) *Linking up Contrastive and Learner Corpus Research. Language and Computer Series 66,* 227–253. Amsterdam: Rodopi.

Hengeveld, K. and Mackenzie, J. L. (2008) *Functional Discourse Grammar: A Typologically-Based Theory of Language Structure.* Oxford: Oxford University Press. http://dx.doi.org/10.1093/acprof:oso/9780199278107.001.0001

Hinkel, E. (2002) *Second Language Writers' Text. Linguistic and Rhetorical Features.* Mahwah, NJ: Erlbaum.

Jespersen, O. (1949) *A Modern English Grammar on Historical Principles. Part VII: Syntax.* Copenhagen: Ejnar Munksgaard.

Klein, E. (1988) A contrastive analysis of focus phenomena in English and German on a functional basis and some implications for a didactic gramma. *Die Neueren Sprachen* 87 (4): 371–386.

Lambrecht, K. (1994) *Information Structure and Sentence Form.* Cambridge: Cambridge University Press.

Lambrecht, K. (2001) A framework for the analysis of cleft constructions. *Linguistics* 39 (3): 463–516.

Lube, K. (2000) *Information Structure and Word Order in the Advanced Learner Variety. An Empirical Study with Applications for the Foreign Language Classroom.* Hamburg: bod.Libri.

Martínez-Caro, E. (1999) *Gramática del Discurso: Foco y Énfasis en Inglés y Español.* Barcelona: PPU.

Martínez-Caro, E. (2007) Pragmatic frames, the thetic-categorical distinction and Spanish constituent order. *Alfa -Revista de Lingüística, São Paulo,* 51 (2): 119–142.

Moreno-Cabrera, J. C. (1999) Las funciones informativas: Las perífrasis de relativo y otras construcciones perifrásticas. In I. Bosque and V. Demonte (eds) *Gramática Descriptiva de la Lengua Española, Vol. 3: Entre la oración y el discurso – Morfología,* 4245–4302. Madrid: Espasa Calpe.

Pinedo, A. (2000) English clefts as discourse-pragmatic equivalents of Spanish post-verbal subjects. *Estudios Ingleses de la Universidad Complutense* 2000 (8): 127–151.

Plag, Ingo (1994) Avoidance in oral L2 production. The encoding of new referents in English interlanguage narratives. In G. Bartelt (ed.) *The Dynamics of Language Processing. Essays in Honor of Hans W. Dechert,* 33–44. Tübingen: Narr.

Prince, E. F. (1978) A comparison of *wh*-clefts and *it*-clefts in discourse. *Language* 54 (4): 883–906. http://dx.doi.org/10.2307/413238

Quirk, R., Greenbaum, S., Leech, G. and Svartvik, J. (1985) *A Comprehensive Grammar of the English Language.* London: Longman.

Rowley-Jolivet, E. and Carter-Thomas, S. (2005) Genre awareness and rhetorical appropriacy: Manipulation of information structure by NS and NNS scientists in the international conference setting. *English for Specific Purposes* 24 (1): 41–64. http://dx.doi.org/10.1016/j.esp.2003.09.003

Schachter, J. and Rutherford, W. (1979). Discourse function and language transfer. *Working Papers in Bilingualism* 19: 1–12.

Siewierska, A. (1994) Word order and linearization. In R. E. Asher and J. M. Y. Simpson (eds) *The Encyclopedia of Language and Linguistics* (vol. 9), 4993–4999. Oxford: Pergamon Press.

Singleton, D., and Lengyel, Z. (1995) *The Age Factor in Second Language Acquisition. A Critical Look at the Critical Period Hypothesis.* Clevedon: Adelaide.

Sornicola, R. (1994) Topic, focus, and word order. In R. E. Asher and J. M. Y. Simpson (eds) *The Encyclopedia of Language and Linguistics* (vol. 9), 4633–4640. Oxford: Pergamon Press.

Stutterheim, C. von. (2003) Linguistic structure and information organisation: The case of very advanced learners. In S. H. Foster-Cohen and S. Pekarek-Doehler (eds) *EUROSLA Yearbook,* 183–206. Amsterdam: John Benjamins.

Sornicola, R. (1994) Topic, focus, and word order. In R. E. Asher and J. M. Y. Simpson (eds) *The Encyclopedia of Language and Linguistics* (vol. 9), 4633–4640. Oxford: Pergamon Press.

Thompson, S. (1978) Modern English from a typological point of view: Some implications of the function of word order. *Linguistische Berichte* 54: 19–35.

Trévise, A. (1986) Is it transferable, topicalization? In E. Kellerman and M. Sharwood Smith (eds) *Crosslinguistic Influence in Second Language Acquisition?,* 173–185. Oxford: Pergamon.

Van Valin, R. D., Jr. and La Polla, R. J. (1997) *Syntax: Structure, Meaning and Function.* Cambridge: Cambridge University Press.

Ward, G., Birner, B. and Huddleston, R. (2002) Information packaging. In R. Huddleston and G. K. Pullum (eds) *The Cambridge Grammar of the English Language,* 1363–1443. Cambridge: Cambridge University Press.

White, L. and Genesee, F. (1996) How native is near-native? The issue of ultimate attainment in adult second language acquisition. *Second Language Research* 12 (3): 233–265. http://dx.doi.org/10.1177/026765839601200301

8 Annotating thematic features in English and Spanish: A contrastive corpus-based study

Jorge Arús, Julia Lavid and Lara Moratón

In this paper we present the preliminary results of an empirical study designed to test contrastive features of the category of Theme in English and Spanish through corpus analysis and manual annotation. Using as our theoretical basis the more general features of the model of thematization proposed in Lavid *et al.* (2010), the study describes the different steps of the methodology used, starting with the selection of the corpus used as a 'training suite', followed by the design of the annotation scheme, and ending with a discussion of the results of two annotation experiments carried out so far to test the reproducibility of the annotation scheme. It is expected that the work reported in this paper has a theoretical impact on the area of contrastive corpus studies and serves as the basis for the (semi)-automatic annotation of thematic features in larger bilingual corpora.

1. Introduction

The study of the linguistic category of Theme from a cross-linguistic perspective has attracted the attention of a number of scholars in the functional linguistic community, given its relevance not only for clausal analysis (Rose, 2001) but also for its impact on discourse organization (Lavid, 1998, 2000a, 2000b, to mention a few).[1] However, to date, there are no studies which investigate the potential of human-coded corpus annotation as a tool to test theoretical aspects of this complex linguistic category in a contrastive manner. As part of a larger research effort within the framework of the CONTRANOT project,[2] in this paper we investigate how certain theoretical issues concerning the semantic definition and the structural delimitation of Theme can be tested through contrastive corpus annotation.

Our methodology is based on a number of steps, borrowed from the standard methodologies used in the computational community, but adapting them for the purpose of testing certain theoretical aspects of the category of Theme in English and Spanish. These steps are explained in detail in the following sections, and are summarized in the Methodology section.

The chapter is organized as follows: Section 2 discusses the problems which arise when applying the standard definition of Theme to the analysis of the Spanish clause, and describes the solutions adopted in this study, based on the theoretical model of thematization proposed in Lavid *et al.* (2010a). Section 3 outlines the methodology followed in our research, specifically describing the corpus selected for the annotation experiments (3.1), the annotation scheme used for testing Theme contrastively in English and Spanish (3.2) and the two annotation experiments designed to test the reproducibility of the annotation scheme, with a discussion of the cases with the poorest agreement among annotators (3.3). Finally, Section 4 provides a summary and some concluding remarks, as well as some pointers to the future.

2. Delimiting Theme in English and Spanish

The standard definition of the category of Theme in the Systemic-Functional Linguistics (SFL) literature is the following: 'The Theme is the element which serves as the point of departure of the message; it is that which locates and orients the clause within its context' (Halliday and Matthiessen, 2004: 64). As stated in Arús (2007, 2010), this definition represents an important improvement over the one available in the first two editions of Halliday and Matthiessen's *Introduction to Functional Grammar* (IFG), in that it no longer alludes to the concept of 'aboutness', which at the time led to a great deal of misunderstanding about the nature of this textual category, notably outside systemic circles (see also Fawcett, 2007: 24 on this issue).

A basic example of Theme is provided in (1), where the highlighted *Everybody* functions as point of departure of the clause. The Spanish translation of (1), below in (2), in turn shows that the standard definition of Theme is in principle applicable to Spanish, *Todo el mundo* ('everybody') being in this case the thematized constituent.

(1)   **Everybody** is having fun
(2)   ***Todo el mundo*** *se está divirtiendo*

Although Examples (1) and (2) seem to suggest that the standard definition of Theme is valid for both English and Spanish, examples where language-specific problems arise are frequent. This is epitomized by realizations such as (3), where a decision has to be made as to whether the Process *llegaron* is the clausal Theme or if this is a clause with unrealized Subject Theme. This is an extremely important issue, since Spanish, as the rest of Romance languages but French, is considered a pro-drop language (Arnaiz, 1997: 48), which results in clause-initial pronominal Subjects constantly being left out in unmarked processes. Either option, i.e., unrealized Subject as elided Theme or Process as Theme, is problematic in light of the existing characterization of Theme. If the unrealized Subject is the Theme, 'the element which serves as point of departure', as stated in the standard definition, is not actually present, which is in itself quite paradoxical, if not contradictory. On the other hand, if the Process is taken to be the Theme, then the fact that the elided Subject is in some way present in the verbal inflection – third person plural *-aron* in (3) – seems to suggest that by considering the Process as Theme we are in fact including the Subject in the Theme. This is not really a problem, since Theme is identified as being realized by 'the first group or phrase that has some function in the experiential structure of the clause' (Halliday and Matthiessen, 2004: 66), and the Process is one and only one experiential element. However, the question arises of what to do in cases such as (4), where the third person plural inflection, *–an,* is part of the Finite, and the Finite is not supposed to have thematic status by itself. As Halliday and Matthiessen say, referring to English yes/no questions, 'since that [the Finite operator] is not an element in the experiential structure of the clause, the Theme extends over the following Subject' (2004: 76). We could then think that, as the Finite *Han* in (4) is not an experiential element, the Theme should extend over the Predicator *llegado*. However, the following consideration should be taken into account before making a decision: could the presence of the inflection referring to the Subject suffice to consider the Finite as Theme, or should the Theme be extended to the Predicator?

> (3)   *Llegaron los primeros*
>   [they] arrived the first
> (4)   *Han llegado los primeros*
>   [they] have arrived the first

As we can see from the discussion above, establishing the *semantic* delimitation of Theme goes hand in hand with establishing its *structural* delimitation, i.e., its boundaries. One does not need to look at Theme cross-linguistically to run into difficulties concerning the boundaries of Theme. Different systemic authors have provided alternative views on this issue;

Berry (1989), for instance, considers the Theme everything that goes before the verb in the clause, whereas Ravelli (1995) speaks of the difficulties to establish the thematic extent. Not even the initial status of Theme can be taken for granted; Fawcett follows Rose (2001) to claim that:

> *[T]here is no necessary connection between 'coming early in the clause' and 'realizing a thematic meaning' - and it is clear that no linguist - and especially no functional linguist - should infer too readily that the set of phenomena that have the characteristic of occurring early in the clause in English have a corresponding generalized meaning at the level of semantics. (Fawcett, 2007: 8)*

As discussed elsewhere (e.g., Arús, 2010; Lavid, 2010; Lavid *et al.*, 2010a), concerning the unrealized-Theme vs. Process-as-Theme choice, we opt for the latter, by which we align ourselves with authors such as Taboada (1995) and McCabe and Alonso (2002). An important reason for not considering the unrealized pronoun as Theme, besides the aforementioned paradox it would entail, is the existence in Spanish of examples such as (5), where the Subject *algunos* ('some') follows the verb *Dicen* ('say'), Process ^ Subject being a fairly common sequence in Spanish. This clearly shows that when the Subject is not present there is no reason to assume that if it had been present it would have been in thematic position. It seems sensible, therefore, to assign thematic status to the first realized element, whether Process or participant. When any of these elements is preceded by a Circumstance, the experiential Theme includes both the Circumstance and the first element from nuclear transitivity, as in (6) below, where *Before the meeting* is a Circumstance, and the Theme extends to, and includes *everybody*.

(5)   *Dicen algunos que es mejor...*
      Say   some   that it is better...
      Some say that it is better...

(6)   **Before the meeting, everybody** was glad to hear the good news

The question remains open, however, as to what to do about the verbal inflection and how to integrate its presence in a theoretically sound model of Theme. As proposed in Lavid *et al.* (2010a), we have found it necessary to (a) create several layers of analysis, and (b) break up the Theme.[3] At the most general level of analysis is the *Thematic Field*, which we define as the '[c]omplex functional zone in clause-initial position serving a variety of clausal and discourse functions' (Lavid *et al.*, 2010a: 299). This rather general definition allows us to consider, within the Thematic Field, all sort of textual and interpersonal meanings, as well as Circumstances, preceding the first experiential element of nuclear transitivity,[4] as well as to defer the identification of the thematic climax, and therefore its end, to a lower stage of analysis.[5] In an unproblematic example such as (6) above, the thematic field would be *Before the meeting, everybody*. In an example starting with textual (*But*) and interpersonal (*surprisingly*) elements, such as (7), the Thematic Field is longer, as shown:

(7)

But, surprisingly, before the meeting everybody	*was glad to hear the news*
Thematic Field	*Rhematic field*

The Thematic Field consists of up to two parts, the *Inner Thematic Field* (ITF), made up by the 'elements from the experiential structure of the clause' (including Circumstances) and an optional *Outer Thematic Field* (OTF), or the 'elements which surround and complete the Inner Thematic Field', i.e., textual and interpersonal ones (Lavid *et al.*, 2010a: 299, 302).[6] The example in (7), above, is reproduced as (8), below, with the specification of ITF and OTF. The inclusion of the Circumstance within the ITF reflects the fact that, although these elements do not belong to nuclear transitivity, they are still part of the experiential structure.

(8)

But, surprisingly,	*before the meeting everybody*	*was glad to hear the news*
OTF	ITF	
Thematic Field		

The OTF consists then of any textual and interpersonal Themes that may precede the ITF. Based on the standard definitions of these two categories in *IFG*, for Lavid *et al.* (2010a: 209-302) Textual Themes are elements which 'are instrumental in the creation of the logical connections in the text, such as linkers, binders, and other textual markers', whereas Interpersonal Themes are 'those elements which express the attitude and the evaluation of the speaker with respect to his/her message, including those expressing modality and polarity'.

The ITF, in turn, has an obligatory element, the *Thematic Head*, and one or more thematic *PreHeads* which, although not really optional, as we will see in due course, are not always present. The Thematic Head is defined as the 'first element with a function in the experiential configuration of the clause which is more central to the unfolding of the text by allowing the tracking of the discourse participants' (Lavid *et al.*, 2010a: 299). This excludes Circumstances, so in (8) above, the Thematic Head is *everybody*, whereas the Circumstance *before the meeting* is the PreHead, which is 'typically realised by *Circumstantial* elements which do not exhaust the thematic potential of the clause' (Lavid *et al.*, 2010a: 301).[7] The analysis reflecting the internal structures of the OTF and the ITF is as shown in (9):

(9)

But,	*surprisingly,*	*before the meeting*	*everybody*	*was glad to hear the news*
Textual Theme	Interpersonal Theme	PreHead	Thematic Head	Rhematic Field
OTF		ITF		
Thematic Field				

Going back to Spanish, Example (10) illustrates a process with a very simple thematic structure, consisting only of the Thematic Head, whereas (11) shows a process from our corpus of newspaper commentaries with a complex ITF.

(10)

El profesor	*comenzó la lección*
Thematic Head	Rhematic field
Thematic Field	

   'The teacher   started the lesson'

(11)

De hecho	*hasta 1954, cuando construyeron la carretera entre Río de Janeiro y Santos,*	*el principal acceso a Paraty*	*era marítimo*
Adjunct	Circumstance	Participant	
PreHead		Head	
Inner Thematic field			Rhematic field

In fact, until 1954, when the road from Rio de Janeiro to Santos was built, the main access to Paraty was by sea.

(12)

Se	*hall-*	*-a*	*ahora ante un proceso de expansión internacional*
'*se*' CLITIC	Find	3PSG. PRES. IND.	
PreHead		Head	
Thematic Field			Rhematic Field

   It finds itself in the face of an international expansion process

The key elements in our analysis that explain thematic choices in a language like Spanish are the PreHead and the Thematic Head. Example (12) shows a process with a number of specific traits of the Spanish language. The clause starts with the *se* marker typical of middle processes. When this clitic appears in thematic position, it is a PreHead, as it is part of the experiential structure (it is part of the middle process *hallarse* ['find oneself']), yet it cannot qualify for Thematic Head because it is not a participant (see Lavid *et al.*, 2010a: 114-118). Although *se* is part of the verb, the first real element from nuclear transitivity to appear in the process is *halla*, but not all of it has the same thematic force. The part which allows the tracking of participants and contributes to the cohesive unfolding of the text is the inflection *–a*, which textually fulfils a similar role to *(s)he* in English. That is why the non-inflectional part of the verb, i.e., *hall-*, is also a PreHead, whereas the inflection is the Thematic Head.

Example (12) quite clearly illustrates the advantage of breaking up the standard ideational Theme into PreHead and Thematic Head, as we can now easily account for the thematic structure of the no longer problematic *han llegado los primeros*, which we now analyse in (13), with the inflection *–an* as Thematic Head and the non-inflectional part of the verb preceding it, i.e., the form *h-*, as PreHead. We thus solve the problem of the extent of the Theme when a process starts with a Finite ^ Predicator sequence. Having identified the Thematic Head as the nuclear element in the ITF, the presence of such an element marks the end of the Theme. Finally, in (12) and (13) we can see why the PreHead, although not an obligatory element, is not always really an optional element: when the verb is in thematic position, as in these two examples, the PreHead has to be present, as it is the non-inflectional part of the verb. In fact, the only PreHeads than can be added to, or removed from, a process without substantial semantic change are certain Circumstances.

(13)

H-	-an	*llegado los primeros*
PreHead	Thematic Head	
Thematic Field		Rhematic Field

3. Methodology

To carry out the research presented here, we followed a number of steps:

(a) Selecting the corpus. This step involves the compilation of those texts to create what is known as the 'training corpus' on which the annotations will be hand-coded both by human experts and by trained annotators.

(b) Delimiting the category to be annotated and its features, as described in Section 2 above.

(c) Designing the annotation scheme and guidelines. This involves instantiating all or part of the features of the selected theoretical model and developing a core and an extended tagset to be used in the process of annotating the training corpus.

(d) Performing annotation experiments on some fragment of the training corpus, in order to determine the feasibility both of the instantiation and the annotator manual.

(e) Measuring the results of the annotations by comparing the degree of agreement between the annotators' decisions. This step also involves deciding which measures are appropriate, how they should be applied, and determining the level of agreement which will be considered satisfactory. Here our goal is to identify all relevant phenomena, test the theory instantiation, and hence validate the underlying theory, investigating the cases of poor agreement.

3.1. Selecting the corpus

Our training corpus consists of a selection of comparable newspaper texts in English and Spanish belonging to two genres – news reports and commentaries. The selection of these texts as our training corpus is motivated by two main factors: (1) their online availability (Hauser, 2001: 291, 292) the fact that they were subject to a previous contrastive analysis (Lavid *et al.*, 2010) using categories from the model of thematization that we want to test in this study. Both reports and commentaries were extracted from online press editions (British press for English, press from Spain for Spanish). The total number of clauses and words are specified in Tables 1 and 2:

Table 1: The English corpus

ENGLISH	# CLAUSES	# WORDS
REPORTS	325	8743
COMMENTARIES	576	13583
TOTAL	901	22326

Table 2: The Spanish corpus

SPANISH	# CLAUSES	# WORDS
REPORTS	111	3338
COMMENTARIES	111	3453
TOTAL	222	6791

The research presented in Lavid *et al.* (2010b) shows that these two genres do show different thematic features in their textual unfolding. These differences concern (a) the experiential roles selected as Thematic Head – e.g., much higher presence of Sayer as Theme in news reports vs. relative preference for Carrier as Head in news commentaries; and (b) the semantic nature of the nominals realizing the Thematic Head characterizing each genre – tendency for concrete nouns referring to individuals, group of people or institutions in news reports vs. higher frequency of abstract nouns in news commentaries; and (c) the internal structure of the Nominal Groups as Thematic Heads – more complex in commentaries than in reports (see Lavid *et al.*, 2010b: 90 for interpretations of these contrasts). In the present work, however, our main concern is not the thematic contrasts between these two newspaper genres but, as established in the introduction, the delimitation of thematic categories for later validation.

3.2. Designing the annotation scheme

Our next step in this study was to design the annotation scheme and guidelines which would allow us to test the theoretical model of thematization, partially described in Section 1 above.[8] An annotation scheme is, according to Leech 'the document describing and explaining the scheme of analysis employed for the annotations' (Leech, 1997: 6). The main challenges in the creation of our annotation scheme were: (a) the identification and definition of the thematic categories to include as part of the core annotation scheme; and (b) the creation of an extended annotation scheme that would help annotators overcome the difficulties posed by the shortcomings of the core annotation scheme.

Tables 3 and 4 show the core tagsets for English and Spanish, respectively, based on the theoretical model outlined in Section 1. It may seem *prima facie* surprising that, after all our efforts to find and define thematic categories that would cover the notion of Theme cross-linguistically, we finally decided to create a different tagset for each language. The reason is that the annotation scheme is going to be the reference for the annotators and, once each thematic category had been identified and defined, we found it more useful for the annotators to be provided with additional information, notably concerning specific realizations. Once realizations come into the fore, language-specific tagsets are unavoidable. Thus, in Table 3 we can see a reference to existential *there* in English as Thematic Head, whereas the tagset in Table 4 refers to the Spanish clitic *se*.

Table 3: Core tagset for Theme types in English

Annotation layer	Thematic field	Description
Unit		Main clause
Core annotation scheme		
Tags:	TH (Thematic Head)	First nuclear constituent (Participant or Process, not Circumstantial) in main clause, or 'There' in Existential clauses.
	PreHead	Any Circumstantial element and/or Finite element preceding the Thematic Head.

| | Textual Theme | Elements which are instrumental in the creation of the logical connections in the text, such as linkers, binders and other textual markers. |
| | Interpersonal Theme | Elements which express the attitude and the evaluation of the speaker with respect to his/her message, such as Vocatives and Modal Adjuncts, including mood and comment adjuncts |

Table 4: Core Tagset for Theme Types in Spanish

Annotation layer	Thematic field	Description
Unit		Main clause
Core annotation scheme		
Tags:	TH (Thematic Head)	First nuclear element (not circumstantial) in main clause, realized by either lexical or morphological means.
	PreHead	Elements preceding the Thematic Head, including: Circumstantials, pronominal 'se', lexical part of Verbal Group.
	Textual Theme	Elements which are instrumental in the creation of the logical connections in the text, such as linkers, binders and other textual markers.
	Interpersonal Theme	Elements which express the attitude and the evaluation of the speaker with respect to his/her message.

On the basis of these core tagsets, we designed two annotation experiments to test the feasibility of the proposed annotation schemes. Given the intrinsic complexity of tagging semantic categories – as opposed, for instance, to POS (Part-Of-Speech) tagging, we did not expect the core annotation schemes for Theme to be final. The annotation experiments were conceived as a probe to find out what was lacking in the core schemes with a view to the design of the extended schemes.

3.3. Annotation experiments

In order to test the annotation scheme, two experiments were conducted. The first one used three human experts with substantial training (namely two linguists and one PhD student in linguistics) who tagged 34 clauses from a randomly-chosen English text from our corpus, and 20 clauses from an English text, also randomly selected, for all the categories in the core annotation scheme, i.e., Thematic Head, PreHead, Textual Theme and Interpersonal Theme.[9] The main purpose of this experiment was to measure the reproducibility of our annotation scheme and, eventually, its stability by having the same annotators tag the same texts. The annotators were given the texts already divided into clause complexes, as shown in Table 5, below. In our research on Theme, we decided to start by looking at this textual category only in the clause complex, to make things easier. Once the thematic categories under scrutiny are stable enough, we will move to the (simple) clause, the 'central processing unit in the lexicogrammar' (Halliday and Matthiessen, 2004: 10). Table 5 shows an extract from the English text annotated in this study. The clauses shown are already tagged by the three annotators for PreHead – in the experiment, of course, none of the annotators could see the others' responses; what we see in Table 5 is a compilation of the three annotators' responses. The annotators were asked to select and to insert in the column under PreHead the chunk of text they thought would correspond to such a thematic element.

Table 5: Annotation exercise on PreHead in English

#	TEXT	Annotator 1	Annotator 2	Annotator 3
		PreH	PreH	PreH
1	The most immediate result of the arrest warrant issued for Sudanese President Omar Hassan al-Bashir by the International Criminal Court last month was the expulsion of most aid agencies from the country.			
2	But this global focus on Sudan's Darfur region, though justified, has overshadowed an even more vital issue: sustaining the quest for a broader peace in all of Sudan.			
3	What is most needed now is to build an international consensus on a strategy to implement fully the 2005 Comprehensive Peace Agreement (CPA) for Sudan.			What i-
4	The CPA ended Africa's longest civil war, which had left behind over two million dead.			
5	That agreement not only contains benchmarks that should lead to self-determination for Sudan's South;			
6	it also spells out a democratization process in Sudan itself.			
7	After all, the oppressive nature of the regime in Khartoum is at the root of the many conflicts that have torn the country apart.			

8	If the government in Khartoum persists in undermining the reform process and derailing the referendum on self-determination promised for the South in January 2011, a return to full-scale civil war, with calamitous consequences for the peoples of Sudan and the entire region, is a real possibility.	If the government in Khartoum … January 2011	If the government in Khartoum … January 2011	If the government in Khartoum … January 2011

After the annotation exercise, agreements and disagreements were quantified, as shown in Table 6, where the figures indicate the number of clauses on which the annotators agree, and then statistically measured to find out about the significance, or not, of the agreement among the three experts. For this, we used *Krippendorff's alpha*, 'a reliability coefficient developed to measure the agreement between observers, coders, judges, raters, or measuring instruments, [which] emerged in the field of content analysis but is widely applicable wherever two or more methods of processing data are applied to the same set of objects, units of analysis, or items and the question is how much they agree' (Krippendorff, 2007: 1).

Table 6: Annotator agreement for thematic categories (experts)

English (34 clauses)			
Category	**3 annotators agree**	**2 annotators agree**	**No agreement**
Thematic Head	29	4	1
PreHead	30	3	1
Textual Theme	27	7	0
Spanish (20 clauses)			
Thematic Head	15	4	1
PreHead	16	3	1
Interpersonal Theme	19	1	0
Textual Theme	20	0	0

A look at Table 6 reveals that total agreement was the norm, although never, except for Textual Theme in Spanish, without flaw. In fact, some categories show high degrees of unreliability, mostly if we consider that for such a small number of sentences there are occasions when the three annotators disagreed. Krippendorff's alpha confirms this: on a scale from 0 (least reliable agreement) to 1 (most reliable agreement), all categories, except for Textual Theme scored closer to 0 than to 1. This pointed to a need for reworking the definitions in our annotation scheme, but, before doing so, we wanted: (a) a corroboration of the results obtained in this experiment; and (b) to answer the question of whether the significant amount of training effort used in the first experiment could be reduced, i.e., whether the use of the annotation scheme as a guide in the annotation process makes linguistic training unnecessary.

With this two-fold purpose, we conducted a second experiment. On this occasion, the annotators were 18 Spanish students of English Linguistics with no prior annotation training and provided only with minimal instruction on Theme. The texts on which they worked contained a roughly similar number of clauses to those in the experiment with experts, and the annotation activities were the same as before. Table 7 shows the results of their annotations. We have grouped the results into 6 columns, ranging from total agreement ('all agree') to no agreement ('none agree'), with partial agreements expressed by the in-between columns. These indicate agreement among two to five students, six to nine, ten to thirteen and fourteen to seventeen. As in Table 6, above, the figures in the cells indicate the number of sentences on which annotators (i.e., students) agree.

Table 7: Annotator agreement for thematic categories (students)

English (33 clauses)						
Category	All agree	14–17	10–13	6–9	2–5	None agree
Thematic Head	6	20	4	3	0	0
PreHead	18	6	9	0	0	0
Interpersonal Theme	13	10	10	0	0	0
Theme Textual	4	9	16	4	0	0
Spanish (16 clauses)						
Thematic Head	2	8	3	3	0	0
PreHead	3	6	5	2	0	0
Interpersonal Theme	8	6	0	2	0	0
Textual Theme	1	1	8	6	0	0

The range of agreement is much more varied here than in Table 6, given the substantially higher number of annotators, and their lack of thematic training resulted in lower reliability coefficients for the tested categories: note that only in one of the categories, English PreHead (18/33), was there total agreement in more than 50% of the clauses, and in all but two categories, English PreHead and Interpersonal Theme, we find clauses on which only ≤ 50% of students agree, notably 6/16 clauses in Spanish Textual Theme. Also note that it makes sense that we found no case of 2–5 or no agreement, because the limited number of participants in each clause virtually precludes the combinatory possibilities necessary for such disagreement among 18 students.

An interesting fact was that several students seemed to confuse PreHead and Textual Theme, as illustrated by (14), where Textual Theme *but* was repeatedly analysed as PreHead, and, conversely, by (15), where PreHead *If ... 2011* was on several occasions chosen as Textual Theme. The same phenomenon was observed in Spanish. This could very well be pointing to a terminological overload, as the Textual Theme, the same as the Interpersonal Theme, occurs in Pre-ITF position.

> (14) **But** this global focus on Sudan's Darfur region, though justified, has over-shadowed an even more vital issue: sustaining the quest for a broader peace in all of Sudan.

> (15) **If the government in Khartoum persists in undermining the reform process and derailing the referendum on self-determination promised for the South in January 2011**, a return to full-scale civil war, with calamitous consequences for the peoples of Sudan and the entire region, is a real possibility.

Another interesting finding was that students occasionally – and this seems to be a problem derived from the lack of training – were at a loss concerning where they should be looking for the thematic elements. Such was the case with (16), where several students had problems discerning *For it should be pointed out* as the main clause, with textual Theme *For* and Thematic Head *it*.

> (16) For it should be pointed out that when the great earthquake occurred, the city's name was not La Antigua Guatemala but Santiago de los Caballeros de Goathemala, graced with the title of 'Very Noble and Very Loyal City', it was one of the oldest and richest metropolises in Spanish America, and as the capital of a Captaincy General, it was the most important city between Lima and Mexico City.

The findings just mentioned have allowed us to draw some preliminary conclusions concerning not only the design of the annotation scheme but also the design of the activities carried out to test the scheme. The task of annotating examples taken directly from the corpus may be too hard for non-trained annotators, which means that at the beginning this task should be simplified as much as possible, e.g., by highlighting the main clause or even by using contrived or selected examples and, once the thematic categories seem reproducible and stable, moving on to the corpus as it is. The terminological overload evinced by the students' confusion between PreHead and OTF makes us think that future experiments with students should avoid testing all the categories in the same session. Devoting one session to testing Thematic Head and PreHead and another one to textual and interpersonal Theme, i.e., the OTF, will most likely improve the rate of agreement.

In any case, it was clear from the experiment with expert annotators that the categories in the annotation scheme needed redefining or extending. In that light, we created an extended annotation scheme where the thematic categories contained not only a definition but also a specification of the possible realizations for each one of them in English and in Spanish. Table 8 below shows the extended tagset for Thematic Head with illustrative examples.

Table 8: Extended tagset for Thematic Head

Thematic Head:
(English)
(a) First nuclear constituent (participant or Process) in main clause.
Realizations:
        Participant:
                Noun Group
E.g., **the cat** *is on the mat;* **Peter** *is at home;* **she** *saw him yesterday*
                Clause (non-finite)
E.g., **Eating** *is vital;* **to live** *is to die*
                Clause (*that-*)
E.g., **that he refused to do it** *worried me*

        Process:
                Verbal Group (command)
E.g., **Eat** *your soup!*
                Verbal Group (finite, preceded by circumstantial pre-Head)
E.g., *On the table* **stood** *a lamp*

 (b) *There* in existential clauses.
Realization:
        There
E.g., **There** *were three people waiting for the bus*
(Spanish)
First nuclear element (participant or process) in main clause, realized by either lexical or morphological means.

Realizations:
        Participant:
                Noun Group
E.g., **El gato** *está en la alfombra;* **Pedro** *está en casa;* **yo** *sí la vi;* **Le** *pareció poco apropiado*
                Se clitic (impersonal, passive, reflexive, reciprocal, *le*-allomorph)
E.g., **Se** *está muy bien aquí,* **Se** *venden libros;* **Se** *insultaron sin piedad;* **se** *lo di ayer*
NOTE: Cf. *Se* **me** *cayó,* where *se* is part of the Verbal Group *caerse* and is, therefore, pre-Head (it fulfils no participant role).
                Clause (non-finite)
E.g., **Corriendo** *no se consigue nada;* **nadar** *me aburre*
                Clause (*que*)
E.g., **que me digas eso** *significa que no me has entendido*
                Verbal inflection (verbal base is pre-Head; both together, ITF)
E.g., *Teng-***o** *frío; ayer v-***i** *a María*
Process:
                Verbal Group (command)
E.g., **Ten** *cuidado!*

Once new experiments are performed and the annotation scheme proves to be reliable, we will embark on an annotation campaign by members of the research group using the tags of that scheme. The annotation campaign will use coding software, i.e., two coding tools being presently tested so as to see which lends itself better to the annotation of such an abstract concept as Theme – as well as the other linguistic categories covered by CONTRANOT: the UAM's Corpus Tool (O'Donnell, 2010), a potentially very useful tool for the kind of annotation carried out by our group, as it is specifically designed to support SFL-based annotation; and the UCAT Coding Tool (University of Pittsburg, 2010), which offers powerful resources for automatic annotation and data analysis.

Although the annotation campaign will take place once the annotation schemes are reliable, this does not mean that annotating the texts will be an easy task, yet the reproducibility of the scheme and the linguistic experience of the annotators should yield satisfactory results. Even less easy will be an eventual further step which currently falls beyond the scope of CONTRANOT but which has to be contemplated as a natural follow-up to the work being done: the development of a semi-automatic annotation programme for Theme, i.e., annotation automatically done by a tagging programme, which is then manually edited by experts. At this point it is not realistic to think of fully automatic tagging for Theme systems. As Matthiessen points out 'probably for the majority of [linguistic] systems – it is not yet possible to carry out automatic analysis: computational analysis tools cannot yet cope with the combination of rich analysis and a flow of registerially unrestricted text' (2006: 141). Even semi-automatic annotation should be expected to require a good deal of editing, given the complexity of this category.

4. Summary and concluding remarks

In this chapter we have explored how certain theoretical issues concerning the semantic definition and the structural delimitation of Theme can be tested through contrastive corpus annotation. Using as our theoretical basis the model of thematization proposed in Lavid *et al.* (2010a), we have described a methodology to test the proposed categories empirically. This methodology, borrowed from the standard ones used in the computational community, consists of a number of steps, starting with the selection of the corpus used as 'training suite', followed by the design of the annotation scheme, with a specification of the core and the extended tagset, and the two annotation experiments carried out so far to test the reproducibility of the annotation scheme.

As pending tasks, we have referred to the need for further tests and evaluation of the extended annotation scheme for a final tune-up, all this with a view to performing an annotation campaign by members of the CONTRANOT project. This campaign has been presented as the final stage of our ongoing project but by no means as the end of our work on annotation for Theme, as future projects should see us engaging in: (a) the expansion of the annotation campaign to other genres; and (b) the development of (semi)automatic annotation systems for Theme.

Before embarking on the development of computerized annotation systems, we need to adapt the linguistic descriptions in our annotation scheme to a machine-readable format that allows (semi)automatic tagging. As said above, there is a long way between the creation of a stable and reproducible annotation scheme and the development of a semi-automatic – let alone automatic – annotation system. The challenge is up for grabs and we expect to rise to it sooner rather than later.

Notes

1.   We would like to thank the anonymous reviewers of this paper for their insightful comments on an earlier draft. Any remaining mistakes are the authors' own.

2.   The CONTRANOT project is financed by the Spanish Ministry of Science and Innovation under the I+D Research Projects Programme (reference number FFI2008-03384). Julia Lavid, as team leader, Jorge Arús, as member of the research team, and Lara Moratón, as doctoral student, gratefully acknowledge the support provided by Spanish Ministry and also the BSCH-UCM grant awarded for the work reported in this paper.

3.   In our description, we propose using the model of thematization put forward for Spanish by Lavid *et al.* (2010), since it offers a wide range of options to cover most of the features displayed by the phenomenon of thematisation both in English and in Spanish. Note, however, that not all the thematic features described in Lavid *et al.* (2010a) are tested in the work reported in this paper. Our aim is to test some general features first, and then proceed with more specific ones.

4.   Following Matthiessen (1995), we take nuclear transitivity as concerning processes and participants and circumstantial transitivity as concerning circumstances.

5.   Once all the categories of analysis are defined, the actual thematic annotation will proceed in the opposite direction, as is to be expected, i.e. from the most specific to the most general units.

6.   *Surround* is not to be taken literally here, as the OTF actually precedes the ITF.

7.   Pending further research, we are for the time being treating all Circumstances as not exhausting the Thematic potential. We are aware, however, that some Circumstances seem to have a more relevant status in the unfolding of text, such as, for instance, *with such attitude* in (i) with such attitude, you'll achieve nothing.

8.   For a complete description of the model upon which this study is based see Chapter 5 of Lavid *et al.* (2010a).

9.   Interpersonal Theme was tagged only on the Spanish text due to an error in the administration of the experiment. This could not be redressed, as we found out about it later, when the annotators had already been exposed to the improved annotation scheme, which would have invalidated the results.

References

Arnaiz, A. R. (1997) An overview of the main word order characteristics of Romance. In A. Siewierska (ed.) *Constituent Order in the Languages of Europe*, 47–73. Berlin: Mouton de Gruyter.

Arús, J. (2010) On Theme in English and Spanish: A comparative study. In E. Swain (ed.) *Thresholds and Potentialities of Systemic Functional Linguistics: Multilingual, Multimodal and Other Specialised Discourses*, 23–48. Trieste: EUT.

Arús, J. (2007) On the aboutness of Theme. In M. Losada, P. Ron, S. Hernández and J. Casanova (eds) *Proceedings of the 30th International AEDEAN Conference* (CD-ROM).

Berry, M. (1989) Thematic options and success in writing. In C. Butler, R. Cardwell and J. Cardwell (eds) *Language and Literature: Theory and Practice. A Tribute to Walter Grauberg*, 62–80. Nottingham: University of Nottingham.

Fawcett, R. (2007) The many types of 'Theme' in English: their semantic systems and their functional syntax. Retrieved on 10 June 2010 from http://www.cardiff.ac.uk/chri/researchpapers/humanities/papers1-10/4Fawcett.pdf

Halliday, M. A. K. and Matthiessen, C. M. I. M. (2004) *Introduction to Functional Grammar*. London: Arnold.

Hausser, R. (2001) *Foundations of Computational Linguistics*. Berlin: Springer.

Krippendorff, K. (2007) Computing Krippendorff's Alpha-Reliability. Retrieved on 21 March 2010 from http://www.asc.upenn.edu/usr/krippendorff/webreliability.doc

Lavid, J. (2010) Contrasting choices in clause-initial position in English and Spanish: A corpus-based analysis. In E. Swain (ed.) *Thresholds and Potentialities of Systemic Functional Linguistics: Multilingual, Multimodal and Other Specialised Discourses*, 49–68. Trieste: EUT.

Lavid, J. (2000a) Contextual constraints on thematisation in written discourse: an empirical study. In P. Bonzon, M. Cavalcanti and R. Nossum (eds) *Formal Aspects of Context*, 37–47. Dordrecht/Boston/London: Kluwer Academic Publishers.

Lavid, J. (2000b) Text types, chaining strategies and Theme in a multilingual corpus: A cross-linguistic comparison for text generation. In J. Bregazzi, A. Downing, D. López and J. Neff (eds) *Estudios de Filología Inglesa: Homenaje a Jack White* 107–121. Madrid: Editorial Complutense.

Lavid, J. (1998) The relevance of corpus-based research for contrastive linguistics and computational studies: Thematisation as an example. In M. T. Turell and E. Vallduví (eds). *IV i V Jornades de corpus lingüistics (1996–1997): els corpus en la recerca semàntica i pragmàtica*, 117–140. Barcelona: Publicaciones del Instituto Universitario de Lingüística Aplicada, Universidad Pompeu Fabra.

Lavid, J., Arús, J. and Zamorano, J. R. (2010a) *Systemic-Functional Grammar of Spanish: A Contrastive Account with English*. London: Continuum.

Lavid, J., Arús, J. and Moratón, L. (2010b) Signalling genre through Theme: The case of news reports and commentaries. In L-M. Ho-Dac (ed.) *Proceedings of the 8th MAD: Signalling*

Text Organisation, 82–92. Moissac (France): University of Toulousse. Available at http://w3.workshop-mad2010.univ-tlse2.fr/MAD_files/papers/LavidArusMoraton.pdf

Leech, Geoffrey (1997) Introducing corpus annotation. In R. Garside, G. Leech and A. McEnery (eds) *Corpus Annotation: Linguistic Information from Computer Text Corpora*, 1–19. London: Longman.

Matthiessen, C. M. I. M. (1995) *Lexicogrammatical Cartography: English Systems.* Tokyo: International Language Science Publishers.

Matthiessen, Christian (2006) Frequency Profiles of some Basic Grammar Systems. In G. Thomson and S. Hunston (eds) *System and Corpus: Exploring Connections* 103–42. London: Equinox.

McCabe, A. and Alonso, I. (2001) Theme, transitivity and cognitive representation in Spanish and English written texts. In *CLAC* 7/2001. Retrieved on 10 February 2009 from http://www.ucm.es/info/circulo/no7/mccabe.htm

O'Donnell, M. (2010) *UAM Corpus Tool.* Available at http://www.wagsoft.com/CorpusTool/

Ravelli, L. J. (1995) A dynamic perspective: implications for metafunctional interaction and an understanding of Theme. In R. Hasan and P. H. Fries (eds) *On Subject and Theme*, 187–234. Amsterdam and Philadelphia, PA: Benjamins.

Rose, D. (2001) Some variation in Theme across languages. *Functions of Language* 8 (1): 109–145.

Taboada, M. (1995) *Theme Markedness in English and Spanish: A Systemic-Functional Approach.* Retrieved on 24 September 2010 from http://www.sfu.ca/~mtaboada/docs/taboada-theme-markedness.pdf

University of Pittsburg (2010) *UCAT Coding Tool.* Available at http://cat.ucsur.pi

9 Topic and topicality in text: A contrastive study of English and Spanish narrative texts

Raquel Hildalgo and Angela Downing

In this study, topic and topicality are explored through the application of a model of analysis to a bilingual sample of English and Spanish written narrative texts in equivalent genres. A Core Annotation Scheme and an Extended Annotation Scheme were designed to search for and test 'aboutness' topics, frame setting topics, and the information status of discourse referents. The texts are also analysed for classes of topics, namely NewTops, GivTops, SubTops and ResTops. All the Annotation categories were tested in both the Spanish and the English texts. The results of the analysis show that aboutness topics and frame-setting topics are cross-linguistically stable categories, although language-specific differences are found in the syntactic coding, for instance in how Spanish marks topicless sentences. The distribution of the information status of discourse referents is also stable, with minor differences between languages and genres. Likewise, the distribution of the different classes of topics tallies with the general principles of topic organization and information structure. A surprising result was to find a higher distribution of Resumed Topics than expected, suggesting that this class has a wider range of discourse functions than is usually noted in the literature.

1. Introduction

Topic and topicality are concepts that have received much attention in linguistics, and in particular, have interested linguists working within a functional approach to grammar (Dik, 1989, 1997), as well as those working with text and discourse (van Dijk, 1981; Goutsos, 1997). Topic has also been explored in its correlation with syntax (Gundel, 1985, 1988; Cadiot, 1992, Lambrecht, 1994) and in oral discourse (Maynard, 1980; Chafe, 1994; Morris, 1998; Hidalgo Downing, 2002, 2003; Downing, 2004). Less has been done, however, from a contrastive perspective and for annotation purposes (Dipper *et al.*, 1998).

In this article we aim to examine differences and similarities in topic organization between English and Spanish, and across genres. The general objective of the research is to provide contrastive analyses of English and Spanish texts based on the functional analysis of comparable and parallel samples in both languages.

In order to achieve this objective, two types of tasks have been performed: the selection and compilation of the sample, and the analysis of the texts. The sample includes narrative texts of various genres in English and Spanish (children's stories, press obituaries, biographies, press news and testimony) pertaining to equivalent genres but avoiding translations or bilingual versions of texts. In the second task, the notions of topic and topicality have been used to propose an Annotation Scheme that can be applied to the analysis of texts in the two languages.

In this article, we shall discuss the results obtained, examining the relative frequencies and distributions of topic and topicality in the compiled texts. The article is organized as follows: in Section 2 we introduce the theoretical framework, discussing the notions of topic and topicality and their application to annotation and text analysis; in Section 3 we briefly describe the data, and in Section 4 we discuss the frequencies and distribution of the categories of topicality in the two languages. The Conclusions and References close the article.

2. Theoretical framework

2.1. Topic and topicality

Despite the differences in the descriptions of topicality and its manifestation in languages, there is common agreement in defining topic in terms of *aboutness*, starting from the intuitive and common use of the term *topic* as 'what a book, a film, a conversation, is about' (Reinhart, 1982):

> The topic of a book, a film, etc., is taken to be what the book or film is about. So 'topic of' expresses the relation of being about. (Reinhart, 1982: 1)

> Topicality is a property of nominal participants of clauses. Propositional information, coded in state or event clauses, tends to be about some topical participant(s) in the state/event. (Givón, 1990: 740)

> The topic presents the entity about which the predication predicates something in the given setting. (Dik, 1989: 16)

It has also been noted that topic is articulated on at least three different levels: from high level to low level, topic can be said to be: (a) the global topic or discourse topic, that is, the topic of a book, an article, a speech etc.; (b) the topic of a paragraph or sequence; and (c) the local topic of a sentence, with regard to that of previous sentences (Reinhart, 1981; van Dijk, 1981). For instance Dik defines the discourse topic as 'a topic expression whose referent is pragmatically salient beyond the limit of a single sentence' (Dik, 1997: 119). This definition also attempts to capture the relation between the three levels of topic, in the sense that topicality is the progressive articulation, and construction of (in retrospect) a global topic through local topics. Those local topics are identified in the discourse as salient entities or participants:

> A discourse, taken in the wide sense of any kind of coherent text (a story, a monologue, a dialogue, a lecture etc.), is 'about' certain entities. For example, this book is 'about' Functional Grammar, this chapter is 'about' pragmatic functions, and this subsection is 'about' Topic and Topicality. For those entities about which a certain discourse imparts information we may use the term Discourse Topic. (Dik, 1997: 313–314)

However, topic does not necessarily manifest itself in language, hence the difficulty for the analyst to pin down topic at all three levels and for all types of discourse. The appearance of certain signals – titles, subtitles, paragraphs, images, meta-discursive expressions and word order – orient the reader/listener in the topic organization of the text. However, such means are not all and always present in texts, and they are not exclusive to marking topic organization, since linguistic expressions perform other functions as well.

2.2. Subdivisions of topic

Indeed, discourse topic and sentence topic are too general as categories to be applied to text analysis, since they do not reflect the way discourse is organized or articulated in different movements, such as maintenance through discourse, progression or shift. Following Dik's (1989, 1997) subdivision of topic categories, we can distinguish: New Topic, Given Topic, Sub-Topic and Resumed Topic.

We define a New Topic as a topic that is being introduced into the discourse (1997: 314). A number of constructions, which show a great degree of uniformity cross-linguistically, are used to introduce new topics into the discourse, such as existential and presentational constructions, post-verbal constituent positions, and metalinguistic expressions which announce the introduction of new topics into the discourse, as in (1):

(1)   I'm going to tell you a story about an elephant called Jumbo. (Dik, 1997: 315)

The second category, Given Topic, stands for a topic which has already been established in the discourse: 'a discourse topic has been introduced into the discourse as a New Topic, it can be treated as a Given Topic in the subsequent communication. Such a GivTop, however, must be kept alive through repeated references in subsequent predications. GivTop reflects the strategy of 'topic maintenance', through several mechanisms such as 'topic chains' (Dixon, 1972) or topic continuity (Givón, 1983; Goutsos, 1989; Dik, 1997: 316).

The intuitions behind these notions are basically the same: speakers apply strategies aimed at maintaining a GivTop as long as it is relevant to communication. Means for signalling topic continuity in languages are, as illustrated in (2), anaphoric reference through an anaphoric personal pronoun (*he*); a variant NP which specifies the class to which the GivTop belongs (*the man*) or provides a personal qualification of the GivTop (*the joker*); finally, through 'zero-anaphora' (deletion of an anaphoric element used with coordinated verbs having the same subject) (*He* wanted me to come ... and (0) gave me the impression, etc.).

> (2)   Yesterday I got a phone call from the tax inspector (NewTop). He/
> the man/the joker (GivTop) wanted me to come to his office, and he/0
> (GivTop) gave me the impression that I was in for some trouble. (Dik,
> 1997: 318).

The third category, Sub-Topic, may be defined as 'a Topic which may be legitimately inferred from a GivTop on the basis of our knowledge of what is normally the case in the world' (Dik, 1997: 324):

> (3)   John gave a party last week, but the music was awful.

Where 'given our knowledge that music is normally one of the features of a party, we may go on to talk about the music as if it had been introduced into the discourse' (Dik, 1997: 323) before. Interestingly, the SubTop relation works both ways, in the following sense: if some entity is treated as SubTop in the discourse, the interpreter will assume that it has some relation with the previous discourse:

> (4)   John and Bill came to see me yesterday. Fred's just bought a new car.
> (Dik, 1997: 324).

Even if 'Fred' has not been mentioned before in the preceding discourse, the addressee will assume that there is a connection between 'Fred' and 'John and Bill'.

When an entity has been introduced into the discourse, but has not been mentioned for some time, it may have to be revived or re-established in the form of a Resumed Topic. This will be particularly the case when several topics (say, A and B) have been introduced, and the discourse has continued for some time about A; resumption or return to B may need some strategy of re-establishment, such as the use of *now* (an indication of topic shift), with a strong form of anaphoric reference, as in (5):

> (5)   John had a brother Peter and a sister Mary … [considerable episode about Peter]. Now, John's sister Mary, who I mentioned before … (Dik, 1997: 325).

Topicality and information status of discourse referents are independent dimensions, yet interestingly related. In Dik's subdivisions of Topic, the four sub-categories – NewTop, GivTop, SubTop, ResTop – are not to be confused or identified with the information status of the referents of such topics.

In our view, subdivisions of Topic can be useful in text analysis because they can capture how a Discourse Topic is articulated through discourse, often prospectively. Therefore, we use the subdivisions of Topic to signal Topic Movements in discourse, that is, the topic progression or organization throughout a stretch of text. In that sense, there are two main topic movements: Topic continuity or maintenance (Given Topic) and Topic shift. Topic shift may be manifested through the introduction of a new topic (NewTop), but also, more frequently, through the introduction of topics related to the given Topic (SubTop) and through the re-introduction or re-establishment of an old given Topic (ResTop).

Dik's subdivions of Topic, in fact, do not reflect the information status of referents with the required precision. In our view, a ResTop is given from the point of view of accessibility (it is known to the reader/hearer) while it is being foregrounded again in the discourse. A SubTop, on the other hand, may be accessible for many different reasons, such as inference, genericity, situation, or givenness.

The advantage of using Dik's subdivisions of Topic is that they provide a fine-grained description of topic construction through text, while a single-category description (with aboutness topic only) fails to show how a discourse topic is built up through discourse. Consequently, we find it necessary to include a fine-grained description of topic organization through these sub-categories.

2.3. Information status of discourse referents

Information status has also received wide attention in linguistics, mostly among functional linguists (Lambrecht, 1994; Prince, 1981), and has been applied successfully to the annotation of texts (Dipper *et al.*, 2007). The information status of discourse referents refers to the degree of novelty of entities in discourse, in terms of the estimation of shared knowledge that speakers assess upon the hearer (Gundel, 1985; Prince, 1981). In this sense, information status is a separate and independent dimension to topicality. Topicality has to do with how a discourse topic (in Dik's sense) is articulated throughout discourse on different levels – through sequence or episode topics and ultimately in sentence topics – by maintaining a general common thread which brings it all together and makes the discourse coherent to the reader or hearer. In terms of linguistic form, sentence topics may be expressed formally through a constituent (usually the subject) while sequence and discourse topics may not be expressed at all.

The information status of discourse referents, on the other hand, also reflects discourse categories and therefore applies to all nominal and prepositional constituents in the clause (NPs and PPs), independently of the fact that those referents may be topics of the predication or not.

The most widespread taxonomy of information values of referents, with minor changes or deviations mostly in the terminology, is Prince's taxonomy of three categories: new, inferable, and given (Prince, 1981). However, we use 'accessible' instead of 'inferable' for the intermediate category. This is because inferable only captures the case where a referent is cognitively accessible via inference, even if it has not been mentioned in the text. Discourse referents, however, may be cognitively accessible for other reasons also: they are accessible because they are present in the situation or because they are part of general knowledge, or because they stand in a metonymic set relationship or part/whole relationship with a referent mentioned before (my father/his friend, etc.).

A discourse referent is said to be new if it has not been mentioned before and is not present in the discourse:

> (6)   John saw an elephant (new).

A discourse referent is said to be accessible if it has not been mentioned before, but the referent can be recovered because it is present in the physical situation (accessible via situation), it can be recovered through inference (accessible through inference), because it is general knowledge (accessible general) or because it is related to a previous known (given) referent (the tax inspector/his office).

A discourse referent is given when it has been mentioned before in the text, or because it is present in the situation (deictics, for instance). Given referents appear normally through common cohesive devices such as anaphora, exophoric reference (through personal and demonstrative pronouns).

Although topicality and information status are separate and independent dimensions, they are closely intertwined. A discourse topic is progressively constructed in the ongoing discourse, and this process is carried out through the successive introduction of the different discourse entities in the discourse; some of these entities will become sentence and even sequence topics. For these reasons, on the one hand, the examination of information values of discourse referents in itself is insufficient to determine the function of those referents in the overall organization of the text; on the other hand, the analysis of sentence topics without knowing the information values of referents only leaves gaps in the understanding of those referents that come to be topics.

A combination of the analysis of topicality (sentence topics) together with the information values of discourse referents should further our understanding of topical organization in text.

2.4. The Annotation Scheme

Grounded on the functional descriptions of topic and the taxonomy of information status presented above, we propose an Annotation Scheme to be used for the annotation of texts in the collected bilingual corpus. The Annotation Scheme is language independent. Here, the Scheme has been used for contrastive purposes. The notions should be applied equally to the two languages, English and Spanish, although the annotation may show similarities or differences between the two languages.

Previous work on information structure annotation (Dipper *et al.*, 2007) provides certain principles that should be taken into account when designing the Annotation Scheme and guidelines. For instance, the guidelines should rely on terms and concepts that are commonly agreed on and whose denotations are not disputable in general; they should also be easy to apply and should focus on the annotation of relevant information. The Scheme and Guidelines should cover both coarse and fine-grained annotations.

In the Annotation Scheme proposed and used in this study, two dimensions or layers of information structure have been selected: Topic (topicality) and Information Status (or givenness). Since the Annotation Scheme developed here has not considered focus, an account is given instead of a more detailed description of topicality in text.

The Core Annotation Scheme presents the basic categories used to describe topicality and information status in texts and reflects broad, coarse distinctions for the two pragmatic dimensions. The tags proposed for the Core Annotation Scheme reflect the basic categories needed to describe topicality in text: aboutness topic and frame-setting topic, for topicality; new, accessible and given, for information status or givenness.

As shown in previous sections, aboutness topic refers to the entity or set of entities about which the predication says something, and is close to the intuitive and common-sense notion of aboutness. For the analysis, we use sentence topic level, taking into account the following basic guidelines:

   i.   Each sentence may have one topic; and

   ii.   A sentence may have no more than one topic; but

   iii.   A sentence may have no topic at all. These are topicless sentences, that is, those which are event-oriented rather than topic-comment oriented. Another common term for this type of sentences is *thetic*. Often such sentences are existential or presentational constructions, impersonals, or sentences with post-verbal subjects.

   iv.   Topic often coincides with the subject; but

   v.   It may coincide with a verbal complement (direct or indirect object) in Topicalizing constructions such as left and right dislocations;

   vi.   Non-inflective clauses – for instance, infinitives or -ing forms – do not have topics, normally their subject is co-referential with the subject of the main clause.

   vii.   Subordinate finite clauses, such as adverbial or non-restrictive relative clauses, may have a topic (for instance the subject). The whole clause, however, may at the same time be a Frame Setting Topic.

   viii.   There are certain tests that can be used to determine the topic of the sentence: asking the question 'what about X?' or using a metadiscursive expression such as 'Talking about X,...' or trying to dislocate or topicalize the constituent: 'As for X, ...'.

   ix.   However, not all types of topic can be determined in this way. The above tests are useful for verifying Resumed Topics.

The Frame setting topic, on the other hand, presents a general domain or setting where the predication which follows holds, and often coincides with adverbial complements or clauses which appear at the beginning of the sentence. The frame setting topic is different from the *aboutness* topic: the former does not say 'what the sentence is about' and cannot be identified with a discourse entity (a pronoun or a NP). Other differences are the following: (i) a sentence may not have a frame setting topic at all (and this happens often); but (ii) a sentence may have more than one frame setting topic; in addition (iii) there is no necessarily direct relation between the frame setting topic and the predication.

The Core tagset for information status of discourse referents consists of the three basic categories: new, accessible, and given, which reflect the three degrees of novelty. As opposed to topic, which is applied to only one NP for each sentence, information status of discourse referents applies to all NPs and PPs in the clause.

The Extended Annotation Scheme is the optional part of the annotation, and attempts to capture fine-grained distinctions in topicality in order to better understand and represent topical progression in text. As explained in Section 2.2., the extended tagset for Topic attempts to capture the various movements which determine topic progression and construct coherence: NewTop, GivTop,

SubTop and ResTop. While NewTop reflects the basic strategy of introducing a new topic into the discourse, Given Topic reflects that of topic maintenance or continuity (usually marked through anaphoric pronouns or zero anaphora, but other means are also possible). Sub-Top signals the introduction of a topic related to the given topic, and ResTop the reintroduction of a given topic which has not been in the foreground in the previous sentence.

3. Data description

As described above, the first task of the research consists in the selection and compilation of a bilingual sample of English and Spanish texts, which correspond to equivalent genres in the two languages.

In order to ensure maximal similarity between the English and the Spanish texts, we have performed a genre and register analysis using a number of variables as they appear in Leckie-Tarry (1995). The various genre and register variables serve as a tool to compare texts in the two languages, with the aim of matching as many values as possible for each variable in the parallel texts. The sample compiled so far includes genres within the narrative text type: children's stories, press obituaries, biographies, press news items (accident and crime reports) and testimony. The latter genre, testimony, is a narrative usually written in the first person and in which the speaker accounts for an event in his or her life, or that of a close person (a relative). In this corpus, testimonies have been collected from survivors of the Holocaust and from the Spanish Civil War.

Table 1: Bilingual sample: English and Spanish narrative texts

Text Title	Language	Genre	Words	Clauses
1. Goldilocks	English	Children's story	678	59
2. Salamo Arouch	English	Obituary	312	18
3. Arafat	English	Biography	890	58
4. Fatal house fire	English	News	718	40
5. Voices of Holocaust	English	Testimony	214	26
6. Pulgarcita	Spanish	Children's story	326	46
7. Tomás Bata	Spanish	Obituary	376	30
8. Velázquez	Spanish	Biography	544	33
9. Siniestro electric	Spanish	News	634	43
10. Guerra civil	Spanish	Testimony	938	79

We have chosen written narrative texts with a clear narrative structure. In such texts, topicality can be best explored and may be more easily applicable than in other text types. Furthermore, as it is a parallel sample, we have tried to collect near-equivalent texts in the two languages, but not translations or the same text in the two languages.

4. Results and Discussion

We have applied the Core and Extended Schemes to the analysis of English and Spanish texts. The results of the analysis are displayed in Tables 2 to 5, followed by a discussion of our findings.

4.1. Aboutness topics in English and Spanish narrative texts

Table 2 shows the results of the text annotation for the number and distribution of aboutness topics in the English and Spanish texts. According to the analysis and annotation of the sample so far, the most frequent pattern is the canonical topic-comment sentence, which accounts for 88% to 97% of the clauses. Results are language independent and are very similar for English and Spanish. Topicless sentences, that is to say, the so-called *thetic* judgement, expressed in general in existential, presentational and event-oriented constructions, appear in 4% to 14% of the total number of clauses.

Table 2: Number of aboutness topics in English and Spanish narrative texts

Annotated Texts	Ab Top		No Topics		CAUSES	
	N°	%	N°	%	N°	%
Text 1 English Children's Story	52	88	7	12	59	100
Text 2 Spanish Children's Story	40	87	6	13	46	100
Text 3. English Obituary	16	89	2	11	18	100
Text 4. Spanish Obituary	29	96.5	1	3.5	30	100
Text 5. English news	37	92.5	3	7.5	40	100
Text 6. Spanish news	40	93	3	7	43	100
Text 7. English biography	56	96.5	2	3.5	58	100
Text 8. Spanish biography	33	100	0	0	33	100
Text 9. English Testimony	24	92.5	2	7.5	26	100
Text 10. Spanish Testimony	77	97.5	2	2.5	79	100

Table 3: Total Frequencies of aboutness topics in genres and languages

Annotated Texts	Ab Top		No Topics		CAUSES	
	N°	%	N°	%	N°	%
Genre 1 Children's Story	92	87.6	13	12.4	105	100
Genre 2 Obituary	45	93.8	3	6.3	48	100
Genre 3 News	77	92.8	6	7.2	83	100
Genre 4 Biography	89	97.8	2	2.2	91	100
Genre 5 Testimony	101	96.2	4	3.8	105	100

Annotated Texts	Ab Top		No Topics		CAUSES	
	N°	%	N°	%	N°	%
Language 1 Spanish	219	94.8	12	5.2	231	100
Language 2 English	185	92.0	16	8.0	201	100

Results are similar in the two languages (Table 3), but vary in texts 1, 2 and 3 (Table 2). In particular, the number of topicless clauses is slightly higher in the first two texts. Such variation may be due to genre; in particular, texts 1 and 2 are traditional children's stories, in which the authors use canonical presentational constructions to introduce characters into the story. Indeed, as shown in Table 3, children's stories have a higher occurrence of topicless sentences than any other genre.

In (7), the author starts with the traditional *había una vez*, the existential construction equivalent to the English *once upon a time* of (8):

> (7) Había una vez una mujer que deseaba un niño pero, como no sabía dónde encontrarlo, se fue a buscar a una hechicera y ésta le dio un grano de cebada.
> There was once a woman who wanted a child, but as she didn't know where to find one, she went to seek a witch, and she/the witch gave her a grain of barley.
>
> (8) Pero en el túnel había una golondrina que yacía muy enferma.
> But in the tunnel there was a swallow lying there very ill.

Topicless sentences may correspond to at least two different syntactic types with different discourse-pragmatic functions: presentational constructions and event-oriented sentences (also called *thetic* judgements). In the first type, a new discourse entity is introduced into the discourse. Such constructions often appear with existential predicates, such as *Había una vez* (7) or *había una golondrina* (8), the function being that of introducing into the discourse an entity which will become topic for at least one clause, such as *Había una golondrina que yacía muy enferma* and which may play a role, either primary (the protagonist of the story) or secondary, in the narrative. In the second type, the event-oriented sentence presents an event but does not predicate anything of a topic or discourse entity. This type of structure does not introduce a character into the story or a discourse entity which will play a role in the story, but, rather, presents or adds background information which may be relevant at a certain point of the narrative. For instance, in example (9), the discourse entity *la primavera* will not appear again in the story and is there to present background information as a whole event:

> (9) Pulgarcita cuidó de ella día y noche hasta que llegó la primavera.
> Tiny Thumb took care of her day and night until springtime.

Syntactically, Spanish topicless sentences typically have post-verbal subjects. This suggests that in Spanish, topicless sentences have a syntactic correlation with the post-verbal subject clause. However, information status of the referents may vary, and the NP may appear as definite (*la primavera*, being an accessible referent) or indefinite (*una flor, una golondrina*, as new referents), depending on its cognitive accessibility to the reader; for instance, *la primavera* represents general knowledge.

In the English texts, topicless sentences match the description of presentational constructions, which introduce new entities into the discourse; syntactically, they are expressed through existential predicates, such as (10) or (11):

> (10)   Once upon a time there were three bears who lived in a little house in a wood. Father Bear was a very big bear. Mother Bear was a medium-sized bear. Baby Bear was just a tiny, little bear.
>
> (11)   Now at the edge of the wood, in another little house, there lived a little girl. Her golden hair was so long that she could sit on it.

Note that the combined analysis of topicality and information status of discourse referents makes for a better understanding of how topic is organized and progresses throughout the text. The existential predicate, *there lived a little girl*, introduces the entity into the discourse (the information status of the referent *a girl* is new, and is marked as indefinite); in the following clause, the discourse referent is treated as known to the hearer and appears as topic of the sentence: *her golden hair was so long* ... This fact supports the view that NPs in presentational constructions such as *there lived a little girl* are not yet topics of the sentence: the discourse referent is new, in terms of degree of novelty, but the sentence does not predicate anything of a topic; it is topicless. However, the presentational construction allows precisely the NP (or an NP cognitively related) to appear as topic in the subsequent clause or clauses.

The second type of topicless sentence, the event-oriented or thetic judgement type, is also found in the English texts, although less frequently than in Spanish.

> (12)   (At 20 he was junior middleweight champion of the Balkans.) Then the Germans invaded, and Arouch and his family were sent to Auschwitz.

Then the GERmans invaded can be considered a topicless thetic sentence on the following grounds: The NP subject *the GERmans* is a Focus expression rather than a topic expression: The syllable *GER* receives tonic prominence (that is, it carries the main pitch movement, a jump in pitch and possibly extra stress), and the verb *invade* is used here as unaccusative. The whole event is in Focus and there is no presupposition such as *someone invaded* (Downing and

Locke, 2006: 242). The function of the sentence as a whole is frame-setting, that is, to add background information necessary at a certain point in the narrative. Furthermore, the tests for Aboutness topics do not apply: the sentence *the GERmans invaded* would not be a natural continuation to the announcement *Let me tell you something about The Germans*. We conclude that only the event structure (thetic) analysis is valid.

As shown in the examples taken from the texts, the discourse function of event-oriented sentences is similar in the two languages, although in Spanish there is a syntactic coding specialized in that function (post-verbal subject) while in English it is the combination of intonation and meaning in context which allows the thetic interpretation.

4.2. Aboutness and frame setting topics in English and Spanish narrative texts

Table 4 shows the distribution of types of topic, aboutness and frame setting topics, in the English and Spanish narrative texts. Aboutness topics are considerably more frequent than frame setting topics (66% to 96% in all texts); such a distribution tallies with the general principles of information structure and text coherence, since most clauses have a sentence topic (often the subject), whereas frame setting topics (usually a complement or an adverbial or participial clause) are optional elements which fulfil more peripheral syntactic functions. Table 5 shows that the distribution of aboutness and frame-setting topics is also quite stable across genres, although with a higher occurrence of frame-setting topics in biographies and obituaries.

Table 4: Aboutness and frame setting topics in English and Spanish narrative texts

Annotated Texts	Ab Top		No Topics		CAUSES	
	N°	%	N°	%	N°	%
Text 1 English Children's Story	52	94.5	3	5.5	55	100
Text 2 Spanish Children's Story	40	91	4	9	44	100
Text 3. English Obituary	16	67	8	33	24	100
Text 4. Spanish Obituary	29	88	4	12	33	100
Text 5. English news	37	92.5	3	7.5	40	100
Text 6. Spanish news	40	93	3	7	43	100
Text 7. English biography	56	89	7	11	63	100
Text 8. Spanish biography	30	75	10	25	40	100
Text 9. English Testimony	24	92	2	8	26	100
Text 10. Spanish Testimony	77	96	3	4	80	100

Table 5: Total frequencies of aboutness and frame setting topics per genre and language

Annotated Texts	Ab Top		No Topics		CAUSES	
	N°	%	N°	%	N°	%
Genre 1 Children's Story	92	92.9	7	7.1	99	100
Genre 2 Obituary	45	78.9	12	21.1	57	100
Genre 3 News	77	92.8	6	7.2	83	100
Genre 4 Biography	86	83.5	17	16.5	103	100
Genre 5 Testimony	101	95.3	5	4.7	106	100

Annotated Texts	Ab Top		No Topics		CAUSES	
	N°	%	N°	%	N°	%
Language 1 Spanish	216	90.0	24	10.0	240	100
Language 2 English	185	88.9	23	11.1	208	100

Frame-setting topics are similar in English and Spanish texts (Table 5); syntactically, they are expressed through adverbial complements and subordinate clauses and often appear in initial clause position, preceding the main predication. The syntactic form, the initial position and the similarity in the two languages, support the idea that frame-setting topics are linguistic expressions which 'frame' the main predication, introducing information which may be necessary in order to understand the main predication or to make the appropriate links with previous stretches of discourse. In the analysed texts, frame-setting topics often introduce adverbial clauses or expressions which connect narrative events in temporal terms, as italicized in (13)–(16):

(13)   *Now at the edge of the wood*, in another little house, there lived a little girl.

(14)   *On that very same morning*, before breakfast, Goldilocks went for a walk in the wood.

(15)   *Cuando los días fueron más luminosos*, la golondrina dijo a la pequeña que si quería ir
con ella.
When the days became brighter, the swallow asked the little girl if she would go away with her.

(16)   *Al escuchar aquellos comentarios*, el abejorro abandonó a la pequeña.
On hearing those comments, the bumble bee abandoned the little girl

The lowest percentage of frame setting topics appears in English testimony (2%), although very close to the Spanish (3%). This can be related to the features of the genre, testimony being a first person narrative, strongly focused on the 'speaker's topic' and written in first person, with no frame setting introducing the topic:

(17)   I went with these girls, they weren't really women, they were young girls.

(18)   So, from what I remember, nobody was over thirty. I never met anybody over thirty after that.

On the other hand, a higher presence of frame-setting topics is found in texts 3 (English obituary) and 8 (Spanish biography), where they amount to 33% and 25%, respectively, of the topics, which is a rather high rate compared to the other texts. These figures can be explained in terms of the genre, and to the way the author has constructed the text. Obituary and biography are very similar, because in both genres chronological information is important. The examples below are all of this kind.

(19)   *Al año siguiente, con 19 años, se casa con Juana Pacheco.*
         The following year, at the age of nineteen, he married Juana Pacheco.

(20)   *Entre 1617 y 1623 se desarrolla la etapa sevillana.*
         Between 1617 and 1623, his Sevillian period developed

(21)   *Born in Salonika in 1923,* Arouch was the son of a labourer.

(22)   During his two years at the concentration camp, he took on 210 opponents.

As shown in (19) to (22), the syntactic form and discourse functions coincide with those seen for the other texts; in these texts such topics frame the biographical narration by temporal ordering.

4.3. Analysis of information status of discourse referents

The results derived from annotation of the information status of discourse referents are shown in Table 6 and Table 7. According to these results, there is regularity in the distribution of the three basic categories (new, accessible, given) and across languages, with minor differences. The most regular pattern refers to the higher distribution of given referents in the two languages and in all the genres (Table 7); this group is always the most frequent and in all cases comprises over 49% of the totality of discourse referents (Table 7). These results are not striking and coincide with the general principles of information structure, where new information is progressively added to given information throughout discourse. If we compare languages (Table 7), the distribution is also similar, although there is a higher occurrence of new referents in Spanish (12% compared to 9% of English texts).

Table 6: Information status of discourse referents in English and Spanish narrative texts

Annotated Texts	New		Accessible		Given		TOTAL REFS	
	N	%	N	%	N	%	N	%
Text 1 Eng Children's Story	5	5.5	10	10.5	80	84	95	100
Text 2 Span Children's Story	12	17	9	12.5	50	70.5	71	100
Text 3. Eng Obituary	6	14	9	21.5	27	64.5	42	100
Text 4. Span Obituary	10	15.5	22	34.5	32	50	64	100
Text 5. Eng news	4	9	18	40.0	23	51	45	100
Text 6. Span news	8	16.5	17	35.5	23	48	48	100
Text 7. Eng biography	9	13	19	27.5	41	59.5	69	100
Text 8. Span biography	2	4.5	15	32.5	29	63	46	100
Text 9. Eng Testimony	4	10	6	15.5	29	74.5	39	100
Text 10. Span Testimony	9	9.5	14	15	70	75.5	93	100

Table 7: Total frequencies of information status of discourse referents per genre and language

Annotated Texts	New		Accessible		Given		TOTAL REFS	
	N	%	N	%	N	%	N	%
Genre 1 Children's Story	17	10.2	19	11.4	130	78.3	166	100
Genre 2 Obituary	16	15.1	31	29.2	59	55.7	106	100
Genre 3 News	12	12.9	35	37.6	46	49.5	93	100
Genre 4 Biography	11	9.6	34	29.6	70	60.9	115	100
Genre 5 Testimony	13	9.8	20	15.2	99	75.0	132	100

Annotated Texts	New		Accessible		Given		TOTAL REFS	
	N	%	N	%	N	%	N	%
Language 1 Spanish	41	12.7	77	23.9	204	63.4	322	100
Language 2 English	28	9.7	62	21.4	200	69.0	290	100

However, an interesting variation in the distribution of given referents is found across genres: in the press obituary of both languages, the frequency of given referents falls to 64% in English and 51% in Spanish, while accessible referents are higher on the scale, totalling 21% in English and up to 34% in the Spanish text.

These results show that within these general principles, where given referents are the most frequent, a certain degree of variation may be found within genres; variation is probably due to the specific features of the genre in terms of the number and distribution of discourse entities. In children's stories, there is a tendency towards repetition of the same discourse entities (characters in the story); in the press obituaries and news, the contrary occurs: the content of the text is somewhat synthesized in order to meet the space restrictions of a newspaper, and more discourse entities (entities related to the persona and life events of the main character) may be introduced within a relatively short text.

In the Spanish texts, most of the new referents appear in post-verbal positions and as indefinite NPs, often as direct or indirect objects, as non-topical constituents which may become topics in the following clause. Promotion of such non-topical constituents is the preferred device for topic introduction and consolidation: first introduce the referent as indefinite, *una mujer, un niño*, etc in (24), then it can subsequently become topic:

> (23)   Había una vez una mujer que deseaba un niño pero, como no sabía
>   dónde encontrarlo se fue a buscar a una hechicera y ésta le dio un grano
>   de cebada. La mujer plantó el grano y, en seguida, brotó una flor.
>   There was once a woman who wanted a child, but as she didn't know
>   where to find one, she went to seek a witch, and she/the witch gave her a
>   grain of barley. The woman planted the grain and immediately a flower
>   bloomed.

Once introduced, the referent may become topic of the next sentence, such as *se fue a buscar a una hechicera, y ésta le dio un grano de cebada*, but then not appear in the story again; or it may become topic of a whole sequence, such as the second paragraph starting with *la mujer*: *la mujer plantó el grano/encontró a una pequeña niña/la llamó Pulgarcita*.

New referents may also appear in pre-verbal positions, as topic and subject of the clause, introducing a new topic into the discourse:

> (24)   Un día, *un viejo sapo* entró por la ventana y mientras Pulgarcita dormía
>   en una cáscara de nuez se la llevó.
>   One day *an old frog* came in through the window and while Tiny Thumb
>   was asleep in a walnut shell, he ran off with her.

The introduction of the new topic is announced by 'un día', signalling the start of a new paragraph and therefore a topic shift (with topic introduction).

When comparing the two languages, the results show regularity in the higher frequency of given referents, but a significant difference in the distribution of new referents: in Spanish, the distribution of new referents is always higher, averaging 15% (14–16%), while in English it is lower (5%) or at least more sensitive to variation (14% in the obituary). Such variation may reflect a language-specific feature, where Spanish would allow for the expression of new entities, probably through flexible word order.

4.4. Classes of topics in English and Spanish narrative texts

In Tables 8 and 9 we show the frequencies of topic subdivisions in the narrative texts.

Table 8: Classes of topics in English and Spanish narrative texts

Annotated Texts	New Top		Sub Top		Giv Top		Res Top		TOTAL TOPS	
	N	%	N	%	N	%	N	%	N	%
Text 1 Eng Children's Story	6	9.5	5	8	33	52.5	19	30	63	100
Text 2 Span Children's Story	7	16	0	0	30	68	7	16	44	100
Text 3. Eng Obituary	1	3.5	6	20	17	56.5	6	20	30	100
Text 4. Span Obituary	3	12	3	12	15	60	4	16	25	100
Text 5. Eng news	7	17	15	36.5	8	19.5	11	27	41	100
Text 6. Span news	3	9	7	21	14	42.5	9	27.5	33	100
Text 7. Eng biography	1	2	13	28.5	24	52	8	17.5	46	100
Text 8. Span biography	1	3.5	9	33.5	11	41	6	22	27	100
Text 9. Eng Testimony	0	0	8	33	11	46	5	21	24	100
Text 10. Span Testimony	3	6	9	18.5	25	51	12	24.5	49	100

Table 9: Total frequencies of topics per genre and language

Annotated Texts	New Top		Sub Top		Giv Top		Res Top		TOTAL TOPS	
	N	%	N	%	N	%	N	%	N	%
Genre 1 Children's Story	13	12.1	5	4.7	63	58.9	26	24.3	107	100
Genre 2 Obituary	4	7.3	9	16.4	32	58.2	10	18.2	55	100
Genre 3 News	10	13.5	22	29.7	22	29.7	20	27.0	74	100
Genre 4 Biography	2	2.7	22	30.1	35	47.9	14	19.2	73	100
Genre 5 Testimony	3	4.1	17	23.3	36	49.3	17	23.3	73	100

Annotated Texts	New Top		Sub Top		Giv Top		Res Top		TOTAL TOPS	
	N	%	N	%	N	%	N	%	N	%
Language 1 Spanish	17	9.6	28	15.7	95	53.4	38	21.3	178	100
Language 2 English	15	7.4	47	23.0	93	45.6	49	24.0	204	100

Differences in topic subdivision frequencies show that several factors determine the shaping of topic progression according to genre conventions, and to the specificity of each language. In general, as shown in Table 8, Given Topics are the most frequent in narrative texts, suggesting that topic maintenance and the creation of topic chains articulate the progression of actions performed by characters in a story. At the opposite extreme, NewTopics are the least frequently used devices by authors of narratives, there being here, however, a difference between languages: in Spanish, NewTops are more frequent than in English (9.6% of New Topics in Spanish, compared to 7.4% in English, Table 9). Such an occurrence in Spanish has to do with constituent order; in particular, with the possibility of having post-verbal subjects marking NewTops. Finally, ResTops are, on the contrary, more frequent in

English (24%, Table 9), reflecting a language-specific preference for marking ResTops.

There are also interesting differences across genres (Table 9), with a lower frequency of Given Topics in news (29.7 %). New Topics, on the contrary, are more frequent in news and children's stories than in other genres (12–13%); at the opposite extreme, biographies and testimonies show lower occurrences of NewTops. Such variation shows that topic is organized differently according to genre conventions.

4.5. Given Topics

Given Topics form topical and referential chains, normally through anaphora; in Spanish, often through verbal agreement (zero anaphora):

(25)   María José Gutiérrez, trabajadora de un colegio situado justo enfrente de la residencia, fue una de las personas que dio la voz de alarma. 0 (GivTop) Estaba a punto de coger un taxi y 0 (GivTop) observó las primeras llamas. Muy afectada, ayer 0 (GivTop)) comentó que lo primero que 0 (GivTop) hizo fue llamar al teléfono municipal 010 «pero no me hicieron caso y me dijeron que llamara al 112».
María José Gutiérrez, a worker in a school just opposite the residence, was one of the people who raised the alarm. She [GivTop] was about to take a taxi and 0[GivTop] saw the first flames. Greatly affected, she [GivTop] said the first thing she [GivTop] did was to ring the municipal 010 number "but they took no notice and told me to ring 112."

It is the normal device used by authors to mark topic continuity in discourse. In narrative texts, Given Topics are particularly frequent since they are about a certain number of characters in the story. This feature is especially evident in children's stories, where often a limited number of characters are the main protagonists throughout the whole story.

In the news article, on the other hand, Given Topics also mark topic continuity, although there may be a higher number of discourse referents and different story foci. Given Topics expressed by lexical variation also show this cohesive device used by writers to construct referential chains and avoid lexical repetition:

(26)   Tomás Bata era uno de esos empresarios que dejan huella, nunca mejor dicho. El magnate de origen checo murió el pasado 1 de septiembre en un hospital de Toronto.
Thomas Bata was one of those businessmen who make their mark, for sure. The tycoon of Czech origin died last 1st of September in a hospital in Toronto.

(27)   La marca Bata es el símbolo de todo un imperio familiar. El negocio lo fundó su padre en 1894, en la ciudad de Zlin, en la antigua Checoslovaquia.

> The Bata make is the symbol of a whole family empire. The business was founded by his father in 1894, in the city of Zlin, in former Czechoslovakia.

(28)   Tomás Bata tomó las riendas de la compañía en 1932. El empresario tenía tan sólo 18 años.

> Thomas Bata took charge of the company in 1932. The businessman was only eighteen years old.

4.6. New Topics

New Topics are less frequent in all genres since other devices for topic introduction are preferred, such as introducing the referent as non-topical and then promoting it to topical position (thus becoming 'given' in terms of novelty status). However, New Topics, that is, constituents that appear in topical positions and that have not been previously introduced are also found. For instance, they are found as proper names and quantified NPs in news, often followed by complementation:

(29)   *María José Gutiérrez*, trabajadora de un colegio situado justo enfrente de la residencia, fue una de las personas que dio la voz de alarma.

(30)   *Jamie Hynds,* who lives across the street from the home, told the Courier Express newspaper that she was awakened at about 2:30 a.m. by a naked woman shouting for help.

(31)   *Ten people*, including nine members of one family, were killed in an early-morning house fire in Jefferson County on Thursday.

Indefinite specific NPs in subject position are also found as NewTops in news in the two languages:

(32)   But *state police and fire officials* increased the number of victims to 10 at a press conference Thursday afternoon.

(33)   *Un accidente de origen eléctrico* se confirma como la causa del incendio que el lunes causó seis muertos y trece heridos.

> *An accident of electrical origin* was confirmed as the cause of the fire which on Monday caused six deaths and thirteen injured.

In fact, these are typical devices of topic introduction and progression in news, where many discourse entities must be introduced within a relatively short text. Such devices account for the high frequency of NewTops (16% in the English news and 9% in the Spanish news) compared with other genres. Interestingly, children's stories also show a higher frequency of New-Tops than other genres; this has to do with the fact that stories introduce a number of discourse entities and secondary characters, which may play a role at certain points in the narrative. Lowest on the scale are two English texts, Testimony and Biography, while the Spanish equivalents are also relatively low compared to the other genres (2%); this fact would suggest that these genres are clearly oriented to the progression of events around one character or discourse topic.

4.7. Subordinate topics

Subordinate topics are the usual way of marking topics that are related to previous topics. In terms of information status, they may be accessible (via inference, situation or generis) or even given; they often include expressions that mark explicit relationship with previous topics. For instance in example (34) *the other two fights* connects with previous topics in the story:

(34)   During his (GivTop) two years at the concentration camp, he (GivTop) took on 210 opponents, of whom he (GivTop) beat 208. The other two fights (SubTop) were drawn.

For these reasons, SubTops are the preferred device used by writers to mark topic progression, shifting from one topic to another that is closely related. Rather than abrupt topic shift or introduction, this type allows the narrative to move and thus foreground different characters or entities in the story:

(35)   By 1945, all Arouch's male relatives (ResTop) had also been killed, his father (SubTop) for being too weak, his brother (SubTop) for refusing to pull out gold teeth from the bodies of the gassed.

That SubTops are related to previous topics is normally made explicit through several cohesive devices, such as possessive pronouns or complementation, as in the examples above. The frequency of SubTops is quite stable across the two languages and genres, accounting for the largest group after GivTops. Again, such results go along with the general principles of topic construction and progression throughout a text. However, some variation is also found here. Children's stories have considerably fewer SubTops than other genres, which would suggest a genre preference for a more hierarchical, traditional narrative style with large topical chains (the main protagonist) and secondary characters (introduced as NewTops) rather than topic-shifting.

4.8. Resumed topics

ResTops are more frequent than expected, mostly in English texts. This frequency suggests that ResTop may fulfil different functions in discourse, contributing to the topic shaping of the text. For instance, ResTops re-introduce a Topic which has been in the background (even for only one sentence), the general function of ResTop being then that of foregrounding a Topic:

(36)   Había una vez una mujer que deseaba un niño pero, como no sabía dónde encontrarlo, se fue a buscar a una hechicera y ésta le dio un grano de cebada. La mujer (Res Top) plantó el grano y, en seguida, brotó una flor.

> There was once a woman who wanted a child, but as she didn't know
> where to find one, she went to seek a witch, and she/the witch gave her a
> grain of barley. The woman [ResTop] planted the grain and immediately
> a flower bloomed.

This is the context usually described for ResTop, where a referent which was topic of previous sentences or sequences of the text is abandoned, while other referents come into the foreground. By ResTop, then, the topic returns to sentence topic. ResTops mark topic shift, or reintroduction of a previous topic. For this reason, the discourse referent(s) of ResTops are normally 'given' in terms of information status, because they represent characters or entities already known to the hearer. This also explains the fact that often they are expressed through definite lexical NPs, such as *la mujer*. Since ResTops mark switch-reference, they do not appear as short pronouns or zero anaphora, but often by repeating the name of the character. For instance, in the English story, ResTops are particularly frequent:

> (37)   Now at the edge of the wood, in another little house, there lived a little
> girl. Her golden hair (SubTop) was so long that she could sit on it. She
> (GivTop) was called Goldilocks. On that very same morning, before
> breakfast, Goldilocks (ResTop) went for a walk in the wood.

The numerous occurrences of ResTops respond, in part, to the genre of which the text is an instance. Stories for very young children tend to have a picture on every other page, at least, illustrating the events narrated in the text. ResTop may serve to call the reader's attention, or to mark a point of advance in the narrative, for instance, a new page with a new picture in children's stories. ResTops are also frequently found at the very end of the narrative, marking topic closure:

> (38)   La sede de la compañía está en Lausanne (Suiza). Bata Shoe (ResTop)
> tiene un museo en Toronto.
> The company's headquarters is in Lausanne (Switzerland). Bata Shoe has
> a museum in Toronto.

In Example (38) the author repeats the referent *Bata Shoe*, foregrounding the topic and giving it a conclusion as a way of synthesizing the global discourse topic. Similar functions of ResTops can be noted in children's stories, where authors repeat the names of the main character(s) in order to bring the story to its final closing:

> (39)   Si vienes conmigo, podrás elegir la flor que más te guste para vivir. Y así
> lo hizo; Pulgarcita [ResTop] se fue con la golondrina. Y en la flor que ella
> escogió para vivir, descubrió asombrada a un jovencito de su mismo tamaño.
> If you come with me you can choose the flower you like best to live in.

> And so she did; Tiny Thumb [ResTop] went away with the swallow. And in the flower that she chose to live in she was astonished to find a young man of her own size.
>
> (40)   When she (GivTop) saw the three bears she (GivTop) jumped off the bed in fright. She (GivTop) rushed to the window, (0Givtop) jumped outside and (0Givtop) ran away quickly into the wood. By the time the three bears (ResTop) reached the window, Goldilocks (ResTop) was out of sight. The three bears (ResTop) never saw her again.

The author of *Pulgarcita* and *Goldilocks* ends in a similar way; the final sequence, which presents the conclusion, foregrounds the protagonists of the stories again as the discourse topic of the whole text.

5. Conclusions

Topic and topicality have been explored here through the application of a model of analysis to a bilingual sample of English and Spanish narrative texts, pertaining to various genres, such as traditional children's stories, press obituaries and news, biographies and testimony. In our analysis, we have searched for 'aboutness' topics and frame setting topics, on the one hand, as well as for the information status of discourse referents; and, on the other, we have analysed the texts for classes of topics, such as NewTops, GivTops, SubTops and ResTops.

The results of the analysis show that aboutness topics and frame-setting topics are cross-linguistically stable categories which apply easily to narrative texts independently of the language, and display similar distributional frequencies. Language-specific differences are found in the syntactic coding, for instance in how Spanish marks topicless sentences. The distribution of information status of discourse referents is also stable, with minor differences between languages and among genres.

The distribution of the different classes of topics also tallies with the general principles of topic organization and information structure, where information is progressively added and text is constructed throughout temporal progression of one or more characters. This principle accounts for the highest frequency of Given Topics (marking topic continuity), Subordinate Topics (marking topic progression or shift) and the lowest for New Topics (topic introduction). A surprising result was to find a higher distribution of Resumed Topics than expected, suggesting that this class has a wider range of discourse functions than is usually accounted for in the literature.

References

Cadiot, P. (1992) Matching syntax and pragmatics: A typology of topic and topic-related constructions in spoken French. *Linguistics* 30 (1): 57–88. http://dx.doi.org/10.1515/ling.1992.30.1.57

Chafe, W. (1994) *Discourse, Consciousness and Time,* Chapter 10 (Discourse Topics). Chicago, IL and London: The University of Chicago Press.

Dik, S. C. (1989) *The Theory of Functional Grammar.* Dordrecht, Foris.

Dik, S. C. (1997) *The Theory of Functional Grammar.* Part II. Dordrecht, Foris.

Dipper, S., Götze, M. and Skopeteas, S. (2007) Information structure in cross-linguistic corpora: Annotation guidelines for phonology, morphology, syntax, semantics and information structure. *ISIS Working Papers of the SFB.* Universitätsverlag Potsdam.

Downing, A. (2004) Achieving coherence: Topicality, conceptualisations and action sequences in negotiating conflicting goals. *Revista Canaria de Estudios Ingleses* 49: 13–28.

Downing, A and Locke, P. (2006) *English Grammar. A University Course* (2nd edn). London and New York: Routledge.

Givón, T. (1990) *Syntax. A Functional Typological Introduction.* Volume II. Amsterdam: John Benjamins.

Goutsos, D. (1997) *Modeling Discourse Topic: Sequential Relations and Strategies in Expository Text.* Norwood, NJ: Ablex.

Gundel, J. (1985) Shared knowledge and topicality. *Journal of Pragmatics* 9 (1): 83–107. http://dx.doi.org/10.1016/0378-2166(85)90049-9

Gundel, J. (1988) Universals of topic-comment structure. In M. Hammond, E. A. Moravcsik and J. Wirth (eds) *Studies in Syntactic Typology,* 209–239. Amsterdam: John Benjamins.

Hidalgo Downing, R. (2002) Orden de palabras y conversación: la tematización sintáctica como introductor de temas discursivos. In J.L.Girón Alconchel *et al.* (eds) *Estudios ofrecidos al profesor J. J. Bustos Tovar,* 167–176. Madrid: Editorial Complutense.

Hidalgo Downing, R. (2003) *La tematización en el español hablado. Estudio discursivo sobre español peninsular.* Madrid: Gredos.

Lambrecht, K. (1994) *Information Structure and Sentence Form. Topic, Focus, and the Mental Representation of Discourse Referents.* Cambridge: Cambridge University Press.

Leckie-Tarry, H. (1995) *Language and Context: A Functional Linguistic Theory of Register.* London: Pinter.

Maynard, D. W. (1980) Placement of topic changes in conversation. *Semiotica* 30 (3–4): 263–290. http://dx.doi.org/10.1515/semi.1980.30.3-4.263

Morris, T. (1988) Topicity vs. thematicity: topic prominence in impromptu Spanish discourse. *Journal of Pragmatics* 29 (2): 193–203. http://dx.doi.org/10.1016/S0378-2166(97)00052-0

Prince, E. F. (1981) Toward a taxonomy of given-new information. In P. Cole (ed.) *Radical Pragmatics,* 223–255. New York: Academic Press.

Reinhart, T.(1982) Pragmatics and linguistics: An analysis of sentence topics *Philosophica* 27: 53–94.

van Dijk, T. A. (1981) Sentence topic and discourse topic. In T. A. van Dijk (ed.) *Studies in the Pragmatics of Discourse,* 177–193. Paris: Mouton.

10 Towards a comparison of cohesive reference in English and German: System and text

Kerstin Kunz and Erich Steiner

The present study is concerned with contrasts in cohesion between English and German, with a special focus on the investigation of cohesive reference. Employing system-based as well as corpus-based methods, we are adding a contrastive to the hitherto dominating monolingual perspectives. Methodologically, we are furthermore attempting to complement the pre-existing system-based accounts with an empirical text-based approach. The paper starts with an overview of different approaches to cohesion, situating and clarifying our own concepts. We then look in more detail at the conceptualizations of cohesive reference and its subcategories before discussing the cohesive resources systemically available in the two language systems for the creation of personal and demonstrative reference. We finally present some preliminary findings from our corpus-linguistic study. These not only test some initial hypotheses derived from the systemic comparison, but also reveal some interesting tendencies with respect to textual frequency and function in the two languages, the registers investigated, and in originals compared to translations. Our study aims at conceptual clarifications, systemic comparisons and some initial textual evidence that may be valuable for basic research as well as language teaching and translator training.

1. Comparing English and German: State of the art

Over the past decades, substantial insights have been gained in the area of contrastive research on English and German. However, the main methodological orientation of this work has been hermeneutic/descriptive and example-based, rather than empirical; it has been system- rather than text-based; and its focus has been on the linguistic levels of morphology, syntax, and to some extent lexis, rather than on text/discourse.

Level \ Methodology	1 — system-based model monolingual		2 — system-based model contrastive	3 — text-based model monolingual		4 — text-based model contrastive
A Lexis	✓ *Oxford English Dictionary, Webster's Dictionary*	✓ *Duden Wörterbuch der deutschen Sprache, Wahrig Deutsches Wörterbuch*	✓ *PONS dictionary, Langenscheidt Collins dictionary, Oxford Duden dictionary, EuroWordNet*	✓ *Collins COBUILD English Language Dictionary*	✓ GermaNet, DWDS	✓ multilingual terminologies in terminology-engineering and translation studies
B Grammar (clause / sentence)	✓ Quirk et al. (1985), Huddleston & Pullum (2002)	✓ *Duden Grammatik der deutschen Gegenwartssprache*, Eisenberg (³1994), Heidolf (1981), Engel (2004), Helbig & Buscha (2001) Zifonun et al. 1997	✓ Hawkins (1986), König & Gast (2007), Königs (2001)	✓ *Longman Grammar of Written and Spoken English* (Biber et al. 1999)	Ø	Ø Teich (2003)
C Text / Discourse (cohesion)	✓ Halliday & Hasan (1976), Brown & Yule (1983), de Beaugrande & Dressler (1981), Schubert (2008), Esser (2009)	✓ Linke / Nussbaumer / Portmann (⁴2001), Brinker (2005), Vater (²2001), Weinrich (1993)	Ø de Beaugrande and Dressler (1981), Doherty 2006, Fabricius-Hansen (1996, 1999, 2005)	Ø		Ø

Boxed (spanning B/C): Halliday & Matthiessen (2004) · Steiner & Ramm (1995), Steiner & Teich (2004), Steiner (2006)

Figure 1: Methodologies and levels

Figure 1 illustrates the different levels on which knowledge about languages can be represented, some basic methodologies, and relevant gaps in the state of the art for English and German. The existing and potential resources for the description and comparison of the two languages are aligned along the following three dimensions: methodology (system-based vs. text-based), language-orientation (monolingual vs. contrastive), and level (lexis vs. grammar vs. text/discourse). The references given in Figure 1 are pointers to relevant strands of research. Of the 12 types of research areas identified, our overall project identifies cells C2 and C4 as our proposed focus of work.[1]

In the available system-based studies, texts are employed as sources for examples only. They have their basis in (pre-existing) studies, lexical resources, grammars, linguistic theories, or sometimes in 'stylistics', depending on the level they focus on. Their coverage for English and German is quite extensive, although there is a gap in C2, that is, there does not appear to exist a system-based contrastive text-grammar English-German.

Text-based approaches differ from those in C1 and C2 in that they use texts as sources for examples as well as for frequencies of collocations. Their sources of knowledge are empirical, for example absolute or relative frequencies of cohesive phenomena. There are several significant gaps in coverage, of which we want to mainly address C4, that is, a text-based contrastive grammar of cohesion for the English-German contrastive pair.

By using a text corpus including aligned translational data for English and German we can benefit from several advantages of a text-based model: first, a broadened perspective in terms of range of phenomena of cohesion; second the possibility of discovering different functions of these resources in different contexts; and third the accessibility of frequencies of use of these resources as indicators of registers. Finally, a text-based approach can yield answers to questions of language contact, apparent in differences between originals and translations language internally, and in the influence of one language on the other in terms of interference/shining-through (cf. Thomason and Kaufmann, 1988; Teich, 2003; Siemund and Kintana, 2008; Matras, 2009).[2] We are furthermore hoping to contribute to empirical methodologies in linguistics in general. (For relevant discussions on the nature of linguistic data, cf. Haspelmath (2009) and other contributions in the same volume, as well as work of the former SFB 441 'Linguistic Data Structures' in Featherstone and Winkler (eds) (2009).)

2. Clarification: Concepts of cohesion

The purpose of this section is to provide a brief clarification of the concept of cohesion as used in the relevant literature.[3] We draw a distinction into perspectives by their main disciplinary and hence methodological and topical preferences, rather than by cultural research traditions or by object language. Accordingly, we distinguish attempts at modelling cohesion arising mainly out of: (1) philosophical; (2) rhetorical/stylistic; (3) psychological; or (4) linguistic orientations, and then focus on 'linguistic orientations', in turn differentiating them into 'grammar-based' perspectives and 'level-based' perspectives.

Among 'philosophical perspectives on cohesion' we subsume those assuming that beyond clause semantics there is something usually called 'coherence' within larger discourse segments. A prime example is Relevance Theory and its discussion of 'explicitness vs. implicitness of linguistic meaning' (cf. Carston, 2002: especially 15ff, 183ff and 222ff), which we have extensively discussed elsewhere (Hansen-Schirra *et al.*, 2007: 242ff): *Linguistic meaning* is the linguistic encoding itself. *What is said* is a propositional semantic representation, including referential instantiation and disambiguation, as well as some forms of 'pragmatic enrichment'. *What is meant* is the full utterance meaning including all sorts of pragmatic implicature. Part of the importance of Carston (2002) can be seen in the claim that there is a much wider gap between *linguistic meaning* and *what is said* than is commonly assumed, particularly in pragmatics. In terms of our discussion here, *what is meant* is the full range of factors to do with textuality, including coherence with context of situation and context of culture. *What is said* seems to cover lexicogrammatical encoding plus cohesion (in the sense of Halliday and Hasan, 1976) and *linguistic meaning* would be the full structural encoding plus its linguistic representations, but nothing more. There are, of course, other philosophically-based approaches, notably 'Discourse Representation Theory' (Asher, 1993; Kamp and Reyle, 1993; Lascarides and Asher, 1993) with its modelling of discourse segments and relations between them, earlier 'Situation Semantics' and its introduction of notions of 'completeness and coherence' of discourse situations and situation types (Barwise and Perry, 1983), and still others. What characterizes these philosophical traditions as far as their treatment of 'cohesion/coherence' is concerned is that they do not make a distinction between the two (cf. Kamp and Reyle, 1993: 53), because their main interest is in what the main types of 'cohesion/coherence' are, rather than on the question of by what kind of linguistic/textual clue they get signalled.

Attempts at modelling aspects of cohesion within rhetorical and/or stylistic traditions are nowadays represented in Rhetorical Structure Theory and similar approaches (cf. Mann and Thompson (1987) and elsewhere, but also Grimes, 1975). They represent further developments of aspects of classical rhetoric, especially in the area of inter-clausal coherence relations. Quite often, they provide interfaces to functional theories of language (Matthiessen and Thompson, 1988; Taboada and Mann, 2006). 'Coherence' within these approaches usually means 'coherence by inter-clausal logical/semantic relations', regardless of whether or not these are openly signalled grammatically and/or by cohesive devices, although both types of signalling are acknowledged and – to some extent – kept apart.

Modelling attempts within psychological (or processing) orientations come in a range of varieties, of which we only mention 'Centering Theory' here (Grosz *et al.*, 1995; Taboada and Zabala, 2008), although names like Ariel, Lambrecht, Gundel and others would also come to mind: these types of modelling attempt to identify cognitive mechanisms of creating 'coherence' between discourse segments, usually by the hearer, and sometimes also by the text producer. They specifically attempt to model the combined function of linguistic information structure and syntax in triggering such coherence.

The three orientations just characterized display certain preferences as to phenomena to be studied and as to preferred methodologies. As for the phenomena:

- philosophical orientations have their foci on co-reference and logical (rather than otherwise 'adverbial') coherence relations, occasionally extended by considerations of temporal relationships and by accounts of 'speech acts' and 'felicity conditions'
- rhetorical/stylistic orientations have their foci on a wider set of coherence relations than philosophical orientations
- psychological orientations privilege mechanisms of access, as well as economy, in processing discourse, and how these are related to linguistic mechanisms or triggers.

As for the main methodologies:

- philosophical orientations show a preference for tracing implications, entailments, presuppositions of utterances
- rhetorical/stylistic orientations share methodologies of the philosophical tradition, though often with less 'logical' rigour, but on the other hand a richer alignment with linguistic structures
- psychological orientations are ultimately geared towards experimental testing, even though this is often neglected in favour of less 'expensive' argumentation of either a philosophical or a linguistic nature.

Let us now focus on 'linguistic orientations', in turn differentiating them into 'grammar-based' perspectives and 'level-based' perspectives.

By a 'grammar-based' linguistic perspective on 'cohesion/coherence', we mean one that starts from an account of the grammar of a language and investigates configurations of linguistic structure at or rather just beyond the limits of grammaticalization. All functionally-motivated linguistic frameworks include this 'inside-out' perspective, often without positing an extra level of 'text/discourse/cohesion'.

By a 'level-based' perspective, we mean one within which a level 'additional' to '(lexico)-grammar' is assumed. It is within this perspective that the question of its precise nature, and of the distinction between 'cohesion' and 'coherence', usually arises. In fact, sometimes a threefold distinction is made into 'Konnexität (syntactic), Kohäsion (semantic) and Kohärenz (pragmatic)', the latter two being conceived of as 'transphrastic' (cf. Schreiber, 1999, particularly pp. 16ff; originally in Hatakeyama *et al.*, 1989), which in Halliday and Hasan's terms would be 'lexicogrammar vs. cohesion vs. coherence' (cf. below).

The view adopted in our research is closest to the formulation in Halliday and Matthiessen (2004: 579), though in a modified re-formulation which we believe is consistent with their overall view of language: the textual resources of English are: (a) structural (thematic, information structure, focus, clause-complexing); and (b) cohesive, with those under (a) 'engendering' grammatical structure in English, and those under (b) being 'realized' in lexicogrammatical structure however engendering semantic/conceptual relations beyond lecogrammar.

In summary, comprehensive discussions of the systemic resources of cohesion exist for English and to a possibly lesser extent for German. In addition, there are corpus-linguistic analyses examining individual linguistic phenomena on text- or discourse level in a monolingual or bilingual perspective (to name but a few: Fabricius-Hansen (1996, 1999); Doherty (2004, 2006) and others on certain aspects of information packaging; and Gundel *et al.* (2004); Bosch *et al.* (2007) and Becher *et al.* (2009), for the investigation of particular cohesive devices). However, no contrastive work is available comparing a broad range of cohesive resources in the two language systems as well as their instantiations in texts across registers. The clarification of the concept of cohesion attempted here is meant as an initial step towards closing some of the gaps in the state-of-the-art identified initially.

3. Contrasts in cohesion E ⇔ G: an initial system-based overview

A preliminary comparison of English-German systemic resources indicates that major differences can be expected in the areas of cohesive reference (in particular demonstrative and deictic reference, but also personal and extended reference, see also Kunz, 2009), ellipsis (more strongly grammaticalized in English, but in less grammaticalized forms very frequent in German), substitution (with different systems and frequencies in English and German), lexical cohesion (different norms for usage of 'general nouns' in English, often reaching the borderline of grammaticalization, vs. German), and of course conjunctive relations, where the frequency of non-finite clauses in English leads to implicitness in one sense, but counteracts this through strong tendencies towards grammaticalization of former non-finite verbs and adverbs, encoding logico-semantic relations.

The classifications of cohesive devices differ considerably across approaches. As a common frame of reference, we shall assume Halliday and Hasan (1976), using them as a basis for transfer comparison. In the following we will provide a reasonably detailed discussion for the category of cohesive reference only, particularly sketching functional and semantic as well as morphological and lexicogrammatic peculiarities in the systems of English and German.

3.1. Cohesive reference

3.1.1. Conceptualization

The methodology employed by Halliday and Hasan (1976) sets out from a particular language, in this case English, but makes the classification on a functional rather than morphosyntactic level (cf. Figures 1 and 2). It represents a compromise in terms of methodology in that it sets up its classifications from the lexicogrammatical, including morphosyntactic, phenomena of one language (English), yet abstracts away from those into a functional/semantic level as an interface for cross-linguistic comparison.

They talk of *co-reference* where different linguistic expressions have the same referent, for example a referring expression, usually an NP, and a pronoun co-referring to that *entity* previously introduced into the discourse world: 'The cohesion lies in the continuity of reference' (1976: 31). Referential devices generating cohesion usually are semantically and formally reduced and cannot be fully interpreted in their own right.[4] Therefore, information as to their reference has to be retrieved from another source. In the case of *exophoric reference*, this source is the situational (and/or cultural) context, whereas in the case of *endophoric reference*, the linguistic environment (antecedent) of the text provides the information required.

Within endophoric reference, Halliday and Hasan (1976) differentiate further between *anaphoric reference* (linking to preceding text) and *cataphoric reference* (linking to following text). Taking into consideration the general *identity* of the information, they establish three types of reference, *personal*, *demonstrative*, and *comparative* reference. The first type can be realized by personal and possessive pronouns, the second by demonstrative pronouns, adverbs like *here* or *there* and the article *the*, and the third type by adjectives and adverbs such as *same, similar, so* or *such*. Note that co-reference, in the strict sense with an individuated discourse entity, here only seems to apply to *personal,* and some subtypes of *demonstrative reference*, because other cases involve type-reference, co-classification or 'sloppy identity'. Importantly for our study, the general distinction into *personal, demonstrative,* and *comparative* is common to English and German; the sub-types, as well as their realization, are not. Between typologically more distant languages, for example, even between Romance, Slavic and Germanic languages, not even the general distinctions would be completely shared, and sub-types and realizations would vary more widely.

The very broad category of *cohesive reference* does not have one exactly co-extensive terminological equivalent in most other approaches; instead, the phenomenon (co-)reference appears in several lexico-grammatical categories realizing cohesion: pro-forms, articles, deixis and the often fully lexically-headed phrases they are part of. De Beaugrande and Dressler (1981), for example, include pronouns, adverbs, demonstrative pronouns, pro-adjectives like German *so* or *solch*, pro-verbs like *tun* or *machen*, and pronominal adverbs, but only the first four would be listed under the heading *reference* in Halliday and Hasan (1976). The same list, except for pro-adjectives and pro-verbs, can be found in Linke *et al.* (2004).

The definite and indefinite articles are usually seen as a form of 'deixis' (e.g., in Linke *et al.*, 2004). They distinguish between *textual* deixis in the case of reference to new information (indefinite article) and given information (definite article), and *deixis to (previous) knowledge* ('(Vor-) wissens-deixis'), where the definite article is used for elements that are new in the text, but, in the opinion of the authors, known to the reader. They mention another form of deixis, that of situational deixis, using this term where the reference is not to another element of the text, but to the situation the text is embedded in.

3.1.2. Systemic differences

Generally speaking, three distinct functional systems of specifically developed items for establishing cohesive (co-)reference are realized in English and German: personal reference, demonstrative reference and comparative reference. As one illustration for the functional/semantic basis of this approach, observe that 'personal reference' is not named 'personal' because English happens to have personal pronouns, but rather, because this kind of reference refers to the 'persons and entities' in the context of situation. For this same reason, personal reference as a semantic phenomenon also occurs in a 'pro-drop' language, or one without pronouns altogether, yet lexicogrammatically realized by ellipsis and/or personal endings on finite verbs. Characteristically, the exposition in Halliday and Hasan (1976) proceeds by semantic/functional distinctions, not by word class or some other morphosyntactic reflex (cf. Figures 2 and 3). In our discussion, we first explore the functional differences in the systems of English and German, before dealing with the formal features of the cohesive devices employed.

Personal reference

'Personal reference is reference by means of function in the speech situation' (Halliday and Hasan, 1976: 37). Figure 4 gives us a bilingual classification fragment on the functional/semantic level for English and German, that is, one classifying all and only the distinctions made by the two languages in combination through cohesive personal (co-)reference. Options in the system network unique to, or at least more elaborated in, German are marked by italics.[5]

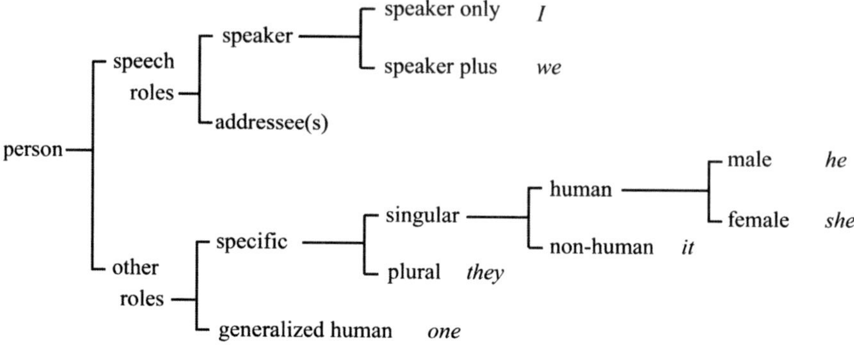

Figure 2: A classification of cohesive personal reference for English (Halliday and Hasan 1976: 44).

Speech roles			Other roles		
			Specific		*Generalized Human*
	Speaker	*Addressee*	*Human*	*Non-human*	
one	I me mine my	you you	he him his his she her hers her	it it [its] its	one one – one's
more than one	we us ours our	yours your	they them theirs their		

Figure 3: Tabular form for the classification in Figure 2 (Halliday and Hasan 1976: 44).

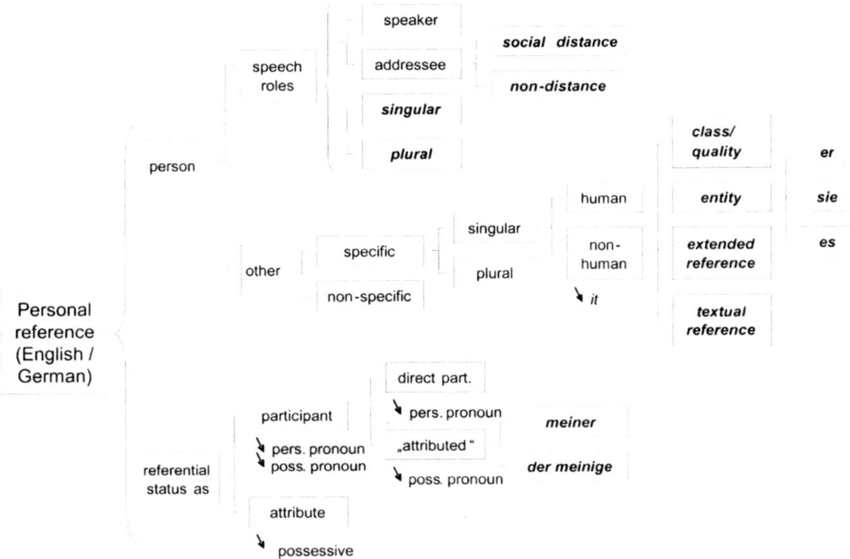

Figure 4: Personal reference in English and German.

Generally speaking, a distinction is drawn in terms of reference to *person/ roles* as *speech role* vs. *other* involved in the act of communication, and in terms of their *referential status* as either *participant*, or as an *attribute*.

First, *person* (where *person* is a generalized category involving all sorts of entities, including complex states and events) are cohesively denoted via different lexical and morphological forms of personal pronouns either as taking an active part in the communication (speech role) or as being involved as some other third-party entity (other). English and German mainly express two speech roles, the speaker(s) (via first person pronouns) and the addressee(s) (via second person pronouns). The languages differ in that German further distinguishes social distance (*Sie*) and non-distance (*du, ihr*) and singular (*du, Sie*) and plural (*ihr, Sie*) in the speech role of the addressee, whereas contemporary modern Standard English does not realize this contrast in terms of personal reference since it uses one form only (*you*). In the speech role of speaker, both languages distinguish between singular and plural. Person-referents[6] that do not take an active part in the speech event are cohesively expressed either as being specific (third person pronouns) or non-specific (*one; man*) in English and German, even if the use of *one* in modern English is much more restricted than German *man*. In many contexts of modern English, *one* is substituted by either general nouns *(people)*, specific pronouns *(we, you)*, or agentless passive.

For specific reference, a further classification is made in German and English for plural and singular referents. With singular referents, English distinguishes human and non-human referents as natural categories, whereas German realizes a threefold grammatical gender distinction in cases of reference to non-human entities (see below). For both languages, there is the further distinction under non-human singular into reference to an entity, extended reference to an event, and textual reference to the fact that an event occurred (cf. Halliday and Hasan, 1976: 52ff). We suspect that these types of reference are: (a) less ambiguous in German than in English; and (b) are differently expressed by personal or demonstrative reference (or ellipsis) in the two languages.[7] German has the additional option of referring to a quality (cf. Examples (3) and (4) below), although we shall argue in a later chapter that this construction is more a type of 'cohesive substitution' than one of reference (cf. Kunz and Steiner, forthcoming).

Second, a difference is made with respect to the *status of referents* either as *attributes* or *participants*. As for reference to *participants*, the two languages further distinguish between referents involved as direct participants in a process and referents which constitute attributed or possessed persons/referents of other referents/persons. The former type is indicated by personal pronouns, the latter by nominalized possessive pronouns (*mine, meiner, der meinige*). At this place in the system, we believe that English nominalized possessives (*mine,* etc.) and the two German options (*meiner/der meinige*) are in terms of function closer to substitution, than they may be to reference. Reference to *attributes* of referents is realized in the two languages via possessive determiners.

We now adopt the perspective from lexicogrammatical realization, describing contrastive differences in terms of morphological forms of the cohesive devices employed in the two languages. Lexicogrammatical realization will be seen to have strong effects on the textual function, for example, creation of ambiguities or otherwise in referential cohesion.

As for personal pronouns, both languages inflect for number, or rather, they use different word stems depending on number. Yet, there are differences with respect to gender and case inflection, and German systemically enforces a choice depending on social distance in the second person (singular and plural), additionally differentiating singular vs. plural for both speaker and addressee speech roles.

The marking of gender in Standard English is primarily determined by natural sex distinctions and metaphorical extensions thereof (Hawkins, 1986: 11ff; König and Gast, 2007: 63). Pronouns referring to entities other than human beings or higher animals are assigned to neuter gender. In German, gender assignment is basically arbitrary, that is, grammatical with a semantic basis allowing for some generalizations (König and Gast, 2007: 60). Most nouns[8] denoting humans and higher or domestic animals are inflected for biological gender; all other nouns are marked arbitrarily, by masculine, feminine or neuter gender. As a consequence, more neuter personal pronouns can be expected in English relative to German. Referential ties of endophoric devices to full lexical noun phrases in German may be more explicit than in English since the former contain gender, number and case inflection whereas English full lexical noun phrases do not inflect for gender (or case). Thus sequences such as the following in German are potentially ambiguous in English, and may locally lead to unnecessary processing costs:

> (1)   Eine verantwortungsbewusste Politik kann diesen Prozess, der zudem von objektiven Faktoren determiniert wird, nicht nur flankieren. <u>Sie</u> muss <u>ihn</u> vielmehr formen.

> (2)   A responsible policy can not only accompany this process, which is additionally determined by objective factors, **it** must moreover shape **it**.

In some registers, particularly in spoken texts, personal pronouns will be preferred in English where demonstrative pronouns are employed in German (see below). Note also that in German, but not in English, third person singular pronoun *es* or demonstrative article *das* can be employed as *Propredicative* (Schreiber, 1999: 153) as in (3) and (4) below, hence our inclusion of personal reference to *quality* as a subtype of *singular* in the upper part of Figure 4:

> (3)   Ist die Suppe heiß? – Ja, sie ist es/ das ist sie.

> (4)   Is the soup hot? – Yes, it is (it/that*).[9]

For possessive pronouns in German and English, there is a form available where the possessive pronoun functions as nominal head and constitutes the only element of the noun phrase: *mine* in English and *mein(e,r)* in German.[10] Both languages use variant stems for expressing variation in speech roles and number. The German and English forms additionally differ with respect to morphological inflection in that German uses gender, number and case inflection whereas English has one invariant form only. German also provides a possessive pronominal form which is introduced by the definite article. In contrast to the form described above the use of the latter is assumed to be delimited to particular registers of formal style and is also considered to underlie regional preferences. In English no such form is available. Possessive determiners are the words known traditionally as possessive pronouns. Different use in particular linguistic environments, such as external possession is well documented between English and German (cf. König and Gast, 2009: 112ff).

Demonstrative reference

Demonstrative reference is one area of the overall field of *deixis*, but in no way exhausts it.[11] 'Demonstrative reference is reference by means of location, on a scale of proximity' (Halliday and Hasan, 1976: 37), extending from concrete spatio-temporal location through abstract space and notably into semiotic space. As we would see it, where this 'reference' uses 'demonstratives', it blends co-reference with 'deixis'.

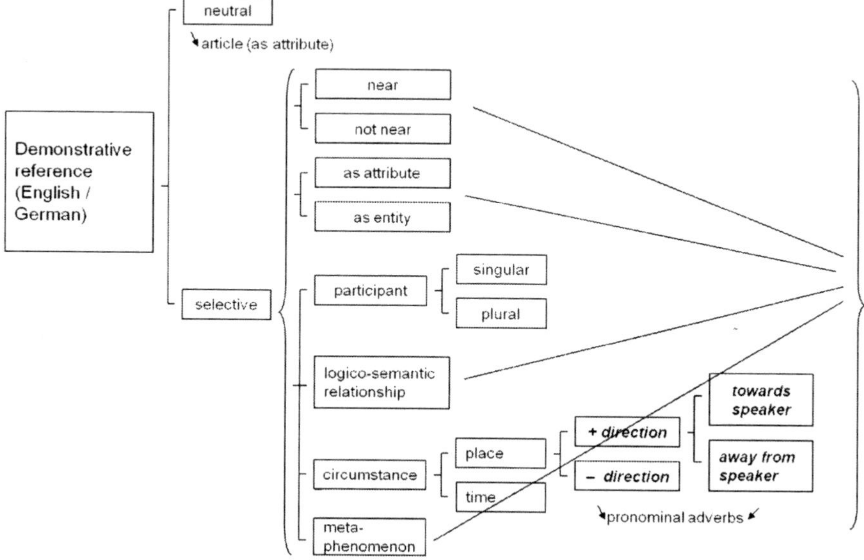

Figure 5: Demonstrative reference in English and German.

Similar systems are available in English and German to some extent, though with substantial differences in *selective→as entity/ participant* demonstrative reference through the existence of a demonstrative article in German[12] (*der, die, das*), plus the invariant *dies,* and substantial differences in *selective → entity/ logico-semantic relationship, circumstance, and metaphenomenon* options, where German has developed (or 'preserved') a full set of demonstratives (adverbs, articles, pronouns) for all the major referents and relations. These are used with high frequency[13] both in the type- and token sense, though not equally productively across the semantic sub-types, and partly subject to register-constraints.[14] They furthermore can be classified into *asserting vs. questioning (darüber* vs. *worüber)* and *near vs. far (darüber* vs. *hierrüber).*

The major systems are structured around *neutral* vs. *selective* demonstrative reference, and within the latter into functions to do with *near* vs. *far, attribute* vs. *entity*, and *participant* vs. *circumstance* vs. *logico-semantic relationship* vs.

meta-phenomenon. Their realization is in phrase types in English (and word classes to some limited extent) and German (where the word classes are more diversified and preferred): demonstratives, determiners introducing referring noun phrases, demonstrative pronouns and articles serving as head of a noun phrase, and adverbs. Within the word class of determiners, we can distinguish demonstratives on the one hand and the definite article on the other.

Demonstrative reference is either *neutral* or *selective.* The option *neutral* encodes some referent as *identifiable,* which in English is realized through the definite article *the,*[15] and in German through the definite article in its inflected forms (gender, number, case). The German *demonstrative article* which can occur as a head will be covered under *selective→as entity* below, although historically, and in some (low-German) varieties, it may be a form of neutral reference encoding simply *identifiable.* This word class does not exist in English.

Selective demonstratives are selective by encoding not only general identifiability, but more specifically identifiability through (semiotic) proximity. Differently from the pro-forms for personal reference, they thus add an important element of 'attention-direction' by 'proximity' to their general meaning of 'being identifiable', which is shared by other pro-forms and the definite article. They are classified in terms of temporal-spatial-textual proximity (*near vs. not near*), in terms of reference as an entity, or, restricted to the demonstrative pronouns, as an attribute (semantically), and in terms of being a participant, a circumstance, a logico-semantic relation, or a meta-phenomenon. Furthermore, if we have selective demonstrative reference to a participant, it may be singular or plural, and if we have selective demonstrative reference to a circumstance, it may be by place or time, with further sub-distinctions for German dependent on place. Finally, if we have demonstrative selective reference other than to a human participant, in German we get a full set of pro-forms, the so-called pronominal demonstrative adverbs.

Let us go through selective demonstratives type by type, giving examples:

(a) Selective, not near, as attribute, participant, singular
     that house/jenes[16] *Haus;* **das**[17] *Haus*

(b) Selective, not near, as attribute, participant, plural
     those houses/jene Häuser; **die** *Häuser*

(c) Selective, near, as entity, participant, singular
     this[18]*/der/die/das*[19]*; dieser/diese/dieses*[20]

(d) Selective, near, as entity, participant, plural
     these/die; diese

(e) Selective, not near, as entity, participant, plural
     these/jene[21]

Observe a few options specific to, or at least preferred, in German:

(f) Selective, not near, as entity, circumstance, place, -direction
     darunter, darauf, davor, dahinter[22]

(g) Selective, near, as entity, circumstance, place, -direction
     hierunter, hierauf, hiervor[23]

(h) Selective, near, as entity, circumstance, place, +direction, towards speaker
     herunter, herauf, hervor

(i) Selective, near, as entity, circumstance, place, +direction, away from speaker
     hinunter, hinauf

(j) Selective, not near, as entity, logico-semantic relationship
     thereof, thereby.../ davon, damit, deswegen[24]

(k) Selective, not near, as entity, meta-phenomenon
     daran, davor, daraus, deswegen,....

Note that there are, of course, English adverbs and prepositional phrases in parallel to (f) (*below, on top, in front, behind*), but they are not *demonstrative*. The +/- *near* distinction (cf. f) vs. (g) is, we think, absent from English at this point in the system, as are the distinctions between (h) and (i).

Finally, and importantly, German uses the questioning variants frequently to express conjunctive relations (cf. 5 below).

(5)   der Zug kam verspätet, was niemand wunderte, worüber niemand lachte, weswegen niemand böse war, etc.

(6)   The train was late, which didn't surprise anyone, about which nobody laughed, because of which nobody was angry, etc.[25]

We now move on to describe contrastive differences between the two languages departing from the respective forms at hand.

Demonstrative pronouns

Demonstratives are described in the literature as a form of verbal pointing (cf. Ahrenholz (2007) for a recent specialized study). In their function as exophoric devices they denote referents that are present in the speech situation (deixis). Employed as endophoric devices, demonstrative pronouns serve as *focus-lifters* (Gundel, 2004; Diessel, 1999; Bosch *et al.*, 2007, etc.), they raise a referent's degree of accessibility from a low to a higher level. Similar to the neuter form of the third person pronoun, they may also serve for extended and textual reference in English and German, yet with their own added 'demonstrative, deictic force'. However, we hypothesize that demonstratives serving as anaphors to complex antecedents (extended reference, meta-phenomena) may be preferred to *it* in English and *es* in German, though to different degrees and with language-specific motivations (cf. Becher, 2011). There are additional preferences to do with syntactic function (Subject vs. others) or semantic type.

Basically, four different forms are available in English: *this/these* and *that/those*. They are inflected for number but do not contain any marking for case or gender. The two forms can be distinguished in terms of proximity (situational, textual, spatio-temporal, possibly others such as affect-oriented proximity). *This/these* mark referents in terms of nearness and *that/those* signal distance to the referent from the view of the speaker.

The two forms in singular, *this* and *that*, are restricted in use in that they cannot denote human beings. According to Halliday and Hasan (1976: 63), the use of the plural demonstrative pronouns *these* and *those* for humans is more acceptable.

In German, a wider range of different forms is available. The invariant[26] forms *dies* and *das*, the inflected forms *diese(r,s)* (dies-pronoun) and *jene(r,s)*, and the inflected forms of *der/die/das* (d-pronoun).

Dies vs. *das* (largely for extended or textual reference) and *diese(r,s)* vs. *jene(r,s)* (largely for person and entity reference) may be distinguished in terms of proximity but the distinction is less clear than in English. Furthermore, *jene(r,s)* is becoming more and more outdated, hence *diese(r,s)* is also used for cases in which *that/those* would be employed in English. Ahrenholz (2007: 247ff), in a corpus-based study yielding frequencies of use, finds in terms of frequency: personal pronoun third person > d-pronoun > dies-pronoun. *Das* with text-reference is particularly frequent, even if it introduces a systematic vagueness. The phonetic distinction between *dies* and *das* is often neutralized towards *des*, a possible sign of grammaticalization processes (Ahrenholz, 2007: 247). Distributions are sensitive to mood-choice, and syntactic positions vary between *Vor-* and *Mittelfeld*.

Equal to *this* and *that* in English used as head in a nominal group, the invariant forms *dies* and *das* are restricted to reference to inanimate objects, or even more often to extended or textual reference. It still remains to be examined more closely, whether the two forms reflect differences in scope and if these differences correspond to the *this*-and-*that* distinction in English.

The demonstrative pronouns (articles) *der/die/das* lack a corresponding form in English, and they freely refer to both animate and inanimate referents, differently to *this/that* in English used as heads. They exhibit gender, number and case inflection. Assumptions are that *der/die/das* occur in certain registers only, and spoken texts in particular. However, they systematically offer a means of referring to participants as entities, and here not through personal reference, but through demonstrative reference, something which does not exist in English.

Since particular demonstrative pronouns can be employed for human beings in German but not in English, a higher overall frequency may be expected for German demonstrative pronouns used as head/entity, relative to English.

The definite article. The definite article is considered by Halliday and Hasan (1976) as the neutral form of verbal pointing: it marks a referring expression as denoting a referent that is somehow known without indicating explicitly which type of knowledge is required. Thus, the information about the referent in question may be retrieved by inferences from long-term memory, the situational context or the linguistic context. In addition no distinction is made with the definite article in terms of proximity. The definite article is combined in the nominal referring expression with a lexical noun functioning as head which establishes a tie of lexical cohesion. Definite noun phrases thus are employed as endophoric devices to establish a relation of co-classification or co-extension or a co-reference relation.

The definite article in English has one invariant morphological form that is neither inflected for number nor for gender and case. Different from that, the article in German (*der/die/das*) is inflected for grammatical gender, number and case, resulting in more explicit textual ties, relative to English. In addition, there are differences between the two languages in the use of the definite article with generic reference, abstract reference and proper names.

Demonstrative determiners. In English, there are two devices available that correspond formally to the demonstrative pronouns described above. However, used as demonstrative determiners, *this/these* and *that/those* only introduce noun phrases with a lexical head. Similar to their pronominal counterparts they are inflected for number and enhance identification of a referent in terms of proximity.

German provides the demonstrative determiners *diese(r,s)* and *jene(r,s)* introducing nominal referring expressions. In contrast to English, the two forms are not only inflected for number but also for gender and case.

Demonstrative adverbs. Halliday and Hasan (1976) only present the four adverbs *now, then, here* and *there* under the heading of demonstrative reference. There are contrasts in meaning with respect to proximity on the one hand, and time and space on the other hand: *now* and *here* mark something as being near, the former in time and the latter in space; *then* and *there* signal distance, the former with respect to time, the latter with respect to space.

The corresponding items in German are *jetzt/nun* (*now*), *damals* (*then*), *hier* (*here*) and *da/dort* (*there*), with the German system at this point encoding a threefold distance distinction (*hier – da – dort*). Other devices such as *after that*, *in this respect*, etc. are assigned by Halliday and Hasan (1976) to the category of cohesive conjunctives (1976: 75f).

In German, a larger set of 'pronominal adverbs' would additionally fall under demonstrative reference since they function as reference markers and/or as devices establishing logico-semantic relations between different textual parts. German provides a broad range of these devices, such as *darauf, dabei, darin, davor, dahinter, hinein, hinaus, damit, dafür, dazu*, etc. (the overall number is estimated at above 100, cf. Becher, 2011). German certainly has a larger and more differentiated system at this point), and even where the two languages have similar systems, textual frequencies are supposed to be lower in English (token-frequency, cf. Becher. 2011, as well as our first initial findings in this area). Corresponding items in English would be *therefore, thereafter, thereof*, etc., yet hardly with reference to locations (*sit thereon? therein?*). These are often antiquated and not assumed to appear in contemporary texts of Standard English with frequencies comparable to those of their German counterparts. As noted in the literature a number of times (e.g., Rohdenburg, 1990: 149), pronominal (demonstrative) adverbs therefore are predicted to occur much more frequently in German than in English:

> German *dafür* – English: *for the problem, for the purpose, for the occasion...*
> German *dabei* – English: *in the process, in the attempt, on the occasion...*

As Becher (2011: 21) rightly notes, these 'composite deictics' in German usually present a blend of the three functions of: (a) explicitly realizing arguments (or modifiers, we would add), (b) establishing textual cohesion, and (c) structuring complex sentences.

4. Preliminary findings from the corpus linguistic analysis

An example-based theoretical and hermeneutic approach to cohesion as presented in the previous sections is particularly valuable for the comparison of the systemic options for establishing cohesion in English and German. As we have seen, it is also an important exploratory step to generate assumptions about the range and use of cohesive devices. The next step, that is, the one from assumptions to actual linguistic evidence, though, is only possible on the basis of a text corpus for both languages. Including translations in the analysis is especially interesting here: not only do they hint at analogies between cohesive devices in the two languages, they also show areas where one-to-one equivalents are not preferred, or even non-existent.[27]

Below we present some preliminary findings from the CroCo corpus[28] as examples of how a corpus-linguistic analysis complements the theoretical and example-based comparison of systemic contrasts described above, thus yielding additional and above all different types of insights about instantiations of cohesion. The analyses were carried out on two subcorpora of the CroCo corpus featuring political essays (ESSAY) and fictional texts (FICTION).

4.1. Personal pronouns

The focus of the first analysis is on personal reference, particularly on the use of the neuter pronoun in English (*it*) and German (*es*). Although both languages have this pronoun, assumptions about contrastive differences in frequency and use were already formulated on the basis of the systemic contrasts discussed in Section 3.

Table 1 shows the findings from the corpus query in the two corpora FICTION and ESSAY.

Table 1: Query *'it/es'* in the CroCo registers ESSAY and FICTION

ESSAY	EO	Etrans	Gtrans	GO	
It/it total	0.45 %	0.49 %	0.39 %	0.48 %	*Es/es* total
Cohesive It	47.9 %	58.3 %	14.29 %	12.20 %	Cohesive Es
FICTION	EO	Etrans	Gtrans	GO	
It/it total	1.06 %	1.02 %	0.88%	0.84%	*Es/es* total
Cohesive It	62.3 %	48.61 %	36.29 %	32 %	Cohesive Es

As Table 1 illustrates, both registers comprise two original subcorpora, one in English (EO) and one in German (GO), as well as subcorpora containing translations from these into the respective other language (Etrans and Gtrans). Queries were made as to the number of all instances of the neuter pronoun inside and at the beginning of sentences in relation to all tokens (*It/it* total for English, *Es/es* total for German), without distinguishing cohesive and non-cohesive occurrences. For cohesive uses in relation to all types of use, we concentrated on occurrences of the neuter pronoun at the beginning of the sentence (Cohesive *It*/Cohesive *Es*) as automatic disambiguation of cohesive vs. non-cohesive use was not possible at this early stage of the project.

First of all, in most respects, there is a greater similarity between originals and translations in the same language than in texts across languages in both registers, pointing to a contrastive difference in terms of frequency of the neuter pronoun. The findings also permit a consideration of the reasons lying behind the differences in frequency, particularly when comparing translations and originals.

The frequencies for cohesive instances of the neuter pronoun occurring at the beginning of the sentence show that for *Es* in German the non-cohesive function predominates, whereas English *It* tends to have a cohesive function as often as a non-cohesive one. The respective cohesive occurrences in the text show that the neuter pronoun is often employed in both registers of English in cases where a personal pronoun indicating feminine or masculine gender is used in the German parallel texts. This is illustrated by an extract from an English original and its German translation below:

(7) The UK has always been a strong supporter of European enlargement and I am very pleased to mark <u>this latest accession of ten new members on 1 May</u>. We welcome it as another important and historic step towards sealing over the artificial divisions created by the Cold War. [EO_ESSAY_003]

(8) Großbritannien hat sich immer schon für die europäische Erweiterung stark gemacht und deshalb begrüße ich <u>den Beitritt von zehn neuen Mitgliedstaaten am 1. Mai</u> von ganzem Herzen. <u>Er</u> ist ein historischer Schritt auf dem Weg, die künstlichen Risse zu kitten, die der Kalte Krieg hinterlassen hat. [GTrans_ESSAY_003]

Thus, the findings corroborate our assumptions concerning English-German differences due to biological vs. grammatical gender, and their implications for possible local ambiguities. Yet, this is not the only reason for the contrast in frequency. Comparing German translations and English originals reveals that an equivalent translation for *it* in German may be realized via a pronominal adverbial (*damit/therewith*) as in (10). Note that the adverbial is additionally focused by the German demonstrative article *das* in the preceding clause, which refers to a wider scope than the English personal pronoun *they* in (9). Another example is the demonstrative pronoun *dies* as in (12), again giving a feature of increased deictic force to the German translation. The same applies to demonstrative *zudem* for English non-deictic *moreover* in the preceding clause. In other German translations full lexical noun phrases are found for anaphoric *it* in English (compare (13) and (14)).

(9) We <u>work for prosperity and</u> opportunity because <u>they</u>'re right. <u>It</u>'s the right thing to do. [EO_ESSAY_006]

(10) Wir <u>arbeiten für Wohlstand und Chancen</u>, weil <u>das</u> richtig ist. Wir tun <u>damit</u> das Richtige. [GTrans_ESSAY_006]

(11) And he answered them courteously that they should speak on, for he had not come so far and so wearily simply in order to turn back. <u>Moreover he was charged by his father with a mission, which he might not reveal in that place</u>. '<u>It</u> is known to us already,' said the three damsels. [EO_FICTION_002]

(12)   Und er erwiderte ihnen artig, daß sie weitersprechen sollten, denn er habe die Mühsal und Beschwerden des weiten Weges nicht auf sich genommen, um nun kehrtzumachen. <u>Und zudem habe sein Vater ihn mit einer Aufgabe betraut, die er an diesem Ort zu enthüllen nicht gesonnen sei.</u> '<u>Dies</u> ist uns bekannt', sagten die drei Jungfrauen. [GTrans_FICTION_002]

(13)   In November 2001 the president directed that we begin to fill <u>the SPR</u> to its 700 million barrel capacity. Today <u>it</u> contains a record 640 million barrels of oil. [EO_ESSAY_001]

(14)   Im November 2001 veranlasste der Präsident das Auffüllen <u>der Strategischen Ölreserve</u>, deren Fassungsvermögen 700 Millionen Barrel beträgt. Heute enthält <u>die Ölreserve</u> die Rekordsmenge von 640 Millionen Barrel. [GTrans_ESSAY_001]

Hence, while in English the neuter personal pronoun is quite frequently used to establish cohesion, German often makes use of demonstrative devices with a deictic force.

Contrasting the frequencies between originals and translations, we notice a greater divergence between the English and the German texts, across registers. Quite interestingly, the divergences lead into different directions: In German there is a clear tendency for the translations in both registers to exhibit higher frequencies of *Es* than the originals, thus pointing to cases of shining through. The English translations of the register FICTION show significantly fewer occurrences of Cohesive *It* than the English originals, which may also be due to shining through of the German originals. In contrast, the English translations taken from ESSAY exhibit the highest frequencies of all subcorpora of the register ESSAY since they are even higher than the English originals. Thus, except for the latter, the findings for the translation corpora may hint at traces of language contact.

Apart from the language contrast identified above, the register itself causes variation. For instance, the distribution of the neuter pronoun is higher in FICTION than in ESSAY across languages; what is more, there are more cohesive instances at the beginning of sentences in FICTION than in ESSAY. As closer examination shows, many of these have a wide and partially ambiguous scope in contrast to most instances traced in ESSAY, which have a more limited and well-defined scope. Finally, the findings for the English registers are more similar to each other than the findings for the German registers. This may result from the tendency in the German FICTION texts that more instances of the neuter pronoun have a wider scope than in the English FICTION texts. Moreover, while the scope of the antecedent can be defined very easily in most cases in ESSAY, the scope in FICTION quite often remains rather vague.

By way of illustration, consider the following extract of a German original text of the register FICTION:

(15)   Er war ein eher ängstliches Kind, sagte die Mutter. Er log nicht. Er war anständig. Und vor allem, er war tapfer, sagte der Vater, schon als Kind. Der tapfere Junge.

So wurde er beschrieben, auch von entfernten Verwandten. Es waren wörtliche Festlegungen, und sie werden es auch für ihn gewesen sein. [GO_FICTION_008]]

In (15), the scope of the neuter pronoun *Es* at the beginning of the last sentence is not uniquely identifiable. *Es* may point to any subset of the preceding propositions. Exactly the same option is not available in English, hence the deictically stronger *these*:

(16)   He was rather a timid boy, said our mother. He didn't tell lies. He was well-behaved, and above all, said our father, he was brave even as a child. People described him as that brave boy, even distant relations.

These were verbatim observations, and <u>they</u> will have been meant for him too. [ETrans_FICTION_008]

4.2. Demonstrative pronouns

Our next findings concern the analysis of different types of demonstrative pronouns, again in the two registers ESSAY and FICTION.

Table 2: Distribution of demonstrative pronouns in the CroCo registers ESSAY and FICTION

	EO_ESSAY	Etrans_ESSAY	EO_FICTION	Etrans_FICTION
this	46.43%	75.31%	63.83%	37.36%
that	45.24%	9.88%	27.66%	54.95%
these	4.76%	11.11%	5.32%	2.2%
those	3.57%	3.70%	3.19%	5.49%
total	0.24%	0.39%	0.25%	0.23%

	GO_ESSAY	Gtrans_ESSAY	GO_FICTION	Gtrans_FICTION
dies	18.85%	27.78%	2.70%	13.14%
das	73.78%	68.1%	76.4%	73%
diese/r/s	4.1%	4.17%	2.70%	1.5%
der/die	3.28%	0%	18.24%	12.41%
Total	0.34%	0.20%	0.40%	0.39%

The total figures (total number of demonstrative pronouns in relation to number of tokens) show a tendency for the German texts to exhibit a higher number of demonstrative pronouns than the English texts, across registers. We may thus infer a higher level of *selective* demonstrative force in the German as compared to the English texts, which may result from the contrast in referring to human beings with demonstrative pronouns (see 3.1.2). Note that both translations of the register ESSAY show features that differ considerably from all other texts in the same language: Etrans_ESSAY exhibits a higher number of demonstratives than all other English texts under investigation and Gtrans_ESSAY shows a much lower distribution of demonstratives than all other German texts. These seem to be clear cases of source text imitation, or even exaggeration of source text strategies. The question of why this divergence only holds for the register ESSAY and not for FICTION requires further investigation.

The distributions of the individual rather than total forms (occurrences of respective forms in relation to the total number of demonstrative pronouns) convey notable differences between the two languages, but also between registers and originals and translations.

As Table 2 displays, more variation in forms is found for German, as already suggested in the frame of the systemic comparison above: in addition to *diese/r/s* the forms *der/die* additionally serve to refer to human beings as well as inanimate and abstract entities, although with significant distributional differences between registers (see below).

Contrasts in frequency between the two languages can partially be interpreted as a reflection of contrasts in function of similar morphological forms. For instance, the figures reflect a distribution of the form *das* in German that is higher than *dies*, whereas in English the form *this* occurs more often than *that*, in both registers. Our first assumption was that the relatively high number of *das* might be due to the German peculiarity of expressing not only extended reference but also reference to noun phrases (inanimate and animate entities), and thus having a limited scope (not possible in English). The respective occurrences however contradict this interpretation as all instances of *das* in the registers investigated refer to clauses and even larger textual parts. Yet, the situation may be different for other registers, particularly of the spoken mode.

Comparing German originals with their translations shows that *das* in the register ESSAY is often used anaphorically where *this* is employed in English, as displayed in (17) and (18) below:

(17)   Mit Ausgaben für Forschung und Entwicklung von etwa 3,5 Milliarden Euro gehört die Branche zwar nach wie vor zu den besonders forschungsintensiven Industrien der Bundesrepublik. Tendenziell ist der Anteil der deutschen Pharmabranche an den globalen Forschungsausgaben der Branche, ebenso wie der Anteil an der Zahl neuer Wirkstoffe, aber rückläufig. <u>Das</u> bereitet den Experten Sorgen.

(18)   The German pharmaceutical sector still spends more on research than most other industries in the Federal Republic – RandD expenditure totals about 3.5 billion euros. Even so, its share of global expenditure on phar-

maceutical research, as well as its share of new active-substance discoveries, is declining. <u>This</u> is a cause for concern among the experts.

The picture in FICTION is different: In most cases, *das* is translated as *that*, which could serve as a source of explanation for the high distribution of 54.95% in Etrans_FICTION.

Other solutions for translating *das* found in the register FICTION, but not ESSAY, are with *it* as in (20), or employing an elliptical construction, as in (22).

> (19) Ich kann dich auch umziehen, Jerzy, wenn du Hilfe brauchst.' (…) 'Ich mache <u>das</u>, sag ein Wort, und ich ziehe dich um.

> (20) I can change your clothes too, Jerzy, if you need help.' (…) 'I'll do <u>it</u>, just say the word and I'll change your clothes.

> (21) Nur weil die anderen sich so gehen lassen, mußt du <u>das</u> nicht auch machen.'

> (22) Just because the others let themselves go like that, you <u>don't have to</u> also.'

The very high number of demonstrative *this* in English translations cannot be interpreted as a direct case of shining-through as neither the invariable nor the variable morphological forms of the lemma *dies* occur with such a high distribution in the German originals. In fact, the values for demonstrative occurrences of *dies* are even lower in all German texts than in the English originals. The high value in English seems to stem, at least in part, from frequent occurrences of the invariable form *das* in the German original texts GO_ESSAY:

> (23) Das Zurückschneiden des Sozialstaats verlangt mehr 'Eigenverantwortung , Krankheit und Alter müssen stärker privat abgesichert werden; <u>das</u> wiederum muss die Politik jungen Leuten klarmachen, für die der Einstieg in den Beruf viel schwieriger geworden ist …

> (24) Politicians have to explain <u>this</u> to young people who can no longer rely on being offered the kind of firm employment …

However, the main source of explanation in Etrans_ESSAY can be found by looking at the corresponding source text sentences in German:

> (25) The participants are aware of <u>this</u>, by the way.

> (26) Den Akteuren ist <u>das</u> übrigens klar

> (27) It is astonishing how little they complain about <u>this</u>.

> (28) Sie klagen <u>darueber</u> erstaunlich wenig.

> (29) There is no straight answer to <u>this</u>;

> (30) Eine eindeutige Antwort <u>darauf</u> gibt es nicht.

(31)   The Old Economy often lacks the spirit to do <u>this</u>.

(32)   <u>Dafuer</u> fehlt in der Old Economy oft der Spirit.

Examples (25) to (32) show that *this* is often used for the translation of pronominal adverbs. It is employed quite frequently in cases where the neuter form of the third person pronoun may have been used in English originals. The strategy employed leads us to assume that, first, the variety of forms available in German seems to cause indecision in the translators, and second, that translators may not be aware of the functional differences of demonstrative and personal pronouns between English and German.

Our corpus linguistic analysis also identifies new tendencies in frequency, function and use of cohesive devices dependent on register. For instance, fewer occurrences of the German demonstrative articles *der/die* are traced in the sub-corpora ESSAY than in FICTION. FICTION is in many respects similar to registers of spoken German, hence these findings seem to support assumptions in the literature that the use of the German demonstrative pronouns *der, die* is largely restricted to registers of spoken language (see Demonstrative determiners, in Section 3.1.2 above).

The following example displays one instance taken from GO_FICTION and its English translation:

(33)   Ich lenkte mich ab, suchte Schlaf, vergaß, sank weg – prompt schoss mir das entscheidende Bild in den Kopf: mein Freund Axel am Tisch der Mensa, neben uns die Zeitung, aufgeschlagen die Seite mit einer Über-schrift zum beginnenden Prozess gegen <u>diesen Richter, der am Volksg-erichtshof mindestens 230 Todesurteile gefällt hatte</u>. Sogleich stellte sich der Ton zu diesem Bild ein, der bittere, verächtliche Satz, den Axel hatte fallen lassen und der mich erst jetzt, im Bett, wie eine böse Erleuchtung traf: <u>Der</u> hat das Urteil für meinen Vater fabriziert, <u>der</u> und der Freisler. [GO_FICTION_001]

(34)   I distracted myself, sought sleep, forgot, drifted off – and promptly the crucial image popped into my head: my friend Axel at the cafeteria table, the newspaper next to us opened to a headline about the start of the trial of <u>this judge who had passed at least 230 death sentences at the People's Tribunal</u>. Immediately the soundtrack to this image kicked in, Axel's bitter, contemptuous words which hit me only now, in bed, like an evil epiphany: <u>He</u> fabricated my father's verdict – <u>him</u> and Freisler. [ETrans_FICTION_001]

The instances identified in FICTION show that *der* and *die* are mostly employed for reference to human beings, which is not possible with demonstratives in English. As the example displays, partial equivalence in meaning can be obtained by a personal pronoun.

Examples (33) and (34) below, taken from the CroCo subcorpus SPEECH, illustrate that a proximate demonstrative pronoun is employed in English for reference to abstract entities where the form *die* is used in German:

(35)   <u>Bei den Gebuehren fuer Rundfunk</u> kann ich es mir, verehrter Herr Ministerpraesident, ganz leicht machen: <u>die</u> duerfen nur die deutschen Laender erheben. [GO_SPPECH_012]

(36)   As for <u>the licence fee issue</u>, I have a very simple answer, for <u>these</u>, Mr Minister-President, are a matter purely for the Laender.' [ETrans_SPEECH_012]

The most notable differences between the two registers investigated in English concern the distributions of *this* and *that*: while the figures for ESSAY lie relatively close together there is a considerable divergence in frequency in the register FICTION, which still requires closer inspection.

Altogether, the heterogeneity in frequency of demonstrative pronouns as shown in Table 2 for the registers ESSAY and FICTION seem to reflect the fact that similar forms are hardly comparable across languages and even register. They seem to serve more different functions than become apparent on the basis of a theoretical consideration of systemic differences and thus call for an intensive investigation of the respective occurrences in the texts.

5. Conclusions and outlook

The above examples of corpus linguistic research may serve as an indication that empirical corpus linguistic studies are an essential step towards a contrast for that model of cohesion in English and German, not only because they yield statistics about the frequency of cohesive devices, but also because they allow a more comprehensive interpretation and because they show a wider range of realizational possibilities for one and the same cohesive relation than one would suspect without corpus evidence. However, in order to gain a more comprehensive picture of the distribution and function of cohesive devices holding for texts produced in English and German, we have to look into all other registers of the CroCo Corpus. In addition, we aim at an expansion of the corpus to registers of spoken language such as interviews or dialogues, since we expect considerable differences as compared to registers in the written mode. Furthermore, an investigation of more linguistic devices establishing cohesion will be necessary together with an analysis of co-occurrences of different means of cohesion in particular texts across registers and languages. In addition, we also intend to analyse how cohesive chains are realized in both languages and thus cover an aspect of cohesion which has largely been neglected in the literature, and even more so in contrastive accounts of cohesion.

Notes

1.   The project is funded by the Deutsche Forschungsgemeinschaft (DFG) under GZ STE 840: 6–1.

2.   For a description of the architecture of our corpus, cf. Culo *et al.* (forthcoming), and for the revised and extended architecture Kunz and Lapshinova-Koltunski (2011) and Amoia *et al.* (2011).

3.   For a more extensive discussion of the current and the preceding section, cf. Steiner (2012).

4.   Note that this applies to grammaticalized structures in general, e.g., verbal inflection signalling person in 'pro-drop' languages.

5.   As we have shown in detail elsewhere (e.g., Steiner, 1994), semantic/functional distinctions specific to some place in the structure of a language will usually be made at some other place of the system in another language.

6.   Not reference to things, interestingly, i.e., there is no 'impersonal pronoun' for things. We are not sure that 'one' or German 'man' actually belongs here, being a means of reference, though not of co-reference. Otherwise, we would have to include the numerous 'indefinite pro-forms' *someone, Jemand/ eine-r/-e/-s, unsereiner/euereines, unseresgleichen/euresgleichen'* (by identiy) and others (Zifonoun *et al.*, 1997, 1: 43) . But none of these establishes co-reference. But then, this applies to reference to speech roles in general (cf. Halliday and Hasan, 1976: 48).

7.   Note also the German tendency towards using *es/das* for cases of extended reference, or possibly rather substitution, where English would use ellipses: *Ich kann ihn sehen, aber Du kannst es/das nicht (I can see him, but you can't)*.

8.   Though not all, cf. *Mädchen* ('the girl', neuter), even if what triggers the neuter here is the diminutive, cf. analogously *das Bübchen* ('the boy', neuter).

9.   But see the English possibility of 'She is nice and *so* is he', which rather comes under 'comparative reference', or possibly even substitution?

10.   Like Halliday and Hasan (1976: 54f) point out, these are cases of reference in so far as they co-refer to a person. We believe they can also be analysed as cases of *substitution*.

11.   See among many others Zifonun *et al.* (1997, 1: 311ff), who discuss person, object, local, temporal, textual (locutionary) and illocutionary deixis, see also Becher (2011), Ehlich (2007) and elsewhere, on the distinction between 'deixis' and 'anaphora'.

12.   See the treatment as a 'Demonstrativpronomen' in Schreiber (1999: 216ff), or as 'Referenzpronomen' in Weinrich 1993: 373f).

13.   See *Präpositionaladverbien* in Zifonun *et al.* (1997, 1: 54f f) and elsewhere; *Pronominaladverbien* in Schreiber (1999: 240ff).

14.   For example, demonstrative articles tending to prefer the more spoken registers, and the pronominal adverbs and pronouns being quite constrained as for co-reference to simple-entity-like participants, but occurring freely with 'meta-phenomena'.

15.   Or, in fact, the third person singular pronoun *it*, but that is covered under *personal reference*. Observe that articles, like other word classes, also have important clause-internal, that is grammaticalized functions, but these are outside our current focus.

16.   Registerially very restricted in modern German.

17.   Demonstrative article.

18.   Only possible with neuter gender and most likely extended reference.

19.   Demonstrative articles quite acceptable in German colloquial register.

20.   Only in contrastive contexts.

21.   Restricted.

22. Observe that the PP-variants preferred in English (*below it, upon it, before it, behind it*) are dispreferred in German, and above all not cases of demonstrative reference.

23. Probably restricted to extended reference nowadays.

24. With possible restricted 'near' variants *hereof, hereby …/hiervon, hiermit …*

25. This is a significant translation problem within the Germanic languages cf. Ramm (2010: 190ff).

26. 'Invariant' at least as to gender and number.

27. It is, of course, important here to include the work of more than one translator in the corpus; otherwise the findings could be due to an idiosyncratic translation strategy.

28. For further details on corpus design see http://fr46.uni-saarland.de/croco/corpus_ design.pdf

References

Ahrenholz, B. (2007) *Verweise mit Demonstrativa im gesprochenen Deutsch. Grammatik, Zweitspracherwerb und Deutsch als Fremdsprache.* Berlin and New York: de Gruyter.

Amoia, M., Kunz, K. and Lapshinova-Koltunski, E (2011) Discontinuous constituents: A problematic case for parallel corpora annotation and querying. In *Proceedings of the 2nd Workshop on Annotation and Exploitation of Parallel Corpora (AEPC2 a RANLP 2011 workshop).* Hissar, Bulgaria. September.

Asher, N. (1993) *Reference to Abstract Objects in Discourse.* Dordrecht: Kluwer. http:// dx.doi.org/10.1007/978-94-011-1715-9

Barwise, J. and Perry, J. (1983) *Situations and Attitudes.* Cambridge, MA: MIT-Bradford.

Beaugrande, R.-A. de and Dressler, W. U. (1981) *Introduction to Text Linguistics.* London and New York: Longman (German version also in 1981 published by Niemeyer).

Becher, V. (2011) Differences in the use of deictic expressions in English and German texts. *Linguistics* 48 (4): 1309–1342.

Becher, V., Höder, S. and Kranich, S. (2009) A tentative typology of translation-induced language change. Paper given at Workshop Multilingual Discourse Production, 6–7 November. University of Hamburg Research Centre on Multilingualism.

Biber, D., Johansson, S., Leech, G., Conrad, S. and Finegan, E. (1999) *Longman Grammar of Spoken and Written English.* Harlow: Longman.

Bosch, P., Katz, G. and Umbach, C. (2007) The non-subject bias of German demonstrative pronouns. In M. Schwarz-Friesel, M. Consten and M. Knees (eds) *Anaphors in Text. Cognitive, Formal and Applied Approaches to Anaphoric Reference,* 145–164. Universität Jena: Studies in Language Companion Series.

Brinker, K. (2005) *Linguistische Textanalyse: Eine Einführung in Grundbegriffe und Methoden.* 6th edition. Berlin: Erich Schmidt.

Brown, G. and Yule, G. (1983) *Discourse Analysis.* Cambridge: Cambridge University Press.

Carston, R. (2002). *Thoughts and Utterances: The Pragmatics of Explicit Communication.* Oxford: Blackwell. http://dx.doi.org/10.1002/9780470754603

Cruse, D. A., Hundsnurscher, F. and Lutzeier, P. (2005) *Lexikologie/ Lexicology. Ein internationals Handbuch zur Natur und Struktur von Wörtern und Wortschätzen.* Berlin/ New York.

Čulo, O., Hansen-Schirra, Neumann, S. and Maksymski, K. (forthcoming). Querying the CroCo corpus for translation shifts. Beyond corpus construction: exploitation and maintenance of parallel corpora. In S. Hansen-Schirra, S. Neumann and C. Oliver (eds) *Beyond Corpus Construction: Exploitation and Maintenance of Parallel Corpora.* Special Issue of the *International Journal of Corpus Linguistics.*

Diessel, H. (1999) The morphosyntax of demonstratives in synchrony and diachrony. *Linguistic Typology* 3 (1): 1–49. http://dx.doi.org/10.1515/lity.1999.3.1.1

Doherty, M. (2004) Reorganizing dependencies. In: *SPRIKreports*, No 23, October 2004.

Doherty, M. (2006) *Structural Propensities. Translating Nominal Word Groups from English into German.* Amsterdam and Philadelphia, PA: Benjamins.

Ehlich, K. (2007) Anadeixis und Anapher. In K. Ehlich (ed.) *Prozeduren des sprachlichen Handelns (Sprache und sprachliches Handeln 2)*, 25–44. Berlin and New York: Mouton de Gruyter.

Eisenberg, P. (1994) *Grundriss der deutschen Grammatik.* 3rd edition. Stuttgart: Weimar: Metzler.

Engel, U. (2004) *Deutsche Grammatik.* Neubearbeitung. München: iudicium.

Esser, J. (2009) *Introduction to English Text-linguistics.* Frankfurt a.M.: Peter Lang.

Fabricius-Hansen, C. (1996) Informational density: a problem for translation and translation theory. *Linguistics* 34 (special issue): 521–565. http://dx.doi.org/10.1515/ling.1996.34.3.521

Fabricius-Hansen, C. (1999) Information packaging and translation: Aspects of translational sentence splitting (German–English/Norwegian). *Studia Grammatica* 47: 175–214.

Fabricius-Hansen, C. (2005) Elusive connectives. A case study on the explicitness dimension of discourse coherence. *Linguistics* 43 (1): 17–48. http://dx.doi.org/10.1515/ling.2005.43.1.17

Featherstone, S. and Winkler. S. (eds) (2009) *The Fruits of Empirical Linguistics. Vol. 1: Process, Vol. 2: Product.* Berlin: de Gruyter.

Grimes, J. E. (1975) *The Thread of Discourse.* The Hague: Mouton.

Grosz, B. J., Joshi, A. K. and Weinstein, J. (1995) Centering: A framework for modelling the local coherence of discourse. *Computational Linguistics* 21 (2): 203–225.

Gundel, J. K., Hedberg, N. and Zacharski, R. (2004) Demonstrative pronouns in natural discourse. *Proceedings of the Fifth Discourse Anaphora and Anaphora Resolution Colloquium* 81–86. São Miguel, Portugal.

Halliday, M. A. K. and Matthiessen, C. M. I. M. (2004) *An Introduction to Functional Grammar.* 3rd edition. London: Arnold.

Halliday, M. A. K. and Hasan, R. (1976) *Cohesion in English.* London and New York: Longman.

Hansen-Schirra, S., Neumann, S. and Steiner, E. (2007) Cohesion and explicitation in an English-German translation corpus. *Languages in Contrast* 7 (2): 241–265.

Haspelmath, M. (2009) Welche Fragen können wir mit herkömmlichen Daten beantworten? *Forum Zeitschrift für Sprachwissenschaft ZfS* 28 (1): 157ff.

Hatakeyama, K., Petöfi, J. S., Sözer, E. (1989) Text, Konnexität, Kohäsion, Kohärenz. In: Conte, E. (ed.) (1989) *Kontinuität und Diskontinuität in Texten und Sachverhalts-Konfigurationen. Diskussion über Konnexität, Kohäsion und Kohärenz.* Hamburg: Buske, 1–55.

Hawkins, J. A. (1986) *A Comparative Typology of English and German: Unifying the Contrasts.* London: Croom Helm.

Heidolf, K. E., Flämig, W. and Motsch, W. (eds). (1981) *Grundzüge einer deutschen Grammatik.* Berlin: Akademie Verlag.

Helbig, G. and Buscha, J. (2001) *Deutsche Grammatik. Ein Handbuch für den Ausländerunterricht.* Berlin, etc.: Langenscheidt.

Huddleston, R. D. and Pullum, G. K. (2002) *The Cambridge Grammar of the English Language.* Cambridge: Cambridge University Press.

Kamp, H., Reyle, U. (1993) *From Discourse to Logic. Introduction to Model-theoretic Semantics of Natural Language, Formal Logic and Discourse Representation Theory.* Kluwer: Dordrecht.

König E. and Gast, V. (2007) *Understanding English-German Contrasts. Grundlagen der Anglistik und Amerikanistik* (revised 2nd edition: 2009). Berlin: Schmidt.

Königs, K. (2000) *Übersetzen Englisch–Deutsch. Systemischer Ansatz.* München: Oldenbourg.

Kunz, K. (2010) *English and German nominal coreference. A study of political essays.* PhD Thesis. Frankfurt am Main: Peter Lang.

Kunz, K. and Lapshinova-Koltunski, E. (2011) Tools to analyse German-English contrasts in cohesion. In *Hamburg Working Papers in Multilingualism* (poster at GsCL 2011 Hamburg).

Kunz, K. and Steiner, E. (forthcoming) Cohesive substitution in English and German – a contrastive and corpus-based perspective. In: K. Aijmer and B. Altenberg (eds). *Advances in Corpus-based Contrastive Linguistics. Studies in Honour of Stig Johansson.* Amsterdam: John Benjamins.

Lascarides, A. and Asher, N. (1993) Temporal interpretation, discourse relations and commonsense entailment. *Linguistics and Philosophy* 16 (5): 437–493. http://dx.doi.org/10.10 07/BF00986208

Linke, A., Nussbaumer, M. and Portmann, P. R. (2004) *Studienbuch Linguistik.* 5th edition. Tübingen: Niemeyer.

Lipka, L. (2002). *English Lexicology. Lexical Structure, Word Semantics and Word Formation.* Tübingen: Niemeyer.

Mann, W. C. and Thompson, S. A. (1987) Rhetorical Structure Theory: A theory of text organization. In *Technical Report ISI/RS-87-190*. Los Angeles, CA: University of Southern California, USC Information Sciences Institute.

Matthiessen, C. M. I. M. and Thompson, S. A. (1988). The structure of discourse and 'subordination'. In J. Haiman and S. A. Thompson (eds) *Clause Combining in Grammar and Discourse*, 275–329. Amsterdam: Benjamins.

Matras, Y. (2009) *Language Contact*. Cambridge: Cambridge University Press. http://dx.doi.org/10.1017/CBO9780511809873

Quirk, R., Greenbaum, S. Leech, G. and Svartvik, J. (1985) *A Comprehensive Grammar of the English Language*. Harlow: Longman.

Ramm, W. (2010) *Satzgrenzenveränderung in der Übersetzung: Satzverbindung und lokale Diskursorganisation im Norwegischen und Deutschen*. Oslo: University of Oslo, Humanistiske Fakultet.

Rohdenburg, G. (1990) Aspekte einer vergleichenden Typologie des Englischen und Deutschen. Kritische Anmerkungen zu einem Buch von John A. Hawkins. In C. Gnutzmann (ed.) *Kontrastive Linguistik. Forum Angewandte Linguistik. Band 19*, 133–152. Frankfurt am Main: Peter Lang Verlag.

Schreiber, M. (1999) *Textgrammatik. Gesprochene Sprache. Sprachvergleich*. Frankfurt am Main: Peter Lang Verlag. (Reihe Vario Linguistica. Nonstandard – Standard – Substandard.)

Schubert, C. (2008) *Englische Textlinguistik. Eine Einführung*. Berlin: Erich Schmid Verlag.

Siemund, P. and Kintana, N. (eds) (2008) *Language Contact and Contact Languages*. Hamburg Studies in Multilingualism Vol. 7. Amsterdam: Benjamins.

Steiner, E. (1994) A fragment of a Multilingual Transfer Component and its Relation to Discourse Knowledge. In W. Ramm (ed.). *Text and Context in Machine Translation: Aspects of discourse representation in discourse processing. Studies in Machine Translation and Natural Language Processing 6*, 77. Brüssel and Luxemburg Europäische Kommission.

Steiner, E. and Ramm. W. (1995) On Theme as a grammatical notion for German. *Functions of Language* 2 (1): 57–93.

Steiner, E. and E. Teich. (2004) Metafunctional profile of the grammar of German. In A. Caffarel, J. R. Martin and C. M. I. M. Matthiessen (eds) *Language Typology. A Functional Perspective*, 77–138. Amsterdam: Benjamins.

Steiner, E. (2006) Construing contextualization through meaning: Some thoughts on a semantics for theme. In S.-Y. Cho and E. Steiner (eds) *Information Distribution in English Grammar and Discourse and other Topics in Linguistics. Festschrift for Peter Erdmann on the Occasion of his 65th Birthday*, 267–288. Frankfurt am Main: Peter Lang.

Steiner, E. (2012) Towards a comparison of cohesion in English and German – the concept of cohesion. In V. Atayan and U. Wienen (eds) '*Sprache – Rhetorik – Translation. Festschrift für Alberto Gil zum 60. Geburtstag*'. Reihe 'Rhethos'. Frankfurt am Main: Peter Lang.

Taboada, M. and Mann, W. C. (2006) Rhetorical Structure Theory: Looking back and moving ahead. *Discourse Studies* 8(3): 423–459. http://dx.doi.org/10.1177/1461445606061881

Taboada, M. and Zabala, W. C. L. (2008) Deciding on units of analysis within Centering Theory. *Corpus Linguistics and Linguistic Theory* 4 (1): 63–108. http://dx.doi.org/10.1515/CLLT.2008.003

Teich, E. (2003) *Cross-linguistic Variation in System and Text. A Methodology for the Investigation of Translations and Comparable Texts.* Berlin/New York: de Gruyter.

Thomason, S. and Kaufman, T. (1988) *Language Contact, Creolization, and Genetic Linguistics.* Berkeley, Los Angeles, CA and Oxford: University of California Press.

Vater, H. 2001. *Einführung in die Textlinguistik.* 3rd edition. München: Fink.

Wanzeck, C. (2010) *Lexikologie: Beschreibung von Wort und Wortschatz im Deutschen.* Göttingen: Vandenhoek und Ruprecht.

Weinrich, H. (1993) *Textgrammatik der deutschen Sprache.* Mannheim: Dudenverlag.

Zifonun, G., Hoffmann, L. and Strecker, B. (1997) *Grammatik der deutschen Sprache.* Berlin and New York: de Gruyter.

11 Genre- and culture-specific aspects of evaluation: Insights from the contrastive analysis of English and Italian online property advertising

Gabrina Pounds

The distinction between evaluative and non-evaluative meaning in discourse is problematic. Many expressions may be purely factual in some contexts and evaluative in others. As argued by Hunston (1999: 199–201), the criteria for evaluation rely in part on shared assumptions that form part of the message of any texts. Evaluation is, therefore, often expressed in ways that are highly implicit and discourse-dependent. The aim of this paper is to illustrate how detailed manual contrastive linguistic analysis comparing equivalent genres (online property descriptions in this case) produced in two different contexts of culture (England and Italy) may be used to: (a) explore the fine variation in the subjective force of evaluative expressions, which might escape automated larger-scale analysis; and, thereby (b) distinguish with some precision between genre- and culture-specific aspects of evaluation. The theoretical framework for the analysis is derived from Appraisal Theory (Martin and White, 2005) and from the author's earlier adaptation and application of the framework to the analysis of English property descriptions (Pounds, 2011). The significance of the findings is discussed with particular reference to further research into genre- and culture-specific evaluative patterns.

1. Introduction

It is notoriously difficult to produce reliable classifications of evaluative expressions as their evaluative nature and strength vary significantly according to discourse type, context and level of observation. Many expressions may actually be purely factual in some contexts and evaluative in others. The aim of this paper is to show that contrastive linguistic analysis may be used to clarify the extent to which evaluation and evaluative strategies are both genre- and culture-specific. The contrastive analysis is applied to a corpus of English and Italian online property descriptions produced by six different estate agents (three for each cultural setting). The analysis focuses on expressions of positive evaluation which realize the promotional function of the discourse. The Italian and English descriptions are subject to very similar constraints since legislation has been introduced in both Italy and England to ensure that estate agents produce sufficiently objective descriptions of the properties they are promoting. This means that the expression of positive evaluation has to be balanced against the requirement to provide accurate factual information. In both Italy and England the descriptions are accompanied by pictures and are made available online in very similar formats. The question, therefore, arises as to whether positive evaluation is similarly encoded in both sets of descriptions. Expressions of positive evaluation are identified in terms of 'appraisal' choices with particular reference to the categories of positive 'appreciation' outlined by Martin and White (2005). The author's earlier adaptation of the framework – used to compare expressions of evaluation in the online property descriptions produced by different English estate agents (Pounds, 2011) – is revisited to establish its suitability to the comparison between the Italian and English samples. The analysis reveals that very similar evaluative strategies are employed in the two sets of descriptions, indicating that they may be genre- rather than language- or culture-specific. Significant differences were, however, also identified, which appear to point towards culture-specific variation centred on particular socio-cultural and interpersonal values. The study further shows the extent to which detailed genre- and context-specific contrastive analysis is needed in order to capture the more subtle aspects of evaluation.

2. The genre of online property advertising

It can be argued that Italian and English online property descriptions belong to the same genre as they share functional, structural and stylistic features as well as content and intended audience. In the existing literature (e.g., Swales, 1990: 58) it is the sharing of all these aspects (particularly the communicative purpose) that forms the principal criterion for the definition of genre. These similarities are partly due to the similar legal constraints under which the descriptions are produced and, possibly, the inevitable tendency towards genre standardization across countries operating in a global market.

This may arguably apply particularly to widely accessible online genres. The shared aspects of the genre are presented and clarified in the following subsections.

2.1. Relevance of the legislation

The requirement of accuracy in property descriptions has increased over the last few decades. In the UK, the Property Misdescriptions Act (PMA) was introduced in 1991 (enforced 1993) which provides for an offence of making 'a *false* or *misleading* statement about a *prescribed matter* in the course of an estate agency business or a property development business' (S1[1], emphasis added). The 'prescribed matters' include 33 categories covering both physical (dimensions and construction) as well as legal matters (tenure and planning). What appears to be admissible (see Hodgson's clarification, 1994) are statements of facts (for which evidence can be provided and as long as they are not false or misleading) and statements of opinion or evaluation that cannot be factually proven as long as *immaterial* (promotional, not directly relevant to subject matter of the negotiation), mere 'puff and wind' (Hodgson, 1994) and clearly expressed as opinion rather than fact. These are expressions shared by most other types of advertising (see Section 2.2).

No Act has been introduced in Italy (to the best of the author's knowledge) that specifically provides against false or misleading statements in property descriptions but Art. 2008 in the Codice Federazione Italiana Agenti Immobiliari (Code of the Italian Federation of Estate Agents) states that 'Il contenuto dell'informazione pubblicitaria non dovrá mai essere ingannevole, elogiativa e comparativa' ('The content of the advertised information should never be misleading, praising or comparative', my literal translation).

2.2. Property descriptions vs. general advertising

A precursory analysis of the English and Italian property descriptions immediately reveals that they do indeed contain primarily factual information about the location, size and price of the properties. While the proportion of explicitly evaluative language has overall increased in traditional advertising over time (Woods, 206: ch. 1), partly precisely because explicit promotion is less subject to regulatory prohibitions (Shimp and Preston, 1981: 24–30), the reverse applies in property descriptions. Explicit evaluation was found to amount to no more than 6% in the study of property advertising in the West of Scotland conducted by Pryce and Oates (2007, 2008).

The study on 'advertising claim objectivity' conducted by Darley and Smith (1993) concluded that the quality and strength of the message claims based on verifiable properties of the product offered (the *facts*) are most effective when consumers are 'interested in learning about the advertised product [because of high relevance] and, therefore, carefully consider the ad's content'. This would, therefore, apply to property advertising independently of the requirements of the legislation. To the extent, however, that properties are also 'value-expressive' products (such as perfume and stylish clothes, Park and Young, 1986) and 'feeling products' (evaluated primarily on the basis of personal preference, Tellis, 2004), some form of subjective evaluation may also be expected. Shimp and Preston (1981: 30) argue that evaluative advertising represents a rather 'risk-free' advertising strategy as it 'may deceive consumers into thinking that the brand is somehow unique or superior to competing offerings, yet regulators are unlikely to challenge the advertising due to the abstract and apparently innocuous nature of the claims'. This would seem to apply in property descriptions (see previous section) even though, on balance, factual formulations prevail.

Shaw's study of evaluative language in promotional genres (2006) shows that agent's particulars share features with other, more traditional forms of 'evaluative interested genres' (aiming at persuading the recipient to do something that will benefit the producer). Such features include: prevalence of positive evaluation, frequency of authorial expression of affect (as in: *we are delighted to offer for sale this three bedroom mid-terrace house*), relatively low frequency of terms whose value is clear in any context (such as *good* or *fine*), uneven distribution of evaluation and, particularly, non-distinctive evaluation (such as *fully functional* or *useful spare room*, Shaw, 2006: 157), that is, evaluation that does not 'discriminate between good and less good cases'.

3. General overview of the corpus

The online descriptions selected for analysis were produced by well-established estate agents in the East of England (Norfolk) and Northern Italy (Lombardy: Monza-Brianza). The six agents (three in each cultural area) were selected so as to represent maximum variation in evaluative content (as estimated on the basis of precursory analysis). For each set one agency was included that appeared to produce more concise and factual descriptions than most of the others. All six agents have their own websites as well as advertising their properties on the most popular general property websites. They typically include a picture, price, location of the property and short description and/or summary of the main features. It is then possible to view further pictures and access the full details including the listing of the various rooms, sizes and contents and specific internal and external features. Further links typically lead the viewer to one or more maps, floor plan and, in some cases, more specific information about travel options and location of services and amenities. Most of the evaluative material is included in the initial description or summary. Ninety descriptions (45 Italian and 45 English) were analysed overall: 15 descriptions per agency. The descriptions of local properties were selected at random across the full range of prices. These ranged from about £150,000 to £5,000,000 for the English descriptions and from about €170,000 to €5,000,000 for the Italian descriptions. Some selection criteria were applied to enable comparison: only urban family properties were included, only houses for the English set and mainly flats for the Italian set. This is because, within the regions concerned, in urban areas, the average family live mostly in houses in England but in flats in Italy. For each agency ten properties were selected from a tighter price range of £300,000/350,000 Euro to £150,000/170,000 Euro so as to avoid major differences due to high price differential. Five amongst the most expensive properties were then added in each case to check for any considerable variation at the very top end of the market. Sections included in the analysis were: main description, list of full details and summary of main features, if applicable. Repeated formulations across full details and summary were excluded. The English set comprised 24,796 words (an average of about 550 words per description). The Italian set comprised 5,595 words (an average of 125 words per description). The difference in word number is due to the fact that the English descriptions contain much longer factual sections listing the measurements and contents of each room. This aspect is considered in the discussion of the findings. Even though there is very little difference between the material appearing on the agency's own website and the version provided on the general online sites (the responsibility for which rests with the agencies), only the former was used in the analysis. No striking differences were observed in the nature or number of the pictures provided. More detailed analysis may reveal subtle and, possibly, significant variation but falls outside the scope of this study. Some reference is made, however, to the reliance on visual material in the discussion of the findings (Section 7.2).

4. Evaluation and its dimensions

The linguistic expression of evaluation is particularly difficult to analyse due to the number of aspects involved (e.g., *subjectivity, affect, modality*). Overlapping terms are used to refer to various aspects, depending on the researcher's perspective (e.g., *evaluation, attitude, stance, appraisal*). Whilst some attitudinal meanings, including levels of certainty and obligation, are associated with specific linguistic items (e.g., modal verbs and adverbs) others, such as positive or negative evaluation are typically realized prosodically over long stretches of text and through varying and unpredictable lexico-grammatical operators. The distinction between evaluative and non-evaluative expression is additionally problematic in that many expressions may be purely factual in some contexts and evaluative in others. As noticed by Hunston and Sinclair (1999: 74), '… evaluation appears parasitic on other resources and to be somewhat randomly dispersed across a range of structural options shared with non-evaluative functions'. As argued by Hunston (1999: 199–201), the criteria for evaluation rely in part on shared assumptions that form part of the message of any text and evaluation is, therefore, often expressed in ways that are highly implicit and context-dependent. In the case of property descriptions, the shared assumption of their promotional function provides the basis for the interpretation of their positive evaluative content.

Variation in the evaluative patterns of discourse produced in different cultural settings is, therefore, likely to be due to pragmatic factors, linked to contextual features and cultural preferences, rather than structural differences in linguistic systems. This is arguably why evaluation is best explored through contrastive genre- rather than contrastive linguistic analysis. This paper is particularly concerned with the expression of positive evaluation and with establishing whether and to what extent similar evaluative meanings and formulations appear in the Italian and English online property descriptions.

Similarities in evaluative patterns would point to genre-specific features that may be found across a number of different language-cultures and for which variant configurations may be observed across different types of promotional genres. Differences in evaluative patterns, on the other hand, may be linked to differences in the socio-cultural and interpersonal dimensions underlying the property-transaction process in the two cultures. This would highlight aspects of evaluative expression that are particularly susceptible to cultural preferences, such as levels of explicitness or emotive involvement, and may underlie other evaluation-rich genres within the same language-culture. The aim, in other words, is to distinguish between two different types of contextual influence on the expression of evaluation, namely genre-specific and cultural-specific factors.

The expression of evaluation in specific genres is typically studied in relation to its structural position within the text it appears in. This means that the lexico-grammatical realizations of evaluation tend to be identified in sections of text which are explicitly *evaluative* (see, for example, Taboada's analysis of online movie reviews, 2011). If it is granted, however, that the overall function of a text (promotional in the case of online property descriptions) provides the basis for the interpretation of its evaluative content (as argued above), formulations which, in other contexts, are factual and descriptive (and appear in *non-evaluative* sections), may be invested with some evaluative meaning. In order to capture, therefore, the finer distinctions between levels of evaluation in context, the property descriptions were analysed in their entirety. It is widely acknowledged that such finer distinctions in the levels of strength and implicitness of the evaluation are difficult to identify in automated analysis of large corpora (see Bednarek, 2006: 46–48, 74) and that the most implicit formulations retrievable over long stretches of text may be missed (see Taboada and Carretero, this volume). The small-scale, non-automated analysis presented in this study, on the other hand, is specifically concerned with identifying context-dependent and implicit formulations and with *grading* evaluative operators according to both theory- and context-derived criteria.

5. The APPRAISAL framework and genre-specific adaptations

Appraisal Theory provides a useful theoretical foundation for the study of evaluation in context. It has been formulated over the past 20 years by a group of scholars based in Australia (noticeably Martin, Rose, White and Rothery) and working within the Systemic Functional approach to discourse analysis. The current theoretical framework (Martin and White, 2005) was derived from the analysis of attitudinal expression in journalistic genres and in the discourse of aesthetic appreciation. As indicated by Martin (1999: 161) and Martin and White (2005: 58), however, it is expected that these categories may need to be modified depending on the discourse observed. Appraisal resources are a set of interpersonal operators that realize speaker/writer's evaluative expression along three main parameters (simplified from Martin and White, 2005):

> ENGAGEMENT: Expression of commitment to what is stated (*she <u>may</u> have betrayed us*)
> ATTITUDE: Expression of:
>> Own or observed emotion: AFFECT (*I am/they are <u>upset</u>*)
>> Judgement of people: JUDGEMENT (*she is very <u>patient</u>*)
>> Appreciation of things end events: APPRECIATION (*the film was <u>great</u>*)
> GRADUATION: Expression that modulates or scales what is said in terms of its intensity/
> FORCE (*this is <u>extremely</u> irritating*) or prototypicality/FOCUS (he is a <u>true</u> friend).

Martin and White (2005: 45) argue that AFFECT is the core attitudinal parameter in that it underlies JUDGEMENT and APPRECIATION, which are, arguably, 'institutionalized' forms of feelings. They (2005: 136) also point out that GRADUATION, although presented as an independent parameter, is central to the ATTITUDE and ENGAGEMENT domains, to which scaling may typically be applied.

Although in the examples provided above the evaluative meaning is directly inscribed and retrievable out of context, Martin and White (2005: 61–68) observe and show that evaluative meaning may often be expressed more implicitly and indirectly. In these cases the interpretation is entirely reliant on the context. Of particular relevance is also the degree to which seemingly factual material may be invested with evaluative meaning in context.

As a form of 'evaluative interested genre' (see Section 2.2) the discourse of property advertising is mainly characterized by the positive evaluation of 'things', values of affectivity and generalized subjectivity. The categories of APPRECIATION and GRADUATION are, therefore, expected to play a key role. AFFECT is also likely to be relevant to the extent that it is often implicated in values of APPRECIATION. The appraisal categories of APPRECIATION have been used as a basis on which the more specific genre-based categories are identified. Table 1 presents the categories of APPRECIATION, as distinguished by Martin and White (2005: 56). The basis for the categorization of APPRECIATION: COMPOSITION is clearly the language of the visual arts and the aesthetic domain. The REACTION categories of IMPACT and quality are, however, generally applicable to a variety of promotional discourse types and appear to include more emotionally charged evaluation than the other categories. In the context of property descriptions, VALUATION, which, as argued by Martin (2005: 57), is particularly field-specific (since the value of things is particularly dependent on the institutional focus), can be further subcategorized to include the elements that make up the value and qualities of a property such as its appearance, functionality, location, size and age.

An earlier version of the appraisal framework is used by Shaw (2006, see Section 2.2) in his analysis of promotional genres (including agent's particulars) but the categories are mainly employed to distinguish between 'interested' and 'disinterested' genres and are, therefore, not developed (refined or extended) for the purpose of finer discrimination between 'interested' (conventional) advertising genres.

Table 1: Categories of APPRECIATION within the appraisal model (Martin and White 2005: 56), showing positive examples only.

	Positive
REACTION: IMPACT: 'did it grab me?'	arresting, captivating, engaging …; fascinating, exciting, moving … lively, dramatic, intense … remarkable, notable, sensational …
REACTION: QUALITY: 'did I like it?'	okay, fine, good … lovely, beautiful, splendid … appealing, enchanting, welcome …
COMPOSITION: BALANCE 'did it hang together?'	balanced, harmonious, unified … symmetrical, proportioned … consistent, considered, logical … shapely, curvaceous, willowy …
COMPOSITION: COMPLEXITY: 'was it hard to follow?'	simple, pure, elegant … lucid, clear, precise … intricate, rich, detailed …
VALUATION: 'was it worthwhile?'	penetrating, profound, deep … innovative, original, creative … timely, long awaited, landmark, inimitable, exceptional, unique … authentic, real, genuine … valuable, priceless, worthwhile … appropriate, helpful, effective …

More genre-specific categories may be derived from the rhetorical analysis of property descriptions undertaken by Pryce and Oates (2007). Their categories are based upon the distinction between LOGOS and PATHOS: LOGOS includes the listing of facts about the property that makes up the majority of the description and PATHOS includes emotive expressions. They distinguish between broad (potentially emotive) and narrow (unambiguously emotive) definitions of PATHOS. The broad group includes four subcategories: expressions related to the ORIGINALITY of the property (*character, individual* ...), its general AMBIANCE (*bright, fresh* ...), its PRESTIGE (*exclusive, executive* ...) and EXCITEMENT (*amazing, fantastic* ...). The narrow group includes expressions such as *preferred, lovely, exceptional* ... Their analysis has the advantage that it relies on a very large corpus and uses discourse-specific categories. As it was computer-aided, however, it was arguably less sensitive to the effects of contextual variation on meaning (finer variation in evaluative strength) than a manual analysis.

6. Categories of positive evaluation in the Italian and English property descriptions

By integrating Pryce and Oates' categories with the APPRECIATION categories from the APPRAISAL system a framework was initially created to compare the evaluative content in the property descriptions produced by different English agencies (Pounds, 2011). It was already clear at that stage that additional categories needed to be included to account for those formulations whose evaluative meaning or impact is either acquired or implied in context. It was also found that dimensions of subjectivity and affectivity appear to play a more important role than apparent in the appraisal framework and may be used to differentiate more clearly between evaluative dimensions. Levels of affectivity could also be identified with more precision than in Price and Oates's and in Shaw's study. One of the aims of the present contrastive study was to review this framework to establish, in the first instance, whether it could be applied to the Italian corpus. The fact that this was found to be the case is viewed as the main evidence of genre similarity and is referred to in Section 7.1 below. The same main distinctions were found to apply and only minor adjustments in subcategories were required. The relevant dimensions are summarized and illustrated in Table 2 (see Appendix) and clarified below.

Table 2: Categories of POSITIVE APPRECIATION identified in the corpus (English examples)

EXPLICIT

EMOTIVE IMPACT (E) Highest subjectivity (values of affect)	*Impressive, breathtaking, exceptional, exciting, amazing, fantastic, a palace/heaven, superb …*
PLEASANTNESS (P) Lower affectivity but still high subjectivity	*Lovely, beautiful, appealing, charming, attractive, pleasant, delightful, well-structured …*
QUALITY (Q) Minimum affectivity and subjectivity	1st -CLASS: higher indeterminacy/subjectivity ORIGINALITY: *original, unique, character, individual, imaginative, innovative, unusual, bespoke…* AMBIANCE: *clean, tidy, immaculate, bright, light, fresh, quiet, private, sunny …* PRESTIGE: *exclusive, executive, enviable, prestigious, popular, luxury, upmarket, prime, first-class…* FUNCTIONALITY: *effective, useful, in good working order, well-maintained…* CRAFTSMANSHIP: *quality, to a high standard, accurate…* 2nd-CLASS: lower indeterminacy/subjectivity LOCATION: *with views …, with (good/easy) access to …, near/close to … on the edge of …* USE: *to be used as …, ideal for …, flexible, versatile …* SIZE/QUANTITY: *large, wide, ample, good-sized, spacious, generous, extended, numerous, well-stocked, comprehensive …* AGE/CONDITION: *modern, modernized, new, refurbished, original, traditional, established, mature …* COST EFFICIENCY: *cheap rates, low consumption, no extra costs…*

IMPLICIT

High subjectivity (1)	OBLIGATION AND DESIRABILITY: *must be seen* IMPLICIT THREAT: *not to be missed* POTENTIAL EMOTIVE EFFECT ON BUYER/ AGENT or 3rd PARTY'S EMOTIVE REACTION: *we are very pleased/delighted to present …; living the dream*
Low subjectivity (2)	ENTAILED POSITIVE APPRECIATION: *the accommodation offer s…; provided with …; enhanced by …*
Factual detail (3)	FAVOURABLE NEGOTIATING BASIS: *no chain; available immediately* POTENTIAL ADDED BENEFIT: *possibility to purchase a double garage* IMPLIED PLEASANTNESS (COMPOSITION: BALANCE): *the property is articulated over two levels* INTENSIFICATION: Lexical: *there is even a breakfast bar; with good access to* Non-lexical: font size, underlining, bold, capitals, exclamation marks

Six main categories were identified: Three for explicit and three for implicit expressions. The three explicit types include:

EMOTIVE IMPACT (E), conflating REACTION: IMPACT and some REACTION: QUALITY with some 'narrow' PATHOS and EXCITEMENT expressions. The included formulations are those that arguably convey the highest level of appraiser's subjective involvement in that they are derived from or refer to values of affection (REACTION: IMPACT) such

as: *impressive, exciting, stunning.* They also include intensified REACTION: QUAL-
ITY expressions such as: *wonderful, fantastic, astonishingly beautiful* and emotively-
charged metaphorical references such as: *a work of art, a dream come true.* In this
latter case the attitudinal category of REACTION: QUALITY can be said to be combined
with a high value of GRADUATION.

PLEASANTNESS (P) conflates the less intense REACTION: QUALITY and 'narrow' PATHOS
expressions and includes some COMPOSITION: BALANCE types (COMPOSITION: COM-
PLEXITY does not appear to apply in the case of property). Examples are: *nice, good,
lovely, beautiful, charming, well-presented.*

QUALITY (Q) includes more specific reference to context-dependent value (VALUA-
TION) and can be divided into two classes according to the level of semantic inde-
terminacy (and, therefore, subjectivity). For the more open-ended evaluation (first
class) the terms used have been borrowed from Pryce and Oates's subcategories of
ORIGINALITY, PRESTIGE and AMBIANCE. Further categories of FUNCTIONALITY and
CRAFTSMANSHIP are also added.

The less undetermined QUALITIES (second class) are those that could easily be
replaced with factual description (measurements of size, quantity, time or space) or
actually have a factual component. They include: LOCATION, USE, SIZE/QUANTITY,
AGE/CONDITION and COST EFFICIENCY. These categories are not included under
Martin and White's APPRECIATION types, nor were they considered in Pryce and
Oates' study. Intensified expressions of QUALITY (e.g., *incredibly bright* and *excep-
tionally spacious*) convey high emotive involvement on the part of the appraiser and
were, therefore, classified as EMOTIVE IMPACT along with the intensified expressions
of PLEASANTNESS. The 'double identity' of these expressions (EMOTIVE IMPACT/QUAL-
ITY) was, however, considered in the discussion of the findings (Section 7.2).

The three implicit forms of positive appreciation include high-subjectivity
expressions, low-subjectivity expressions, and factual expressions, as outlined
below.

6.1. High-subjectivity expressions

OBLIGATION AND DESIRABILITY such as: *Viewing is a must* or *viewing essential.*
Here the strength of the request implies that the description does not fully do
justice to the property and, therefore, indirectly adds to the positive evaluation of the property.

Implicit THREAT (see Lorenzo-Dus, 2006: 741), that is hinting at the negative implications of non-persuasion. This is often combined with DESIRABILITY as in: *Early viewing recommended to avoid disappointment.*

Expressions referring to the potential emotive effects on the buyer of having
the property in question as their home as in: *Living the dream; entering the
room you are immediately taken aback by ...* or the agent's or third party's

own EMOTIVE REACTION to the property or some of its features as in: *we <u>are</u> <u>delighted to present</u> this newly renovated two bedroom house ...* The presence of this type of affectivity was also noted by Shaw (2006, see Section 2.2).

6.2. Low-subjectivity expressions

VERBS OR PHRASES ENTAILING POSITIVE APPRECIATION of their object/s (often factual features in themselves) as in: *The property <u>benefits from</u> double glazing, central heating ...; the property <u>offers</u>/<u>enjoys</u>/<u>boasts</u> ...*

Factual expressions strongly cue positive appreciation in that:

1. Assumed potential negative aspects deriving from the purchasing process are explicitly denied as in: *no onward chain* or *immediately available.*

2. Potential added benefits are mentioned: *extension options.*

3. Pleasantness (position, structure) is implied through lexical choice: *the living room is directly connected to/ leads to/ is positioned exactly between/completes ...*

4. They are emphasized through lexical or non-lexical intensification. Values of GRADUATION/INTENSIFICATION are involved but in combination with factual rather than subjective expressions. Relevant lexical formulation include: *with good access to ...; last but not least the study.* Particular factual features may be emphasized through the use of different font colour and size, underlining, bold, capitals and exclamation marks.

Frequency of use tends to generally erode evaluative impact at all levels, though this is difficult to measure (for further clarification of some of the finer discriminating factors see Pounds, 2011).

In summary, the analysis of the evaluative expressions in both corpora shows that they may be classified according to levels of subjectivity and affectivity (*subjective force*) arising from:

1. Intensity of appraiser's affective involvement: higher in E than P and Q.

2. Referential specificity, whereby the reference to specific values in Q can be seen to be less subjective than the general attribution of pleasantness in P.

3. Semantic indeterminacy, whereby the less indeterminate second-class qualities can be seen to be less subjective than the more indeterminate first-class ones.

Implicit formulations may also be distinguished according to levels of subjectivity and factuality.

7. Findings from the contrastive analysis

A full overview of the instances and frequency of positive APPRECIATION identified in the two sets of property descriptions is presented in Tables 4, 5 and 6 in the Appendix. Table 4 shows instances and frequency of POSITIVE APPRECIATION by category and agency, Tables 5 and 6 show the distribution of POSITIVE APPRECIATION by category and agency (or set of descriptions: English = EN and Italian = IT) based on the total number of evaluative expressions (divided between explicit and implicit occurrences). Similarities, differences and their significance are summarized and discussed in the following sections.

7.1. Similarities and genre-specific evaluative patterns

As mentioned in Section 6, the same main categories could be used to classify expressions of positive evaluation in both sets of descriptions. The similarities extend to the general frequency of evaluative expressions and their distribution according to *subjective force* and explicitness (see Appendix/Table 4). The frequency is overall very low in both sets: from 0.95% to 2.99% in EN and from 4.86% to 7.56% in IT. In both sets, evaluation is mostly expressed explicitly but mostly through QUALITIES (particularly the less indeterminate type), that is, low-affectivity/subjectivity and high-specificity, fact-based formulations, whose evaluative impact is highly context-dependent. The more indeterminate type of QUALITIES (see Appendix, Table 2) accounts for 28.20% (EN) and 33.79% (IT) of the total explicit evaluation. The less indeterminate, more factual QUALITIES account for 52.99% (EN) and 46.09% (IT) of the total explicit evaluation.

Within the implicit expressions, low subjectivity and factuality also dominate, accounting for 57.42% of the overall implicit expressions in EN and for 94.42% in IT. Both the English and Italian agencies exploit the positive evaluation implicitly communicated through reference to factual detail: the potential added benefits and balanced composition of a property (IT) and the favourable negotiating conditions (EN and IT).

This distribution may be typical of promotional genres in which factuality is foregrounded, possibly due to constraints on subjective content imposed by the legislation (as in this case) and/or the type of product ('high-relevance', see Section 2.2).

When considering the high-subjectivity categories of EMOTIVE IMPACT and PLEASANTNESS, in the explicit expressions, the former is, on the whole (with the exception of one of the English agency, Abbotts, that has low values overall), noticeably more frequent than the latter, possibly because highly subjective evaluation may escape criticism as it can be clearly seen as opinion rather than fact (as mentioned in Section 2.2).

In both sets there is some noticeable variation across agencies in the length of the descriptions and frequency of evaluation but the distribution of the evaluative expressions is proportionally similar overall, as seen above.

Further research could be carried out to establish whether the identified categories and discriminating criteria (based on values of subjectivity, affectivity, factuality and explicitness) identified in this contrastive analysis of property descriptions may be used to classify other types of evaluative genres, independently from language and culture.

7.2. Differences and culture-specific evaluative patterns

As well as the similarities summarized above some significant differences between the two sets of descriptions were noticed. Some of these differences relate to the distribution of QUALITY types across the two sets of agencies. The relevant types are summarized in Table 3. Occurrences include examples of the intensified QUALITIES that are classified under EMOTIVE IMPACT in the main summary of results (Appendix: Table 4).

Some of the differences clearly reflect predictable culture-specific differences in the structure and features of properties such as the almost obligatory presence of a garden and wider space between dwellings in urban areas in England, explaining the frequent reference to the size of the garden, the established plants there and the position/views in EN. Other differences, such as the frequent reference in EN to 'age' (as a positive factor) and to (restored) 'condition' in IT reflect the fact that more value is generally ascribed in England to historical properties and period features (although 'new' status is also highly appreciated) while Italians prefer new and newly restored properties, at least in urban areas.

Table 3: Most commonly mentioned QUALITIES in each set of descriptions by number of occurrences in comparison to the other set

QUALITIES	English prevalent	
	EN	**IT**
Prestige: Location	33	14
Size/quantity: Garden	30	3
Potential use of rooms	29	3
Age: Old: Plants	20	0
Location: Position/views	20	1
Originality	19	2
Age: Old: Accommodation	10	3

	Italian prevalent	
	IT	EN
Condition	35	7
Ambiance	30	17
Craftsmanship	22	5
Functionality	13	6
Cost efficiency	5	0
	Similar high frequency	
	EN	IT
Size/quantity: Accommodation	55	69
Location: Amenities/Services	25	12
Prestige: Accommodation	23	21
Age: New	16	9

Further differences appear to derive from less clearly obvious cultural values pertaining to practical aspects of the properties, such as the importance of identifying an appropriate 'use' for rooms in EN and the 'cost efficiency' and quality of the building work and material ('craftsmanship') in IT. Other differences reflect more abstract property values, such as its 'originality' and the 'prestige' of the location in EN (perhaps still related to the preference for more independent individual accommodation) and the overall 'ambiance' in IT. The 'prestige' of the accommodation itself and the convenience of the 'location' (close to services and amenities) appear to be highly valued in both cultural contexts. The most frequently-mentioned quality in both sets of descriptions, but particularly in IT, is, however, not surprisingly, the large size of the accommodation and of each individual room. On the basis of a wider contrastive study of 'preferred' QUALITIES in particular domains, it may be possible to develop 'maps' of salient evaluative lexical choices by domain and culture.

Other differences appear to reflect more subtle, culture-specific promotional strategies in which interactive preferences pertaining to the negotiation process appear to play a role. The distinction between Low-Context and High-Context (LC and HC) communication styles may be helpful in qualifying some of these preferences. The distinction was firstly introduced by Hall (1976) and then developed by Hofstede (1980). Hall distinguished between cultures (such as Scandinavian and German) in which communication occurs predominantly through explicit verbal statements (LC cultures) and cultures (such as Japanese and Chinese) in which a lot of the information is not explicitly expressed but is expected to be retrieved in context (HC cultures). Although it is now widely recognized that rigid categorizations of cultures is problematic if only because any differences may be temporary and context-specific, these dimensions still appear to have some relevance in the study of culture-specific communication. They seem to play a significant role, for example, in explaining differences in the design of promotional websites across cultures, as repeatedly shown in a number of studies, including Würtz (2005), Hermeking (2005), Liao *et al.* (2008), Manca (2008), Fu and Wu (2010) and Usunier and Roulin (2010). In spite of the fact that the genres analysed in this body of research are all promotional, the focus tends to be on the structural features of the websites rather than on their evaluative content. Some of the observations and findings are, however, relevant to the expression of evaluation. Würtz (2005: 1), for example, argues that 'visual communication is a high priority in the design of High-Context websites'. Hermeking (2005) shows that website communication in HC cultures uses 'soft sell' appeals (indirect approaches creating emotions and atmosphere by visuals and symbols) while LC cultures favour 'hard sell' strategies, highlighting product features with explicit information. Liao *et al.*'s study (2008) found that LC communication cultures particularly value the rational appeal of products and tend to employ direct, textual, factual and analytical argumentation in advertising and marketing.

According to Usunier and Roulin's classification (2010: 215) (drawing on Hall's classification and further sub-categorization into Low, Low/Medium, Medium, Medium/High and High Context communication styles) both English (British) and Italian cultures belong in the Medium-Context group. According to Katan (2004: 261), however, the situation varies depending on the communication type. In 'transactional' communication, in which the focus is on the transmission of facts, British cultural style is deemed to be Low-Context and the Italian High-Context, while in 'interactional' communication, focusing on the transmission of feelings and views, the reverse applies. Katan further argues, however, that, in the case of advertising, the situation is even more complex because:

> The advertising of goods and services *in theory* is transactional communication. In practice, the function is not the dissemination of information but the desire to influence … the default tendency is that, for most products, an LCC culture is going to expect more attention paid to the text both in terms of eye-catching wordplay and in terms of factual information. An HCC culture will focus more on the overall picture and the aesthetics or feelings created by the advert. (2004: 283, my italics)

In a comparison of Italian and British online 'farmhouse' holiday advertising websites, Manca (2008) found that the British websites make wider use of LC strategies as they are more content-oriented and provide detailed and explicit descriptions while the Italian websites prefer HC strategies aiming at eliciting and evoking positive feelings around the holiday.

The findings from the analysis of the property descriptions in this study appear to confirm these preferences to the extent that the English descriptions contain a higher proportion of factual data while the overall much shorter Italian descriptions rely more heavily on the evaluative component and the pictures. If one considers the nature of the emotive/subjective component, however, it appears that the 'interactional' mode applies: The Italian expressions of EMOTIVE IMPACT tend to be more explicit in that they include 25 (out of 42) instances of intensified QUALITY, such as 'extremely bright room' (EMOTIVE IMPACT + QUALITY: AMBIANCE) while the English descriptions consist mostly of more generalized formulations, such as 'a beautiful property' (EMOTIVE IMPACT only) and only have eight (out of 46) instances of intensified QUALITY. Although very infrequent in both sets, expressions of generalized PLEASANTNESS are particularly rare in IT, again possibly due precisely to their lack of specificity. So it looks like the English agencies favour a combination of mostly highly factual description with rare instances of highly subjective expressions. The Italian agencies, on the other hand, appear to prefer shorter descriptions, including a higher proportion of highly subjective yet more specific evaluation and, thereby, rely more heavily on the visual appeal of the pictures and, possibly, the face-to-face more explicit negotiating process with the estate agent and property buyer/seller.

Implicit evaluation is also altogether rarer in IT (16.94% of the overall evaluation) than in EN (31.45%). The most highly subjective implicit formulations are almost non-existent in IT: There are no examples of EMOTIVE EFFECT/REACTION or THREAT and only rare examples of OBLIGATION/DESIRABILITY. The low-subjectivity ENTAILMENT type is also noticeably more frequent in EN. Likewise, expression of intensification in, otherwise, factual description is overall relatively frequent in EN but almost non-existent in IT. One of the Italian agencies is, however, making a very high use of non-lexical intensification (font size, underlining, exclamation marks), showing perhaps again a higher reliance on the visual impact.

Of course, other factors, including corporate demographics and industry-related variables (such as financial and legal constraints) would also have a bearing on communicative choices and would need to be investigated to obtain a fuller understanding of the expressive strategies.

8. Conclusion

The findings from the contrastive analysis of evaluation undertaken in this study highlight its dependence on both genre- and culture-specific factors. The similarities in evaluative patterns, that is, the similar distribution of more or less subjective options across the English and Italian property descriptions, clearly point to the connection between genre and levels of subjectivity, affectivity and explicitness. Further cross-linguistic analysis may reveal typical distributions for other promotional genres.

The differences in evaluative patterns, including differences in the ratio evaluation/description, implicit and explicit choices as well as levels of specificity and reliance on non-verbal contextual aspects, on the other hand, may be linked to culture-specific factors. The question arises, in other words, as to whether differences in the evaluative content of equivalent promotional genres produced in different cultural settings may, at least partly, be explained through underlying differences in cultural communicative styles (such as the LC and HC distinction referred to above). Further contrastive analysis of promotional genres in England and Italy would be needed to identify non-genre-specific differences in evaluative style, linked to cultural communicative preferences in the domain of promotional discourse.

The study also crucially shows that a comprehensive analysis of evaluation needs to identify not only the semantic orientation (levels of positivity or negativity) and the target of the evaluation (objects, emotions or behaviours) but also its *subjective force* (varying levels of subjectivity and affectivity) and level of explicitness. In the case of property descriptions, semantic orientation (positive) and target (objects) are invariant and the analysis focused on the other two dimensions. While semantic orientation and target can be identified through automated analysis (as in the study by Taboada and Grieve, 2004), a detailed manual analysis that takes full account of the overall communicative function of the text is clearly more appropriate in order to account for *subjective force* and levels of explicitness. Once genre-specific formulations have been identified in this way, however, it would be possible to carry out further automated analysis on a wider corpus to obtain a fuller picture.

References

Bednarek, M. (2006) *Evaluation in Media Discourse*. London: Continuum.

Darley, W. K. and Smith, R. E. (1993) Advertising claim objectivity: Antecedents and effects. *Journal of Marketing* 57 (4): 100–13. http://dx.doi.org/10.2307/1252222

Fu, C-S and Wu, W-Y. (2010) The means-end cognitions of web advertising: A cross-cultural comparison. *Online Information Review* 34 (5): 686–703. http://dx.doi.org/10.11 08/14684521011084573

Hall, E. T. (1976) *Beyond Culture*. New York: Doubleday.

Her Majesty's Government. (1991) Property Misdescriptions Act (c. 29 Sections 1–7). http://www.opsi.gov.uk/ACTS/acts1991/ukpga_19910029_en_1 (accessed 7 July 2009).

Hermeking, M. (2005) Culture and internet consumption: Contributions from cross-cultural marketing and advertising research. *Journal of Computer-Mediated Communication* 11 (1): 192–216. http://dx.doi.org/10.1111/j.1083-6101.2006.tb00310.x

Hodgson, J. (1994) The Property Misdescriptions Act 1991. *Structural Survey* 12 (1): 26–32. http://dx.doi.org/10.1108/02630809410041741

Hofstede, G. (1980) *Culture's Consequences: International Differences in Work-Related Values.* Beverley Hills, CA: Sage.

Hunston, S. (1999) Evaluation and the planes of discourse: Status and value in persuasive texts. In Hunston, S. and Thomson, G. (eds) *Evaluation in Text,* 176–206. Oxford and New York: Oxford University Press.

Hunston, S. and Sinclair, J. (1999) A local grammar of evaluation. In Hunston, S. and Thomson, G. (eds) *Evaluation in Text,* 74–100. Oxford and New York: Oxford University Press.

Katan, D. (2004) *Translating Cultures* (2nd edn) Manchester: St Jerome.

Liao, H., Proctor, R. and Salvendy, G. (2008) Content preparation for cross-cultural e-commerce: A review and a model. *Behaviour and Information Technology* 27 (1): 43–61. http://dx.doi.org/10.1080/01449290601088424

Lorenzo-Dus, N. (2006) Buying and selling: Mediating persuasion in British property shows. *Media, Culture and Society* 28 (5): 740–61. http://dx.doi.org/10.1177/0163443706067024

Manca, E. (2008) From phraseology to culture. Qualifying adjectives in the language of tourism. *International Journal of Corpus Linguistics* 13 (3): 368–85. http://dx.doi.org/10.1075/ijcl.13.3.07man

Martin, J. (1999) Beyond exchange: Appraisal systems in English. In S. Hunston and G. Thomson (eds) *Evaluation in Text,* 142–175. Oxford and New York: Oxford University Press.

Martin, J. and White, P. R. R. (2005) *The Language of Evaluation.* Basingstoke and New York: Palgrave.

Park, C. W. and Young, S. M. (1986) Consumer response to television commercials: The impact of involvement and background music on brand attitude formation. *Journal of Marketing Research* 23 (1): 11–24. http://dx.doi.org/10.2307/3151772

Pounds, G. (2011) 'This property offers much character and charm'. Evaluation in the discourse of online property advertising. *Text and Talk* 31 (2): 195–220. http://dx.doi.org/10.1515/text.2011.009

Pryce, G. and Oates, S. (2007) Pathos and patter in real estate parlance. *SHEFRN.* Discussion paper. http:// www.gpryce.com and www.shefrn.org (accessed 12 July 2009).

Pryce, G. and Oates, S. (2008) Rhetoric in the language of real estate marketing. *Housing Studies* 23 (2): 319–348. http://dx.doi.org/10.1080/02673030701875105

Shaw, P. (2006) Evaluative language in evaluative and promotional genres. In G. Del Lungo Camiciotti, M. Dossena and B. Crawford Camiciottoli (eds) *Variation in Business and Economics Discourse: Diachronic and Genre Perspectives,* 152–165. Rome: Officina Edizioni.

Shimp, T. A. and Preston, I. L. (1981) Deceptive and non-deceptive consequences of evaluative advertising. *Journal of Marketing* 45 (1): 22–32. http://dx.doi.org/10.2307/1251717

Swales, J. M. (1990) *Genre Analysis: English in Academic and Research Settings.* Cambridge: Cambridge University Press.

Taboada, M and Grieve, J. (2004) Analysing appraisal automatically. In Proc. of AAAI *Spring Symposyum on Exploring Attitude and Affect in Text*, 158–161. Stanford. http://dx.doi.org/10.1515/text.2011.011

Taboada, M. (2011) Stages in an online review genre. *Text and Talk* 31 (2): 247–269.

Tellis, G. J. (2004) *Effective Advertising*. London: Sage Publications.

Usunier, J-C. and Roulin, N. (2010) The influence of high- and low-context communication styles on the design, content and language of business-to-business websites. *Journal of Business Communication* 47 (2): 189–227. http://dx.doi.org/10.1177/0021943610364526

Woods, N. (2006) *Describing Discourse*. London: Hodder Arnold.

Würtz, E. (2005) A cross-cultural analysis of websites from high-context cultures and low-context cultures. *Journal of Computer-Mediated Communication* 11 (1): Article 13.

Appendix: Property descriptions

English sites (accessed July-September 2009):

Abbotts. http://www.abbotts.co.uk
William H Brown. http://www.sequencehome.co.uk/properties
Haart. http://www.haart.co.uk

Italian sites (accessed April-May 2010):

Tecnocasa. http://www.tecnocasa.it
Primalux. http://www.primalux.net
Gabetti. http://www.gabetti.it

Table 4. Instances and frequency (based on total number of words) of POSITIVE APPRECIATION by category and agency.

APPRECIATION CATEGORY	ENGLISH			ITALIAN		
	Haart 8146 words	H W Brown 9713 words	Abbotts 6937 words	Tecnocasa 2797 words	Primalux 1746 words	Gabetti 1052 words
EXPLICIT (Total)	**157 1.92%**	**159 1.63%**	**52 0.74%**	**116 4.14%**	**100 5.72%**	**53 5.03%**
Emotive impact	**32 0.39%**	**10 0.10%**	**4 0.05%**	**15 0.53%**	**17 0.97%**	**10 0.95%**
Pleasantness	**10 0.12%**	**6 0.06%**	**7 0.10%**	**1 0.03%**	**1 0.05%**	**2 0.19%**
QUALITIES 1 (Total)	**50 0.61%**	**40 0.41%**	**14 0.20%**	**46 1.64%**	**28 1.60%**	**17 1.61%**
Originality	10	5	4	2	0	0
Ambiance	7	8	1	14	5	8
Prestige:	28	21	7	12	16	7
Location	11	18	4	6	7	1
Accommodation	17	3	3	6	9	6
Functionality	1	6	0	7	5	0
Craftsmanship	4	0	1	11	2	2
QUALITIES 2 (Total)	**65 0.79%**	**103 1.06%**	**27 0.38%**	**46 1.64%**	**54 3.09%**	**24 2.28%**
Location: Amenities/	9	28	6	7	2	2
Services	5	19	1	6	2	2
Position/View	4	9	5	1	0	0
Use	21	5	3	0	1	2
Size/quantity	29	58	6	24	31	14
Accommodation	23	27	3	23	30	13
Garden	6	21	3	1	1	1
Other		10				
Age/condition	19	22	12	14	16	6
Old	8	16	6	2	1	0
Accommodation	2	4	4	2	1	0
Plants	6	12	2	0	0	0
New	8	5	3	2	4	3
Condition	3	1	3	10	11	3
Cost efficiency	0	0	0	1	4	0

IMPLICIT (Total)	87	1.06%	68	0.70%	14	0.20%	20	0.71%	32	1.83%	3	0.28%
High subjectivity												
Obligation	13		17		0		0		3		0	
Threat	4		6		0		0		0		0	
Emot. effect/reaction (buyer/3rd party)	21		1		0		0		0		0	
Low subjectivity												
Entailment	21		23		10		6		5		0	
Factual detail												
Favourable negot.	5		6		2		5		3		0	
Added benefit	0		0		0		8		4		2	
Implied pleasantness	0		0		0		present		present		0	
Intensification	13		15		2		1		17		1	
Lexical	13		15		2		1		2		0	
Non-lexical	0		0		0		0		15		1	
TOTAL	244	2.99%	227	2.33%	66	0.95%	136	4.86%	132	7.56%	56	5.32%

Table 5. Distribution of POSITIVE APPRECIATION by category and agency based on total numbers of explicit and implicit evaluative expressions per agency

EXPLICIT	Haart	H W Brown	Abbotts	Tecnocasa	Primalux	Gabetti
Emotive impact	20.38%	6.28%	7.69%	12.93%	17%	18.86%
Pleasantness	6.36%	3.77%	13.46%	0.86%	1%	3.77%
Qualities 1	31.8%	25.15%	26.92%	39.65%	28%	32.07%
Qualities 2	41.40%	64.77%	51.92%	39.65%	54%	45.28%
IMPLICIT						
High subj.	55.17%	35.29%	0%	0%	9.37%	0%
Low subj./ Fact	44.82%	64.71%	100%	100%	90.63%	100%

Table 6. Distribution of POSITIVE APPRECIATION by category, based on total average number of explicit and implicit evaluative expressions per set of descriptions (EN and IT)

APPRECIATION CATEGORY	EN (average)	IT (average)
EXPLICIT		
Emotive impact	12.53%	15.61%
Pleasantness	6.26%	1.48%
Qualities 1 (higher indeterminacy/ subjectivity)	28.20%	33.79%
Qualities 2 (higher indeterminacy/ subjectivity)	52.99%	46.09%
IMPLICIT		
High subjectivity	42.58%	5.58%
Low subjectivity/ Factuality	57.42%	94.42%

12 Contrastive analyses of evaluation in text: Key issues in the design of an annotation system for attitude applicable to consumer reviews in English and Spanish

Maite Taboada and Marta Carretero

This paper reports on part of the research on evaluative language currently carried out within the CONTRANOT project,[1] which aims at the creation and validation of contrastive functional descriptions through corpus analysis and annotation in English and Spanish. More concretely, we will present the coding scheme designed for Attitude, a subcategory of Appraisal as studied within Systemic-Functional Linguistics (White, 2003; Martin and White, 2005). The criteria for selection and annotation of spans of Attitude in the coding scheme are specified and illustrated with examples from the Simon Fraser University Review Corpus (Taboada, 2008), a corpus of consumer-generated reviews on hotels, books and movies, and a small-scale English-Spanish contrastive analysis of these reviews has been carried out. The scheme is to be used for the future annotation of evaluation in an English-Spanish corpus, CONTRASTES (Lavid, 2008; Lavid *et al.*, 2007, 2010). Once annotated, the reviews will be part of this corpus.

1. Introduction

Evaluative language, from the point of view of the Appraisal framework, refers to the linguistic expressions that indicate 'the subjective presence of writers/speakers in texts as they adopt stances towards both the material they present and those with whom they communicate' (Martin and White, 2005: 1). The study of evaluative language has intrinsic interest, in that we all use language to evaluate, appraise and classify objects and people on an everyday basis. It has also received a surge of attention lately from more applied venues, in particular with regard to computational applications (see Pang and Lee, 2008, and references therein). The web is now teeming with opinions, which are of interest to marketers, policy makers and the public in general.

The field of sentiment extraction, or semantic orientation detection, is a growing area within computational linguistics. The approach typically taken consists of counting the number of positive and negative words in a text (usually adjectives), and averaging their values, determined by a pre-existing dictionary (e.g., Esuli and Sebastiani, 2006; Kennedy and Inkpen, 2006; Turney, 2002). Other approaches follow Machine Learning techniques, often involving little linguistic information (e.g., Pang *et al.*, 2002; Goldberg and Zhu, 2006). Some researchers have found the categories and classifications provided by the Appraisal framework of use, and are creating appraisal lexicons for this task (Taboada and Grieve, 2004; Whitelaw and Patrick, 2004; Whitelaw *et al.*, 2005; Bloom *et al.*, 2007). This proved efficiency of the Appraisal system for the creation of lexicons of evaluative expressions, together with the accessibility of its labels for use by non-linguists, are the reasons why we have adopted this theory for our analysis of evaluation. Among other approaches, we will quote Douglas Biber's approach, based on the quantitative analysis of clusters of grammatical and lexical features (Biber, 1988, 1995; Biber and Finegan, 1989a), and a few others which focus on the contribution of modality to express evaluation, stance or opinion in text (Stubbs, 1986; Biber and Finegan, 1989b) and the role of evidentiality in expressing subjectivity (Chafe and Nichols, 1986).

The Appraisal framework, which originated in Australia within the Systemic Functional School of Linguistics, was developed in response to the need to cope with (and, ideally, to be proficient in) the expression of interpersonal meaning. More concretely, Appraisal Theory was developed as part of the Disadvantaged Schools Program's *Write It Right* literacy project, which concerned writing in the workplace and secondary school (from 1990 to 1995 approximately). Its main proponents are Jim Martin and Peter White (see, for instance Martin, 2000; Martin and White, 2005, among other publications), but many other academics also participated (for example, Joan Rothery, Cate Poynton, Mary Macken-Horarik, Maree Stenglin, Rick Iedema and Susan Feez). In Martin and White's words (2005: 9), Appraisal concerns 'how evaluation is established, amplified, targeted and sourced'.

The framework for the present study is a project which aims at developing contrastive corpus analyses, and then systems of annotations, for a number of linguistic categories, some of which (apart from evaluation, the focus of this paper) are coherence relations, tense, aspect and modality. The systems of annotation are to be designed for use by non-academic annotators, who will be provided with relatively simple sets of instructions. According to this aim, our approach to evaluation will have to be restrictive, giving preference to the individual evaluative charge of words and expressions against the overall evaluative effect of all the expressions in a given text. It could even be stated that in reality every word has its charge of evaluation: when we speak or write, even in those messages whose main role is to transmit information with a high degree of objectiveness, we design our utterances with the purpose of presenting a certain world view to the addressee.[2]

A related project focuses on detecting sentiment automatically, making use of linguistic information, and drawing on the insights provided by the Appraisal system. Preliminary work in the project has resulted in a collection of book, movie, and consumer product reviews (Taboada, 2008), a software program (Taboada *et al.*, 2008a), and a few publications and presentations (Taboada and Grieve, 2004; Taboada *et al.*, 2006a, b, 2008b, 2011; Voll and Taboada, 2007). This project is applied, seeking to develop an automatic system for the extraction of sentiment and evaluation in text. The work described in this paper is more theoretical, in the sense that the goal is to understand evaluation in text, and to provide an annotated corpus. This work will also draw on previous work on modality and its role in the expression of the speaker/writer's attitude (Carretero, 2002, 2004, 2007).

The goal, then, was to create a system for annotating evaluation in text. The first step involved a detailed analysis, based on a corpus of authentic texts. In this way, a wide variety of patterns and relations that convey evaluation can be found, and are labelled for analysis. For its purposes, the analysis has to meet two characteristics: (1) rigour and clarity, so as to ensure inter-rater reliability; (2) simplicity, with the view that this analysis will be the basis of an annotation system designed for use by non-specialists.

2. The corpus and its annotation

The corpus selected for analysis is part of the larger Simon Fraser University Review Corpus, which consists of 1,600 movie, book, and consumer product reviews, 800 in English and 800 in Spanish. The English reviews were extracted from the web page Epinions.com. A first data collection (400 texts) took place in 2004, and a second round of the same number was collected in 2008. For Spanish, we used two web sites: Ciao.es and Dooyoo.es, all of it collected in

2008. The reason to have two rounds for each language was that we used one set to develop dictionaries and other resources, and thus we needed a set for independent evaluation purposes. The reviews are divided into eight categories: books, cars, computers, cookware/appliances, hotels, movies, music and phones.

The reviews are all written by non-experts. The contributors are mostly avid web users who enjoy sharing their experiences with others. In addition, Ciao promises a small monetary compensation if a sufficiently large number of reviews are posted and they are considered useful by readers of the site. The language is typically informal, with many colloquial expressions, typos and abbreviations. In the examples provided in the paper, we have left punctuation, spelling and grammar as they originally appeared.

3. Categories within the Appraisal system

Within the Appraisal system, the types of evaluation are divided into three broad categories: Attitude, Graduation and Engagement. The main proponents of the Appraisal System, James R. Martin and Peter R. R. White, have acknowledged that these labels are not unarguable; for example, White (2002: 7), writing about Attitude and its subtypes, states that they have been designed 'as a resource for those who need something to manage the analysis of evaluation in discourse, and as a challenge to those concerned with developing appropriate reasoning'. Appraisal in fact has been criticized for the arbitrariness of the labels and the difficulties that it poses for inter-rater reliability. However, we believe that it is still possible to design a system that guarantees this kind of reliability, even if some of the decisions made will unavoidably have some degree of arbitrariness.

3.1. Attitude

Attitude concerns the expression of feeling, and is subdivided into three types:

- **Affect**, which covers the explicit expression of positive or negative feelings by the speaker/writer or someone else, as in *I am **happy**, She **likes** him, He left the office **sadly**.*
- **Judgement**, which 'deals with attitudes towards behaviour, which we admire or criticise, praise or condemn' (Martin and White, 2005: 42). Judgement concerns social esteem and ethical evaluations, and applies mostly to persons or institutions. Examples of this category are *They acted **honestly*** or *She is an **efficient** worker.*
- **Appreciation**, which 'involves evaluations of semiotic and natural phenomena, according to the ways in which they are valued or not in a given field' (Martin and White, 2005: 43). Examples of Appreciation are *This book is **fas-***

cinating or *The plot is **conventional***. The evaluations are aesthetic or functional, and they refer mostly to works of art or literature and to non-human physical objects, rather than to humans.

From the description above it may be inferred that Affect evaluates the entity through the expression of feeling (the speaker/writer's, or that of someone else), whereas Judgement and Appreciation evaluate the entity by attributing a quality to it.

Among all three categories, Attitude will be the main concern of this paper, and at the first level of analysis. Each of the Attitude categories, Affect, Judgement and Appreciation, is divided into subcategories, but these will not be taken into account for the sake of simplicity.

3.2. Graduation

Graduation consists of the use of linguistic expressions for emphasizing or downtoning other expressions. Expressions of Graduation differ from those of Attitude in that they do not have intrinsic positive or negative values by themselves, but acquire them in context. Some expressions of Graduation are intensifiers applied to nouns (*real, true, genuine*) or to adjectives (*very, really*), and softeners (*kind of, sort of, or something*). Graduation is divided into two broad subtypes: Focus and Force.

- **Focus** involves Graduation according to prototypicality, that is, 'by reference to the degree to which they match some supposed core or exemplary instance of a semantic category' (Martin and White, 2005: 137). Focus is divided into the subtypes **Sharpen** and **Soften**, which indicate proximity and distance, respectively, to a core or exemplary member of the category. Some examples of expressions realizing Sharpen are *real, true, genuine(ly), effective(ly)* ... and instances of Soften are *kind of, sort of, of sorts, -ish (fourish), bordering on* ...
- **Force** serves speakers or writers to modulate the impact of what they say. Force is divided into the following categories:
  - o **Intensification**, which can apply to a quality (*slightly sad*) or to a process (*greatly disturbed me*), but no difference will be made in this respect concerning annotation. Some realizations of intensification are *a bit, somewhat, relatively, fairly, rather, very, extremely, utterly;* self-pronouns when their use is optional (1); the comparative and superlative forms or constructions with adjectives. Intensification may also apply to an entity, as in (2):

(1)   He did it *himself*.

(2)   This is the *very* book I was reading the other day.

  - o **Quantification**, which is divided into the following categories:
    - ▪ Number: *a few, lots of, many, streams of*. Exact numbers are not considered to be Appraisal devices, since they refer to objective quantities.

- Mass/presence: *tiny, small, large, huge, gigantic*
- Extent:
  - Proximity:
    - Time: *recent, ancient*
    - Space: *nearby, distant*
  - Distribution:
    - Time: *long-lasting, fast*
    - Space: *narrow, broad*

In this chapter, Graduation will be considered only when it is within the scope of an evaluative span of Attitude. For example, in (3), the evaluative span is *a little excited*: the key expression is *excited* (Affect), which is modified by the expression of Graduation *a little*:

(3)   I got **a little excited** that things were looking up only to find out that it really was nothing. (Books no, 3)

3.3. Engagement

Engagement 'deals with sourcing attitudes and the play of voices around opinions in discourse' (Martin and White, 2005: 35). Examples of Engagement are epistemic modal expressions (*He **might** have finished his studies by now*), evidential expressions (***Apparently**, he has recovered from his illness*) or denials (*This hotel **is not** near the sea as you said*). Engagement will only be marginally discussed in borderline cases with Attitude (see 5.6).

4. The experiments

For a qualitative analysis, we did a first experiment with 12 reviews, distributed evenly according to these features: language (six English, six Spanish); kind of evaluation (six positive, six negative); product evaluated (four books, four movies, four hotels). After the reviews had been analysed in terms of problematic issues and the results discussed, we designed a second experiment. This time we restricted the experiment to books and movies which, in contrast to hotels, are intellectual products that have authors, plot and characters. The analysis took place in two steps: the first was the selection of the markables; once agreement was reached, we undertook the labelling of these markables. For this second experiment, we selected eight reviews, four for each language, equally divided between reviews of books and movies, and positive and negative reviews. We found that selecting the markables was the most difficult task, whereas labelling them was easier, and led to higher agreement. Table 1 shows the results for the selection of markables for the eight reviews. We see that the initial total agreement is quite high. The precision (calculated as the number of units for the annotator with the lowest number of units, Annotator

2, over the number of units for Annotator 1) is quite high. More importantly, both total and partial recall (number of agreements over the number of units for Annotator 1) is very high.

Table 1: Agreement for annotation experiment

Units (Annotator 1)	348
Units (Annotator 2)	315
Total agreement	281
Partial agreement	31
No agreement	47
Recall	90.52%
Precision (total)	80.75%
Precision (partial)	89.66%

Once we were confident that our annotations were reliable and showed high degree of agreement, we proceeded to annotate further texts. The entire corpus discussed in this article (see Section 2) consists of 32 reviews, 16 in each language. Throughout the paper, we will refer to examples from the corpus; occasionally, examples from other reviews will also be used. When examples from this corpus are used, the product reviewed and the number of the review will be specified. Non-labelled examples are constructed by the authors.

5. Selection of markables of Attitude

5.1. Application of the evaluation to the products evaluated

Evaluation was restricted to the cases in which it refers to the products evaluated and related entities that reflect the quality of the product, such as the author, the plot and quality features of the character of books (*believable, deep* ...), or performances of actors and actresses in movies. We have excluded evaluative spans included in the descriptions of the plot or characters in books and movies: a director may well have chosen an ugly suburb of a city as scenario or a stupid person as the protagonist so as to suit best his/ her purposes. Examples of non-included evaluative spans are (4) and (5). However, trailers and covers of books were considered as part of the movie or book; consequently, the evaluative expressions referring to them were included (6).

(4)   The Spruills have a son who is a rather large bully (Books no, 3)

(5)   This book was about a lawyer who worked in a firm as a litigator and was around the most defiant and high up men there were in the city. (Books no, 1)

(6)   The trailer did manage to make the film look fun (Movies yes, 1)

5.2. Evaluative and non-evaluative occurrences of the same word or expression

Some words or expressions have an inherent evaluative meaning, so that they are always considered as cases of Appraisal. These include many adjectives (*disastrous, excellent, fair, great ...*) and their derived words. Among other kinds of evaluative words other than adjectives and their derived words, there are quantifiers, such as *too (much)*, which is negative in that indicates excess; nouns (*joy, sorrow*) or verbs (*excel, improve, disappoint*). This is also the case of some grammatical constructions, such as *all that* and its Spanish correlate *todo ello*, literally 'it all' or *no hace más que* 'does nothing but', which have an evaluative meaning (negative in these cases).

Concerning expressions that indicate manner, Martin and White (2005: 146) follow Stillar's (1998) argument that circumstances of manner (7) always implicate the speaker/writer's subjectivity, since they do not lend themselves to objective accounts in the same way as time, place or cause do. Accordingly, we have always included these expressions as evaluative spans.

(7)   she comes out *very shrilly*. (Movies no, 1)

Other items, however, may be considered evaluative or not, depending on the context. Some examples from the reviews in which the expressions can be considered as evaluative due to the context are (8) and (9). In (8), *típica* 'typical' has negative connotations, but this adjective can be easily imagined in a neutral context ('the typical costume of the village'). In (9), *generic* has the sense of 'clichéd, stereotyped' and has therefore been considered as the head of an Appraisal span; however, it has non-evaluative uses, as in *generic software*, which means software for a wide range of computers.

(8)   A la protagonista nos la presentan como a la *típica* mujer que sabe que consigue más luciendo carne, que utilizando el cerebro, en fín en una palabra decepcionante. (Libros no, 1.14).

'The protagonist is introduced as the *typical* woman who knows that she achieves more showing her flesh than using her brain, to sum up, in a word disappointing.'

(9)   her character was *just totally generic* (Movies no, 1)

5.3. Invoked evaluations

In contrast to cases where the evaluation is due to the lexical meaning of a word or expression (which is called Inscribed evaluation), in other cases there are facts that imply positive or negative evaluation. In those cases, the evaluation is Invoked. In our annotation system, spans that could possibly be considered as invoked evaluations have been excluded in many cases, for the sake of simplicity. For example, (10) is part of the argument that the treatment of the role of women in the 1950s is inaccurate, and deviates from what was really the case. The reviewer suggests that this lack of authenticity may be due to the audience to which the film was addressed. Similarly, (11) refers to a fact (*hacer taquilla*, which literally means 'make box office') which may well be considered as morally questionable. As we stated above, these cases will not be included in our evaluation analysis.

(10)   I know women were the core audience of this film, particularly young college women. (Movies no, 1)

(11)   Steven está claro a lo que ha ido que es a hacer taquilla (Películas no, 1.11)

'It's clear that what Steven wanted was big box-office numbers.'

However, we have included invoked evaluations in a number of cases, in which the linguistic clues facilitate the consideration as such:

1.   **Complex clauses,** one of which suggests (not) to read or view the product evaluated and the other provides argumentation for this suggestion (*if*- conditionals or similar constructions). In these cases the evaluation is not communicated by lexical meaning, but by implicature. Both (12) and (13) are spans with an implicated negative evaluation, the book reviewed being *The Da Vinci Code*. The evaluation is even more indirect in (13), since it mentions other novels, hinting that the reviewed book should not be read.

(12)   For an example of how marketing hype can overcome critical judgment and influence popular taste, read 'The Da Vinci Code'. (Books no, 1)

(13)   If you're looking for an intellectually challenging mystery story, read or reread Eco's 'The Name of the Rose', or 'Foucault's Pendulum'. (Books no, 1)

2.   When **comparison** is used for evaluative purposes. An example is (14): Although the phrase 'like Sherlock Holmes on speed' is not negative *per se*, it is here used as criticism for the hectic pace of the book. In certain cases, the comparison is not with entities, but with situations (15):

(14)   Well actually, you have until Saturday Night so there's time to run around *like Sherlock Holmes on speed* and solve the mystery just minutes before the news media puts your company out of business. (Books no, 19)

(15)   Descriptions of places – Louvre, Westminster Abbey – are lifeless, and read as if plagiarized from a do-it-yourself walking tour guide by one of the less gifted of the author's former prep school students. (Books no, 1)

3.   When **metaphors** are used for evaluative reasons. We have to specify that our approach to metaphor is more restricted than that commonly used in

cognitive linguistics (e.g., Lakoff and Johnson, 1980; Coulson, 2001; Fauconnier and Turner, 2008), according to which many cases of transfer of domain are considered as metaphors. For example, *go into* in (16) would be considered as metaphorical, since it does not express physical movement. We will consider as metaphors only those cases in which the writer clearly has consciousness of this transfer of domain. One such example is (17), in which *Madame Bovary* is an expression of evaluation (and the ensuing paraphrase gives a clue of the sense of this evaluation).

(16)   He went into the matter carefully. (Cf. 'He went into the labyrinth carefully')

(17)   No solemos dudar del amor que nuestra madre nos profesa ni del que tenemos a nuestros hijos o amigos, y sin embargo, no necesitamos reafirmarlo con expresiones verbales. […] Sin embargo ¿por qué sí lo esperamos de nuestras parejas? Yo intuyo que es por una necesidad creada por la literatura (en su conjunto) de ser *Madame Bovary*, es decir, la protagonista de nuestra propia novelita rosa. (Libros yes – 4.11.)

'We don't usually doubt the love that our mother has for us nor that we have for our children or friends, and nevertheless, we do not need to reaffirm it with verbal expression. […] However, why do we expect that from our lovers? I believe that it is because of a need created by literature (as a whole) to be *Madame Bovary*, that is, the protagonist of our own little romance novel.'

5.4. Emotional outbursts and vocatives

Martin and White (2005: 68) classify swearing as Involvement, a meaning which, like Appraisal, is included within Tenor, and concerns the distinction between proximal and distal stance towards the text and the addressee. We believe that in our corpus these expressions (*my God, hell,* etc.) as well as vocatives (*honey, my dear, idiot, son of a bitch* …) have, above all, an evaluative role of Affect, since they express strong positive or negative feelings. The same may be stated about emotional outbursts different from swearing: In (18) *ooooh* intensifies the absurdity of the conspiracy, and therefore could be considered as a span of negative Appreciation, and in (19) the initial outburst lays emphasis on the bad quality of the film:

(18)   *Ooooh* … big conspiracy … it would be nice if James Patterson explain why. (Books no, 24)

(19)   *Bufffffffffff*, por donde empiezo? (Películas no, 2-10)
         'Buffffffffffff, where do I start?'

5.5. Inclusion of markables in elliptical expressions or expressions replaced by a pronoun

We have included the spans in which an evaluative word or expression is inferable from the linguistic context and omitted by ellipsis (20) or substitution (21).

> (20)   I guess I just thought that this movie would be as good as the Grinch, but unfortunately, it *wasn't*. (Movies no, 13)

> (21)   tenía cierto miedo a que mis queridos Simpson perdieran en su aparición en la pantalla grande. Pero *no ha sido así*. (Películas yes, 4-2)
>
> 'I was quite afraid that my dear Simpsons would lose in their appearance on the big screen. But it hasn't been so.'

5.6. Overlaps between Attitude and Engagement

There are some expressions that overlap between Attitude and Engagement. Negative or non-assertive linguistic devices are a subtype of Engagement, in the sense that the contents communicated (have the potential to) clash with previous expectations, and will be considered as such in our annotation scheme, but at the same time they point to evaluations (22–23):

> (22)   she *doesn't* really bring *anything* that we *haven't* seen before (Movies no, 1)

> (23)   the reader *still* has gotten *few* clues about matters (Books no, 1)

Another case in point are epistemic and deontic modal expressions. Epistemic modality, which may be defined as the estimation of the chances that a state of affairs has of being or becoming true, has a high degree of overlap with Attitude (Carretero and Taboada, to appear). We have classified these cases within Attitude or within Engagement, depending on the relative importance of the emotional or the epistemic meaning. Expressions of credibility (24), sincerity (25), (ab)normality (26), and (dis)agreement with expectations (27) are classified under Attitude, while those of probability due to quality (28) are classified under Engagement.

> (24)   One of the few positives of the film is the cinematography by Anastas N. Michos, that has lovely moments of colorful images and that *authentic* 1950s look. (Movies no, 1; Appreciation)

> (25)   *Sinceramente* me esperaba que fuese peor. (Películas yes, 5–11)
>
> '*Frankly*, I expected it to be worse.'

> (26)   Dos policías. – el más joven intenta imponer su ley ante la vecindad desesperada. *Lógicamente*, NO lo conseguirá. (Películas no, 1–5)
>
> 'Two policemen.- the youngest one tries to impose his law on the despairing neighbourhood. *Obviously*, he WON'T manage it.'

> (27)   el filme *no me ha decepcionado en absoluto* (Películas yes, 4–2)
>
> 'The movie did not disappoint me at all'

> (28)   it's *likely* not to get any Oscar nominations for anyone involved except the costume and production designs. (Movies no, 1)

Deontic modality, that is, obligation, recommendation and permission, is characterized in Martin and White (2005: 111) in terms of Engagement, with the argument that this modality 'explicitly grounds the demand in the subjectivity of the speaker – as an assessment by the speaker of obligation [or of permission] rather than as a command'. However, we believe that these expressions have an important semantic feature of Judgement: Obligations and recommendations, as in (29), are morally desirable events, and permissions are morally acceptable events. Therefore, we will classify these expressions under Judgement.

> (29)   Newell still *should be given* credit for trying to make things interesting since the pacing of the film is attentive but it's given a weak script with no sense of a singular direction to begin with. (Movies no, 1)

Rhetorical questions are also devices that express Attitude, but we believe that their main meaning belongs to Engagement, in that they have a strong implicature of positive or negative polarity. For example, the evaluative span in (30) has been classified under Engagement, but could also be considered as negative Appreciation, since the reviewer criticizes an inconsistency of the book.

> (30)   …While talking about conspiracies involving the Whitehouse, James Patterson mentions the Whitewater Scandal. *How can that be if Clinton was never the President in Patterson's story?* (Books no, 24)

5.7. Inclusion of expressions of Graduation within spans of Attitude

In some cases, the evaluative expression of Attitude is intensified or downtoned by a word or expression of Graduation that syntactically modifies it. In these cases, the modifier is included in the evaluative span (31–32). We will only annotate the realizations of Graduation by independent words: our approach will not consider scalar terms, as in the series of terms *contented/ happy/joyous* (Affect), *competently/skilfully/brilliantly* (Judgement) or *warm/ hot/scalding* (Appreciation). On the other hand, we will adopt Martin and White's (2005: 143) inclusion under Graduation of the expressions with a lexical meaning of Attitude, such as <u>*reasonably*</u> *happy* or <u>*dreadfully*</u> *cold*, on the grounds that their effect in these contexts is to intensify the meaning of the evaluative expression that they modify. In other words, they undergo delexicalization, even though it might be argued that their meaning of Attitude is not entirely lost.

> (31)   There is just something about the way he says his lines that makes them *so funny*. (Movies no, 13)

> (32)   That's probably *the biggest detriment* to the book (Books no, 17)

5.8. Length of the text spans

Due to the overall aim of the analysis (to annotate a large quantity of text spans), we restrict the spans to the evaluative lexical item, leaving aside the constituents of the syntactic unit to which it belongs. For example, in (33) the span is restricted to *free* instead of the whole constituent (*free parking for hotel guests*), and in (34), the span includes only *decrepitud* 'decrepitude', rather than *la decrepitud de Ender*.

> (33)   I would definitely recommend the Golden Nugget (oh, and did I mention *free* parking for hotel guests?) (Hotels yes, 22)

> (34)   la *decrepitud* de Ender (Libros no, 1.1)
>
> 'Ender's decrepitude'

However, some spans consist of more than one word, since the kind of evaluation that they express depends on the expression as a whole. In (35) the span is *bajando la calidad*, since neither *bajando* nor *la calidad* convey the negative evaluation expressed by the whole:

> (35)   y después fue *bajando la calidad* hasta llegar a su final (Libros no, 1.1)
>
> 'and afterwards *quality kept going down* until it reached the end'

In certain cases, especially when the expressions of Attitude are modified by expressions of Graduation, the evaluative spans are discontinuous, with non-evaluative items in the middle. However, the non-evaluative words have been included within the spans for reasons of easiness of quantification:

> (36)   *lo peor* [que he leído] *en mucho tiempo* (Libros no, 1. 11)
>
> 'the worst that I have read in a long time'

5.9. Coordinated and juxtaposed evaluative expressions

When evaluative expressions are joined by a coordinating conjunction, they are considered as a single span, since they can be the scope of a single Graduation expression (37). This is not the case of juxtaposed spans, which are consequently considered as separate spans (38). However, when two coordinated spans are modified by different expressions of Graduation, they are considered as separate spans (39).

> (37)   Julia Navarro ha conseguido que la historia sea *interesante y apasionante desde el principio hasta el final*. (Libros yes, 5–10)

'Julia Navarro has managed to make the story interesting and exciting from beginning to end'

(38)   It's a *brazen/daring/no-holds-barred comic* assault on many of the values that we hold most dear (Movies yes, 23)

(39)   I also found Block's transformation from a money-hungry associate striving to make partner in a large firm to an idealistic lawyer hoping to change the world *a bit forced* and *somewhat unconvincing*. (Books no, 11)

6. Labelling of the markables

6.1. Criteria for signalling subcategories within Attitude

Ethics and aesthetics

In order to annotate the spans as instances of Judgement or Appreciation, the first distinction to consider is that between **ethics** and **aesthetics**. Evaluations about ethics are under Judgement, and evaluations about aesthetics are under Appreciation, independently of whether the target is human or non-human: in this way, *a fair referee* and *a fair decision* are both classified under Judgement, while *an ugly dress* and *an ugly person* are both cases of Appreciation.

Human and non-human targets

When the evaluation cannot be easily categorized into ethics or aesthetics, it is classified under Judgement if the target is human (*an efficient actor*) and otherwise as Appreciation (*an efficient computer*). However, entities named by abstract nouns are classified as Judgement, since they are nominalizations of the actions of persons or institutions. For example, (40) could equally be expressed by 'the publisher worked unusually hard on the marketing':

(40)   The success of the book must be attributed to the publisher's (Doubleday) *unprecedented marketing effort*. (Books no, 1)

The influence of the context

Some lexical items are associated with Judgement, and others with Appreciation. However, lexical items normally associated with one of these categories can occasionally realize the other. For example, the adjective *stupid* is associated with Judgement, but realizes Appreciation in *a stupid novel*. According to Bednarek (2009: 182), these instances provoke the effect of 'a collocational clash and a particular flavour of appraisal meaning'. For example, the periphrastic construction with *poder* 'can, be able' with a human subject is normally associated with capacity (Judgement), but in (41) the determining factor for this capacity does not lie in the value of children, but in the value of the movie, and hence the span has been classified as Appreciation.

(41)   Los peques *podrán aprender*, gracias a Wall-e, el valor de cuidar el planeta
        para que nos dure un poquito más. (Movies yes, 5–10)

        'Kids will be *able to learn*, thanks to Wall-e, the value of taking care of the
        planet so that it will last a little longer.'

Another point is the distinction between Affect and Judgement in terms such as *guilty, embarrassed, proud, jealous, envious, ashamed ...* (Martin and White, 2005: 60). We classify these expressions under Affect when they express feelings, i.e., *John is jealous of some of his wife's male colleagues*, and under Judgement when they express character traits of individuals, as in *John is a jealous person*.

Adjectives of reaction

Some adjectives indicate the emotions that the entity in question provokes in the reader. However, the adjective conceptualizes this emotion-triggering as a quality, so that they are classified under Judgement or Appreciation, not as Affect:

(42)   Even in the tense, dramatic moments, it doesn't feel *suspenseful* nor in the
        lighter moments, it comes out as fluff. (Movies no, 1)

(43)   Unfortunately, isolated examples can't create the *mind-numbing* effect of
        page after page of this tedious bloviating. (Books no, 1)

6.2. Polarity

Within the Appraisal framework, positive and negative polarity are associated with favourable and unfavourable evaluations, as in Examples (44) and (45), respectively.

(44)   Janet Evanovich's series of books starring Stephanie Plum, an inept
        bounty hunter, was one of the *most enjoyable* books I've read in a while.
        (Books yes, 3)

(45)   What *really put me off* was that it was *not clean* (hairs in the tub, dust in
        the mini-bar, etc.) (Hotels no, 1–11)

In the examples listed above, polarity is determined by lexical meaning. In other cases, it depends heavily on context. In (46) the negative polarity is due to the entity evaluated: if it had been a medicine or curative plant instead of a book, irony would be out of place and the polarity would be positive. In (47), the counterfactual conditional reverses the polarity. In (48), the positive lexical item occurs in a comparison with other related entities, so that the polarity of the span is negative.

(46)   contra el insomnio es *infalible* (Libros no, 1.14).

        'against insomnia it is *infallible*'

(47)   si tuviera un *buen* sumario (Libros no, 1.12)
        'if it had a *good* index'

(48)   I just felt her other novels were *much more exciting and interesting.*
        (Books no, 17)

7. Comparison of Appraisal realization across languages

The annotations were carried out on 32 texts, 16 per language, for a total number of words of 11,990 in English and 19,507 in Spanish. This being such a small corpus, we cannot make any broad generalizations about the type of phenomena found across the two languages. Here, we will merely show some differences that seem to be developing as trends in the corpus.

The two corpora contained different numbers of tokens of Attitude: 237 in English (one per 50.59 words) and 687 in Spanish (one per 28.39 words). In spite of this quantitative difference, when it came to distribution by Attitude type, the percentages were quite similar, with Appreciation having the overwhelming majority of the tokens, and Affect and Judgement more or less sharing the balance. In terms of polarity, the two languages also show similar trends, with a majority of positive tokens, albeit Spanish has a wider gap between positive and negative tokens. Table 2 summarizes these statistics.

Table 2: Feature statistics for the corpus

	English		Spanish	
	Tokens	Percentage	Tokens	Percentage
Attitude (tokens)	237		687	
Affect	45	18.99%	136	19.80%
Judgement	52	21.94%	168	24.45%
Appreciation	140	59.07%	383	55.75%
Positive polarity	121	51.05%	425	61.86%
Negative polarity	116	48.95%	262	38.14%

8. Conclusions and suggestions for future research

In this paper we have described the scheme for Attitude within the CON-TRANOT project, based on two experiments, the first of which included annotation of consumer reviews of books, movies and hotels and the second was restricted to books and movies. Concerning the selection of the evaluative spans, the signalling is restricted to the cases in which it refers to the products evaluated and related entities, trailers of movies and back covers of books. The words and expressions that have an inherent evaluative meaning are therefore systematically included in spans, while others are only evaluative in certain contexts. Invoked evaluations (that is, evaluations by implicature), are mainly comparisons and metaphors, as well as complex clauses containing a suggestion about the product reviewed as well as argumentation for this suggestion. Other kinds of evaluative spans are emotional outbursts and vocatives, spans containing omitted evaluative lexical items by ellipsis or substitution and expressions of deontic modality. Some areas of overlap between Attitude and Engagement, such as epistemic modality, rhetorical questions and some instances of negation and non-assertion, have been discussed with regard to the selection of the Attitude spans. As for the length of the text spans, the tendency is to restrict it as far as possible. An exception to this tendency is the inclusion of expressions of Graduation within the scope of those of Attitude. Evaluative lexical items joined by coordinating conjunctions are considered as a single span, but not if they are juxtaposed.

With regard to the annotation of markables, the key criteria for signalling subcategories are ethics and aesthetics, as well as human and non-human targets. Some lexical items are mainly associated with Judgement and others with Appreciation, but their value may vary depending on context. Concerning polarity, the main perspective adopted is that of the entity reviewed, so that in certain cases the positive or negative value of the span is the opposite of its lexical meaning.

Due to the complexities involved in the design of a coding scheme for Attitude, the two experiments were necessary so as to reach a satisfactory degree of agreement between the annotators. Even though we cannot make broad generalizations due to the size of the corpus, we should state that the percentages of the three subtypes of Attitude (Affect, Judgement and Appreciation) were similar in the English and in Spanish reviews; differences were found in the number of spans, which was higher in Spanish both in absolute terms and in frequency per number of words, and also in polarity, in that positive polarity displayed a higher percentage in the Spanish reviews while the opposite occurred with negative polarity.

This scheme for Attitude could be further refined by analysing a higher number of consumer reviews and by diversifying the kinds of products, in order to arrive at an easily reproducible and transparent standard of annotation.

Notes

1.   The CONTRANOT project is financed by the Spanish Ministry of Science and Innovation under the I+D Research Projects Programme (reference number FFI2008-03384). As mem-

bers of the team, we gratefully acknowledge the support provided by Spanish Ministry and also the BSCH-UCM grant awarded to our research group.

2.   The system has been designed considering a discussion on the Appraisal Analysis e-mail list initiated by Marta Carretero, which took place in January 2010. We thank Monika Bednarek, Geoff Thompson, Alexanne Don and Donna Miller for their contributions. The short-comings and inconsistencies of the resulting system are our responsibility.

References

Bednarek, Monika (2009) Language patterns and ATTITUDE. *Functions of Language* 16 (2): 165–192. http://dx.doi.org/10.1075/fol.16.2.01bed

Biber, Douglas (1988) *Variation across Speech and Writing*. Cambridge: Cambridge University Press. http://dx.doi.org/10.1017/CBO9780511621024

Biber, Douglas (1995) *Dimensions of Register Variation: A Cross-Linguistic Comparison*. Cambridge: Cambridge University Press. http://dx.doi.org/10.1017/CBO9780511519871

Biber, Douglas and Finegan, Edward (1989a) Drift and the evolution of English style: A history of three genres. *Language* 65 (3): 487–517. http://dx.doi.org/10.2307/415220

Biber, Douglas and Finegan, Edward (1989b) Styles of stance in English: Lexical and grammatical marking of evidentiality and affect. *Text* 9.1: 93–124. http://dx.doi.org/10.1515/text.1.1989.9.1.93

Bloom, K., Garg, N. and Argamon, S. (2007) Extracting appraisal expressions, *Proceedings of HLT/NAACL* 308–315. Rochester, NY.

Carretero, Marta (2002) The influence of genre and register on epistemic modality in spoken English: A preliminary study. *Estudios Ingleses de la Universidad Complutense* 10: 11–41.

Carretero, Marta (2004) The role of evidentiality and epistemic modality in three English spoken texts from legal proceedings. In J. Marín-Arrese (ed.) *Perspectives on Evidentiality and Modality in English and Spanish*, 25–62. Madrid: Editorial Complutense.

Carretero, Marta (2007) Subjectivity in English epistemic modality: A two-resource based approach. *BELL New Series* 5 (5): 97–111.

Carretero, Marta and Taboada, Maite (to appear) The annotation of Appraisal: How attitude and epistemic modality overlap in English and Spanish consumer reviews. In J. R. Zamorano (ed.) *Thinking Modally: English and Contrastive Studies on Modality*. Berne: Peter Lang.

Chafe, Wallace and Nichols, Johanna (1986) *Evidentiality: The Linguistic Coding of Epistemology*. Norwood, NJ: Ablex.

Coulson, Seana (2001) *Semantic Leaps: Frame-shifting and Conceptual Blending in Meaning Construction*. Cambridge: Cambridge University Press. http://dx.doi.org/10.1017/CBO9780511551352

Esuli, Andrea and Sebastiani, Fabrizio (2006) Determining term subjectivity and term orientation for opinion mining, *Proceedings of EACL-06, the 11th Conference of the European Chapter of the Association for Computational Linguistics*. Trento, Italy.

Fauconnier, Gilles and Turner, Mark (2008) Rethinking metaphor. In R. Gibbs (ed.), *Cambridge Handbook of Metaphor and Thought*, 53–66. Cambridge: Cambridge University Press.

Goldberg, Andrew B. and Zhu, Xiaojin (2006) Seeing stars when there aren't many stars: Graph-based semi-supervised learning for sentiment categorization, *Proceedings of HLT-NAACL 2006 Workshop on Textgraphs: Graph-based Algorithms for Natural Language Processing*, 45–52. New York.

Kennedy, Alistair and Inkpen, Diana (2006) Sentiment classification of movie and product reviews using contextual valence shifters. *Computational Intelligence* 22 (2): 110–125. http://dx.doi.org/10.1111/j.1467-8640.2006.00277.x

Lakoff, George and Johnson, Mark (1980) *Metaphors We Live By*. Chicago, IL: University of Chicago Press.

Lavid, Julia (2008) CONTRASTES: An online English-Spanish textual database for contrastive and translation learning. In B. Lewandowska-Tomaszczyk (ed.), *Corpus Linguistics, Computer Tools, and Applications – State of the Art*. Frankfurt: Peter Lang Verlag.

Lavid, J., Arús, J. and Zamorano, J. R. (2007) *Working with a Bilingual English-Spanish Database using SFL*. Paper presented at the 34th International Systemic-Functional Congress, Odense, Denmark.

Lavid, J., Arús, J. and Zamorano, J. R. (2010) *Towards an Annotated English-Spanish Corpus with SFL Textual Features*. Paper presented at the 37th International Systemic-Functional Congress, Vancouver, Canada.

Martin, James R. (2000) Beyond exchange: Appraisal systems in English. In S. Hunston and G. Thompson (eds) *Evaluation in Text: Authorial Distance and the Construction of Discourse*, 142–175. Oxford: Oxford University Press.

Martin, James R. and White, Peter R. R. (2005) *The Language of Evaluation*. New York: Palgrave.

Pang, Bo and Lee, Lillian (2008) Opinion mining and sentiment analysis. *Foundations and Trends in Information Retrieval* 2 (1–2): 1–135. http://dx.doi.org/10.1561/1500000011

Pang, B., Lee, L. and Vaithyanathan, S. (2002) Thumbs up? Sentiment classification using Machine Learning techniques, *Proceedings of Conference on Empirical Methods in NLP*, 79–86.

Stillar, Glenn (1998) *Analyzing Everyday Texts: Discourse, Rhetoric and Social Perspectives*. London: Sage.

Stubbs, Michael (1986) 'A matter of prolonged field work': Notes towards a modal grammar of English. *Applied Linguistics*, 7 (1): 1–25. http://dx.doi.org/10.1093/applin/7.1.1

Taboada, Maite (2008) SFU Review Corpus [Corpus]. Vancouver: Simon Fraser University, http://www.sfu.ca/~mtaboada/research/SFU_Review_Corpus.html.

Taboada, Maite, Anthony, C., Brooke, J., Grieve, J. and Voll, K. (2008a) *SO-CAL: Semantic Orientation CALculator*. Vancouver: Simon Fraser University.

Taboada, Maite, Anthony, C. and Voll, K. (2006a) Creating semantic orientation dictionaries, *Proceedings of 5th International Conference on Language Resources and Evaluation (LREC)* 427–432. Genoa, Italy.

Taboada, M. Brooke, J., Tofiloski, M., Voll, K. and Stede, M. (2011) Lexicon-based methods for sentiment analysis. *Computational Linguistics* 37 (2): 267–307. http://dx.doi.org/10.1162/COLI_a_00049

Taboada, M., Gillies, M. A., and McFetridge, Paul (2006b) Sentiment classification techniques for tracking literary reputation, *Proceedings of LREC Workshop: Towards Computational Models of Literary Analysis* 36–43. Genoa, Italy.

Taboada, Maite and Grieve, Jack (2004) Analyzing appraisal automatically. In Y. Qu, J. G. Shanahan and J. Wiebe (eds) *Proceedings of AAAI Spring Symposium on Exploring Attitude and Affect in Text (AAAI Technical Report SS-04-07)* 158–161. Stanford University, CA: AAAI Press.

Taboada, M., Voll, K. and Brooke, J. (2008b) *Extracting Sentiment as a Function of Discourse Structure and Topicality* (Technical Report No. 2008-20): Simon Fraser University.

Turney, Peter (2002) Thumbs up or thumbs down? Semantic orientation applied to unsupervised classification of reviews, *Proceedings of 40th Meeting of the Association for Computational Linguistics* 417–424. Philadelphia, PA.

Voll, Kimberly and Taboada, M. (2007) Not all words are created equal: Extracting semantic orientation as a function of adjective relevance, *Proceedings of the 20th Australian Joint Conference on Artificial Intelligence* 337–346. Gold Coast, Australia.

White, Peter (2002) Appraisal. In J.-O. Östman and J. Verschueren (eds) *Handbook of Pragmatics* 1–27. Amsterdam: John Benjamins.

White, Peter R. R. (2003) *An Introductory Course in Appraisal Analysis*. Retrieved March 16, 2009 from http://www.grammatics.com/appraisal

Whitelaw, C., Garg, N. and Argamon, S. (2005) Using Appraisal groups for sentiment analysis, *Proceedings of ACM SIGIR Conference on Information and Knowledge Management (CIKM 2005)* 625–631. Bremen, Germany.

Whitelaw, Casey and Patrick, Jon (2004) Selecting systemic features for text classification, *Proceedings Australasian Language Technology Workshop,* 93–100. Sydney, Australia.

13 An annotation scheme for dynamic modality in English and Spanish

Juan Rafael Zamorano-Mansilla and Marta Carretero

This chapter describes the results of a series of annotation experiments that focused on a number of prototypical expressions of dynamic modality in English and Spanish. This kind of modality may be defined as possibility and necessity due to natural factors (Perkins, 1983) and comprises meanings such as inevitability, tendency, ability and circumstantial possibility. The work reported is part of a larger project – CONTRANOT – aimed at the creation and validation of contrastive functional descriptions through corpus analysis and annotation, and at the production of a bilingual English-Spanish corpus annotated with different layers of discourse and grammatical features (see Arús *et al.*, this volume; Lavid, 2008; Lavid *et al.*, 2007, 2010a, 2010b, 2010c). The results display striking similarities between inter-annotator agreement in the two languages, in terms of both the global percentages of agreement and the percentages of the individual expressions and their respective correlates in the other language. The main problem for inter-annotator agreement was the distinction between dynamic modality and the other two modalities (epistemic and deontic).

1. Introduction

This study is based on the results of a series of experiments in which the authors annotated examples of a set of expressions in English and Spanish that are considered to be prototypical realizations of dynamic modality. These experiments are part of the CONTRANOT project, currently going on at the Universidad Complutense de Madrid under the supervision of Prof. Julia Lavid. The aim of the project is to create functional descriptions of various areas of the grammar of English and Spanish and to validate them through experiments in which inter-annotator agreement is measured. The results reported here have been produced by the team working on the category of modality.

By comparing the level of agreement attained by two different expert annotators, it was possible to identify the examples that were readily identified as instances of dynamic modality and those for which annotation was more problematic. By reflecting on these examples, a discussion is offered of the factors that favour an unproblematic identification of dynamic modality, as well as those that lead to inter-annotator disagreement.

The article is organized as follows: Section 2 briefly describes the expressions analysed in English and Spanish and the data used in the experiments; Section 3 presents the definition of dynamic modality used by the authors in the annotation process; Section 4 offers an overview of the results obtained in the experiments; finally, Section 5 deals with the main areas of disagreement between the annotators as well as the factors that cause this disagreement.

2. The annotation: data and method

The results described in this paper were obtained in a series of annotation experiments in which 40 corpus examples of prototypical expressions of dynamic modality in English and Spanish were classified by the authors. The selection of the expressions analysed here was motivated by the inclusion of these expressions in previous studies of dynamic modality (see Section 3), as well as the existence of narrow correlates in the two languages. All these expressions have other modal meanings (epistemic and/or deontic) apart from their dynamic meaning. The expressions selected are the following:

- The English verbs *must* and *have to* (the latter both in the present and past tenses).
- The Spanish equivalents of English *must* and *have to*, respectively: the verbs *deber (de)*[1] and *tener que* (the latter both in the present and past tenses to enable comparison with English *have to*).
- The English verb *can* (both in the present and in the past tenses).
- The Spanish equivalent of *can*: *poder* (both in the present and past tenses).
- The English adverb *possibly* and its Spanish equivalent *posiblemente*.

The 40 examples of each of the expressions listed above were extracted at random from the *British National Corpus* (BNC) and the *Corpus del Español* (CdE). The BNC (http://corpus.byu.edu/bnc/) contains approximately 100 million words, of which 90 per cent are taken from written language and 10 per cent from spoken language. The spoken section comprises both context-governed texts (leisure, educational, business and public-institutional) and non-context-governed or 'demographic' texts, and the written section includes imaginative texts (drama, prose fiction and poetry) as well as informative texts (leisure, world affairs, commerce and finance, etc.). Most of the texts were produced from 1975 onwards.

The CdE (http://www.corpusdelespanol.org) contains over 100 million words of Spanish texts belonging to different periods and genres. However, for the purposes of this paper the searches were restricted to the twentieth century (about 25 million words). The texts belonging to this century are grouped into four categories (academic, literature, news and oral), each representing approximately 25% of the total.

Every example was then classified as conveying deontic, epistemic or dynamic modality by the two authors of this paper, who had previously done joint research on modality (Carretero *et al.*, 2007; Zamorano-Mansilla and Carretero, 2009) and had previously agreed on the concept, scope and meanings of dynamic modality presented in Section 3. Occasionally, the annotators chose more than one annotation for the same example when they did not find it easy to decide which label applied. These were regarded by Coates (1983) as cases of either ambiguity (lack of clarity between two modal meanings) or merger (co-occurrence of two modal meanings) between two modality types.

The annotations produced by the two annotators were compared in order to quantify their level of agreement, using two measures:

(a) The percentage of examples that showed agreement.
(b) Cohen's Kappa coefficient, a statistical test specifically designed to quantify inter-annotator agreement (Cohen, 1960).

These measures give an idea of the reliability of the definitions used for the different types of modality when used by more than one annotator.

The examples shown in what follows derive from the *British National Corpus* (BNC) or the *Corpus del Español* (CdE). Examples constructed by the authors are not identified as belonging to either of these two corpora.

3. A characterization of dynamic modality

3.1. Dynamic modality: concept, scope and meanings

The label 'dynamic modality', together with those of 'epistemic modality', 'deontic modality' and less commonly 'boulomaic modality' and others, corresponds to a semantic typology based on modal logic and often used in linguistics for dividing modality into types (Hermerén, 1978; Perkins, 1983; Palmer, 1990; Carretero, 1995; Silva-Corvalán, 1995; Nuyts, 2001, 2005; Wärnsby, 2006;

Collins, 2009). These works show variation in the types proposed as well as in the defining criteria for each of them. For our definition of dynamic modality, we follow Perkins' (1983) monograph on modal expressions in English, also adopted in Carretero (1995) for epistemic modality in English and in Silva-Corvalán (1995) for the Spanish verbs *poder* ('can, may') and *deber (de)* ('must'). Perkins takes as point of departure the eight categories of modal logic distinguished in Rescher (1968): alethic, epistemic, temporal, boulomaic, deontic, evaluative, causal and likelihood. Rescher characterizes all the modalities by means of scales, based on the possibility-necessity axis. Taking into account other works on the adaptation of this typology to linguistics (Wertheimer, 1972; Miller, 1978), Perkins reduces Rescher's types to three: epistemic, deontic and dynamic, and proposes a monosemantic approach for English modal expressions, according to which the meaning of each expression is based on the following elements:[2]

(a) A system of organized beliefs K, which is divided into rational laws (for epistemic modality), social laws (for deontic modality) and natural laws (for dynamic modality).

(b) A set of circumstances C, in which K is relevant.

(c) A variable X, which represents the truth of a proposition in the case of epistemic modality and the occurrence of an event in the case of deontic and dynamic modality.

Perkins covers a wide range of English modal expressions, including the modal auxiliaries and semi-auxiliaries, adjectival, participial and nominal expressions, adverbs and lexical verbs. Among these expressions, he devotes considerable space to the modal auxiliaries, which he classifies in terms of the following features:

(a) A possibility-necessity axis, which results in three degrees of strength:
- Possibility: K (C does not preclude X);
- Probability: K (C is disposed towards X);
- Necessity: K (C entails X).

(b) Primary versus secondary modals. Secondary modals have a semantic component of conditionality, which varies depending on context: hypotheticality, past time, formality, politeness, etc. We believe that the secondary modals can be considered as the past tense of the primary modals.

(c) The combination of these two features results in the following characterization of the modals:
- Possibility. Primary: *can, may*; secondary: *could, might*;
- Probability. Primary: *shall, will*; secondary: *ought to, should, would*;
- Necessity. Primary: *must*; secondary: none.

(d) Individual specifications of K, C and X for each modal. These specifications are complex and will not be considered in this chapter for reasons of space.

Our approach to the modals differs from Perkins' in two respects: first, we consider that *shall, will* and *would* mean K (C entails X). *Will* clearly expresses stronger modality than other modal expressions which have a less strong positive bias, such as *probably* (compare (1) and (2)). *Would* is the secondary counterpart of *will*, so that it is advisable to classify it as an expression of necessity too. As for *shall*, its strength is comparable to that of *will*; we will not go into detail here, since neither of these expressions is included in our analysis.

(1)   John **will** be in class now.

(2)   John is **probably** in class now.

Second, we agree that the strength of each modal auxiliary (and of each modal expression in general) is by and large pervasive in (nearly) all its uses, but in our view this feature by itself cannot motivate the consideration of the modals as monosemantic. All of them can be used with more than one of the types of sets of beliefs K (rational, social and natural laws): in other words, they all can express more than one kind of modality. In our view, this versatility is a sound reason for considering them as polysemantic: the different modalities may well be considered as different meanings. For example, we consider that *must* has three different meanings, since it can express epistemic modality (high probability (3)), deontic modality (socially imposed obligation (4)) and dynamic modality (necessity due to natural properties (5)). The Spanish equivalents of *must,* the verbs *tener que* and *deber (de),* also share these three meanings.

(3)   I rather pity the young who live in London because they **must** be having a particularly difficult time. (BNC BN6)

(4)   A subject that always causes controversy is whether head teachers should advise or instruct members of staff on their dress and appearance. Not many heads would go as far as one who insists that male members of staff **must** wear their jackets in classrooms even on the warmest of days. (BNC AND)

(5)   You simply can't use coir in exactly the same way as you would use peat. It just won't work. Coir must be watered differently and it **must** be fed after three to four weeks instead of the six to eight weeks recommended for peat. If you use it wrongly, which is what happened at Which?, you'll get bad results. (BNC ACX)

Along the lines described above, we propose a definition of dynamic modality as the set of meanings that configure the axis possibility-necessity determined by natural circumstances. Dynamic modality may be considered to be a semantically heterogeneous category, since the relations between the different meanings are not easy to perceive. After examining several sources on the semantics of modal expressions (Perkins, 1983; Palmer, 1990; Silva-Corvalán, 1995; Westney, 1995; Nuyts, 2001, 2005; Wärnsby, 2006; Collins, 2009), we concluded that the main dynamic meanings are those expressed below. They are valid for both English and Spanish, but for the sake of simplicity we will use only examples from English.

High degree: necessity

(a) Necessity due to inherent properties of an entity: in (6–7), the sources of the necessity are Mary's character and the nature of flesh and blood, respectively:

(6)   Mary's different. She **can't help** hating me because I'm single and she's a widow. (BNC HRA)

(7)   Her heart was rioting madly, and her limbs were going weak, but a gleam entered her eye. 'You might let me go just a little. I know you call me a ghost, but flesh and blood **must** breathe! Laughing, he loosened his hold enough so that she could pull her arms free. (BNC HGV)

(b) Necessity due to external circumstances. This is the case of (8): the need to sleep is not a specific feature of the referent of 'you', but shared by all humans and other living beings:

(8)   She suddenly realized how tired she was, but she made an effort and told him that she was travelling to Rome to join her aunt and uncle. You have a long journey, signorina, her companion told her. The lines are not fully repaired after the war. We go to Florence via Genoa and La Spezia. It takes much time. But you are tired. You **must** sleep. (BNC CEY)

(c) Habit or strong tendency, which may be due to inherent properties. For example, *will* in (9) expresses a tendency due to the properties of the pumice, and *would* in (10) a habit connected with the professor's character; however, inherent properties are not so obvious in other cases, such as in (11):

(9)   First, a word about pumice itself. The pumice that we know from painful experience in the bathroom consists of material containing over 65 per cent of silica, and there is a general tendency to associate pumice only with acid rocks such as rhyolites. Strictly speaking, though, pumice is only a kind of highly vesicular glassy rock with a low density, so low that many types **will** float on water, and it may be anywhere between basalt and rhyolite in composition. (BNC ASR)

(10)   They had lived in London for many years and Ilsa drifted to the Polish cafés and Hungarian tea-rooms where she could talk with other emigres and drink Viennese coffee in fluted glasses. They argued! They talked!

They banged tables and a little old professor **would** shout and stab the air with his cigar. (BNC HGF)

(11)   Every evening the small party **would** sit under the stars and listen to his stories of life in the African interior, his extensive travels and explorations, his war years and his friendship with the Swiss psychologist Carl Jung. (BNC A7H)

Median degree: tendency of lesser strength

(12)   Water shortage was often acute, especially in the Lower Volga area. In general, conditions of land tenure, communal arrangements, and cultural traditions differed considerably in the Volga provinces from those in the West and the centre of European Russia. For instance, members of Volga communes **were apt** to be more outward-looking than those in Kursk guberniia because of their wider market ties and better transport facilities. (BNC A64)

Low degree: potentiality

(a) Occasional tendency:

(13)   Ferguson simply has a precious gift for going past defenders. Deceptively strong, he **can** surprise opponents by riding heavy challenges. (BNC A2E)

(b) Ability:

(14)   They'll know we **can** speak English, at least. (BNC H0F)

(c) Possibility due to inherent properties of an entity:

(15)   The solvent used tends to be methylene chloride thickened with SCMC to a gel consistency to slow down the evaporation of the solvent and to make the product easy to apply. In this form it is brush applied to cold surfaces and therefore marketed as a cold oven cleaner. Used hot it **can** be dangerous. (BNC APV)

(d) Possibility due to external circumstances:

(16)   But you won't get in it easily now the tide's up. Wait until it goes down and you **can** walk in without getting your feet wet. (BNC H85)

Not surprisingly, different proposals are found in the literature on dynamic modality as for the range of meanings covered. For instance, Palmer (1990) does not draw the line between deontic and dynamic modality in terms of social versus natural laws, but in terms of the addresser being or not the source of the modality, so that deontic modality is restricted to the cases in which the addresser imposes the obligation or prohibition, or gives the permission. In this way, he considers social obligation as dynamic when it is not imposed by the addresser, as in (17–18), two examples cited from the *Survey of English Usage* (Palmer, 1990: 113). However, we believe that in these cases the addresser subscribes to the obligation and is therefore involved in it, even if it is not imposed by him/her. Hence, the distinction between social laws and natural laws seems to be a clearer borderline.

(17)   If the ratepayers **should** be consulted, so too must be the council tenants.

(18)   Yes, I **must** ask for that Monday off.

Hermerén (1978) and later Wärnsby (2006: 15–19) consider that the possibility due to external circumstances is part of epistemic modality. We do not agree with this classification, since this meaning does not express an assessment of the likelihood of a proposition to be or become true, but the potential for something to be or become true; this potential may be activated or not. For instance, in (16) above *can* indicates that, when the tide goes down, the natural circumstances (in this case the dryness of the ground) will make it possible for the addressee to walk in without getting his/her feet wet, independently of whether s/he will do so or not. Therefore, we consider these cases as dynamic.

In his turn, Perkins (1983) considers volition as dynamic, in that it is inherent to an entity, which in the case of (19) is the referent of the subject. We believe, however, that volition is closer to deontic than to dynamic modality: volition shares with obligation and permission an element of human will, which was already noted in Jespersen (1924: 819–821), the difference being that obligation and permission have a semantic trait of (lack of) imposition that volition does not have.[3] Therefore, we will not consider volition as part of dynamic modality.

(19)   Daniel put his hand on Peter's arm. 'Thank you, but no. I **will** go alone, if I may.' (BNC CMJ)

3.2. Dynamic modality as a peripheral category of modality

The peripheral status of dynamic modality in the literature

The peripheral status of dynamic modality among the types of modality can be noticed in many ways. For a start, some approaches to modality based on logico-semantic categories, which cover the meanings of dynamic modality listed above, do not use the label 'dynamic': the term 'root modality' is frequently used as a term covering dynamic and deontic modality (Coates, 1983; Talmy, 1988, 2000; Sweetser, 1990); similarly, Westney (1995), in his comparative study of modal auxiliaries and their periphrastic equivalents, studies some of the meanings listed above, such as ability, possibility and necessity, but does not use the term 'dynamic'. In their turn, Halliday and Matthiessen (2004: 621) state that the category of ability/potentiality is 'on the fringe of the modality system'. Moreover, one may venture to say that the literature on dynamic modality is less abundant than that on deontic modality, the difference with epistemic modality being still greater. The lesser coverage of dynamic modality in comparison to the other two may be seen in the subject indexes of monographs on modality, as well as in the titles of articles in compilations on modality (Bybee and Fleischman, 1995; Facchinetti *et al.*, 2003; Facchinetti and Palmer, 2004; Marín-Arrese, 2004; Klinge and Müller, 2005; Tsangalidis and Facchinetti, 2009; among others).

This situation may well be due to the peripheral status of dynamic modality within a more general category of modality. In this respect, it is admittedly difficult to find general features of modality, to the extent that some references argue against considering dynamic, deontic and epistemic modality as a single supercategory (Nuyts, 2001: 25–27; Nuyts, 2005). However, modality in general has most often been identified with two semantic features (Carretero *et al.*, 2007: 92–93):

(a)   irrealis (non-factuality or counterfactuality);
(b)   subjectivity, in the sense that modality often expresses an attitude of the addresser to what is communicated.

As will be shown in the rest of Section 3.2, dynamic modality is not connected with these two features to the same extent as epistemic and deontic modality are.

Dynamic modality and irrealis

Givón (2001: 301–302) makes the distinction between realis assertions, i.e., propositions strongly asserted to be true, and irrealis assertions, i.e., propositions weakly asserted to be either possible, likely or uncertain (epistemic sub-modes) or necessary, desired or undesired (valuative-deontic sub-modes). Realis assertions, in contrast to irrealis assertions, implicate strong belief on the part of the addresser. Consequently, epistemic expressions place the propositions under an irrealis scope (20–21) except for those that express total certainty, which are not often considered as prototypical epistemic expressions (22). Propositions with deontic expressions are also under an irrealis scope (23–24) except when the deontic modality refers to the past, in which case the deontic modality is also expressed by a non-prototypical deontic expression (25):

(20)   I never knew Marie was married. **Maybe** she told me and I forgot. (BNC A74)

(21)   '**Surely** your sister must know where Jeopardy is', Cleo suggested. (BNC GW2)

(22)   I **know** that you're an historian by profession. (BNC KRG)[4]

(23)   My goals are clear-cut. I **must** seek knowledge, the truth that derives from knowledge. (BNC AN8)

(24)   And they kept her there when they **could** have sent her to hospital. (BNC ALP)

(25)   We **had to** pay for our own training in those days. (BNC H4C)

On the other hand, the relation between dynamic modality and irrealis is different. In many of the examples of the different meanings of dynamic modality (6–16), the modal expressions can be roughly paraphrased with realis assertions: in (6), (9) and (14), *can't help, will* and *can*, are replaceable with unmodalized Verbal Groups in the present tense; in (10) and (11) the modalized Verbal Groups with *would* can be substituted by unmodalized Verbal Groups in the past; as for *were apt to* in (12) and *can* in (13) and (15), they are paraphraseable by unmodalized Verbal Groups combined with adverbials of frequency such as *often* or *sometimes*. In all the cases mentioned in this paragraph, dynamic modality refers to properties of entities or to habits, in spite of the fact that the main verb depicts a non-stative situation. Such situations retain all the typical properties of non-stativity (such as perfectivity), and they can even be temporarily ordered relative to other situations, as in *When I was younger, I could stay out all night long and get up early the next day*. However, the whole process is not located at any particular time. Therefore, they can be classified under Givón's (2001: 286) category of habitual tense, as 'an event (or state) that either occurs always or repeatedly, or whose event time is left unspecified'. Givón (2001: 305) states that habitual clauses are non-challengeable strong assertions just as realis clauses are, but lack the property that he considers most important of realis assertions, namely reference to specific events occurring at a specific time. Therefore, these meanings of dynamic modality could be said to be in the realis-irrealis borderline.

The remaining meanings of dynamic modality, i.e., necessity and possibility due to external circumstances (as in (8) and (16)) are nearer realis assertions in that the circumstances refer to a specific time; however, emphasis is not laid on the truth of these circumstances but on the potential for the event to be actualized; therefore, their status may also be characterized as borderline between realis and irrealis.

Dynamic modality and subjectivity

Epistemic modality, at least in its most prototypical realizations, is subjective insofar as it is the addresser's estimation of the chances that the state of affairs (SoA) has of being or becoming true. This estimation may be done by someone else in the so-called 'descriptive' cases (Nuyts, 2001), but these play a peripheral role within epistemic modality (26). As for deontic modality, subjectivity has often been associated with the addresser's being the source of the obligation or permission; however, even if s/he is not the source, in many cases s/he still subscribes to it (27). Both epistemic and deontic modality can be considered to have a strong association with subjectivity insofar as estimations of probability, obligation and permission in many contexts can be open to individual differences of perception.

(26)   He repeatedly says he **believes** that she will lead the Conservatives into the next election and emerge victorious. (BNC EDU)

(27)   He says that it has been the foundation of Europe's post-war success, the implication being that we **must** adopt the same system in Britain if we are to become a modern, prosperous nation. (BNC AJ6)

As for dynamic modality, its reference to a permanent or temporary property of an entity or a circumstance may be considered to have a subjective element, in that the property itself is not directly perceivable but inferred by knowledge of the world obtained by reception of repeated experiences. Givón (2001: 305) states that 'a habitual assertion may be a well-founded generalization supported by knowledge of many specific past instances – hence its high subjective certainty'. This may be stated not only about the meanings connected with habit or tendency, but about all the meanings of dynamic modality: concerning inherent and external necessity, the knowledge obtained from repeated experience in (7) is that 'flesh and blood', i.e., human beings, need to breathe in order to live, and in (8), that people need to sleep when they are tired; likewise, ability and external possibility may also be derived from previous knowledge (see Examples 14, 15 and 16). In spite of this, it may be stated that the subjectivity of dynamic modality is, by and large, weaker than that of the other two modalities, in that it is less prone to individual variation than them, and this weaker subjectivity contributes to its consideration as a peripheral modality. However, the potential for variation depends on concrete cases, even if the same expression is used: for example, in (7) (almost) everyone knows that flesh and blood need to breathe, while in (8) the addressee's need to sleep might be more challengeable.

A brief note on the pragmatics of dynamic modality

The weak association of dynamic modality with irrealis and subjectivity, in comparison to epistemic and deontic modality, probably motivates the relatively scant attention paid to the former from the pragmatic viewpoint in comparison to the other two. Epistemic modality is often used in strategies in which the main intention on the part of the addresser is to provoke certain effects on the addressee rather than to give an accurate estimate of probability (Carretero, 1992, 1995; Kärkkäinen, 2004; Simon-Vandenbergen and Aijmer, 2007). As for deontic modality, pragmatic issues have also been broadly studied in the literature, since it is a common device for realizing directive speech acts with varying degrees of politeness. Dynamic modality is also of interest from the viewpoint of pragmatics: for example, the use of dynamic *can/could* to express requests and suggestions (28–29) and the use of *will/would* to express habit with a nuance of disapproval (30) are well-known. However, dynamic modality as a whole does not lend itself to generalizations about its pragmatics in the same way as epistemic and deontic modality do.

(28)   **Can** you pass me the butter? Thank you. (BNC KCH)

(29)   You **could** help me find out if I've made a terrible mistake coming here. (BNC AEB)

(30)   And after dinner sometimes he will sit down in that chair and go to sleep! I say to him, if he did more gardening, more real gardening, more digging, he **would** keep more lissom. (BNC AC7)

4. Dynamic modality in English and Spanish: overview of the results

In this section we present the quantitative results obtained in the experiments in which the authors annotated 40 examples of each of the lexical items listed in Section 2. The purpose of the experiment was to measure the validity of the definition used for the category of dynamic modality. A high level of agreement between the annotators would mean that the definition is sufficiently precise and detailed, and therefore suitable for producing similar results when used by different individuals. Conversely, a low level of agreement would mean that the characterization of dynamic modality is not sufficiently differentiated from other types of modality and would consequently have to be refined.

We start with the overall results obtained for the total of 480 examples annotated in English and Spanish, shown in Table 1. This includes two different measures of the reliability of the whole coding scheme of modality used in the annotations. One is the percentage of examples where we find coincidence between the two annotators. The second is Cohen's kappa coefficient.

Table 1: Agreement in the annotation of English and Spanish examples

	Examples annotated	**Percentage of agreement**	**Kappa coefficient**
English	240	80.30 %	0.693
Spanish	240	76.52 %	0.649
Both	480	78.87 %	0.676

The most significant result worth mentioning from Table 1 is the striking similarity between English and Spanish. This is evidence of the similar role of modality in both languages with regard to the expressions selected, and confirms that the definitions of the different types of modality used in the annotations were adequate as cross-linguistic categories.

The degree of inter-annotator agreement displays a percentage of agreement ranging from 76% to 80% and a kappa coefficient just over 0.60. Consequently, the agreement can be considered to be acceptable, but there is still room for improvement, which, we believe, could easily be achieved by reaching an agreement about the problematic cases described in Section 5.

The results discussed above quantify the reliability of the definitions of the different types of modality when applied to the totality of examples annotated. However, such quantification provides a generalization that conceals the differences between each lexical item. Table 2 offers the degree of agreement observed by lexical item.

Table 2: Agreement by lexical item

Lexical item	Percentage of agreement	Kappa coefficient
posiblemente	100.00%	1.000
must	92.86%	0.854
deber(de) (present)	85.71%	0.713
can	85.71%	0.671
possibly	84.09%	0.647
have to (past)	79.17%	0.565
poder (past)	81.40%	0.552
could	73.33%	0.536
poder (present)	68.00%	0.443
tener que (past)	64.44%	0.373
have to (present)	70.21%	0.371
tener que (present)	65.12%	0.291

Table 2 shows very similar tendencies for the English and Spanish items that are semantically equivalent. The adverbs *possibly* and *posiblemente* and the verbs *must* and *deber (de)* are the ones that offer a higher degree of agreement, whereas the annotation of *have to* and *tener que* seems less reliable.

We now turn our attention to the concept of dynamic modality and its characterization relative to the two other types of modality: epistemic and deontic. Tables 3 and 4 specify the modality types involved in the cases of disagreement in English and Spanish. For instance, 'deontic/dynamic' means that disagreement arose because the same example was classified as 'deontic' by one of the annotators and as 'dynamic' by the other. The column 'all three types' includes those cases of disagreement that were classified by one or both annotators as belonging to more than one type of modality (that is to say, as cases of ambiguity or merger). The tables give us an indication of the modality types that were more often present when disagreement between the annotators took place. The information is organized by lexical item. The tables also offer in brackets the relative frequencies of each kind of disagreement within the total number of cases of disagreement.

Table 3: Disagreement types in English

Disagreement type / Lexical item	deontic/ dynamic	epistemic/ dynamic	epistemic/ deontic	All three types
must	3	–	–	–
can	8	4	4	–
could	9	3	1	1
have to (present)	15	–	–	–
have to (past)	10	–	–	–
possibly	2	4	1	–
Total	47 (72.31 %)	11 (16.92 %)	6 (9.23 %)	1 (1.54 %)

Table 4: Disagreement types in Spanish

Disagreement type / Lexical item	deontic/ dynamic	epistemic/ dynamic	epistemic/ deontic	All three types
deber (de) (present)	4	–	2	–
poder (present)	6	9	4	–
poder (past)	6	3	2	1
tener que (present)	13	1	–	–
tener que (past)	14	–	–	1
posiblemente	–	–	–	–
Frequency	**43 (65.15 %)**	**13 (19.70 %)**	**8 (12.12 %)**	**2 (3.03 %)**

Tables 3 and 4 reveal once again striking similarities between English and Spanish. In both languages the distinction between deontic and dynamic modality is responsible for the majority of cases of disagreement. In fact, this is not only the most common type of disagreement, but also the one that is found with all lexical items. It is also interesting that the highest number of disagreements concerning deontic and dynamic modality is found with the semantically equivalent verbs *have to* and *tener que* (both in the present and past tenses). In Section 5.1 we discuss the reason for this.

The second most common source of disagreement in both languages is also the distinction between dynamic and epistemic modality. This type of disagreement, which is largely restricted to the semantically equivalent verbs *can* and *poder*, is explained in Section 5.2.

These results suggest that dynamic modality is the modal category that poses most problems for its detection; this may be due to its peripheral nature within modality (treated in 3.2). The confusion between dynamic and deontic modality, and – to a lesser extent – between dynamic and epistemic modality accounts for about 90% of all cases of disagreement in English and Spanish. The boundaries between dynamic and deontic modality seem to be particularly fuzzy, especially when the meaning of modal necessity (present in the constructions *have to* and *tener que*) is involved.

5. Dynamic modality in English and Spanish: problematic cases

5.1. Unclear cases between deontic and dynamic modality

As was seen in Section 4, by far the most common type of disagreement between the annotators concerned the distinction between deontic and dynamic modality. It was also the only disagreement type that was found with every lexical item, except *posiblemente* in Spanish, all of whose occurrences were classified as epistemic by both annotators. The cause of disagreement can be said to have two main sources:

(a) The difficulty to distinguish between obligation that stems from social laws and obligation that stems from natural laws with the verbs *must/ deber (de)* and the verbs *have to/tener que*. The disagreement was much more frequent with the verbs have to/tener que, probably because *must/deber (de)* displayed more cases of epistemic modality in both languages. The kind of epistemic modality conveyed by these verbs was hardly ever confused with dynamic modality.

An analysis of the examples that were unanimously annotated as dynamic or as deontic reveals the factors that define prototypical instances of both types of modality. In the dynamic examples, the sense of obligation is recognized as stemming from natural laws when the main process is clearly outside a participant's control. These sentences seem to emphasize a component of inevitability or absence of choice:

(31)   The scenario depicted is that decreased hospital stay means that older people (or indeed patients of any age) are being sent home with high levels of dependency; community services/informal carers cannot cope and the person **has to** come back into hospital. (BNC ECE)

(32)   la agitación lo dominó y **tuvo que** apoyarse contra el árbol. (CdE)

he was overwhelmed with emotion and had to lean against a tree.

By contrast, examples easily identified as deontic depict an obligation in which the component of responsibility, duty or liability is more prominent than that of inevitability:

(33)   I **had to** do this three months before Mussolini's visit because the security arrangements were intense; there were many Slavs in the city with anti-Fascist feelings. Every family had to notify the police of the number of members of the family who would be present on the day, and give the names of any guests who would be staying in the house. (BNC G3B)

(34)   uno **tenía que** usar camisa blanca, corbata, etcétera. (CdE)
one **had to** wear a white shirt, a tie, etc.

Another element that made the recognition of dynamic modality easier was the presence of a purpose clause. In these examples the modalized clause presents a prerequisite for the process contained in the purpose clause. Such logical relation between two processes is felt to correspond with natural laws:

(35)   Body Position All the weight **has to** be used to make the tail dig in, so the posture needed is exactly that of a very bad carve gybe, ie straight front leg, leaning back and pulling the rig towards you. (BNC AT6)

By contrast, the problematic examples typically included no conclusive element that helped the annotators decide if the sense of obligation had a natural or a social origin:

(36)   Moreover she had the real comfort of knowing that her community appreciated what she was doing; more, her life excited such admiration that after her death the interment **had to** be delayed for some days for fear of riots. (BNC ACL)

(37)   Pero encontró unos amigos y se fue con ellos para mirar la carrera. Un rato nomás **tenía que** ser. (CdE)
But he came across some friends and he went with them to the races. It had to be a short while only.

(b)   The difficulty posed by the verbs *can* and *poder* as regards the distinction between their dynamic meanings (occasional tendency, inherent and circumstantial possibility, and ability), and their deontic meaning of permission. There are three ways in which the convergence of dynamic and deontic modality occurs.

First, the addresser may depict a process as possible or impossible without specifying whether this (im)possibility stems from social or natural factors. For example, in (38), *could possibly* admits a deontic interpretation (in the sense that holds in ships are supposed to meet certain requirements when ships are built and obscurity is one of them) and a dynamic interpretation (the gleams and reflections were really strange, given that there were no natural conditions which could make them visible). Likewise, the possibility in (39) to write the autobiography may be due to the absence of impeding social factors (deontic modality) or to mere enabling conditions (dynamic modality).

(38)   The hold was very dark, but not quite as dark as Willis had expected. In fact, it was not as dark as it should be. There were gleams and reflections where none **could possibly** be. (BNC H0R)

(39)   Los expertos han barajado varias teorías: que Neck Adam, el protagonista, era el trasunto de Hemingway, que así **pudo** escribir su autobiografía. (CdE)

The experts have put forward different theories: [one is] that Neck Adam, the main character, was a representation of Hemingway, who thus could write his autobiography.

This indeterminacy often occurs as a face-saving strategy used to disguise the addresser's role as deontic source. For example, it is not entirely clear whether *can* in (40) is used to grant permission (deontic) or to report that the video is technically fit at the time of speaking (dynamic).

(40)   You've, you've got you've got a video which is scheduled for one thirty because you've got something else at two o'clock, but you **can** have it now if you prefer to have it now rather than one thirty. (BNC F8E)

Second, stating or asking about the addressee's ability or possibility to carry out an action is a common strategy to request him/her to do something in English and Spanish, and this conversational implicature is easily confused with the deontic meaning of permission. Such use of the dynamic modality can be highly conventionalized as a mere indicator of politeness (41), but circumstantial possibility or ability can still be highly relevant even if the request is also present (42).

(41)   **Can** you pass me the salt?

(42)   **Can** you help me with this software problem?

Third, there are cases in which a deontic element of reasonability and common sense is present, but this element is dependent on adequacy to natural circumstances (dynamic), that is, on how reality actually is. (43) and (44) are two examples of this type of occurrences. With these cases, the verb modified by the modal often means belief or expectation (*believe, think, expect*) or classification (*classify, distinguish, divide* …).

(43) One problem with this cosy consensus, and its greatest irony, is that as a nation we take our pubs too much for granted. We **can** believe that the pub is universally respected and prized and that there is common cause and common understanding between owners, operators and users alike. (BNC A0B)

(44) There were such reams of documents that it simply wasn't possible to read them all. A quick scan was the best you **could** hope for before launching into the preparation of a cross-examination. (BNC AN9)

5.2. Unclear cases between epistemic and dynamic modality

These cases, which mainly involve the verbs *can/poder*, can be classified into three main subtypes.

(a) Possibility in generic statements. The verbs *can/poder* and the English adverb *possibly* are often used in generic statements to indicate that, whenever certain circumstances occur, there is potential for the event to take place, i.e., that nature does do not prevent it from occurring (dynamic modality), and also that for each time that these circumstances occur, there is probability for the event to occur (epistemic modality). Consequently, these cases could be considered as merger between dynamic and epistemic modality, since it is hard to tell if the sentence is stating that the main process is just possible or that there is a possibility that the main process will actually happen in the future. This kind of merger is even more common in the Spanish examples, perhaps because in this language the only verb used is *poder*, whereas in English both *can* and *may* are used: the difference between them seems to be that *can* puts more emphasis on the dynamic meaning (45) and *may* on the epistemic meaning (46). As may be seen in our translation of these examples, the verb *poder* does not indicate the predominance of either of these meanings. It must be noted that *may* does not express dynamic modality in other kinds of statements, and for this reason it has not been included among the expressions studied in this chapter.

(45) The ideas outlined here may seem a bit odd, cranky even, and certainly inconvenient and impractical. Yet I think that in fact they **can** make life easier for mother and baby.

(BNC ANM)

Las ideas bosquejadas aquí pueden parecer un poco raras, estrafalarias incluso, y sin duda inadecuadas y poco prácticas. Sin embargo creo que de hecho **pueden** hacer la vida más fácil a la madre y al bebé

(46)   The pathogenesis of the calculi found in patients with primary sclerosing cholangitis **may** depend on several factors. (BNC HU2)

La patogénesis de los cálculos hallados en pacientes con colangitis esclerótica primaria **puede** depender de varios factores.

(b)   Indeterminacy between epistemic and dynamic impossibility. The distinction between negative epistemic and dynamic modality of high degree is not always clear-cut. This fuzziness occurs because the meaning of dynamic impossibility can be used as the evidence from which an inference is made. The result is epistemic impossibility, which can be viewed as the negative equivalent of epistemic *must* in English. The problem is that very often, even when an utterance is identified as conveying epistemic modality, it can be argued that the dynamic element is still present, as we will see below.

Clear cases of dynamic impossibility can be identified because of the absence of a subjective element. The addresser's communicative intention is not to present the content of the utterance as deriving from indirect evidence, but simply to describe what is not possible because of physical limitations:

(47)   and this means that often a machine will have 4 or 8 MBytes of memory that a simple spreadsheet just **cannot** make use of. (BNC HAC)

(48)   … pero dado que los anfibios **no pueden** masticar … (CdE)
… but since amphibians **cannot** chew …

Clear cases of epistemic modality are identifiable because it is evident that the addresser does not know whether the content of the utterance is true or not. The addresser presents a statement as based on judgement or common sense through the use of *cannot/no poder*, but it is apparent that such estimation is not based on dynamic impossibility, but merely on personal impressions:

(49)   Nada, hijo, una gotitas todas las noches **no pueden** hacer ningún daño. (CdE)

Come on, son, a few drops every night **cannot** be harmful.

The problematic cases occur with examples in which we can detect the addresser's judgement behind the use of *can/poder* and such judgement is inferred from physical circumstances close to impossibility:

(50)   A cold, distant voice that **could not possibly** come from her spoke at my side. (BNC FAP)

(51)   Al principio me negaba a creerlo. No **podía ser posible**. Si tomó el avión a las cinco, ya debería estar llegando a Nueva York. (CdE)

At first I refused to believe it. It **couldn't be possible**. If he took the plane at five, he should be arriving in New York by now.

Examples like (50–51) are difficult to classify because the meaning of physical impossibility is used by the addresser as the evidence that supports his/her epistemic subjective evaluation. Furthermore, even if the addresser seems to know the truth, the expressions of impossibility serve to convey epistemic nuances such as disbelief or incredulity.

(c)   Indeterminacy between epistemic and dynamic possibility in questions. An interesting source of disagreement between the annotators involved epistemic and dynamic possibility in cases like (52), in which the interrogative mood is present.

(52)   But Mill considers what, what reasons **could** there **possibly** be for having this two stage process. (BNC HUF)

Example (52) was interpreted by one of the annotators as dynamic, i.e., as a question about the naturally possible reasons. The other annotator considered that the question was about an epistemic qualification, i.e., a speculative question whose answer neither the addresser nor the addressee knew. The explanation for this discrepancy is perhaps that questions most often implicate the addresser's lack of total certainty about the truth of the utterance, and this is precisely the crucial factor that distinguishes epistemic modality from other types of modality. Consequently, there is perhaps very little difference between asking about outcomes that are physically possible and outcomes that are not certain.

6. Conclusions and suggestions for further research

The results obtained in the annotation experiments have revealed striking similarities between the annotators. These similarities have different implications on the issue of modality in English and Spanish:

- The definitions of the different types of modality used by the annotators (epistemic, deontic and dynamic) are equally valid for English and Spanish. Likewise, the role of modality seems to be very similar in both languages, as regards the expressions concerned.
- Dynamic modality is the least well defined of all three types of modality in both languages, since it accounts for the majority of disagreement cases between the annotators.
- The confusion between dynamic and deontic modality is the most common source of disagreement in the annotation of English and Spanish examples. It is mainly found with the verbs *have to*/*tener que*, due to the difficulty in distinguishing between social and natural laws as the origin of the obligation.

- The confusion between dynamic and epistemic modality is mainly found with the verbs *can/poder*, due to the difficulty in distinguishing between epistemic evaluations about specific events and statements about potential developments.
- The expressions examined in English and Spanish were paired according to their semantic equivalence. Such equivalence was confirmed by the very similar results obtained in the experiments for the two languages, and suggests that the expressions perform analogous functions in both languages. The most notable exception are the adverbs *possibly/posiblemente*: whereas the latter expresses only epistemic modality, the former has a dynamic meaning in some cases of combination with *can*.

Notes

1.   Spanish grammars have traditionally stated that, in correct usage, *deber* + infinitive expresses obligation and necessity (in our terms, deontic and dynamic modality), while *deber de* + infinitive expresses deduction (in our terms, epistemic modality). However, language users tend to ignore this difference and employ the two periphrases interchangeably for both meanings. Given this situation, we have opted for including the two periphrases in our analysis.

2.   The present description has been simplified, so as to concentrate on the most operative factors.

3.   The narrow relationship between obligation and permission is further strengthened by the high frequency with which volition has a conversational implicature of obligation, as in the following example:

Will you be quiet for a moment and stop struggling? (BNC HGT)

4.   Some epistemic expressions, such as the adverbs certainly, definitely and obviously, can express total and non-total certainty depending on the context in which they occur, but this issue will not be treated here.

References

Arús, J., Lavid, J., and Moratón, L. (in press) Annotating thematic features in English and Spanish: a contrastive corpus-based study. In M. Taboada, S. Doval Suárez and E. González Álvarez (eds) *Contrastive Discourse Analysis: Functional and Corpus Perspectives*. London: Equinox.

Bybee, J. and Fleischman, S. (eds) (1995) *Modality in Grammar and Discourse*. Amsterdam/ Philadelphia, PA: John Benjamins.

Carretero, M. (1992) The role of epistemic modality in English politeness strategies. *Miscelánea* 13: 17–35.

Carretero, M. (1995) *La pragmática de las expresiones de modalidad epistémica en el inglés hablado*. PhD Thesis downloadable at http://eprints.ucm.es/3368/

Carretero, M., Zamorano, J. R., Nieto, F., Alonso, C., Arús, J. and Villamil, A. (2007) An approach to modality for higher education studies of English. In M. Genís, E. Orduna, and D. García-Ramos (eds) *Panorama de las lenguas en la enseñanza superior. ACLES 2005*. CD-ROM. 91–101. Madrid: Universidad Antonio de Nebrija.

Coates, J. (1983) *The Semantics of the Modal Auxiliaries*. London: Croom Helm.

Cohen, J. (1960) A coefficient of agreement for nominal scales. *Educational and Psychological Measurement* 20 (1): 37–46. http://dx.doi.org/10.1177/001316446002000104

Collins, P. (2009) *Modals and Quasi-modals in English*. Amsterdam: Rodopi.

Facchinetti, R., Krug, M. and Palmer, F. (eds) (2003) *Modality in Contemporary English*. Berlin: Mouton de Gruyter.

Facchinetti, R.. and Palmer, F. (eds) (2004) *English Modality in Perspective: Genre Analysis and Contrastive Studies*. Frankfurt am Main: Peter Lang.

Givón, T. (2001) *Syntax: An Introduction*. Vol. 1. Amsterdam/Philadelphia, PA: John Benjamins.

Halliday, M. A. K. and Matthiessen, C. M. I. M. (2004) *An Introduction to Functional Grammar*. Third edition. London: Edward Arnold.

Hermerén, L. (1978) *On Modality in English: The Study of the Semantics of the Modals*. Lund: Gleerup.

Jespersen, O. (1924) *The Philosophy of Grammar*. London: Allen and Unwin.

Kärkkäinen, E. (2004) *Epistemic Stance in English Conversation*. Amsterdam/Philadelphia, PA: John Benjamins.

Klinge, A. and Müller, H. H. (eds) (2005) *Modality: Studies in Form and Function*. London: Equinox.

Lavid, J. (2008) CONTRASTES: An online English-Spanish textual database for contrastive and translation learning. In B. Lewandowska-Tomaszczyk (ed.) *Corpus Linguistics, Computer Tools, and Applications – State of the Art*. Frankfurt: Peter Lang Verlag.

Lavid, J., Arús, J. and J.R. Zamorano (2007) *Working with a bilingual English-Spanish textual database using SFL*. Paper presented at the 34th International Systemic-Functional Congress. Odense (Denmark), July 2007.

Lavid, J., Arús, J. and Moratón, L. (2010a) *Investigating thematic meaning in English and Spanish: A methodological proposal*. Paper presented at the Euro International Systemic-Functional Conference. Koper (Eslovenia), July 2010.

Lavid, J., Arús, J., and Moratón, L. (2010b) *Towards an annotated English-Spanish corpus with SFL textual features*. Paper presented at the International Systemic-Functional Congress. Vancouver (British Columbia, Canada), July 2010.

Lavid, J., Arús, J. and Moratón, L. (2010c) *Corpus annotation within the CONTRANOT project*. Paper presented at the Interdisciplinary Conference of AHLisT (Association of History, Literature, Science and Technology), Universidad Complutense de Madrid, 23–25 June.

Marín-Arrese, J. (ed.) (2004) *Perspectives on Evidentiality and Modality*. Madrid: Editorial Complutense.

Miller, G. A. (1978) Semantic relations among words. In M. Halle, J. Bresnan and G. A. Miller (eds) *Linguistic Theory and Psychological Reality*, 60–118. Cambridge, MA: MIT Press.

Nuyts, J. (2001) *Epistemic Modality, Language and Conceptualization: A Cognitive-Pragmatic Perspective*. Amsterdam/Philadelphia, PA: John Benjamins.

Nuyts, J. (2005) The modal confusion: On terminology and the concepts behind it. In A. Klinge and H. H. Müller (eds) *Modality: Studies in Form and Function*, 5–38. London: Equinox.

Palmer, F. R. (1990 [1979]). *Modality and the English Modals*. London and New York: Longman.

Perkins, M. R. (1983) *Modal Expressions in English*. London: Frances Pinter.

Rescher, N. (1968) *Topics in Philosophical Logic*. Dordrecht: Reidel.

Silva-Corvalán, C. (1995) Contextual conditions for the interpretation of 'poder' and 'deber' in Spanish. In J. Bybee and S. Fleischman (eds) *Modality in Grammar and Discourse*, 67–105. Amsterdam/Philadelphia, PA: John Benjamins.

Simon-Vandenbergen, A-M. and Aijmer, K. (2007) *The Semantic Field of Modal Certainty. A Corpus-Based Study of English Adverbs*. Berlin and New York: Mouton de Gruyter. http://dx.doi.org/10.1515/9783110198928

Sweetser, E. (1990) *From Etymology to Pragmatics*. Cambridge: Cambridge University Press.

Talmy, L. (1988) Force dynamics in language and cognition. *Cognitive Science* 12 (1): 49–100. http://dx.doi.org/10.1207/s15516709cog1201_2

Talmy, L. (2000) *Toward a Cognitive Semantics. Volume I: Concept Structuring Systems*. Cambridge, MA: The Massachusetts Institute of Technology Press.

Tsangalidis, A. and Facchinetti, R. (eds) (2009) *Studies on English Modality. In Honour of Frank Palmer*, 229–258. Bern: Peter Lang.

Wärnsby, A. (2006) *(De)coding Modality. The Case of* Must, May, Måste *and* Kan. Lund Studies in English 113. Lund: Lund University.

Wertheimer, R. (1972) *The Significance of Sense: Meaning, Modality and Morality*. Ithaca, NY: Cornell University Press.

Westney, P. (1995) *Modals and Periphrastics in English*. Tübingen: Niemeyer.

Zamorano-Mansilla, J.R. and Carretero, M. (2009) The expression of deduction referring to past time within the verbal group: An English-Spanish contrastive analysis. In A. Tsangalidis and R. Facchinetti, *Studies on English Modality. In Honour of Frank Palmer*, 229–258. Bern: Peter Lang.

14 Corpus analysis and phraseology: Transfer of multi-word units

Juan Pedro Rica Peromingo

This paper presents an analysis of the production of multi-word units present in English argumentative texts written by non-native speakers of the language. The aim of this study is to examine the potential influence of the mother tongue on learners' production of both correct and incorrect multi-word units that are typically used in English for creating textual cohesion: lexical bundles, in particular, linking adverbials. Several corpora will be used: non-native students from the ICLE Corpus, and the CEUNF, an original corpus of Spanish non-native students of English who study English as a subject outside their curriculum. These will be contrasted with two native corpora: the American university students' corpus (LOCNESS) and the corpus of the professional editorialists writing in English (SPE). The taxonomy used has been taken from Biber (2004), Biber *et al.* (2004, 1999) for the linking lexical bundles. Results suggest that transfer of L1 multi-word units occurs very often in the learners' production and that it plays an important role for both correct and incorrect textual cohesion. Teaching effect will also be considered as an important factor correlating with transfer.

1. Introduction

EFL learners have been shown to overuse a limited number of frequent English phraseological units but to underuse a whole set of native-like multi-word units (Granger, 1998; Jarvis, 2000; De Cock, 2003; Rica, 2007, 2009, 2010; Paquot, 2008). These studies have also pointed to the potential influence of the mother tongue on learners' multi-word units. For example, Rica

(2009) finds that the overuse by Spanish university writers of some grammatical collocations with verbs of communication and mental states (*I think that*, for example) may be due to transfer factors because of the similarity (and existence in Spanish) of such units with the Spanish writers' native tongue (*Creo que*), while they underuse some multi-word units most typically used by native writers (*I believe that*, for example). Granger (1998) states that French learners typically use those English collocations involving intensifiers that have a direct translation equivalent in French (*closely linked* 'étroitement lié'). Jarvis found that for the Finnish-speaking and Swedish-speaking Finn students who participated in his study '[their] referential word choices pattern better according to L1 background than according to other variables' (2000: 298). Paquot (2008) finds that French learners overuse the multi-word unit *let's take the example of* as a direct translation of the French unit *prenons l'exemple de.*

Some early studies on transfer (Kellerman, 1977, 1979) suggested that L2 learners seem to work on the hypothesis that there are constraints on how similar the L2 can be to the L1, and these constraints seem to hold, even when the two languages are closely related and the structures congruent. Some more recent studies (Nesselhauf, 2003, 2005) have acknowledged the potential L1 influence on native-like multi-word units produced by non-native writers, and have also correlated this L1 influence with the so-called *teaching effect*: some units are more likely to be transferred either due to their similarity (or existence in the L1) of such units with their L1, or due to the way those units are included in the syllabus for teaching English as a second or foreign language (specially lack of systematic training of multi-word units in a university context), as Paquot (2008: 114–115) states: 'L2 word-like units tend to be overused by learners especially if there are similar units performing similar functions in their L1s. The overuse is often reinforced by instruction as teaching materials tend to focus exclusively on these units.' Other authors have also studied the effect class instruction may have on the overuse, for example, of non-native writers' production of multi-word units, which may be due to 'the direct consequence of the long lists of connectors found in most ELT textbooks, which classify connectors in broad semantic categories (contrast, addition, result, etc.) but fail to provide guidelines on their precise semantic, syntactic and stylistic properties, thereby giving learners the erroneous impression that they are interchangeable' (Granger, 2004: 135).

Our study is based on corpus linguistics and phraseology. Corpus linguistics has been considered by many authors as the most important methodological trend since the Chomskyan revolution of the 1950s. The field of study in those years basically consisted of, first, the study of those lexical phrases based on meaning and, second, their co-occurrence with other words. It has been extensively proved in later years that, for second language acquisition (SLA) or foreign language acquisition (FLA), the use of linguistic corpora constitutes a very useful tool. On the one hand, linguistic corpora are necessary in order to provide students with more practical teaching and first-hand experience in a natural context. On the other hand, it seems to be a very useful tool for teachers developing analytic and pedagogical models for their classes. It has also been proved that the use of linguistic corpora is useful for the research and teaching of pragmatics and discourse analysis, among others, in order to determine language behaviour patterns through texts, as well as to identify the typical and unusual selection of the users, and describe the interaction among multiple variables (Conrad 2002: 78). But it has especially been in the field of translation, lexicology and elaboration of dictionaries where the use of linguistic corpora has been spectacular, in particular dictionaries, grammar books and reference books that take into account word frequencies, collocations and phraseology, as well as variation, lexis and grammar (Hunston, 2002: 96). In short, the use of student corpora enables us to analyse and compare native and non-native students' written production. This has been called *Contrastive Interlanguage Analysis* (Granger, 2002), the aim of which is, first, to identify the over-and underuse of specific linguistic aspects in the students' language and, second, to identify the transfer from and interference of the students' L1. Our intention is, as well, to foster the use of linguistic corpora for teaching English as a Foreign Language (EFL) in a Spanish university context and the use of multi-word units in the classroom, especially for advanced students of EFL, as compared to native writers' production (Siyanova and Schmitt, 2007).

Alongside corpus linguistics, this study has taken phraseology as its theoretical background. Phraseology (Howarth, 1998; Cowie, 1998; Cowie and Howarth, 1996; Meunier and Granger, 2008) is the linguistic trend that studies phraseological units, and although there seems to be a terminological confusion about what to call a *phraseological unit*, it should not prevent us from focusing on the most important aspect of these units: the more or less free combination of terms in order to constitute units with meaning. To avoid such terminological confusion, in this article we will use the term *phraseological unit* (or *multi-word unit*) as the generic structure that includes all kinds of collocations (lexical and grammatical) and lexical bundles (linking adverbials).

2. The study: Data and methodology

The study we present here consists of an analysis of the production of multi-word units that are present in English argumentative texts written by non-native speakers of the language, all of them part of the ICLE corpus and with different L1 backgrounds, and an original corpus (CEUNF) of Spanish university writers of English from different fields.

The aims for this study include: first, to analyse the use of multi-word units (lexical bundles) by non-native writers with B1 and B2 levels (as stated in the *Common European Framework of Reference for Languages: Learning, Teaching, Assessment,* Council for Cultural Co-operation Committee, 2001); second, to identify the most problematic areas in the employment of multi-word units; third, to detect teaching effect and the influence of transfer factors from the students' L1 to their L2; and, finally, to devise teaching materials which enable us to find out about the use of phraseological units by non-native university writers and show the importance of including the study, teaching and learning of this type of units in the curriculum of EFL within the university educational curriculum. As Wray (2002: 183) points out, 'collocations can only be learned if they are present in the input learners are exposed to'.

Several corpora[1] have been used for such purposes: non-native students' production from the ICLE Corpus (*International Corpus of Learner English*), and especially the Spanish subcorpus (SPICLE), and CEUNF (*Corpus de Estudiantes Universitarios No Filólogos*), the latter being an original corpus of non-native students of English from different fields (Audiovisual Communication, Fine Arts, Computer Science, etc.) who study English as a subject outside their curriculum. All their production has been contrasted with two corpora that include writings from native speakers of English: the American university students' corpus (LOCNESS) and the corpus of the professional editorialists writing in English (SPE). The taxonomy used has been taken from Biber (1993, 2004), Biber *et al.* (1999, 2004) for the lexical bundles (linking lexical bundles).

The reason for choosing such particular lexical patterns is that linking lexical bundles – together with grammatical collocations with verbs of verbal and mental processes (Rica, 2009) – are structures commonly used in argumentative writing. Lexical bundles, and especially linking adverbials, fulfil organizational and rhetorical functions which are basic in academic writing: introducing a topic, summarizing, adding information, contrasting, exemplifying, explaining, concluding, etc. Their primary function, according to Biber *et al.*, is 'to state the speaker/writer's perception of the relationship between two units of discourse' (1999: 875). Table 1 shows the taxonomy for linking adverbials used for this study. This taxonomy includes both adverbs and multi-word units in each of the categories.

Table 1: Taxonomy for the lexical bundles analysed in this study[2]

Lexical bundles: linking adverbials
Enumeration and addition **Enumeration:** First, Second, Firstly, Secondly, Thirdly, In the first place, In the second place, First of all, For one thing, For another thing, To begin with, Next, Finally, Lastly **Addition:** In addition, Further, Furthermore, Similarly, Also, By the same token, Likewise, Moreover
Summation: All in all, In conclusion, Overall, To conclude, To summarize, To sum up, In sum, To conclude.
Apposition: Which is to say, In other words, i.e., that is, e.g., for example, for instance, Namely, specifically
Result/inference: Therefore, Consequently, Thus, As a result, Hence, In consequence, So, Then
Contrast/concession **Contrast:** On the one hand, On the other hand, In contrast, Alternatively, Conversely, Instead, On the contrary, By comparison **Concession:** Though, And anyway, However, Yet, Anyhow, Besides, Nevertheless, Still, In any case, At any rate, In spite of that, After all
Transition: By and by, Incidentally, By the way, Now, Meanwhile

Two hypotheses have been stated for this study: first, that non-native students from the ICLE and the CEUNF corpora are expected to use a number of multi-word units which is quantitative and qualitatively different from used by the native writers (both the university students of the LOCNESS and the professional editorialists of the SPE); and second, that transfer and teaching effect are the two main factors for the non-native writers' overuse and underuse of certain phraseological units.

Wordsmith Tools 3.0 (Scott, 2008) has been used for the quantitative analysis of the results, *t*-test for statistical significance, and the norming of all corpora word numbers by 10,000 in order to eliminate differences in number of words between corpora (Biber *et al.*, 1998: 263). The analysis of the data and the use of these appropriate statistical tools allow us to emphasize the importance of implementing multi-word units in the students' production of written texts in the university context, especially in the Spanish educational context (McCarthy and O'Dell, 2005), and to try to identify transfer factors (Odlin, 2005).

3. Lexical bundles: Linking adverbial use

In the following pages we present the results of the use of linking adverbials in the written production of both native and non-native speakers of English. We will focus first on those differences found in the two Spanish writers' corpora. Second, we will present those differences compared to the native writers' production and, finally, the rest of the non-native students from the ICLE corpus.

In general, the Spanish non-native students from the CEUNF use more linking lexical bundles than the other Spanish non-native writers from the SPICLE and/or the native university students from the LOCNESS and the professional editorialists from the SPE. Table 2 presents the total results (top part of the results column) of the different categories of linking adverbials and the normed results (bottom part of the results column, in bold).

Table 2: Linking adverbials in the CEUNF and SPICLE and LOCNESS and SPE

	Enu-merat.	Addit.	Summa.	Apposit.	Result/Inferenc.	Contrast	Concess.	Transit.	Results
CEUNF	209	122	143	276	82	135	218	39	1224 **79.62**
SPICLE	247	84	64	269	211	135	226	17	1253 **64.30**
LOCNESS	80	76	16	85	156	50	236	8	707 **47.20**
SPE	46	19	1	25	34	23	86	16	250 **24.18**

Results show that there are important differences if we compare the production of the CEUNF (79.62) with the SPICLE (64.30), the Spanish university writers with the American university writers of the LOCNESS (47.20) and even more with the native professional writers of the SPE (24.18). As can be seen, the Spanish university writers of the CEUNF use lexical bundles twice as much as the American university writers and three times as much as the professional editorialists.

In order to find out whether these differences are meaningful or not, we have applied the *t*-test with the results shown in Table 2. The differences are extremely significant with respect to the Spanish non-native university writers, and also with respect to the American native writers of the LOCNESS ($p<0.02$), although in the latter case, the difference is less significant than in the case of the CEUNF and the SPICLE (Table 3).

Table 3: Lexical bundles: linking adverbials in the Spanish and native corpora; *t*-test

	Enumerat.	Addit.	Summa.	Apposit.	Result/Inferenc.	Contrast	Concess.	Transit.	*t*-Test
CEUNF	209	122	143	276	82	135	218	39	$p<0.002$
SPICLE	247	84	64	269	211	135	226	17	$p<0.003$
LOCNESS	80	76	16	85	156	50	236	8	$p<0.02$
SPE	46	19	1	25	34	23	86	16	

If we compare the total production of the CEUNF and the SPICLE with the rest of the non-native writers from the ICLE corpus (Table 4), only the Polish students (PICLE) use more linking adverbials (90.53) than the Spanish university writers of the CEUNF (79.62), and closer to the CEUNF are the French non-native students (FRICLE: 78.92). The differences grow bigger with respect to the rest of the non-native students: the Czech students of the CZICLE (46.10), the German students of the GERICLE (54.55), the Russian students of the RICLE (46.07) and the Swedish students of the SWICLE (58.95). The differences found are smaller with respect to the Dutch students of the DICLE (75.03), the Finnish students of the FINICLE (70.68) and the Italian students of the ITICLE (73.13).

Table 4: Linking adverbials in the ICLE

	Enum.	Addit.	Summa.	Apposit.	Result/ Inferenc.	Contrast	Concess.	Transit.	Results
CZICLE	174	30	13	175	131	171	235	26	955 **46.10**
DICLE	303	116	52	357	376	120	437	22	1783 **75.03**
FINICLE	194	110	26	436	322	127	544	8	1767 **70.68**
FRICLE	319	216	83	553	400	262	421	16	2270 **78.92**
GERICLE	199	67	20	141	207	107	337	33	1111 **54.55**
ITICLE	246	223	100	320	279	159	324	9	1660 **73.13**
PICLE	326	186	42	302	449	148	663	12	2128 **90.53**
RICLE	162	45	12	271	170	112	185	30	986 **46.07**
SWICLE	173	78	44	258	207	135	308	17	1220 **58.95**

All these numbers account for all linking adverbials, both adverbs and multi-word units. All categories of linking adverbials are widely used by the non-native writers although some are significantly used more than others: those which show concession (17.10) are the ones mostly used by the students, together with those that show apposition (14.24) and result and inference (11.72). Enumeration (10.88), contrast (6.87) and addition (5.60) adverbials are used less and, finally, summation linking adverbials (2.50) and transition ones (0.98) are the least used by all non-native students (see Table 5).

Table 5: Linking adverbials categories: results in non-native writers

Linking adverbials categories	Total and normed results
Enumeration	2,632 (10.88)
Addition	1,353 (5.60)
Summation	606 (2.50)
Apposition	2,443 (14.24)
Result / Inference	2,834 (11.72)
Contrast	1,661 (6.87)
Concession	4,134 (17.10)
Transition	237 (0.98)

Contrasting with the results found by Biber *et al.* (1999: 880) or Conrad (1999: 7), the non-native students do not use more enumeration, addition, apposition and summation linking adverbials in academic writing. Summation linking adverbials are precisely one of the least used groups by the students from the ICLE, being the concession linking adverbials the ones most used in all the non-native students' groups. Biber *et al*.'s results do not coincide either with the result and inference linking adverbials as being the most widely used by the non-native writers. On the contrary, our study and Biber *et al*.'s study do coincide with the lack of transition linking adverbials.

Within the category of linking adverbials we find two groups of items: those single adverbs which do not constitute any multi-word unit and those lexical bundles (adverb phrases, prepositional phrases, finite clauses and non-finite clauses) which do constitute phraseological units.

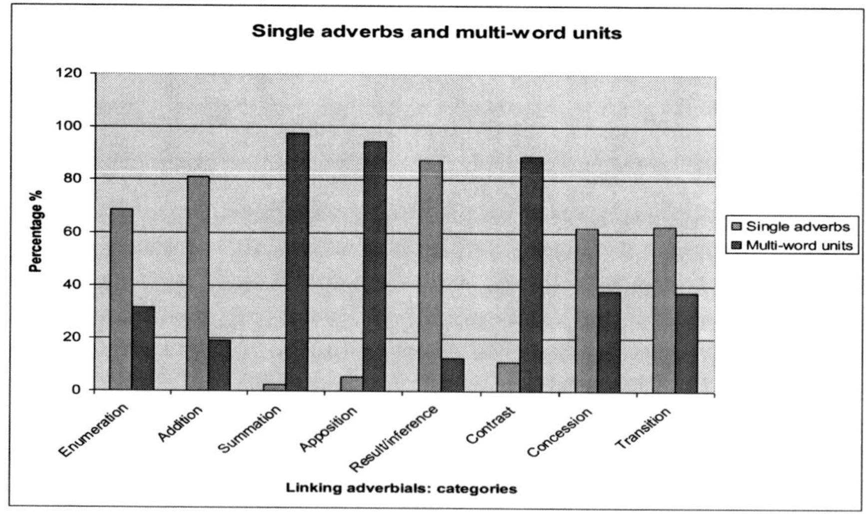

Figure 1: Use of single adverbs or multi-word units by the non-native writers (CEUNF e ICLE).

Figure 1 shows which structure is more used by the non-native writers compared to the native production, indicating whether the students tend to use more single adverbs or multi-word units in their writings. As can be observed, and after norming the results by 10,000 words, the use of single adverbs (35.03) is almost similar to the use of multi-word units (35.06), with a slightly higher use of phraseological units.

We may say, then, that non-native students rely on both single adverbs and phraseological units in order to state their ideas in argumentative writing. It is true, though, that the non-native students use more enumeration, addition, result/inference, concession and transition single adverbs and more recapitulation, apposition and contrast phraseological units in their production, but that may be due to the kind of terms included in the taxonomy used for this study.

If we compare all this production by the non-native writers with that of the native writers (both the American university students of the LOCNESS and the professional editorialists of the SPE), we find the first relevant difference: after norming the results, both LOCNESS and SPE writers use more single adverbs (27.84) than phraseological units (10.03), as can be seen in Figure 2.

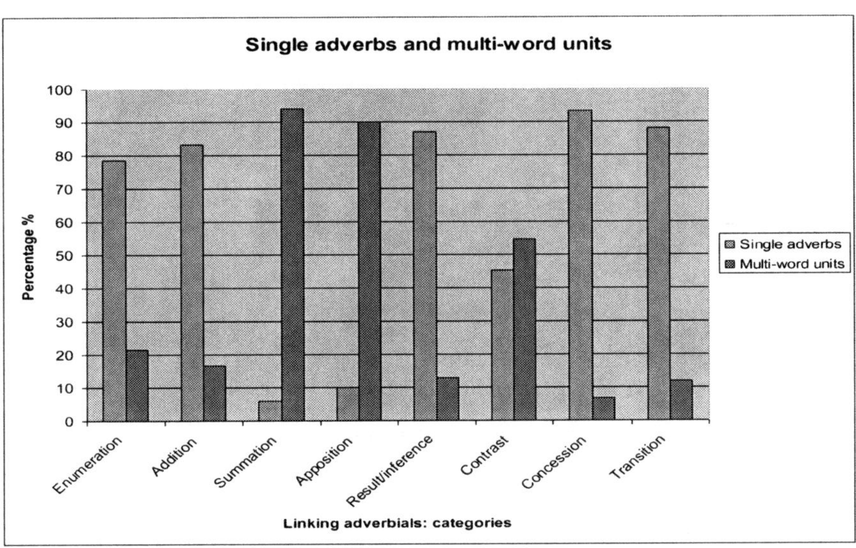

Figure 2: Use of single adverbs or multi-word units by the native writers (LOCNESS y SPE).

The native writers use more enumeration, addition, result/inference, concession and transition single adverbs and more multi-word units with respect to summation, apposition and contrast linking adverbials.

It seems evident, therefore, that the non-native writers use significantly more multi-word units than the native writers. If the use of both single adverbs and multi-word units was not significantly different in the case of the students' written production ($p<0.9$), that difference is significant in the case of the native writers ($p<0.03$) (Figure 3). This means that, contrary to common belief and previous studies on multi-word units use (Howarth, 1996; Biber *et al.*, 1999, 2004; Conrad, 1999; Nesselhauf, 2003, 2005), non-native writers use significantly more phraseological units than native writers. These studies have identified the use of lexicalized units as a more typical strategy for native writing than for non-native ones: complex multi-word units use is normally associated with native-like production rather than with non-native-like ones.

Therefore, it is not only the case that the Spanish university writers of the SPICLE and the CEUNF are the ones who widely use more multi-word units, rather all the non-native writers of the ICLE do so as well. And curiously, within the group of native writers, the LOCNESS university students also use more phraseological units than the professional editorialists.

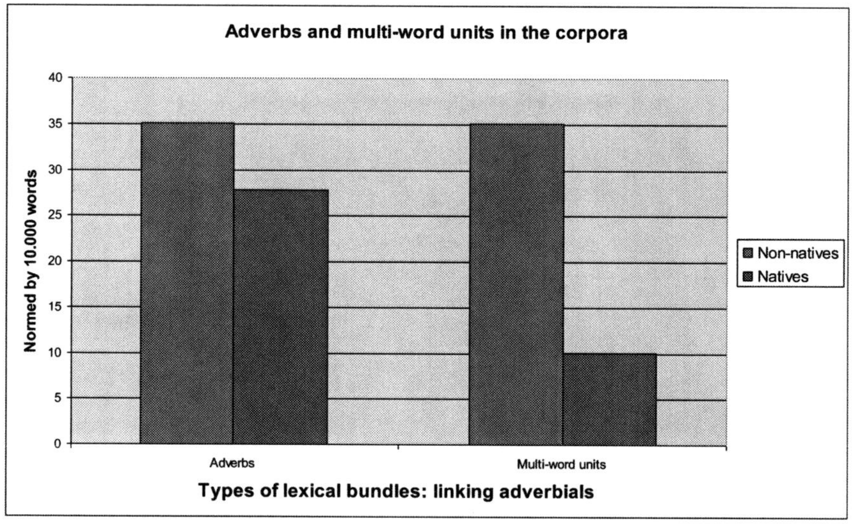

Figure 3: Use of single adverbs and multi-word units by all corpora.

Both native and non-native writers coincide in what type of linking adverbials are realized with either single adverbs or phraseological units. In both groups, summation linking adverbials (specially the lexical unit *In conclusion*), apposition (*For example*) and contrast (specially the multi-word unit *On the other hand*) are the ones mostly expressed with phraseological units. On the contrary, for the other types of linking adverbials the use of single adverbs is predominant: enumeration (specially the adverb *Finally*), addition (*Also*), result and inference (*However*) and, finally, transition (*Now* and *Meanwhile*).

Nevertheless, it should be mentioned that in Biber *et al.*'s linking adverbials taxonomy there is a supremacy of single adverbs over multi-word units. We may mention, for example, the case of the result and inference adverbials: out of seven types of adverbials four are single adverbs (*therefore, consequently, thus* and *hence*) and three are multi-word units (*as a result, as a consequence* and *in consequence*); in other cases, the single adverbs are less common in English than the multi-word units included in the taxonomy, as the case of *at any rate* or *after all* versus *however*. That is why for this study we searched both adverbs and multi-word units.

If we take, for example, the relation of those adverbs and multi-word units mostly used by the two Spanish corpora and the two native ones, we can see that there are many coincidences in their use of lexical bundles: most of them coincide in the most phraseological unit used for enumeration (*First of all*), addition (*In addition*), result/inference (*As a result*), contrast (*On the other hand*) and transition lexical bundles (*By the way*). With respect to the most recurrent adverb we also find coincidences: *Specifically* for apposition lexical bundles, *Therefore* for result/inference, *Instead* for contrast and *However* for concession lexical bundles. In the Table 6 we present a relation of the most used adverbs and multi-word units in the two Spanish corpora (CEUNF and SPICLE) and, in the two native ones (LOCNESS and SPE).

Table 6: Multi-word units and adverbs most used in the CEUNF, SPICLE, LOCNESS and SPE

	Linking lexical bundles			
	CEUNF	SPICLE	LOCNESS	SPE
Enumeration	First of all (2.92)	First of all (1.53)	First of all (0.6)	First of all (0.19)
	Finally (3.51)	First (3.64)	Finally (1.67)	First (2.32)
Addition	In addition to this/ that (0.97)	In addition (0.51)	In addition (0.46)	In addition (0.38)
	Also (2.27)	Moreover (2.46)	Also (3.07)	Also (0.48)
Summation	In conclusion (5.26)	In conclusion (1.23)	In conclusion (0.66)	All in all (0.09)
	Overall (0.26)	Overall (0.10)	Overall (0.06)	------------------
Apposition	For example (13.4)	For example (6.36)	For example (3.60)	For instance (0.87)
	Specifically (0.26)	Specifically (0.15)	Specifically (0.26)	Specifically (0.19)
Result / Inference	As a result (1.49)	As a result (1.07)	As a result (1.46)	As a result (0.48)
	Therefore (2.01)	Therefore (4.67)	Therefore (5.40)	Therefore (1.35)

Contrast	On the other hand (5.72)	On the other hand (4.46)	On the other hand (1.46)	On the other hand (0.29)
	Instead (0.39)	Instead (0.25)	Instead (1.40)	Instead (1.06)
Concession	In spite of this/that (0.39)	In spite of this/that (0.41)	After all (0.53)	After all (0.96)
	However (6.05)	However (6.51)	However (11.68)	However (4.06)
Transition	By the way (0.13)	By the way (0.10)	By the way (0.06)	By the way (0.09)
	Now (2.14)	Meanwhile (0.56)	Now (0.4)	Meanwhile (0.87)

There also seems to be a coincidence of some multi-word units and adverbs even if the four groups do not exactly coincide: *Finally* and *First* for enumeration lexical bundles, *Also* and *Moreover* for addition, *In conclusion* and *All in all* (as multi-word unit) and *Overall* (in the three groups except the SPE, who do not use any adverb) for summation lexical bundles, *For example* and *For instance* for apposition, *In spite of this/that* and *After all* for concession, and, finally, *Now* and *Meanwhile* for transition lexical bundles.

If we study the multi-word units used in all corpora (native and non-native writers), we realize that, in general, non-native students use fewer single adverbs than phraseological units, as mentioned before. Besides, the group of non-native students use fewer different multi-word units than the native writers and concentrate their production (overuse) on a specific number of phraseological units, whereas the native university students and the professional writers use a wider variety of multi-word units.

All non-native writers' use of phraseological units range between 26 different types of multi-word units (CZICLE and RICLE) and 32 types (SPICLE and DICLE), including the other group of Spanish university students (CEUNF: 30), whereas the American university writers (LOCNESS: 22) and the professional editorialists (SPE: 21) are the two groups in all 13 corpora analysed in this study who use less different types of phraseological units. There is, therefore, a very clear difference between native and non-native writers.

All non-native students widely use more multi-word units than native writers. *For example* is the most used phraseological unit in all non-native corpora (except the French students, for whom *For instance* is the most used unit, and the Czech students, for whom *On the other hand* is the most used unit). There is, nevertheless, a very clear difference with respect to the professional editorialists, for whom *After all* is the most used multi-word unit, followed by *For instance* and, in the third place, *For example*. It is also noticeable the clear difference in the use of the unit *For example* in the case of the CEUNF (13,40) and the rest of the corpora, including the other group of Spanish university writers (SPICLE: 6,36).

Another aspect that should be mentioned is that there is a clear difference in the use of multi-word units if we divide the groups between Romance languages and Indo-European Languages: the students from Romance languages (CEUNF, SPICLE, FRICLE and ITICLE) use a wider range of phraseological units in their writings than the other groups of non-Romance language, although that difference is not significant.

If we take all the multi-word units presented in Table 6 before and analyse those results in groups, we find that the apposition linking adverbials group is the one in which most of the writers (both native and non-native) use more phraseological units (94.68%). On the contrary, the addition, result and inference and concession linking adverbials groups are the ones in which most of the writers (again, both native and non-native) use more single adverbs (addition: 19.07%, result and inference: 12.38% and concession: 38% of multi-word units).

As can be observed from the previous table, there is a group of multi-word units which are used by all corpora (*for example* and *for instance*), another group of units used by most of the non-native writers (*first of all, i.e., on the other hand*) and, finally, a group of lexical units which are only used by the native students and professionals: *in addition (to this/that), in contrast* (only by the SPE) and *in any case* (only by the SPE). It should also be noticed the fact that there is a group of multi-word units which is only used by one of the non-native corpora: *at first* (only by the CZICLE), *to sum up* (only by the SPICLE), *that is* (only by the SPICLE), *in spite of this/that* (only by the CZICLE) and *by the way*, only used by the GERICLE.

Comparing these general results with the ones obtained by Biber *et al.* (1999) in their study, we find important differences in the use of linking adverbials by non-native writers: if 80% of all the linking adverbials used in Biber *et al.*'s study corresponded to single adverbs, in the case of the non-native writers the use of single adverbs (35,03%) and the multi-word units (35,06) is almost the same, although there is a slightly higher number of examples of phraseological units than of single adverbs. We may state, then, that the non-native students in this study rely more on multi-word units than those who constitute Biber *et al.*'s corpus. In another very relevant study on the same issue (Conrad 1999: 9) it was found that in both conversation and academic writing linking adverbials are realized by single adverbs and not so much by phraseological units. Our study does coincide with Durrant and Schmitt's study, in which they found that non-native writers 'rely heavily on high-frequency collocations, but that they underuse less frequent, strongly associated collocations (items which are probably highly salient for native speakers)' (2009: 157).

We may, therefore, refute Kjellmer when he says that 'in building his utterances, the native speaker makes use of large prefabricated sections. The learner, on the other hand, having automated few collocations, continually has to create structures that he can only hope will be acceptable to native speakers [...]. His building material is individual bricks rather than prefabricated sections.' (1991: 124).

4. Results and conclusion: transfer of L1 multi-word units

Results show, first, that contrary to common belief, non-native writers (*p*<0.03) significantly resort to multi-word units more often than do native speakers of English, and their production is marked by an over- and underuse of certain lexical units. And, second, that those phraseological units mostly used by the non-natives (and, in most of the cases, overused) are structures which are similar to those used in the L1 (*First of all, En primer lugar, Zunächst, Tout d'abord; In conclusion, Como conclusión, Zum Abschluß, En conclusión*, etc.), whereas they underuse some typical native structures found in the two native corpora (SPE and LOCNESS).

We may say, therefore, that the use of single adverbs to mark the connection between ideas seems to be more difficult for the students of English as a foreign language than the use of certain lexicalized structures, which are memorized as such, and which have the same function that could be expressed with single adverbs. This so-called *rote-learning* of certain structures means less mental process for learning them. As Howarth (1996: ix) explains: 'the significance of such multi-word units is that they are stored in the mental lexicon as wholes and are used as conventional expressions to facilitate fluent production and rapid comprehension', and are, at the same time, structures which are 'stored together with some indication of their grammatical structure and syntactic and pragmatic function' (Howarth, 1996: 6).

In the previous section of this paper we showed the use of multi-word units (lexical bundles) by non-native writers with B1 and B2 levels, which was one of our initial aims; second, we have already identified the most problematic areas in the employment of multi-word units. Our third aim for this study was to detect the influence of transfer factors from the students' L1 to their L2 and teaching effect, which connects with the second hypothesis that we stated at the beginning of this chapter: transfer and teaching effects are the two main factors or the non-native writers' overuse and underuse of certain phraseological units.

With respect to transfer or interference from the L1 of the non-native students, most of the multi-word units which are overused by the non-native writers are very similar to those structures which are used in the L1 to express similar meanings to those expressed in English. If for teaching German, French, Finnish, Italian or Spanish, for example, those units are widely used and, at the same time, are the first ones taught in the EFL classes, it is expected that the non-native students use their knowledge of their L1s and apply it to the production of phraseological units in their foreign language, especially if they confirm that such structures are very similar to those that exist in their L1s. These structures will, therefore, be used as a 'helpful tool' for their L2 multi-word unit use. Previous studies in the field have shown that the similarity among phraseological units in different L1s may cause some problems for L2 students, but at the same time, they may foster the acquisition, learning and use of certain phraseological units: on some occasions, thanks to the exact similarity of some lexical units (*for example*), and on other occasions due to the existence in the students' L1s of certain units that carry out the same function as those equivalent counterfeits in the L2 (*I think/I believe that* in order to introduce your personal opinion and stance towards an idea).

It is true, nevertheless, that it is very difficult to scientifically show whether the use of a certain group of multi-word units by a group of students is due to transfer factors from the L1. However, we can understand and accept this phenomenon as possible, as Nesselhauf (2005: 180–181) says: 'L1 influence will be assumed to be likely if there is a fairly obvious similarity between an L2 expression produced and an L1 expression that would be appropriate in the context'. This seems to be the case of some multi-word units like *for example, in conclusion,* or *on the other hand*: since they exist in most of the ICLE's L1s, are at the same time very similar and are used in similar contexts in their L1s, the fact that these students overuse this type of phraseological units is more likely to be due to interference from their native languages.

This idea partly coincides with the results found by Kaszubski (2000) and Granger (1998), who found that the Polish and French students' overuse of some collocations frequently took place when those structures formally corresponded to the collocations in their L1s. We may confirm those similarities with three real examples taken from three sources (Spanish, French and German) from professional writings and examples taken from the ICLE and CEUNF students (Table 7). We may identify some of the most used phraseological units in the non-native writings and those equivalent units in their L1s (Spanish, French and German).

It is interesting to note that what constitutes a multi-word unit in English is also a multi-word in Spanish, French and German, and that most of the multi-word units which are overused by the non-native students of the ICLE and CEUNF corpora are those which are widely used in their L1s. In order to check how widely phraseological units are used in all languages, Table 7 shows the concordance lines from original newspaper texts in the three languages and examples from the Spanish (SPICLE and CEUNF), French (FRICLE) and German (GERICLE) non-native students. The examples in German and

French are taken from two prestigious newspapers: *Frankfurter Allgemeine* and *Le Monde diplomatique*. The examples for Spanish are taken from two sources: from the MAD reference corpus[3] and from one of the most prestigious newspapers in Spain: *El País*.[4]

Table 7: Multi-word units in original texts in different L1s and non-native students from the ICLE and CEUNF corpora

	N Concordance
Spanish	**MAD Corpus** Te tiene informado de lo que pasa tanto dentro de tu país como en el extranjero (**por ejemplo**, te informa de guerras, crisis en otros países, los problemas de tu ciudad, etc.). Últimamente, De esta manera se puede elegir aunque esta forma no está muy difundida todavía y es difícil adquirirla. **En conclusión** es un medio de comunicación muy útil.
	El País a casi una decena de agentes que ahora dejan de tener el cobijo orgánico que antes tenían. **Por ejemplo**, nadie sabía en dicha consejería qué labores realizaban los funcionarios históricos José Manuel Pinto o José Palomo.
	CEUNF 25 where there isn't food and the waiters don't go. I think this is excessive, because, **for example**, what will happen if you go out with friends who are smokers? **SPICLE** 22 and in such Faculty as Fine Arts has more tendency to receive more theoretical students than talented. **In conclusion**, there are mainly three problems related to the University. The first problem is the problem
French[5]	**Le Monde diplomatique** Les raisons en sont à la fois politiques, économiques, sociales, culturelles et religieuses… mais souvent fort éloignées des idées toutes faites. Ainsi, **par exemple**, les familles les plus riches ne sont pas les moins sélectives.
	FRICLE 5 This motto becomes very obsessive for quite a lot of people and this happens at any age. **For example**, when you are a child, your main preoccupation is to buy the little red car
German[6]	**Frankfurter Allgemeine Zeitung** ein umstrittenes Feld geblieben ist, spielen Risikoprofile eine immer wichtigere Rolle. **Zum Beispiel** dann, wenn über vorzeitige Haftentlassungen entschieden werden soll.
	GERICLE 19 it is a symptom of a problem an individual may be experiencing. **For example**, many may eat excessive amounts of food when they are depressed. Others may have low self esteem or

The problem we encounter is that there are very few studies in the literature of transfer and interference from an L1 that have researched the strategy of transfer from an L1 in the production and use of multi-word units, and there seems to be a contradiction between those studies that state that the lexicon is one of the areas in a foreign language in which L1 interference plays a crucial role and those that state the opposite. There do exist studies that have focused their research on lexical collocations (Howarth, 1998; Nesselfhauf, 2003, 2005), but not on multi-word units, specifically, on lexical bundles.

With regards to the second factor that correlates with transfer, teaching effect, we believe that the kind of instruction that the non-native students receive in their EFL classes – at least in a Spanish university context – is not appropriate regarding the use of phraseological units. We believe that the use of multi-word units is presented to the students in a non-systematic way. In our opinion, one of the reasons, apart from interference from an L1, why non-native students overuse or underuse certain phraseological units is the lack of systematic training of these units within the curriculum for English as a foreign language. It is true that this more systematic way of teaching multi-word units is starting to be implemented in EFL classes, although it seems to be still far from being satisfactory (Granger, 2004: 135).

At the same time, specific difficulties for students to face phraseology are not taken into account in the EFL classes. Those multi-word units which are included are basically lexical collocations (noun plus verb, noun plus adjective, noun plus preposition/adverb, etc.) and, on some occasions, typical lists of multi-word units based on the so-called *connectors* or *linking words* that are used in composition writing.

We are convinced that one of the most important aspects of our study is that the non-native students of English be aware, first, of phraseological issues (as proposed by some authors like Howarth, 1996, 1998; Hill, 2000; Rica, 2007) thanks to the specific activities devised by the university teachers in order to practise – using corpus linguistics and concordance lines (Wiechmann and Fuhs, 2006), for example, from native and non-native corpora – lexical bundles and other kinds of multi-word units; and second, we believe that it is essential that the non-native students be provided with some learning strategies that foster the learning of phraseological issues, not only in argumentative writing but also in other kinds of discourse.

In general, the systematic teaching of multi-word units that combines creativity, fluency and usefulness should be fostered. Some authors (Nesselhauf and Tschichold, 2002; Lewis, 2000) have suggested that teaching lexicalized units should be based on some criteria, such as frequency of use, students' needs, familiarity of the units, difficulties and regularity. This training may be made easier with the use of corpus linguistics (Halliday *et al.*, 2004), since students may find and analyse the production of such units by native writers (both students and professionals) and, most importantly, by other non-native students.

All this will help us fulfil the last of the aims we stated at the beginning: to devise teaching materials for the teaching and learning of multi-word units in academic writing in a university context (Gilquin *et al.*, 2007). The results of the study presented here show the relevance of including corpus analysis in the classroom and, most importantly, the need for teaching the inclusion of multi-word units in a more systematic way (Granger, 2004: 135), since it is one of the most important strategies that non-native writers make use of in their production of EFL writing. Nonetheless, phraseological units also play a crucial and basic role in foreign language teaching and learning. Teaching EFL should be based on a more exhaustive method on what a multi-word unit is because, as Howarth states, 'the dominance of the communicative approach in the teaching of English as a foreign language has tended to place much greater emphasis on learners' ability to use their vocabulary resources creatively in order to 'negotiate meaning' spontaneously, and this approach has consequently had little interest in studying prefabricated language' (1996: 134). Fortunately, as we have already said, in the literature on previous phraseological studies the importance of including this type of lexical studies in the syllabus for teaching EFL has already been acknowledged (Alonso *et al.*, 2000; Allerton *et al.*, 2004; Granger, 2005; Charles, 2006; Paquot, 2007; Liu, 2008; Naciscione, 2010). The findings presented in this study also support the view of contrastive rhetoric in the sense that 'the linguistic patterns and rhetorical conventions of the L1 often transfer to writing in ESL and thus cause interference' (Connor, 2002: 494).

This analysis is the starting point for further research studies which centre on other factors: age differences (Muñoz, 2008), gender differences (Kissau and Quach, 2006), register differences (Cortes, 2004; Biber and Barbieri, 2007; Hyland, 2008; Durrant, 2009), and contrastive studies between non-native writers and professional ones (COEPROF, Rica, 2011a) or, for example, audio-visual translation contrastive studies in the area of subtitling (CORSUBILIN, Rica 2011b), which will be carried out in the near future. We cannot agree more with Brown when he says that 'we read and speak in "chunks" of language' (1974: 2). No doubt that apart from reading and speaking, we also *write* in 'chunks' of language.

Notes

1.   ICLE corpora: 2,066,926 (FRICLE, GERICLE, DICLE, SWICLE, FINICLE, PICLE, CZICLE, BICLE, RICLE and ITICLE), SPICLE: 194,845, CEUNF: 153,721, LOCNESS: 149,790, and SPE: 103,367. The total number of words in the corpora used for this study is 2,871,446.

2.   From Biber *et al.* (1999: 875–879).

3.   The MAD Corpus is a contrastive corpus (Spanish-English) from the Departamento de Filología Inglesa I (Universidad Complutense de Madrid) which consists of 100 argumenta-

tive compositions written by native Spanish students from the first and fourth courses of English Studies at the Universidad Complutense de Madrid and the Universidad de Alcalá de Henares (Neff *et al.*, 2002).

4.   Extracted from the article *Espías remodelados*, by Francisco Mercao, July 2009 in *El País*.

5.   Extracted from the article *L'Asie manque de femmes*, by Isabelle Attané, July 2006 in *Le Monde diplomatique*.

6.   Extracted from the article *Gibt es den geborenen Verbrecher?*, by David Rose, November 2006 in *Frankfurter Allgemeine Zeitung*.

References

Allerton, D. J., Nesselhauf, N. and Skandon, P. (2004) *Phraseological Units: Basic Concepts and their Application*. Basel: Schwabe.

Alonso, C., Neff, J. and Rica, J. P. (2000) Cross-linguistic influence in language learning. *Estudios de Filología Moderna* 1: 65–84.

Biber, D. (1993) Co-occurrence patterns among collocations: A tool for corpus-based lexical knowledge acquisition. *Computational Linguistics* 19 (3): 531–538.

Biber, D. (2004) Lexical bundles in academic speech and writing. In B. Lewandowska-Tomaszczyk (ed.) *Practical Applications in Language and Computers. PALC 2003*, 165–178. Frankfurt am Main: Peter Lang.

Biber, D. and Barbieri, F. (2007) Lexical bundles in university spoken and written registers. *English for Specific Purposes* 26 (3): 263–286. http://dx.doi.org/10.1016/j.esp.2006.08.003

Biber, D., Conrad, S. and Cortes, V. (2004) If you look at …: Lexical bundles in university teaching and textbooks. *Applied Linguistics* 25 (3): 371–405. http://dx.doi.org/10.1093/applin/25.3.371

Biber, D., Conrad, S. and Reppen, R. (1998) *Corpus Linguistics. Investigating Language Structure and Use*. Cambridge: Cambridge University Press. http://dx.doi.org/10.1017/CBO9780511804489

Biber, D., Johansson, S., Leech, G., Conrad, S. and Finegan, E. (1999) *The Longman Grammar of Spoken and Written English*. London: Longman.

Brown, D. (1974) Advanced vocabulary teaching: The problem of collocation. *RELC Journal* 5 (2): 1–11. http://dx.doi.org/10.1177/003368827400500201

Charles, M. (2006) Phraseological patterns in reporting clauses used in citation: A corpus-based study of theses in two disciplines. *English for Specific Purposes* 25 (3): 310–331. http://dx.doi.org/10.1016/j.esp.2005.05.003

Connor, U. (2002) New directions in contrastive rhetoric. *TESOL Quarterly* 36 (4): 493–510. http://dx.doi.org/10.2307/3588238

Conrad, S. (1999) The importance of corpus-based research for language teachers. *System* 27 (1): 1–18. http://dx.doi.org/10.1016/S0346-251X(98)00046-3

Conrad, S. (2002) Corpus linguistic approaches for discourse analysis. *Annual Review of Applied Linguistics* 22: 75–95. http://dx.doi.org/10.1017/S0267190502000041

Cortes, V. (2004) Lexical bundles in published and student disciplinary writing: Examples from history and biology. *English for Specific Purposes* 23 (4): 397–423. http://dx.doi.org/10.1016/j.esp.2003.12.001

Council for Cultural Co-operation Committee (2001) *Common European Framework of Reference for Languages: Learning, Teaching, Assessment.* Council for Cultural Co-operation Committee, Modern Languages Division. Strasbourg: CUP.

Cowie, A. P. (ed.) (1998) *Phraseology. Theory, Analysis, and Applications.* Oxford: Clarendon Press.

Cowie, A. P. and Howarth, P. (1996) Phraseological competence and written proficiency. In G. M. Blue and R. Mitchell (eds) *Language and Education,* 80–93. Clevedon: Multilingual Matters.

De Cock, S. (2003) *Recurrent Sequences of Words in Native-Speaker and Advanced Learner Spoken and Written English: a Corpus-driven Approach.* Unpublished PhD thesis. Leuven: University of Leuven.

Durrant, P. (2009) Investigating the viability of a collocation list for students of English for academic purposes. *English for Specific Purposes* 28 (3): 157–169. http://dx.doi.org/10.1016/j.esp.2009.02.002

Durrant, P. and Schmitt, N. (2009) To what extent do native and non-native writers make use of collocations? *IRAL – International Review of Applied Linguistics in Language Teaching* 47 (2): 157–177. http://dx.doi.org/10.1515/iral.2009.007

Gilquin, G., Granger, S. and Paquot, M. (2007) Learner corpora: The missing link in EAP pedagogy. *Journal of English for Academic Purposes* 6 (4): 319–335. http://dx.doi.org/10.1016/j.jeap.2007.09.007

Granger, S. (1998) *Learner English on Computer.* London: Longman.

Granger, S. (2002) A bird's-eye view of learner corpus research. In S. Granger, J. Hung and S. Petch-Tyson (eds) *Computer Learner Corpora. Second Language Acquisition and Foreign Language Teaching,* 38–51. Lund: Lund University.

Granger, S. (2004) Computer learner corpus research: Current status and future prospects. In U. Connor and T. Upton (eds) *Applied Corpus Linguistics: A Multidimensional Perspective,* 123–145. Amsterdam: Rodopi.

Granger, S. (2005) Pushing back the limits of phraseology. How far can we go? In C. Cosme, C. Gouverneur, F. Meunier and M. Paquot (eds) *Proceedings of the Phraseology 2005 Conference,* 1–4. Leuven: University of Leuven.

Halliday, M. A. K., Teubert, W., Yallop, C. and Čermáková, A. (2004) *Lexicology and Corpus Linguistics. An Introduction.* London: Continuum.

Hill, J. (2000) Revising priorities: From grammatical failure to collocational success. In M. Lewis (ed.) *Teaching Collocation. Further Developments in the Lexical Approach* 47–69. Hove: LTP.

Howarth, P. (1996) *Phraseology in English Academic Writing. Some Implications for Language Learning and Dictionary Making,* Tübingen: Niemeyer.

Howarth, P. (1998) Phraseology and second language proficiency. *Applied Linguistics* 19 (1): 24–44. http://dx.doi.org/10.1093/applin/19.1.24

Hunston, S. (2002) *Corpora in Applied Linguistics.* Cambridge: Cambridge University Press.

Hyland, K. (2008) As can be seen: Lexical bundles and disciplinary variation. *English for Specific Purposes* 27 (1): 4–21. http://dx.doi.org/10.1016/j.esp.2007.06.001

Jarvis, S. (2000) Methodological rigor in the study of transfer: Identifying L1 influence in the interlanguage lexicon. *Language Learning* 50 (2): 245–309. http://dx.doi.org/10.1111/0023-8333.00118

Kaszubski, P. (2000) Selected aspects of lexicon, phraseology and style in the writing of Polish advanced learners of English: A contrastive, corpus-based approach. http://www.staff.amu.edu.pl/~przemka/przemek.html (accessed January 2011).

Kellerman, E. (1977) Towards a characterization of the strategy of transfer in second language learning. *Interlanguage Studies Bulletin* 2 (1): 58–145.

Kellerman, E. (1979) Transfer and non-transfer: Where are we now? *Studies in Second Language Acquisition* 2 (1): 37–57. http://dx.doi.org/10.1017/S0272263100000942

Kissau, S. and Quach, L. (2006) Student control in the second language classroom: an analysis of gender differences. *Journal of Applied Linguistics* 3 (1): 49–67.

Kjellmer, G. (1991) A mint of phrases. In K. Aijmer and B. Altenberg (eds) *English Corpus Linguistics,* 111–127. London: Longman.

Lewis, M. (2000) *Teaching Collocation. Further Developments in the Lexical Approach.* Hove: LTP.

Liu, D. (2008) Linking adverbials. An across-register corpus study and its implications. *International Journal of Corpus Linguistics* 13 (4): 491–518. http://dx.doi.org/10.1075/ijcl.13.4.05liu

McCarthy, M. and O'Dell, F. (2005) *English Collocations in Use.* Cambridge: Cambridge University Press.

Meunier, F. and Granger, S. (eds) (2008) *Phraseology in Language Learning and Teaching.* Amsterdam: John Benjamins.

Muñoz, C. (2008) Age-related differences in foreign language learning. Revising the empirical evidence. *IRAL – International Review of Applied Linguistics in Language Teaching* 46: 197–220.

Naciscione, A. (2010) *Stylistic Use of Phraseological Units in Discourse.* Amsterdam/Philadelphia, PA: John Benjamins Publishing Company.

Neff, J., Blanco, M., Dafouz, E., Díez, M. and Prieto, R. (2002) *The Madrid Corpus (MAD).* English Department, Universidad Complutense de Madrid.

Nesselhauf, N. (2003) The use of collocations by advanced learners of English and some implications for teaching. *Applied Linguistics* 24(2): 223–242. http://dx.doi.org/10.1093/applin/24.2.223

Nesselhauf, N. (2005) *Collocations in a Learner Corpus.* Amsterdam: John Benjamins.

Nesselhauf, N. and Tschichold, C. (2002) Collocations in CALL: An investigation of vocabulary-building software for EFL. *Computer Assisted Language Learning* 15 (3): 251–279. http://dx.doi.org/10.1076/call.15.3.251.8190

Odlin, T. (2005) Crosslinguistic influence and conceptual transfer: what are the concepts? *Annual Review of Applied Linguistics* 25: 3–25. http://dx.doi.org/10.1017/S0267190505 000012

Paquot, M. (2007) *EAP Vocabulary in native and learner writing: From extraction to analysis*. PhD. Dissertation. U. catolique de Louvain, September 2007.

Paquot, M. (2008) Exemplification in learning writing. In F. Meunier and S. Granger (eds) *Phraseology in Foreign Language Learning and Teaching*, 101–119. Amsterdam: John Benjamins.

Rica, J. P. (2007) *Estudio fraseológico del uso de colocaciones gramaticales y grupos léxicos en textos argumentativos nativos y no nativos: análisis de corpus de estudiantes*. Unpublished PhD Thesis. English Department I, Universidad Complutense de Madrid (UCM).

Rica, J. P. (2009) Colocaciones gramaticales en la producción escrita de estudiantes universitarios españoles. *Revista Reduca* 1: 1–26.

Rica, J. P. (2010) Lingüística de corpus en la enseñanza de inglés como lengua extranjera (ILE). In J. L. Cifuentes *et al.* (eds) *Los caminos de la lengua. Estudios en homenaje a Enrique Alcaraz Varó*, 1405–1427. Alicante: Publicaciones de la Universidad de Alicante.

Rica, J. P. (2011a) Corpus de Escritores Profesionales (COEPROF): COEPROES (Corpus de Escritores Profesionales en Español) and COEPROIN (Corpus de Escritores Profesionales en Inglés). Madrid: UCM. Unpublished document.

Rica, J. P. (2011b). CORSUBIL: Corpus de Subtítulos Bilingües inglés-español: CORSUBILIN (Corpus de Subtítulos Bilingües en Inglés) and CORSUBILES (Corpus de Subtítulos Bilingües en Español). Madrid: UCM. Unpublished document.

Scott, M. (2008: online) *Wordsmith Tools. Version 3.0. Online manual.* Available at: http://www.lexically.net/wordsmith/ (accessed January 2011).

Siyanova, A. and Schmitt, R. (2007) Native and nonnative use of multi-word vs. one-word verbs. *IRAL – International Review of Applied Linguistics in Language Teaching* 45: 119–139. http://dx.doi.org/10.1515/IRAL.2007.005

Wiechmann, D. and Fuhs, S. (2006) Concordancing software. *Corpus Linguistics and Linguistic Theory* 2 (1): 107–127. http://dx.doi.org/10.1515/CLLT.2006.006

Wray, A. (2002) *Formulaic Language and the Lexicon.* Cambridge: Cambridge University Press. http://dx.doi.org/10.1017/CBO9780511519772

15 Lying as metaphor in a bilingual phraseological corpus (German-Spanish)

Ana Mansilla

The aim of this chapter is the exploration of the conceptual metaphors that are activated in a set of German and Spanish phraseologisms covering concepts to do with lying, deceit and falsehood. The exploration is based on a bilingual onomasiological corpus that is part of the current research project FRASESPAL ('The idiomatic structure of German and Spanish. An onomasiological corpus-based cognitive study'. Code HUM2007-62198/FILO). Theoretically rooted in the experientialist approach (Lakoff and Johnson, 1980) and using the phraseologisms from our own corpus as an empirical basis, the chapter examines different metaphorical expressions and cognitive models for the images that underlie the conceptual fields of 'lying', 'deceit' and 'falsehood'. Metaphor analysis is an extremely useful tool for revealing the way in which each linguistic community construes extralinguistic reality and for describing both the particularities of each language and the features common to them both, which may be systematized in 'supranational' metaphorical models.

1. Introduction

Taking the principles of cognitive semantics as our point of reference, the aim here is to analyse the metaphorical images which support the concept of lying and its variants – in this case deceit and falsehood – within the field of contrastive phraseology (German-Spanish language pair). We base our analysis on an onomasiological bilingual corpus which is part of a research project entitled FRASESPAL 'The idiomatic structure of

German and Spanish. An onomasiological corpus-based cognitive study' (HUM2007-62198/FILO).[1]

Our goal is to analyse the metaphors that are activated in both languages and identify the affinities and divergences that exist in both linguistic systems when it comes to understanding reality, that is, the way in which each linguistic community tackles the verbal action of lying and its variants from a cognitive point of view through phraseology.

2. The FRASESPAL project

FRASESPAL 'The idiomatic structure of German and Spanish. An onomasiological corpus-based cognitive study' (HUM2007-62198/FILO) is an interuniversity research project led by Dr Carmen Mellado Blanco from the University of Santiago de Compostela. Researchers from different universities across the Iberian peninsula also participate.

This project is divided into two clearly distinguishable parts. In the first part, a bilingual thesaurus (German-Spanish) following the principle of onomasiological arrangement in line with inductive methodology has been developed. Due to the fact that it is not possible to include all the conceptual fields in our study – given time and space constraints – we came to the decision that we would limit the number of fields to three, namely HABLAR/CALLAR – REDEN/SCHWEIGEN (SPEAK/BE SILENT), VIDA/MUERTE – LEBEN/TOD (LIFE/ DEATH) and SALUD/ENFERMEDAD – GESUND/KRANK SEIN (HEALTH/ILLNESS). These three fields were chosen as they cover a large group of phraseological units and provide a good, solid basis for some very interesting metaphor research.

Following the principles of cognitive linguistics (Dobrovol'skij, 1995: 69–70), a taxonomy was drawn up representing the classification schema of the idiomatic expressions or *phraseological units* (hereafter abbreviated to PU) belonging to each field. We were able to compile this corpus successfully – at present it contains some 3,000 units – by extracting entries from some of the leading semasiological and onomasiological monolingual dictionaries of idioms. For German we consulted the alphabetical dictionary *Duden* (2008) and used the German onomasiological dictionaries Dornseiff (2004), Hessky and Ettinger (1997) and Schemann (1989); and for Spanish we consulted the alphabetical dictionaries Rodríguez-Vida (2004), Seco *et al.* (2004) and Cantera and Gomis (2007).

This corpus of PU contains information relating to their denotative meanings, stylistic labels, examples of use, conceptual fields, conceptual subfields, pragmatic information and cross-linguistic equivalences. We are currently developing an online version of the bilingual thesaurus which can be accessed at www.usc.es/frasespal. The electronic version includes a database featuring seven tables: German PU, Spanish PU, style, conceptual field, conceptual subfield, pragmatic observations and metaphor model.

In the second part, cognitive models are studied that underlie the PU belonging to the different conceptual subfields in order to uncover the parallels and divergences between German and Spanish phraseology from a cognitive perspective. We revise the notion of 'conceptual metaphor' as described by Lakoff and Johnson (1986: 140). We also take into account the motivation generated between source and target domains both intra- and interlinguistically. Our theoretical framework is therefore based on cognitive semantics as well as on model theory (Lakoff and Johnson, 1986, 1999; Baranov and Dobrovol'skij, 1991, respectively). We proceed from the premise that, in order to understand the meaning of certain PU and their linguistic expression, it is necessary to establish a connection between the mechanisms that the human mind generates and their experience of the surrounding reality. Abstract realities (target domain) which are conceptualized through language are understood in concrete terms thanks to palpable experiences (basic or source domain: perception, psychomotor faculties and 'embodied' experience). Once we have scrutinized the immediate experience, we then categorize the reality and group a series of PU under the same pattern or cognitive model (propositional structures, image-schematic structures, metaphorical and metonymical projections). The cognitive models represent the different processes and elements which intervene in any given psychological activity.

We also ascribe to the linguistic theory of prototypes (Rosch, 1973), whereby the conceptual fields we analyse include those PU deemed semantic prototypes in relation to the *taxa* or cognitive model in which they are grouped.

3. The varying manifestations of lying in our SPEAK/BE SILENT (HABLAR/CALLAR) corpus

This study is based on the corpus compiled as part of the research project FRASESPAL (see Section 2). The phraseological units (PU) of the HABLAR-SPRECHEN (SPEAK)/CALLAR-SCHWEIGEN (BE SILENT) cognitive field amount to 1,430 units.

The macrofield HABLAR is divided into a series of subfields defined by taxa which represent non-discrete categories (opposition among categories may occur), where the different subfields may present varying levels of prototypicality with the possibility of also being interrelated.

Nuances and focalizations related to HABLAR in the different variants of the act of 'lying' and which have idiomatic relevance, that is, are sorted into themes in phraseology, have been verified in this corpus. Hence, the PU that are directly or indirectly linked to the varying manifestations of 'lying' are grouped in the different subfields of our onomasiological corpus for German and Spanish PU related to these subfields:

A.4.   TO SPEAK A LOT IN RELATION TO THE INTERLOCUTOR

A.5.   FOOLISH TALK

F.   TRUST AND NOT TO BE TRUSTWORTHY (TO LIE/TO DECEIVE)

G.   TO PRAISE FALSELY

Lying can present itself in spoken speech in a number of ways. The first of these subfields, HABLAR MUCHO (TO SPEAK A LOT), is indirectly related to lying through the act of convincing someone. When we try to persuade somebody for a specific purpose, we resort to all kinds of tricks by using our ingenuity, and, if necessary, by manipulating the truth. It is therefore not surprising that the quantity of information generated by the speaker is plentiful.

The different types of deceit expressed through language are varied and include, among others, the acts of insult and slander. When it comes to hiding the truth, we can highlight similar mechanisms such as concealment and falsification. Someone with something to hide holds back from telling everything he or she actually knows, whereas someone who falsifies not only keeps what they know to themselves, but also presents false information as true. We have grouped these manifestations of lying under section F: CONFIAR Y NO SER FIABLE (TRUST AND NOT TO BE TRUSTWORTHY (TO LIE/TO DECEIVE). In addition to the types of lying previously mentioned, other acts include confusing somebody, hiding one's true intentions, and betrayal. The last subfield added to this study is G: ALABAR (TO PRAISE FALSELY). This notion shows similarities with the verb *halagar* (to flatter), which we will address later on in this paper.

We bear in mind the pragmatic aspects of language in our phraseological corpus and, as a result, value both the attitude of the speakers and the nature of the message in relation to them with equal measure. The illocutionary force in a specific context allows us to recognize, with greater precision, each participant's commitment in the communicative act and the speaker's ultimate intention in relation to the listener. Idiomatic expressions are characterized by certain semantic nuances which, thanks to the situational context, are more precise (Solano, 2006: 156).

4. Definition of lying and its variants

According to Hannah Arendt (1973), lying is the deliberate negation of phatic truth. Lying involves twisting the truth or withholding it either partially or totally. The reasons behind wanting to manipulate the truth are numerous and varied in nature (Falkenberg, 1982: 75). The speaker may resort to lying in order to:

(a) obtain something specific from another person
(b) protect their image
(c) cover up a delicate matter in which they or their interlocutor may be implicated
(d) deceive
(e) hide their intentions
(f) discredit the interlocutor, etc.

All of the aforementioned intentions associated with lying complicate interpretation in dialogue. However, they are in consonance with the intrinsic aspect of language itself: the word encompasses a variety of meanings according to its context. In fact, the truth is much bolder and more difficult to express than the lie.

According to Eco (2000), every truth tends to hide a concealed or veiled lie. Lying has found its way into many fields, one of them being rhetoric (irony, hyperbole, litotes, etc.), where the art of persuasion, for example, hides a subtle deceit. It is also present in the political arena as a weapon of manipulation in order to achieve the goals proposed by the politician. From a religious viewpoint, when the eighth commandment which prohibits lying and slander is broken (you shall not bear false witness against your neighbour), this is seen as an attack against the truth.

There are many facets to lying, with deceit and falsehood being two which are synonymous with this notion. Deceit is a simulation of the truth, that is, leading someone to believe that something is a fact when it is not. The difference between lying and deceit lies in the purpose. The first is the mere act of denying the reality, whereas the second is linked to obtaining something specific – an economic return, for example. In this particular case, it is a question of fraud (a crime against patrimony and property). Falsehood, on the other hand, is all that which is untrue, removed from the truth. It also refers to acts which lack authenticity and which go against legal principles. Moreover, falsehood is associated with hypocrisy: when an individual pretends to believe something that they do not really believe. In the legal arena, falsehood is a crime which has to do with altering the truth of facts and things (forging documents, using counterfeit money, bribery and so on.)

5. Theoretical framework: The topic of lying in phraseology

As the theoretical foundation to this topic, we consider it relevant to mention some studies which address, in a concise manner, the relationship that lying and its variants share with phraseology and, more specifically, with metaphor.

Dobrovol'skij and Piirainen (1997: 37) expose the existing relationship between extralinguistic phenomena, understood as universal and cultural mechanisms and language. We as humans understand reality through a world of signs, semiotic entities. Symbols, which are an integral part of semiotics, occupy an important place within the sign system; they are valued not only in culture (literature, art, mythology, etc.), but also in phraseology, where they reflect a way of shaping reality (Dobrovol'skij and Piirainen, 1997: 21).

The symbol, in semiotic terms, can be understood as an entity which expresses something different to that which it designates, unlike a sign which does represent what it designates. The reality evoked by the symbol has a meaning which requires some extralinguistic knowledge to facilitate understanding. Hence, the symbol falls between iconicity and arbitrariness. When we state that the colour 'green' symbolizes immaturity, we think about the colour of fruit, not yet ready to be eaten. We are able to visualize in our mind its symbolic meaning, that is, it appears as an iconic sign. However, as soon as we say that 'blue' symbolizes inebriation in German, we do not establish an immediate relationship between the signifier and the signified, that is, we move in the realm of the arbitrariness of symbols.

Both Dobrovol'skij and Piirainen compare the concept of metaphor with the symbol and hold that whilst metaphor is somewhat closer to iconicity and can therefore be detected and identified by the speaker more quickly, the symbol, in turn, requires further knowledge which makes the identification with the signified a more difficult task: 'Metaphern basieren auf der bildlichen Grundlage, sind "images", also Bilder im weiten Sinne' (Metaphors have a figurative basis, that is, they are 'images' in the broadest sense of the word) (Dobrovol'skij and Piirainen, 1997: 38).

Metaphor is associated with idiomaticity (the final meaning does not derive from the sum of the meanings of each PU component). The symbol, meanwhile, is the result of a single component: a colour, an animal, a numerical figure, an object, among other things, which contribute relevant symbolic information.

The authors draw a distinction between *Kultursymbole* (cultural symbols) and *Sprachsymbole (linguistic symbols)*. The *Kultursymbole* represent a high level of cultural conventionalization, that is, they evoke specific aspects of a culture. They are then further divided into *starke* (strong) and *schwache* (weak) *Kultursymbole*; for example, the dove as a symbol of peace (a strong, universally recognized symbol) and the butterfly as a symbol of the soul (a weak, not universally recognized symbol). The *Sprachsymbole* make up elements of the linguistic sign which combine both denotative and connotative aspects. For example, the compounds *Angsthase* (lit. fear-rabbit: scaredy-cat), *eiskalt* (ice-cold) and *pflegeleicht* (lit. easy-care: low-maintenance) all contain relevant symbolic information.

In relation to our field of study, the colour blue, as it appears in the etymological dictionary, has to do with 'Sinnestäuschung', a distorted perception of reality or hallucination. This gives rise to PU like *jmdm. blauen Dunst vorm-achen* (to pull the wool over sb's eyes) and *sein blaues Wunder erleben* (to get the shock of one's life). Another meaning of the concept 'blue' is associated with the intensifier 'much', where we can find the PU *das Blaue vom Himmel* (lit. the blue from the sky) used with verbs of speaking such as *versprechen* (to promise), *herunterlügen* (to lie), *reden* (to talk), *schwatzen* (to chat), and so on. On the one hand, the PU *das Blaue vom Himmel* is motivated by the immense expanse of the sky and the colour associated with it, and on the other, by the very nature of the object 'sky' which can neither be trapped nor captured. The Spanish language does not share the same symbolism of the colour blue. The equivalent of *jmdm. das Blaue vom Himmel herunterlügen* in Spanish would be the PU *mentir como un bellaco* (lit. to lie like a rogue/ equivalent: to lie through one's teeth).

It goes without saying that phraseology reflects a way of shaping and adapting reality. Human beings conceptualize the physical and experiential world and project this experience onto other more abstract and conceptual domains: 'The essence of metaphor is *understanding and experiencing* one kind of thing in terms of another' (Lakoff and Johnson, 1980: 5).

One way of getting closer to understanding interlingual and intralingual phraseology is through a cognitive conception of language and the metaphor-ical models which underlie the phraseological units. Nevertheless, as some theorists argue, the cognitive approach as defined by Lakoff and Johnson with regard to contrastive phraseology can be fruitful, albeit subject to certain limitations (Dobrovol'skij, 2004: 126). It is not always possible to apply certain metaphorical models to various languages (Burger, 1998: 91).

Dobrovol'skij (2007) calls into question the cognitive approach to metaphor and advocates the theory of frame semantics as developed by Charles J. Fillmore (1976). Knowledge is analysed in terms of semantic frames, frame meaning a schematic representation of a system of related concepts, in such a way that the use of a single concept activates the whole conceptual system. In this sense, and as part of our metaphorical analysis, the model LA VIDA ES UN JUEGO (LIFE IS A GAME) connects with other interrelated, subordinate meta-phorical models such as MENTIR ES HACER TEATRO (to lie is to act), MENTIR ES JUGAR (to lie is to play), etc.

Krukowska (2004) focuses on the semantic field of lying by looking at the verb *lie* from a contrastive perspective (German-Polish). Religion, philoso-phy and anthropology are just some of the fields which have addressed the phenomenon of lying. Worthy of special mention is the essay *Lingüistik der Lüge (Linguistics of Lying)* by Harald Weinrich (1966). If up until this point the analysis of lying was limited to religion and philosophy, then Weinrich was the first to consider this topic from a linguistic point of view. Lying, understood as the assertion of something false, can be broken down into six subtypes from the point of view of the speaker's intention.

From a symbolic point of view, Krukowska focuses on four concepts, namely *Honig* (honey), *Weihrauch* (incense), *Schwarz* (dark) and *Blau* (blue), which perfectly reflect the act of lying:

(a) **Honig** (honey) to flatter someone: *jmdm. Honig um den Bart/ums Maul schmieren* (lit: to smear honey around sb's beard/mouth), *honigsüß reden* (lit: to speak honey-sweet, to butter sb up)

(b) **Weihrauch** (incense) related to adulation: *jmdm. Weihrauch streuen* (to heap praise on), *sich selbst beweihräuchern* (to indulge in self-adulation)

(c) **Schwarz** (black) refers to the prohibited, the 'black market' and the illegal: *Schwarzarbeit* (to work illegally), *Schwarzgeld* (illegal money), *schwarzfahren* (to fare-dodge)

(d) Blau (blue) associated with lying and deceit: *das Blaue vom Himmel lügen/herunterlügen/herunterreden* (to promise sb the blue in the sky). Along the same lines, worthy of mention is the PU *jmdm. einen blauen Dunst reden/vormachen* (to pull the wool over sb's eyes).

Sabine Geck (2003) tackles the metaphorical conceptualization of emotions in interpersonal actions. To this end, Geck bases her study on Lakoff and Johnson's theory. She focuses on two emotional states: admiration and flattery. The latter is materialized in the verbs *schmeicheln* and *adular*. These two verbs are lexicalized in a different way in both languages: intransitive in German and transitive in Spanish. *Schmeicheln* places greater emphasis on the action itself and not on the effect it has on the patient, something which we can see occur in Spanish. Geck proposes the following cognitive scenario:

halagar es hablar de forma bonita
to flatter is to talk in a nice way

schönreden; Schönredner; schöne Worte machen; decirlo con palabras bonitas
(to whitewash/to blandish)

halagar es untar
to flatter is to spread

jmdm. Hönig um den Bart/ums Maul schmieren; dar betún a alg.; dar jabón a alg.
(lit. to smear honey around sb's beard/mouth; to butter sb up)

6. Metaphorical models

6.1. *Mentir es jugar* (Lying is playing)

By using the metaphorical model LA VIDA ES UN JUEGO (LIFE IS A GAME), we come across the metaphor FINGIR ES HACER TEATRO (FAKING IS ACTING A

ROLE). This metaphor is based on the idea of language as a game. According to Wittgenstein, the games that children play enable them to learn language and this can be transferred to everyday use. If we consider that language is to be understood in terms of a game, we are able to affirm that a feigned attitude is similar to a game in the sense of a reality that does not exist. Game/play is analogous to the arts (theatre, literature, etc.). When we play a role, we act out a 'recreated' reality. In one way or another, life always has been and continues to be a stage upon which human grandeur and misfortune are played out. Theatre, or acting, is considered a safe-conduct of the human condition. At some point in our lives we have taken on different roles, and we end up shaping who we are. Hence, the 'realities' we perform depend on several factors, such as the stage, the actors and the rules of each act.

In German:	jmdm. Theater vormachen/vorspielen; Kömodie spielen; so ein Theater aufführen; das ist nur Schau; eine Szene machen; jmdm. eine Schau/Show abziehen.
In Spanish:	montar un show/una escena/escenita/ un espectáculo/número; hacer comedia; echarle mucho teatro a algo; tener mucho teatro; ser puro teatro.

(to show off, to make a scene, to blow smoke, to be play-acting, to play-act, to make a spectacle of oneself)

In German, the lexemes *Theater* (theatre/carry-on), *Schau* (show) and *Szene* (scene) are activated when exaggerated *behaviour* carried out mostly by a third party is being criticized. However, in Spanish, *escena*, *número* and *espectáculo* are employed to a greater extent. *Teatro* is only used with the lexeme *echar* in the PU *echarle mucho teatro a algo*, whose equivalent in German would be *Theater spielen (lit. to play theatre)*.

The PU *das ist (doch alles) nur (oder nichts als) Theater* (it is all just play-acting) is usually uttered by a speaker who criticizes the attitude of a third party to his or her interlocutor. With this view in mind, we can see that the situation described above is examined from a perspective removed from the actual action (Kalisch, 1996: 79).

The fact that metaphors cannot be analysed in isolation gives us cause to state that, based on the metaphor LA VIDA ES UN JUEGO (LIFE IS A GAME), other cognitive metaphors fit here that are closely related to the arts: theatre, literature, painting and so on. Hence, FINGIR ES HACER TEATRO (FAKING IS ACTING A ROLE) and MENTIR ES CONTAR UNA NOVELA (LYING IS RELATING A STORY).

It goes without saying that lying and fiction go hand in hand. If we apply this fiction/lie binomial to language, we can see that certain literary genres provide a metaphorical basis to illustrate our ability as humans to tell stories lacking in any real truth.

In German: Geschichten erzählen; keine Geschichten/Märchen erzählen; jmdm.
              Romane erzählen.
In Spanish: decir cuentos; dejarse de cuentos chinos; tener mucho cuento; con-
              tar novelas.

(to tell stories)

Fiction in literature stems from the fact that stories do not have to justify themselves in a concrete empirical reality. The writer creates an imaginary world and, at the same time, is able to make the reader believe that he or she is telling an important truth. The speaker transmits his or her message in a similar way. However, whereas in literary fiction an agreement between the writer and the reader whereby 'I'm going to tell you a lie and you're going to believe it' is in place, in communicative discourse this notion of complicity with the interlocutor is not generated. Despite this, other types of internal cooperative agreements are created which should support the direction of effective conversation.

These agreements are, in some respects, linked to Grice's (1975) conversational maxims (quality, quantity, relation and manner), with the end purpose being to produce the best communicative situation. A violation of these maxims carries the message over to a more implicit and ambiguous dimension, which results in having to turn to conversational implicatures.

It is necessary to draw attention to the negative assessment of 'lying' or lack of sincerity in terms of its phraseological use. This fact corroborates the important role Grice's quality maxim plays in assertive acts, given that lying goes against the principles of transcultural ethics. Throughout history, this mode of behaviour has been harshly condemned, especially in the fields of philosophy and religion.

The maxim that interests us the most in this study on lying is the maxim of quality, which is about making your contribution one that is true (that uttered by the speaker).

Etymologically, the verb *erzählen* (tell/explain) carries with it the idea of '*jmdm. etw. Unwahres (als Wahrheit) sagen, jmdn. anführen, ihn zum Narren halten*' (to tell sb an untruth, lead sb on, to make a fool of sb) from Middle High German, that is, deceiving or making someone believe a lie. From this it follows that structures which include the verb *erzählen* are closely related to the notion of lying: *du kannst mir viel erzählen* (lit. you can tell me a lot. 'I don't believe you'), *erzähle mir doch keine Geschichten* (lit. don't tell me stories), *das kannst du deiner Großmutter/deinem Frisör erzählen* (lit. you can tell that to your grandmother/hairdresser. 'Tell that to the Marines') and so on. PU that include the verb *erzählen-contar* (to tell) translate into Spanish as *cuéntaselo a tu abuela/a tu tía, no me cuentes rollos/historias*, etc.

The lexeme *cuento* (story/fairytale), which is a derivative of the verb *contar* (tell), appears in the following PU: *déjate de cuentos; tener mucho cuento; tener más cuento que Calleja; cuento chino* (don't tell stories; to have a lot of stories; to have more stories than Calleja [children's author]; Chinese tale/tall tale).

The *cuento* genre has two German equivalents, namely *Erzählung* (story, narration) and *Märchen* (fairytale), with the latter being used in an idiomatic context: *jmdm. Märchen erzählen* (lit. to tell someone fairytales). It should be pointed out that the PU *jmdm. Märchen erzählen* is frequently used in negative imperative sentences. On the one hand, the speaker urges the interlocutor to not digress (to get to the point), and on the other, to tell the truth. These PU may perform the direct illocutionary function of ordering someone to be brief.

In German: Erzähle mir keine Märchen/Geschichten
In Spanish: No me cuentes cuentos chinos/historias/historietas

(lit. Don't tell me any fairy tales/stories)

These PU reveal the consequence of 'speaking a lot' which results in talking nonsense, making tactless remarks, digressing, not focusing on the topic and the tendency to distort reality. This nuance can be seen in the PU *el cuento de nunca acabar* (a never-ending story), which in German is expressed as *eine unendliche Geschichte*.

If *cuento* in Spanish is the genre par excellence to hide the truth, then in German it is *Märchen* or *Geschichte* (fairytale).

6.2. *Mentir es tejer* (Lying is spinning/weaving)

Animals demonstrate univocal and stable behaviour patterns and are a source domain for designating attitudes and behaviours characteristic of humans (Cinkure, 2006: 11). They represent one of the most productive and illustrative models within contrastive phraseology.

The intellectual action of lying, characteristic of humankind, can be found in terms of the animal kingdom, specifically the spider. In this sense, a person who lies is perceived as being as harmful as a spider. One of the symbolic meanings attributed to the spider is that of its creative power, as exemplified in the spinning of its web. This arachnid is also known for its aggressive nature. Other elements which should not go unmentioned relate to the spider's ability to inject venom through its fangs as well as being skilled at catching its prey, thanks to the complex webs it spins. These webs are used to confuse the spider's prey, and upon ignoring the imminent danger, insects, birds and other creatures find themselves in a situation with no means of escape.

As we have seen, the spider is associated with rather negative connotations, and the animal source domain is linked to the web's destructive effect which is projected on human psychic and verbal activity, much like the act of lying. The cognitive process of metaphor connects the abstract domain, that is, the intellectual activity of lying – as target domain – with the source domain of structure, in this case the web, which is assigned the qualities 'deceitful, liar, confusing'.

German PU which convey this metaphorical meaning are *ein Netz von Lügen/ein Lügengespinst/Lügengewebe spinnen/weben; (wie) ein Spinnennetz von Lügen* (aufbauen/aussehen) (lit: to spin a web of lies/build a spiderweb of lies). In Spanish: *tejer/hilvanar mentiras; tejer una maraña de mentiras; una telaraña de mentiras* (to weave a tangled web of lies).

Among all the meanings the verb *tejer* offers, we arrive at the activity of 'interweaving threads, cords, esparto, etc. to make fabrics, matting and other similar things'. The lexemes *Gespinst, Gewebe* (weave) in German and *madeja* (hank), *ovillo* (ball of wool) in Spanish fit in with this idea. As we have seen, this activity is not only the work of human beings; the spider and certain other creatures like the silkworm together 'spin/weave' their webs: *tejer una maraña de mentiras*. In Spanish, lies are 'tacked' *(hilvanar)*, an expression which comes from the art of sewing. However, this nuance is not found in the German language, as the verbs *weben* and *spinnen* are employed instead.

In fact, the images behind these aforementioned PU lie in another structural metaphor, that of UN DISCURSO ES UN TEJIDO (SPEECH IS A WEB). In speech, ideas can be tacked both effectively and poorly, the thread being the subject of the conversation, e.g., *hilo conductor* or *perder el hilo (den Faden verlieren)* (to lose the thread/to lose one's train of thought). When we try to persuade someone and talk non-stop to get what we want, in German we say *sich den Mund fusselig reden* (to talk until one is blue in the face). This PU comes from the word *fusseln* (fray: the threads in the cloth separate causing loose threads). Speech can *enredarse* (become entangled) much like a skein or a ball of yarn.

The *urdimbre* (warp) serves a metaphorical function in all discursive activity, be it spoken or written: *tramar una historia, bordar un discurso, hilvanar un texto*, and by extension also applies to the realm of lying: *tejer/tramar/ urdir/hilvanar/enhebrar/zurcir mentiras, trama/sarta de mentiras*.

The activity 'coser' (sewing) is employed to a lesser extent in German. However, the verbs *anzetteln* (to incite) and *andichten* (to incite/instigate) are used in some PU to denote lying. The verb *anzetteln* appears more often with lexemes such as *Kriege* (wars), *Ärger* (anger), *Diskurs* (discourse) and *Verschwörung* (conspiracy). In Spanish, the verb *hilvanar* (to tack) is used more frequently in the context of lying, whereas *tramar* (plot to) and *urdir* (to warp/ hatch) tend to be associated with the image of cleverly planning a deceitful deed, a tangled web of lies or an act of betrayal, as well as plotting something against someone. In German, the verb *einfädeln* (enhebrar) (to thread) can be used in lexical combination with *Netz* in the PU *ein Netz aus Lügen einfädeln* (lit. thread a web of lies).

The Spanish noun *trama* (weft, plot) is more closely aligned to crimes such as forgery and corruption, for example, *trama de fraude/blanqueo/corrupción* (a fraud/money laundering/corruption plot or scheme). The German equivalent of *trama* is *Anzettelung* (plot/scheme), which is used in combination with the lexemes *Straftat* (criminal act), *Krieg* (war) and *Aufstand* (insurgency). In Spanish, a number of lies grouped together, metaphorically speaking, are referred to as *sartas* (strings of beads), whereas in German, this image is conveyed through sacks or piles: *Sack voller Lügen/Haufen Lügen* (a sack full of/ pile of lies).

If the lie is repeated over and over again, there comes a moment when the speaker finds himself or herself tangled up in a web of lies, falling into their own trap. For this reason, it is necessary to untangle the web of lies created.

In German: sich im Gewebe der/seiner (eigenen) Lügen/Intrigen/… verstricken/(verfangen); sich im eigenen Netz/im Netz der eigenen Lügen/ Intrigen/… verstricken/(verfangen).

In Spanish: enredarse en una madeja/ovillo de mentiras.

(lit. to get/become entangled in a web of lies)

6.3. *Mentir es desviar algo de su posición habitual* (Lying is diverting something from its usual position)

According to Lakoff, speech is an object positioned in space. The intellectual activity of speaking comes under the idea of a manual activity, that is, words are understood in terms of physical, specific, easily-grasped and tangible objects. Ideas in speech take on a spatial dimension and are conceived as placed objects, in terms of their greater or lesser importance. They may be in a visible place, e.g., *poner algo encima de la mesa* (put something on the table/a question presented at a meeting), completely out of sight, or moved from the speaker's field of vision, e.g., *apartar/abandonar una idea* (drop an idea). These PU underlie the orientational metaphor LO IMPORTANTE ES CENTRAL y LO ACCESORIO/SECUNDARIO ES PERIFÉRICO (IMPORTANT THINGS ARE CENTRAL AND SECONDARY THINGS ARE PERIPHERAL) (Jäkel, 2003: 158).

Thought is both tangible and understandable, and by extension so are words. In the case of lying, when words are shifted from their usual position they change place, acquire another dimension and, therefore, take on a different kind of meaning. Confusing the interlocutor by removing ideas from their original position is, in some respects, a way of not telling the truth.

In Spanish: torcer las palabras (to twist words); trastocar una idea (to mess up an idea; to change an idea); trabucar una idea (to overturn an idea); distorsionar la realidad (to distort the truth; poner (un discurso/un texto) patas arriba, (to mess up a speech/text), etc.

In German: das Wort im Munde herumdrehen (to twist sb's words); den Spieß umdrehen (to reverse/turn the tables); jdn. Durcheinanderbringen (to confuse sb); jdn. In Unordnung bringen (to confuse sb/to upset sb); die Wahrheit mit Worten umstellen (lit. to convert the truth with words).

The image MENTIR ES DESPLAZAR/MOVER/GIRAR (LYING IS DISPLACING/ MOVING/TURNING) is registered in both languages in the PU *torcer las palabras – das Wort im Munde herumdrehen* (to twist sb's words). The German PU stands out for its metaphorical relationship with the cognitive model CENTRO and PERIFERIA (CENTRE AND PERIPHERY): LO IMPORTANTE ES CENTRAL Y LO SECUNDARIO ES PERIFÉRICO (IMPORTANT THINGS ARE CENTRAL AND SECONDARY THINGS ARE PERIPHERAL). If we start from the premise that 'the important thing' is central, in other words, the truth is central and lying is peripheral, the act of lying in German involves the concept of a movement which goes around a central point, whereas in Spanish, lying refers to a twisted movement. We must take into account that WORDS ARE OBJECTS. The semantic content of the verb *herumdrehen* (twist) expresses the relevance of truth. In the case of the Spanish PU, the words do not turn. Rather, they are diverted from their usual position, in that they are not upright. 'Lying' implies disconcerting or disorientating the interlocutor, taking a different route. Likewise, disorder is synonymous with confusion. This is conveyed in the Spanish PU *trastocar un plan; alterar un tema/un discurso/un argumento* (to mess up a plan; change a topic/speech/argument). In German, the most representative verb refers to *etwas durcheinander bringen* (lit. to bring sth into chaos: to mix something up). The lexeme *durcheinander* is also synonymous with confusing, disconcerting or stirring something (moving things from one place to another). In short, it conveys the idea of distancing oneself from the central point of the matter at hand. If we start from the premise that 'speech is synonymous with path', then the very nature of the path determines to what extent there is clarity in speech.

'Turning objects upside down or mixing them up' also reflects a way of distancing from the truth. In Spanish, the legs of a table in the PU *poner algo patas arriba* (lit. to put something legs up, to turn upside down) express this notion, with the intention of dislocating facts that at first seem to be correct and plausible, while in German the same idea is conveyed but this time using a part of the body: *etw. auf den Kopf stellen* (lit. to stand sth on its head). In the majority of cases, both PU are used to designate an act of disordering things, moving in a physical space, and are used to a lesser extent to show the attitude of the speaker who fails to make a clear argument. The PU *etwas in ein anderes Licht rücken/setzen/stellen* (to present sth in a different light) is not always associated with lying. Rather, it refers to the act of showing reality from a different angle, without it of course affecting the veracity of the facts. Another German PU which includes the same lexical component, that of *Licht* (light), and where the seme of 'lying and deceit' reigns is *jdn. hinters Licht führen* (lit. to lead sb behind the light: to dupe). This PU underlies two metaphorical models: LA MENTIRA ES OSCURIDAD y LA MENTIRA ES DESPLAZAMIENTO (LYING IS DARKNESS/LYING IS DISPLACEMENT).

All kinds of situations can be visualized under the prism of movement and spatial location, even the most abstract ones (Inchaurralde, 1991: 104). Gradations in space – up/down, left/right, front/back – can be established. In the case in question, truth would be represented by a frontal position, with lying positioned to the back.

Truth can be understood in directional terms via the parameters DENTRO-FUERA (INSIDE-OUTSIDE). That which remains inside is a sign of silence and that which is directed outside indicates honesty: *aus sich herausgehen; heraus mit der; abrirse; desembuchar* (come out with it/spit it out). On many occasions, we come across the FRONT schema when we want to explain something clearly: *decirle algo a la cara a alg.; jmdm. die Wahrheit ins Gesicht schleudern* (to tell the truth to sb's face).

The PU *jdn. hinters Licht führen* (to lead sb behind the light/to dupe) activates the directional schema LO FRONTAL ES VERDAD Y LO POSTERIOR ES MENTIRA (THE FRONT IS TRUTH AND THE BACK IS LYING). There is no similar image in Spanish.

The magnitude of the lie causes a distortion of reality, something which can be seen, in a figurative sense, in the German PU *lügen, dass sich die Balken biegen* (to lie like a cheap watch). In Spanish, this idea is expressed through the image of the 'bellaco' or villain. In other words, a liar is a wicked and vile person. Goodness which personifies truth contrasts with lying, which is considered despicable moral behaviour: *mentir como un bellaco* (lit. to lie like a villain).

Other synonymous PU in Spanish such as *mentir más que hablar, mentir con toda la boca, por la barba/más que la gaceta* (to lie more than to talk, to lie with one's full mouth, to lie through one's teeth) make use of parts of the body on the one hand, and the persuasive nature of the press on the other. This last image can be found in the German PU *lügen wie gedruckt)/wie gefunkt* (to lie like it's in print/broadcast)/*wie der Wehrmachtsbericht* (to lie like an armed forces report).

7. Conclusions

The versatility of the concept of lying and all its variants is obvious to us all. From a cognitive point of view, the study of lying is highly productive. By basing this study on our bilingual (German-Spanish) phraseological corpus, taken from the FRASESPAL research project, we have made an attempt to determine what aspects of the concept of *lying* and its variants are most addressed in phraseology within the framework of both Lakoff and Johnson (1999) and Dobrovol'skij's (1995) cognitive theories.

Lying and theatre, for example, go hand in hand. Lying is performance (*Schau, Theater, Szene* versus *escena, número, espectáculo*) as well as a fictional reality. In German it entails the phraseological unit *Geschichten/Märchen erzählen* and in Spanish is represented by the noun *cuento*. The spider's web is associated with acts of trickery and deceit. This animal activity leads us to the metaphorical pattern UN DISCURSO ES UN TEJIDO/SPEECH IS A WEB. In these terms, we can see that the idea of lying activates the field of 'sewing' more in Spanish than in German. Another aspect within the field of lying refers to the notion of words as objects, which shift from their usual position, change place, go around a central point, acquire another dimension and, therefore, take on a different kind of meaning. In German words go around (*das Wort im Munde herumdrehen*, to turn words in the mouth), whereas in Spanish words become twisted (*torcer las palabras*, to twist words).

Similar cognitive models used to designate the various facets of lying have been identified across both languages, hence reinforcing the theory that, on the one hand, languages underlie universally recognized cognitive patterns, and, on the other, not all universal cognitive patterns may operate in every language. The cognitive conception of language, according to Lakoff and Johnson, presents certain limitations.

Note

1.   This paper is part of a research project about contrastive phraseology financed by the Spanish Ministry of Education (HUM2007-62198/FILO) and ERDF funds.

References

Arendt, H. (1973) *Crisis en la República*. Madrid: Taurus.

Baranov, A. and Dobrovol'skij, D. (1991) Kognitive Modellierung in der Phraseologie: zum Problem der aktuellen Bedeutung. *Beiträge zur Erforschung der deutschen Sprache* 10: 112–123.

Burger, H. (1998) *Phraseologie. Eine Einführung am Beispiel des Deutschen*. Berlin: Erich Schmidt Verlag.

Cantera Ortiz de Urbina, J. and Gomis Blanco, P. (2007) *Diccionario de fraseología española: locuciones, idiotismos, modismos y frases hechas usuales en español.* Madrid: Abada.

Cinkure, I. (2006) Semantische Analyse der phraseologischen Vergleiche mit Tiernamen im Deutschen und im Lettischen. *Studies about Languages* 9: 11–16.

Dobrovol'skij, D. (1995) *Kognitive Aspekte der Idiom-Semantik. Studien zum Thesaurus deutscher Idiome.* Tubingen: Narr Verlag.

Dobrovol'skij, D. and Piirainen, E. (1997) *Symbole in Sprache und Kultur. Studien zur Phraseologie aus kultursemiotischer Perspektive.* Bochum: Brockmeyer.

Dobrovol'skij, D. (2004) Idiome aus kognitiver Sicht. In K. Steyer (ed.) *Wortverbindungen mehr oder weniger fest,* 117–143. Berlin: de Gruyter.

Dobrovol'skij, D. (2007) Cognitive approaches to idiom analysis. In H. Burger, D. Dobrovol'skij, P. Kühn and N. Norrick (eds) *Phraseologie/Phraseology. Ein internationales Handbuch zeitgenössischer Forschung/ An International Handbook of Contemporary Research,* 789–818. Berlin: de Gruyter.

Dornseiff, F. (2004) *Der deutsche Wortschatz nach Sachgruppen,* (CD-ROM). Berlin: de Gruyter.

Duden (2008) *Redewendungen. Wörterbuch der deutschen Idiomatik.* Mannheim: Bibliographisches Institut GmbH.

Eco, U. (2000) *Entre mentira e ironía.* Madrid: Lumen.

Falkenberg, G. (1982) *Lügen. Grundzüge einer Theorie sprachlicher Täuschung.* Tübingen: Niemeyer.

Fillmore, C.J. (1976) Frame semantics and the nature of language. Annals of the New York Academy of Sciences, Conference on the Origin and Development of Language and Speech 280: 20–32.

Hessky, R. and Ettinger, S. (1997) *Deutsche Redewendungen. Ein Wörter- und* Übungsbuch *für Fortgeschrittene.* Tübingen: Narr.

Geck, S. (2003) Jemandem Honig ums Maul schmieren. La conceptualización metafórica de las acciones interpersonales en alemán y español. *Forum* 10. Retrieved on 28 March 2011 from http://usuaris.tinet.cat/asgc/Forum/Autors/geck/geck2.html.

Grice H. Paul (1975) Logic and conversation. In P. Cole and J. L. Morgan (eds) *Speech Acts,* 41–58. New York: Academic Press.

Inchaurralde, C. (1991) Metáforas coloquiales del lenguaje coloquial y su procesamiento. *Procesamiento del lenguaje natural* 10: 97–105.

Jäkel, O. (2003) *Wie Metaphern Wissen schaffen: Die kognitive Metapherntheorie und ihre Anwendung in Modell-Analysen der Diskursbereiche Geistestätigkeit, Wirtschaft, Wissenschaft und Religion.* Hamburg: Dr. Kovac.

Kalisch, E. (1996) Handeln in einer Gesellschaft von Zuschauern. Die Actor-Spectator-Beziehung im Denken von Adam Smith. In J. Fiebach and W. Mühl-Benninghaus (eds) *Spektakel der Moderne. Bausteine zu einer Kulturgeschichte der Medien und des darstellenden Verhaltens,* 79–100. Berlin: Berliner Theaterwissenschaft.

Krukowska, E. (2004) Die Lüge hat viele Namen. Zum Wortfeld des Verbs 'lügen' im Deutschen und im Polnischen. In H. Eggert and J. Golec (eds) *Lügen und ihre Widersacher*, 24–39. Würzburg: Königshausen & Neumann.

Lakoff, G. and Johnson, M. (1980) *Metaphors We Live By*. Chicago, IL: University of Chicago.

Lakoff, G. and Johnson, M. (1986) *Metáforas de la vida cotidiana*. Madrid: Cátedra.

Lakoff, G. and Johnson, M. (1999) *Philosophy in the Flesh: The Embodied Mind and its Challenge to Western Thought*. New York: Basic Books.

Rodríguez-Vida, S. (2004) *Diccionario temático de frases hechas*. Castelldefels: Columbus.

Rösch, E.H. (1973) On the internal structure of perceptual and semantic categories. In T. E. Moore (ed.) *Cognitive Development and the Acquisition of Language*, 111–144. New York: Academic Press.

Schemann, H. (1989) *Synonymwörterbuch der deutschen Redensarten*. Straelen: Straelener Verlag.

Seco, M., Andrés, O. and Ramos, G. (2004) *Diccionario fraseológico documentado del español actual*. Madrid: Aguilar.

Solano Rodríguez, M. (2006) Tout a l'heure? Tu parles! *Estudios románicos* 15: 155–186.

Weinrich, H. (1966) *Linguistik der Lüge*. Heidelberg: Lambert Schneider.

Index

References to tables are entered as, for example, 247t.

9 781908 049759